book is to be returned on or before
the last date stamped below.

OXFORD
Children's
Encyclopedia

Volume 6

OXFORD
Children's
Encyclopedia

Abraham to Zhou Enlai

Oxford University Press

Oxford University Press, Walton Street, Oxford OX2 6DP

Oxford   New York   Toronto
Delhi   Bombay   Calcutta   Madras   Karachi
Kuala Lumpur   Singapore   Hong Kong   Tokyo
Nairobi   Dar es Salaam   Cape Town
Melbourne   Auckland   Madrid
and associated companies in
Berlin   Ibadan

Oxford is a trade mark of Oxford University Press
© Oxford University Press 1991
Reprinted 1991 (twice)
Revised and reprinted 1992

ISBN 0 19 910151 5 (complete set)

Volume 6: 0 19 910157 4 (not for sale separately)

A CIP catalogue record for this book is available from the British Library

Printed in Great Britain by
William Collins Sons and Company Ltd, Glasgow

Editor	Mary Worrall
Design and art direction	Richard Morris
Cover design	Philip Atkins
Assistant editors	Jane Bingham
	David Burnie
	Tony Drake
	Deborah Manley
	Sarah Matthews
	Pamela Mayo
	Stephen Pople
	Andrew Solway
	Catherine Thompson
Copy preparation	Eric Buckley
	Richard Jeffery
Proof reader	Richard Jeffery
Index	Radmila May
Photographic research	Catherine Blackie
	Libby Howells
	Linda Proud
	Suzanne Williams

How to use the Oxford Children's Encyclopedia

The articles in this Biography volume are in alphabetical order, listed under the surname (family name) as in a telephone directory.

In ancient times and in the Middle Ages surnames were not common, so you will find many people under their first names: **Archimedes**, **Moses**, **Plato**. Spellings of historical characters vary, and you may have to search over a few pages to find people like **Cnut** (Canute) or **Jiang Jieshi** (Chiang Kai-Shek).

Cross references

After reading about someone, you may want to find out more information about the job they did or what they are famous for. For instance, you might read the article about **Shakespeare** in the Biography. At the end of the article, the **See also** lists **Drama**, **Poems and poetry** and **Theatre**. So, if you want to know what theatres in Shakespeare's lifetime were like, look up the article on **Theatre**. If you want to know more about sonnets, look up **Poems and poetry**.

Special features

At the end of Volume 6 there are four special features: **British Royal Family**, **Film**, **Pop and Rock** and **Sport**. These articles have been grouped together because many people in sport and entertainment are famous for only a short period.

See also

Drama
Poems and poetry
Theatre

Contents

Abraham

Dates of birth and death unknown. He may have lived about 1800 BC.
Hebrew ancestor of both Jews and Muslims

According to the book of Genesis in the Bible, Abraham lived in the city of Ur in Mesopotamia (now mainly in Iraq). He had led an ordinary life until he was about 75, when God told him that he must leave his country and go to a new land. So Abraham took his household, and that of his nephew Lot, and set out for Canaan, the promised land.

He settled there, and in time God spoke again, and told him that Sarah, his wife, would give birth to a son, Isaac. When Isaac had grown into a boy, God told Abraham to sacrifice him by placing him on an altar and killing him. Together they went into the mountains and prepared an altar. But just as Abraham stretched out his hand to kill the boy God stopped him. 'Now I know how much you obey me,' God said, 'since you were prepared to give me even your son. I will bless you both, and Isaac's children will be as many as the stars in the sky and the sand on the sea-shore, and they will be the founders of a great nation.'

Abraham is important to Jews because God led him to the promised land of Israel, which the Jews have called their own ever since. He is important to Muslims because he obeyed God and was ready, when the call came, to sacrifice his son. (According to Muslim tradition, Ishmael was the son nearly sacrificed.) And he is important to Christians because they see him as someone whose trust in God's promises makes him their own forefather in living a life of faith.

The stories of Abraham are found in the Book of Genesis, chapters 11 to 25, in the Old Testament of the Bible. ■

See also

Hebrews
Mesopotamia

Akbar

Born 1542 in Umarkot, Sind (now in Pakistan)
Became Emperor of the Mughal empire in northern India.
Died 1605 aged 63

Akbar ruled the Mughal empire in India at the same time as Elizabeth I was Queen of England. By the end of his reign, his lands covered an area as big as Europe, and he was more powerful than any European monarch.

Akbar was only 14 when he became emperor, and had to fight hard to build up his power. Sometimes he was ruthless. When he destroyed a rebel fort at Chitor, he built his enemies' heads into the walls of a tower. But Akbar preferred peace, and won most of his lands through treaties and marriages. The Mughal emperors were Muslims but the majority of Akbar's subjects were Hindus. To show that he respected their beliefs, he married a Hindu princess. He also showed friendship to Christian priests from Portugal. Akbar was much more tolerant than European rulers living at the same time. In Europe in the 16th and 17th centuries, Catholic and Protestant rulers forced their subjects to follow their own beliefs. Heretics were burnt at the stake and wars fought between Catholics and Protestants.

Akbar had splendid palaces with beautiful gardens. He loved hunting with cheetahs, riding fierce camels and war elephants, and playing polo. He was good at painting, and made tapestries and carpets. Though he never learnt to read easily, he enjoyed discussions, and collected a huge library. He built the magnificent city of Fatehpur Sikri near Agra. It is still there today, almost unchanged, to remind us of Akbar's India. ■

See also

Indian history

▲ In keeping with the traditions of Genghis Khan and Tamerlane, Akbar's army built a victory pillar with the heads of their enemies after a battle in 1556. This picture shows how such a pillar was constructed.

Alcott, Louisa May

Born 1832 in Philadelphia, USA
Best known as the author of *Little Women,* her classic novel of family life during the American Civil War
Died 1888 aged 55

When Louisa was a child her father abandoned all efforts to earn a living and decided to devote his life to becoming 'a perfect human being'. She and her three sisters grew up with the double difficulties of having hardly any money and of being expected to be good all the time, without fail. The family diet was often only bread, apples and water, but, in spite of everything, Louisa turned out to be a vigorous girl. She had dark deep-set eyes, thick chestnut hair, a stormy temper and a 'great yearning nature'. She listed her faults as 'idleness, impatience, selfishness, wilfulness, independence, activity, vanity, pride and the love of cats'.

When she grew up she tried to earn money to support her family by writing romantic thrillers for magazines. Then, at 35, she wrote *Little Women,* an idealized version of her own difficult childhood with the heroine, Jo, modelled on herself.

The book was a huge success. The popularity of *Little Women,* and of the follow-up volumes which Louisa wrote, freed her family from money worries. But her health had been damaged when she spent a brief spell as a nurse during the American Civil War, and this, together with long-established habits of hard work and self-denial and her shyness with strangers, made it difficult for Louisa to enjoy her fame. She died at the age of 55, two days after her father's death. ■

Alexander the Great

> **Born** 356 BC in Pella, a town now in northern Greece
> A great king and general who conquered the Persian empire
> **Died** 323 BC aged 32

Alexander became King Alexander III of Macedonia at the age of 20. He devoted his reign to making Macedonia greater still than his father Philip had made it, and to conquering the huge Persian empire to the east. He achieved this in a few years in a succession of brilliant battles and sieges. He reached India, and sent an expedition by sea from the mouth of the Indus to Babylon. He would have gone further, but his army refused.

We do not know what Alexander intended to do with his empire, because he died of a fever in Babylon before he had a chance to organize it properly. There were many different accounts of his achievements written during his life or soon after, but they have all been lost over the hundreds of years since he lived. The best information about Alexander comes from historians writing much later under the Roman empire. They copied the earlier accounts freely and saw things from their own point of view, so it is very difficult to form a clear idea of what Alexander wanted.

One thing is fairly certain: Alexander did not just want to create a huge Macedonian kingdom. His ideas changed as he went further and won

▲ This bronze statue of Alexander the Great shows him on his famous horse Bucephalus. He is armed for battle. Notice that he rode without stirrups, which had not yet been invented.

more territory. As a boy he had been taught by the philosopher Aristotle to be proud of being Greek. But he formed his own ideas about different nations living in friendship. By the time he died he had shown that he wanted both Greeks and Persians to be rulers. He appointed Persians as well as Macedonians to high offices. He angered his army by adopting customs from the Persians, some of which involved honouring him as if he were a god.

Alexander had a famous horse called Bucephalus which his father had given him when he was a boy. When the horse died in the east Alexander built a city and named it after him. He built many new cities called Alexandria and settled soldiers and other Greeks in them. The most famous is the one in Egypt which is still an important city today.

Alexander had a ruthless, brutal side. Once he had a violent quarrel with one of his companions and killed him in rage. The Persian royal palace at Persepolis was burnt down after a drinking party. He often had strange moods and sulked. Some things upset him dreadfully, and when his close friend Hephaestion died suddenly, he was overcome with grief.

When Alexander died no one was able to keep the newly won empire together. After years of war among his generals it was split up into smaller kingdoms, including Macedonia itself, Babylonia, and Egypt. ■

◉ See also

Egyptian ancient history
Greek ancient history

Biography
Aristotle
Philip II of Macedon

Alfred

Born 849 in Wantage, England
Established a kingdom in southern
England in the face of the Danish
invasions.
Died 899 aged 50

Among the early kings of England, Alfred is the most famous. He lived at a time when there was no settled kingdom of Britain. Instead, the country was made up of many separate kingdoms. Alfred was the fifth and youngest son of Aethelwulf, King of the West Saxons, whose kingdom of Wessex extended from present-day Devon to Hampshire. Like his brothers, Alfred was brought up to hunt and fight, but he was also interested in learning and might even have gone into the Church as a monk.

Alfred's first taste of real fighting came in 870. A year later the armies of the Danes, who had occupied Northumbria and East Anglia, launched an attack on Wessex. The Saxon army was lined up against the Danes at Ashdown in Berkshire. In this great battle it was Alfred, not his brother Aethelred who

was then king, who showed he had the courage and vigour to beat off the Danes. When Aethelred died, the Saxons chose Alfred as their king. He was 22 years old.

This was not the end of the fighting, but rather the beginning. At first Alfred tried to buy peace, paying the Danes not to attack (this payment was called the 'Danegeld' — gold for the Danes). But by 878 the Danes had conquered the neighbouring kingdoms, and Alfred was forced to flee for his life.

There is a famous legend that while Alfred was hiding in the Somerset marshes, he begged for shelter in a swineherd's cottage. Alfred was so exhausted that he fell asleep in front of the fire when he should have been watching the cakes baking there. When she discovered her burnt cakes, the swineherd's wife scolded him angrily for his carelessness, not recognizing Alfred as her king.

Eventually Alfred managed to raise a new army and he succeeded in beating back the Danes in the battle of Edington (in Wiltshire). The Danes were forced to accept his terms for peace, and Alfred set about establishing a proper 'English' kingdom in southern England.

Alfred was as famous for his peacetime work as his wartime exploits. He

founded a number of new fortified towns called *burhs*. Several modern towns, such as Wareham in Dorset and Cricklade near Cirencester, show signs of Alfred's town planning. He issued a new code of laws and encouraged the country's religious life by re-founding monasteries that had been destroyed.

Alfred wanted his people to be able to read in their own language. He was responsible for translating Bede's *The History of the English Church and People* from Latin, and during his reign the *Anglo-Saxon Chronicles* were begun, a record of important events in the kingdom, written from the start in Anglo-Saxon. ∎

⟲ See also

Anglo-Saxons
Vikings

Biography
Bede

▼ Alfred's decisive victory against the Danes at Edington in 878 led to the signing of the Treaty of Wedmore, in which the Danish leader Guthrum agreed to withdraw his forces to East Anglia and become a Christian.

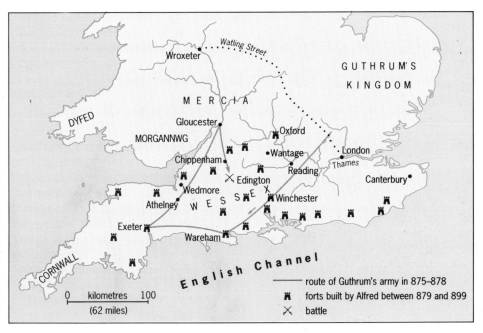

route of Guthrum's army in 875–878
forts built by Alfred between 879 and 899
battle

▲ This ornament was found near the Isle of Athelney in Somerset in 1693. It was made in the 9th century and has an inscription: *Aelfred mec heht gewyrcan.* This is in the language of the Saxons. It means 'Alfred ordered me to be made.' The portrait shows a man holding two sceptres. This is probably Alfred himself.

Amundsen, Roald

Born 1872 at Vedsten, near Sarpsborg, Norway
First man to reach the South Pole
Died 1928 aged 55

Amundsen began a career studying medicine, but gave it up to go to sea. Soon, the idea of polar exploration excited him, and he decided to try to sail through the North-West Passage from the Atlantic to the Pacific Ocean: that is, through the Arctic Ocean north of Canada. He set out in 1903 aboard a tiny sloop, the *Gjöa*, which had sails and an auxiliary engine. He had a crew of only six. He had to set out secretly to avoid his creditors, because he owed a lot of money.

The expedition took just over three years. Amundsen had to make camp for two long polar winters while the sea was iced over. But he completed the journey, the first person to do so.

Amundsen next decided to try to reach the North Pole. Just as he was about to set sail he heard that an American naval officer, Robert Peary, had reached the Pole. So he secretly changed his plans and sailed for Antarctica instead. It was to be a race between Amundsen and a British expedition led by Robert Falcon Scott, which had set out earlier. Amundsen and four companions, using sledges hauled by teams of dogs, reached the South Pole on 14 December 1911. It was another first for Amundsen.

In 1928 Amundsen heard that his friend Umberto Nobile, an Italian aviator, was missing on an airship flight over the North Pole. Amundsen set out to search for him, but his own plane was never seen again. Nobile was later rescued unharmed. ■

See also

Antarctica
Arctic Ocean

Biography
Scott, Robert Falcon

▼ In 1906 Amundsen completed the first voyage from the Atlantic to the Pacific through the Arctic waters north of Canada. Five years later he discovered the South Pole.

Andersen, Hans Christian

Born 1805 in Odense, Denmark
He wrote some of the best children's stories in the world: *The Tin Soldier, Thumbelina, The Little Mermaid,* and hundreds more.
Died 1875 aged 70

▲ An illustration for the story *The Marsh King's Daughter* by Hans Christian Andersen.

In many ways, Hans Andersen was like a person out of one of his own stories. He once said, 'Most of what I have written is a reflection of myself. Every character is from life.'

He was the only son of a poor shoemaker and of a mother who could hardly read. When he was 11 years old, his father died. Andersen left school and worked in a factory. Even though he was talented and could sing well, people used to laugh at him because he was so ugly; he was very tall and clumsy, with a long nose and small eyes. When he was 14 he walked to Copenhagen to try his luck in the big city. At 17 he was put in a school to learn with twelve-year-olds. The headmaster and the children mocked and bullied him, just as the animals in one of his most famous stories, *The Ugly Duckling,* mock the ugly

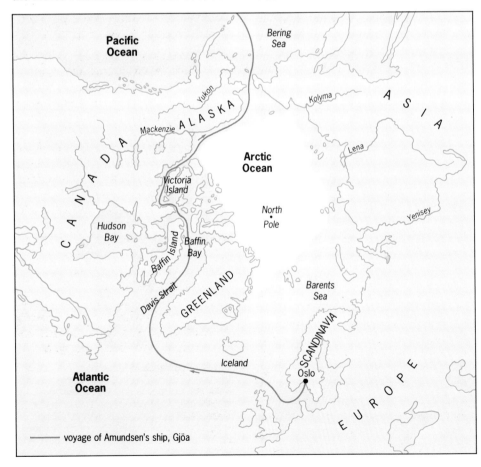

Pacific Ocean

Bering Sea

Yukon

Mackenzie ALASKA

Kolyma

ASIA

CANADA

Victoria Island

Arctic Ocean

Lena

Hudson Bay

Baffin Island

Baffin Bay

North Pole

Davis Strait

GREENLAND

Barents Sea

Yenisey

Iceland

SCANDINAVIA

Oslo

Atlantic Ocean

EUROPE

——— voyage of Amundsen's ship, Gjöa

duckling, who, of course, turns into a beautiful swan in the end.

In time, Andersen wrote plays and novels which were published, but it was his tales for children that brought him worldwide praise. He wrote them exactly as he would have told them to a child, and many other writers began to copy the kind of simple language he used. As his fame grew, he was honoured in many countries, but he remained a shy and lonely man. ■

Andrew, Saint

Born about the same time as Jesus, in Palestine
One of Christ's apostles, who became the patron saint of Scotland
Died about AD 60, possibly in Greece

Andrew was a fisherman who lived in Capernaum. He was a disciple of John the Baptist and then became an apostle of Jesus. Jesus had told both Andrew and his brother, Simon Peter, that they would be 'fishers of men'. He went out into the world preaching the Gospel. We cannot be sure exactly where he went. But the people of Patras in Greece claimed that he was crucified there.

A later legend said that in the 4th century, a native of Patras called Rule had a dream. In this dream an angel told him to take some of Andrew's bones to a land in the north-west. Rule obeyed, and travelled until he reached Scotland. The angel then told him to stop in Fife, where he built a church to hold the bones. The church was later called St Andrews. It became a centre for converting the Scottish people to Christianity. For this reason, Andrew was chosen to be the patron saint of Scotland. His feast day is 30 November. ■

◎ See also

Apostles
Christians
Saints

Biography
Jesus
John the Baptist

Anne, Queen

Born 1665 in London, England
She was the last Stuart monarch, and ruled from 1702. In her reign, in 1707, England and Scotland were joined as one nation.
Died 1714 aged 49

Anne did not have an easy life. She had seventeen children, all of whom died before they grew up. This ruined her health. She became very fat, and had to be carried to her throne when she was crowned.

She became queen when political parties were just starting, and it was difficult to control them. Perhaps because of this, she relied on her friend Sarah Churchill, who was a proud and difficult woman. Sarah's husband John became the Duke of Marlborough. He was a brilliant soldier, and won many victories against the French in Anne's reign. But in the end Anne decided it was time to make peace, and quarrelled with Sarah.

Anne was a firm supporter of the Church of England, and although she was not well educated, she was a sensible woman, who understood how most of her subjects felt. ■

◎ See also

Scotland's history
Stuart Britain

Biography
Marlborough

Archimedes

Born about 287 BC in Sicily
The greatest mathematician and engineer of ancient Greece
Died 212 BC aged about 75, killed by a Roman soldier

Archimedes was born in the town of Syracuse in Sicily, at that time ruled by the Greeks. He was the son of an astronomer and spent his life studying geometry and using his ideas to develop new types of machines. One of the most famous is the Archimedean screw for pumping out water, though the Egyptians may have invented this.

There are lots of stories about Archimedes and if some of them are not completely true they still give a glimpse of what this great man was like. We know he was a wealthy man and a friend of the King of Syracuse.

There is a story that one day the king set him a particularly difficult problem. He wanted to know if his crown was made of pure gold or whether the goldsmith had cheated and mixed in some cheaper metal. Archimedes could not solve this until one day, stepping into his bath, he suddenly realized that the water level rose higher the more of his body he immersed. He leapt out of the bath and ran naked through the streets shouting 'Eureka! Eureka!' which means 'I've got it! I've got it!' The experiment was done with the crown. He could tell the volume of the crown by the rise of water level when he put it in a bath. Next he took a piece of pure gold weighing the same as the crown and immersed it in the water. Did it occupy the same volume as the crown? Did the water level rise to the same height? No! The crown could not have been made of pure gold, and the goldsmith was executed.

Other stories tell of the amazing war machines Archimedes invented to protect Syracuse from the invading Romans. Cranes to lift Roman ships and turn them upside-down; large mirrors that focused the Sun's rays on the Roman fleet and set them on fire. Syracuse was eventually captured, but the Roman general Marcellus ordered that Archimedes should be taken alive and treated with honour. But Archimedes, who was found drawing a mathematical figure in the sand, was killed by a Roman soldier. Marcellus ordered a special funeral and arranged, according to Archimedes' wishes, that his tombstone should be inscribed with a sphere inside a cylinder so that he would be remembered for his outstanding work in geometry. ■

◎ See also

Geometry
Irrigation
Mathematics

Biography
Euclid

Aristotle

Born 384 BC at Stageira in northern
Greece
Philosopher, teacher and writer in
ancient Greece
Died 322 BC aged 62

The town of Stageira where Aristotle was born was then ruled by the kings of Macedon. His father was a doctor to the royal family. When he was about 17, Aristotle travelled to Athens to join the famous Academy, a school run by the philosopher Plato. He stayed there for 20 years. Later he became a teacher himself, and also wrote books about politics and ethics, the study of whether particular things are right or wrong.

When Plato died in 347 BC, Aristotle left the Academy and crossed the Aegean Sea to settle on the island of Lesbos. During this time he continued to study and tried to work out what was special about human beings. He decided that humans were the only animals who lived together in towns and cities. He later wrote down these ideas in his most famous book, *The Politics*, whose title comes from the Greek word for city: *polis*.

In 343 BC Aristotle returned to Macedonia because he had been invited by King Philip to become tutor of his young son. The boy was later to become Alexander the Great. A few years later, Aristotle went back to Athens to set up his own school, the Lyceum. He liked to teach his students while walking up and down under the trees. He wrote many books and often disagreed with the ideas of the earlier philosophers, Socrates and Plato. ■

See also

Greek ancient history
Biography
Alexander the Great
Philip II of Macedon
Plato
Socrates

Arkwright, Sir Richard

Born 1732 in Preston, Lancashire,
England
Invented machines which took over much
of the work done by people in the
manufacture of textiles.
Died 1792 aged 59

Richard Arkwright was the youngest of thirteen children. He had no schooling and did not learn to read and write until he was a wealthy middle-aged man. At the age of 10 he was sent to work in a barber's shop. While working there he discovered a method for dyeing hair that did not fade, and this enabled him to make a great deal of money as a barber and wigmaker. But Arkwright's real claim to fame is his invention of the 'spinning frame', a machine for spinning cotton. He made it with the help of a skilled watchmaker called John Kay.

Arkwright went on to invent and improve other machines used in textile manufacture. Many workers found their jobs were taken over by the new machines. They became very angry and tried to destroy the machines and even threatened Richard Arkwright. But he was a very determined man and his factories helped Lancashire become the centre of the world's cotton industry. ■

See also

Cotton
Industrial Revolution
Spinning

▲ The spinning frame which Arkwright invented in 1768 was driven by a water wheel.

Armstrong, Louis

Born about 1900 in New Orleans, USA
Jazz trumpeter, entertainer and singer
Died 1971 aged about 71

Louis Armstrong was born into a very poor home. His father left his mother before he was born, and the family sometimes had very little to eat. Nevertheless, there was great love in the Armstrong home, and all his life Louis recalled his mother with great affection and pleasure. He was a cheerful, mischievous lad, but one day when he was 13 he went a bit too far. He took a pistol out of the house and fired it in the street. It was meant as a harmless prank, but he ended up being taken to a children's home. This turned out to be good for him, because he was already interested in music, and at the home he had music lessons and played cornet in a band.

He left the home as a teenager and gradually started to earn a living playing his cornet. In the twenties, after playing in other bands, he formed various small groups of his own, such as 'The Louis Armstrong Hot Five', and made some records. These

▲ Louis Armstrong put so much into his performances that he nearly always held a handkerchief with which to mop his brow.

recordings brought him worldwide fame among jazz fans.

Louis was more than just a player. His big smile and his antics on stage made him into something special. In 1936 he appeared in his first film, *Pennies from Heaven* with Bing Crosby. From then on he gradually became a popular entertainer. More and more he was heard as a singer, his gravelly, cheerful voice having an attraction all of its own. His biggest popular song hits were 'Hello Dolly', recorded in 1964, and 'What a Wonderful World', recorded in 1968. Neither of these records is in the same class, musically, as his early jazz performances, but lots of people like them.

In the 1950s, Peter Black of the *Daily Mail* wrote about Louis, 'When he blew his trumpet you would not have been surprised if the whole man had suddenly gone off bang. He looked the incarnation of the spirit of fun.' ∎

See also

Jazz

Armstrong, Neil

Born 1930 in Wapakoneta, Ohio, USA
He was the first human to set foot on the Moon.

Neil Armstrong was always very interested in flying as a young man. He was given his pilot's licence at the age of 16, even before he had learnt to drive a car. The following year he became a naval air cadet, and went on to fly in the Korean War.

Later in the 1950s he became a test pilot for NASA (National Aeronautics and Space Administration) before joining the US space programme in 1962. His first mission in space, on Gemini 8 in 1966, ended earlier than expected when he had to make an emergency landing in the Pacific Ocean.

In 1969 he joined astronauts Aldrin and Collins on the Apollo 11 mission, and July 20 he became the first person to walk on the Moon. As he stepped off the lunar landing module, he said, 'That's one small step for a man, one giant leap for mankind.' ∎

See also

Gravity
Moon
Space exploration

▲ It was not hard for astronauts Armstrong and Aldrin to turn 'small steps' into 'giant leaps' on the Moon's surface because there is very little gravity there.

Arthur, King

Dates of birth and death unknown
A great legendary hero, possibly based on a real British chieftain who may have lived in the 5th or 6th century AD

There are countless tales about Arthur, in Welsh, English, French, German, and many other languages. The first written tales date from around 800. But Celtic people in Britain probably told stories about Arthur before then. So who exactly was he? The simple answer is — we don't know. There was definitely no British king called Arthur. But there might have been a chieftain of that name, around the year 500. Such a chieftain could have led an army against the Anglo-Saxon invaders of Britain. Then again, he could have led an army against fellow Britons in a civil war. Some historians say his headquarters were in the West Country. Others believe that his base was in northern England, or even Scotland.

The Arthur of legend was a perfect Christian king who ruled all Britain and conquered most of western Europe. He held court at Camelot with his lovely queen, Guinevere. His twelve most trusted warriors were called the Knights of the Round Table. And at last, after the battle of Camlann, he was taken to 'Avalon' to be healed of his wounds. But no one ever saw him again. ∎

See also

Arthur and his knights
Chivalry
Dark Ages

Ashcroft, Peggy

Born 1907 in Croydon, England
A famous English actress
Died 1991 aged 84

Edith Margaret (Peggy) Ashcroft's mother was a keen amateur actress, and encouraged Peggy in her career. Peggy made her first stage appearances at Birmingham Repertory Theatre when she was 19. She was soon noticed and given parts in London. She played Desdemona in Shakespeare's *Othello* in 1930, and in 1935 gave a memorable performance as Juliet in *Romeo and Juliet*. She continued to build her career with a long series of excellent performances right up into the 1980s.

As a young actress, Peggy Ashcroft was known for her simplicity and ability to show sadness and tragedy without weeping and wailing. Later in life she still showed the same ability to appear calm and natural, to seem not to be 'acting' at all. When she was over 70 she reached a new audience on television, with performances in *Edward and Mrs Simpson* and *Jewel in the Crown*. She continued to return to the stage, however, which she considered her first love. ∎

Ashley, Laura

Born 1925 in Dowlais, Glamorgan, Wales
With her husband she built up a multi-million fashion business from very small beginnings.
Died 1985 aged 60

Laura was the daughter of a civil servant. She grew up in a Baptist family. She was 17 and Bernard Ashley was 16 when they met at a youth club. They married after both serving in World War II.

In 1952, when she was expecting her first child, an exhibition of patchwork inspired her to design a tea-cloth. The Ashleys printed it on a silk screen frame on their kitchen table and sold it to a shop. Laura began to search for more designs in fabric collections of the 18th and 19th centuries. Slowly, hampered by lack of funds, they extended their range to include printed cotton fabrics and dresses. When they opened a shop in Kensington in London and started advertising, the business took off. By 1985 when the firm became a public company there were 200 shops around the world.

Laura Ashley's pretty, old-fashioned style has a constant appeal. The use of natural fabrics, moderate prices, and the suitability of her designs for both the young and the middle-aged ensure their continuing popularity. Laura Ashley herself was practical and straightforward. She saw to it that her office staff had well-cooked meals at midday and that her factory workers in Wales were home before their schoolchildren. She is remembered with affection. ∎

See also

Textiles

Ashoka

Dates of birth and death not known
Emperor of India from about 272 to 232 BC

Ashoka was the grandson of Chandra Gupta Maurya, the founder of the Maurya empire in ancient India. He extended his empire to cover what is now Afghanistan, Pakistan and most of India.

After coming to the throne Ashoka waged many wars to extend his empire, but was deeply moved to see the suffering of wounded soldiers during one of his campaigns to annex more territory in eastern India. He was then converted to Buddhism. He declared that he would fight no more wars, and devoted the rest of his life to the spread of Buddhism in India and abroad.

He governed according to the Buddhist principles of toleration and humanitarianism and believed in concern for human life and abstaining from harming animals. He asked his subjects not to eat meat. Ashoka spread the teachings of Buddha throughout his empire by erecting pillars of stone with the main teachings of the Buddhist religion inscribed on them. He sent missionaries to neighbouring countries.

Ashoka was a fair and just ruler who made the social welfare of his subjects his main aim. ∎

See also

Buddhists
Indian history

Asimov, Isaac

Born 1920 in Petrovichi, Russia
A scientist who became well known as an excellent science fiction writer
Died 1992 aged 72

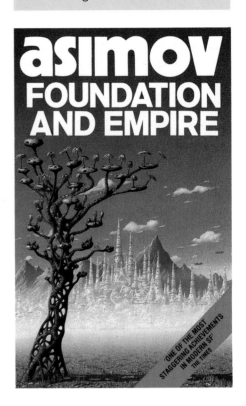

▲ The cover of Asimov's second book in the *Foundation* trilogy, published in 1952. He continued the series 30 years later with two more books.

Isaac was born in Russia, but at the age of 3 he moved with his parents to the USA where his father kept a sweet shop. He studied chemistry at university and worked in the subject called biochemistry, where scientists look at the chemistry going on inside living things.

He wrote more than a hundred books. Many of them set out to explain the marvels of science to people who know nothing about science. He also produced some thrilling science fiction stories of which those in his *Foundation* trilogy (*Foundation*; *Foundation and Empire*; *Second Foundation*) are the best known. ∎

See also

Science fiction

Atahualpa

Born about 1500 in the Inca empire, South America
Last ruler of the South American empire of the Incas
Executed 1533 aged about 33

Atahualpa and his brother Huascar were the sons and heirs of the great Inca emperor Huayna-Capac. After his death in 1525, civil war broke out between the two brothers. Huascar was captured and finally killed, and Atahualpa became emperor, the supreme Inca.

As emperor, he was thought to be a god descended from the Sun. People approached him with great respect. He was served by specially chosen women. He used only the richest of objects, which were kept for him alone. He had complete power over his people, but he was expected to be fair and generous and to follow the ancient traditions of the Incas.

Atahualpa was captured by a small Spanish army in 1532. The Spanish described him as wise, witty and cheerful. Even in captivity he continued to rule his people with strength and authority. But despite paying a huge ransom of gold and silver, he was executed the following year and the Spanish, led by Pizarro, conquered the Inca people. ■

See also

Incas
Spanish colonial history
Biography
Pizarro

Atatürk, Kemal

Born 1881 in Salonika, Greece
The first president of the Republic of Turkey, from 1923 to 1938
Died 1938 aged 57

Mustafa Kemal was born the son of a customs officer in the Turkish part of Salonika. At an early age he decided he wanted to join the army, so he went to military college in Istanbul, then capital of the Ottoman empire. He was so good at mathematics there that he was given the name Kemal which is Arabic for 'perfection'.

He then entered the army and rapidly rose to the highest ranks. He fought in World War I when the Ottoman empire joined the German side. After the armistice (agreement to stop fighting) in 1918, Kemal joined other Turkish politicians in calling for Turkey to become an independent nation free of foreign control.

His military skill was needed again when Greece and Turkey went to war in 1921. With his help, the Turks defeated the Greeks. Shortly after that, the Ottoman sultans were deposed and a Turkish National Assembly was elected with Kemal as president of the new republic.

As president he worked hard to modernize Turkey. In particular, he developed an education programme so that more people would learn to read and write. He also tried to give Turkish women more rights. In 1934, he introduced the idea of surnames into Turkey and took the surname Atatürk ('father of Turks') for himself. The strain of all the work he did, both in the army and as his country's president, led to his death in 1938. ■

See also

Ottoman empire
Turkey

▼ Attila's army raided the divided Roman empire, reaching Constantinople before turning towards the West, where they were forced to retreat after a fierce battle at Châlons. In 452 Attila invaded Italy but had to withdraw when his army was hit by hunger and disease.

Attila

Born 406 somewhere in eastern Europe
He led the barbarian Huns against the Roman empire.
Died 453 aged 46

Attila was born into the tribe of the Huns, a race of warring nomads who had moved from the Asian steppes right up to the borders of the Roman empire in the West.

When he became king of the Huns in 434, his first act was to unite his scattered people in a campaign against the Roman empire. For the next 20 years the Huns under Attila 'ground almost the whole of Europe into dust',

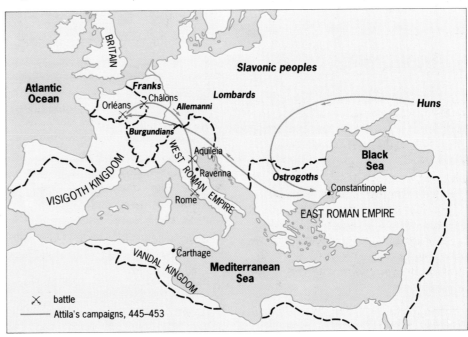

BRITAIN
Atlantic Ocean
Slavonic peoples
Franks
Châlons
Lombards
Orléans
Allemanni
Huns
Burgundians
Aquileia
Black Sea
Ravenna
Ostrogoths
Rome
Constantinople
WEST ROMAN EMPIRE
VISIGOTH KINGDOM
EAST ROMAN EMPIRE
VANDAL KINGDOM
Carthage
Mediterranean Sea

✕ battle
—— Attila's campaigns, 445–453

conquering, plundering and demanding vast sums in tribute. In 447 they laid waste the lands between the Black Sea and the Mediterranean, defeating the Roman emperor three times. In 451 they attacked Gaul (now France), and the next year they invaded Italy. Most of all Attila wanted to destroy Rome, and the Pope had to pay him huge sums of money to save the city.

While his followers lived in luxury, Atilla ate only meat out of a wooden bowl. He was a short man, with a large head, a flat nose, deep-set eyes and a gaze which was hard and arrogant. Although far from handsome, he was married many times; some say he had 300 wives.

When Attila died, probably by poison, the Huns cut their cheeks so that they could mourn their leader with tears of blood. ■

See also

Dark Ages
Roman ancient history

Attlee, Clement

Born 1883 in Putney, London, England
Leader of the Labour Party and Prime Minister of Britain from 1945 to 1951
Died 1967 aged 84

Clement Attlee was born into a middle-class family in London and went to private school and Oxford University. In 1906 he qualified as a barrister, but became a college tutor instead. When he taught at the London School of Economics he lived amongst poor people in the East End and was disturbed to see the problems they faced.

This led to him joining the Labour Party and, after fighting as a soldier in World War I, he was elected Mayor of Stepney in 1919. Three years later he became MP for Limehouse. Eventually he became leader of the Labour Party in 1935.

In 1940 Winston Churchill became prime minister and invited the Labour Party to join his wartime coalition

government. In 1942 Attlee became deputy prime minister. Then, when the war ended in 1945, the Labour Party won an outstanding election victory over the Conservatives and Attlee replaced Churchill as prime minister.

Attlee was convinced of the need to grant independence to India and to Britain's Asian colonies. India, Pakistan, Burma and Ceylon (Sri Lanka) all became independent in 1947. At home his government immediately began to carry out major changes in Britain. State benefits and pensions were increased and the National Health Service, to provide everyone with free medical care, was started in 1948. The railways and the

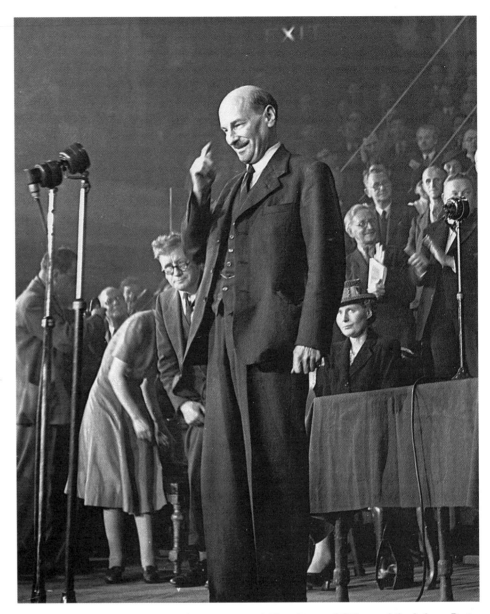

▲ The victory of Attlee and the Labour Party in the 1945 general election to the House of Commons came as a great surprise to many people because the Conservative Party leader Winston Churchill had been such a popular wartime leader. Here is the new prime minister being cheered by his supporters.

coal, gas and electricity industries were nationalized (taken over by the state). The Labour Party was defeated by the Conservatives in 1951. Then in 1955 Attlee retired from being leader of the party. He was made a peer and, as Earl Attlee, became a member of the House of Lords. ■

See also

British history 1919–1989

Augustine of Canterbury, Saint

Born date and place not known
Augustine was sent by Pope Gregory to convert the Angles (the English) to Christianity.
Died 604 or 605

There had been Christians in Britain while it was a Roman province, and there were Christian communities worshipping in western Britain when Augustine arrived in 597.

Pope Gregory I had decided to send Augustine to convert the people in Britain. Augustine was then the prior (deputy head) of St Andrew's monastery in Rome. He set off for Britain with 40 of his monks and landed at the Isle of Thanet in Kent. There they met the King of Kent, Ethelbert. His wife, Bertha, was already a Christian and she persuaded her husband to allow Augustine's mission to begin.

On Christmas Day 597 he converted 10,000 people. The main place for worship was the capital of Kent, Canterbury. Augustine was made Archbishop of Canterbury and Primate of Britain (chief bishop) by Pope Gregory in 601. Augustine founded the first monastery in Britain in Canterbury. ■

See also

Christians

Augustine of Hippo, Saint

Born 354 in Numidia, North Africa
One of the most important early Christian writers
Died 430 aged 75

Augustine grew up in a small town in North Africa, which was then part of the Roman empire. His magistrate father was proud and stubborn, while his mother was intensely loving and protective: he was a pagan, but she

▲ This picture of Saint Augustine was painted by Sandro Botticelli, an Italian Renaissance artist. He depicted Augustine in a building of his own period, and did not try to imagine what the surroundings had really been like in Augustine's lifetime.

was a Christian and had the greater influence on Augustine.

Both parents wanted a university education for their talented son, and at the age of 16 he went to study law at Carthage. At university, Augustine worked hard and played hard. By the time he was 22 he had a mistress and an illegitimate son, but was able to support himself by teaching. Six years later he moved to Milan in Italy, where he taught the art of speech-making.

As he looked back on his early life, what Augustine remembered was not his career success, but the time he stole pears from a neighbour's garden with a gang of friends, and his grief at the death of his close friend. Since then, Augustine felt, he had grown further and further away from his mother's religion, and from his true father, God.

One day, while he was walking in a garden, Augustine thought he heard a child singing: 'Take and read.' He rushed home to open his Bible at: 'Let us walk honestly, as in the day; not in rioting and drunkenness . . . not in strife and envying' (Romans chapter 13, verses 13–14). It was then that he

took the agonizing decision to give up his career and devote the rest of his life to God. His *Confessions* tells the story of his childhood, youth and conversion.

When he wrote the *Confessions*, Augustine had just become Bishop of Hippo, a city near his home town in Africa. He had not been able to stay out of public life for long; the people of Hippo had used force to make him bishop. He remained there until his death, running the local church, leading the Church in North Africa, and by his writings reaching the Christian community throughout the Roman world.

At this time the Roman empire was under attack from barbarians and was falling apart. In his most important work, *The City of God,* Augustine urged Christians not to trust in Rome or in anything that it stood for, but to think of themselves instead as belonging to God's city in heaven. ■

See also

Christians
Roman ancient history

Augustus, Emperor

Born 63 BC in Italy
The first Emperor of Rome. He took power after the assassination of Julius Caesar and the civil war which followed.
Died AD 14 aged 76

Augustus started life as Gaius Octavius. His mother was the niece of Julius Caesar, and after his father died when Octavius was only 4, Caesar adopted him and made him his heir.

At the time of Caesar's murder, Octavius was studying in Greece. He hurried back to Rome to avenge Caesar's death. He joined forces with Marcus Antonius (Mark Antony) against the murderers Brutus and Cassius. After they had won, Octavius and Antony fought against each other in a civil war. On 11 January, 29 BC, Octavius declared peace throughout the Roman world.

He was now the most powerful man in Rome and took the name given to him by the senate, Augustus (that is 'a person to be respected'). The word 'emperor' comes from another title, *imperator*, but he was also called Caesar. Augustus was careful to appoint the right people in powerful positions. He established a new system of government: that of rule by one man. He added various countries to the Roman empire and created peace for the Roman people for over 30 years.

During his long reign he transformed the city of Rome. One writer said that he 'found Rome built of sun-dried bricks and left it covered in marble'. On the deaths of his two grandsons he adopted Tiberius (son by his wife's first marriage) as his heir and the next emperor of Rome. He died in Nola, in Italy. ■

See also

Roman ancient history

Biography
Caesar

Austen, Jane

Born 1775 in Hampshire, England
She wrote some of the best novels in the world.
Died 1817 aged 41

Jane was the seventh child of a country clergyman. He and his wife always encouraged their children, converting the rectory barn into a little theatre for plays put on by the family during the summer holidays. By the age of 12, Jane was writing her own stories, reading them out to the rest of her household.

Later on as a young woman she had several romances but never married, although she came close to it once. She accepted a young man one evening, but then turned him down the next morning.

She devoted her life to her numerous nieces and nephews, and to the writing of six outstandingly witty novels. In her stories attractive heroines always

▲ Cassandra, Jane Austen's sister, made this sketch of her in 1810, when Jane was about 35 years old.

find a husband in the end even though this often seems unlikely because of various misunderstandings and obstacles standing in their way.

In *Pride and Prejudice*, which Jane Austen wrote in 1797, when she was 21, the heroine Elizabeth first of all refuses her proud friend Mr Darcy but later wishes she had accepted him when she knows him better. Despite many discouragements everything finally works out happily.

In *Emma*, one of her last books, the heroine also makes some mistakes but ends by marrying not the first man she liked but a nicer one she had previously rather taken for granted. The other four novels written by Jane Austen are entitled: *Northanger Abbey*, *Sense and Sensibility*, *Mansfield Park* and *Persuasion*.

Jane Austen did not simply write love stories, though. She was also very amusing at the expense of certain pompous, shallow characters who always come off very badly in her novels. And she describes the life led by people like her at the time that she was writing so memorably that readers afterwards often feel they have been there themselves. ■

Babbage, Charles

Born 1792 in Totnes, Devon, England
Mathematician obsessed with the idea of building a great calculating machine
Died 1871 aged 78

Babbage studied mathematics at the University of Cambridge. Here he began to improve the standard of English mathematics by making sure that English mathematicians knew about the work of clever European mathematicians. He also calculated a correct table of logarithms so that mathematical calculations could be done very accurately. But most of his life was filled with his determination to build a magnificent calculating machine.

He persuaded the British Government to invest £17,000 in the project (a very large sum of money in those days). He himself provided £6,000, money he had inherited from his father who had been a banker.

The project was never completed, mainly because the sort of machine that could be built at that time was too clumsy for what Babbage wanted to do. But Babbage is often called the 'grandfather of the modern computer' because of his original ideas. ■

See also

Calculators   **Biography**
Computers   Napier
Mathematics   Pascal

Bach, Johann Sebastian

Born 1685 in Eisenach, Germany
The greatest member of a remarkable family of musicians
Died 1750 aged 65

We know of more than 50 members of the Bach family who were musicians of one sort or another. The greatest of them all was Johann Sebastian.

He first studied music with his elder brother, but seems to have taught himself to compose by copying out the music of the composers he most admired. When he was 15 he found work in the choir in Lüneburg. Two years later he became an organist in Arnstadt. He then worked as a court musician, first for the Duke of Weimar and then for Prince Leopold of Cöthen. His last and most important post was as organist and choirmaster of St Thomas's Church, Leipzig.

When working as a court musician Bach wrote mainly chamber and orchestral works, including the six Brandenburg Concertos. When working for the church, he wrote organ music, cantatas, and great choral works, such as the *St Matthew Passion*. He wrote music as part of the daily routine of his job. The fact that he was a great genius probably never occurred to his employers.

Although he was very famous in his day (particularly as an organist), Bach's music was soon forgotten after his death. It was not until the 19th century that people began to realize how great it was.

He married twice and had 20 children. Two of them, Carl Philipp Emanuel (1714–1788) and Johann Christian (1735–1782), became, for a time, even more famous than their father. ■

See also

Choirs
Concertos

▼ St Thomas's church and school in Leipzig, Germany, in 1723, at the time when Bach was organist and choirmaster there.

Bacon, Sir Francis

Born 1561
Elizabethan politician and writer
Died 1626 aged 65

Francis Bacon was often ill as a child and spent a great deal of his time studying. He went to Cambridge University at the age of 12 and, after training to become a lawyer, spent most of his life working for the government.

Bacon is most famous for his essays. An essay is a fairly short piece of writing on a particular subject. Bacon's were about ideas such as 'Truth', 'Revenge' and 'Ambition'. He published 58 essays altogether. People still enjoy reading what he had to say about human beings, their beliefs and the world they live in.

Francis Bacon was knighted in 1603 and two years later published the *Advancement of Learning*, which gave his opinions on education at that time. In this and other books, he urged people to collect and classify facts about the world. He tried also to work out a method of using the facts collected to develop new scientific knowledge. He was one of the first people to predict that the world could be transformed by this kind of science. In 1618 he became Lord Verulam and was also given his most important government position, Lord Chancellor of England. He continued to write a great deal until his death. ■

Baden-Powell, Lord Robert

Born 1857 in London, England
The founder of the worldwide Scouting movement
Died 1941 aged 83

Robert Baden-Powell was one of ten children, and his father died when he was 3. When Robert was 19 he joined the British army. He was sent to southern Africa during the Boer War disguised as a reporter. His job was to collect important information and to correct maps of country held by the Boers. Later he was commanded to train some black African soldiers to scout out enemy country. He was so good at it that his enemies called him 'the wolf that never sleeps'. He taught his scouts to notice details in the countryside, organizing them into small groups so that they could act more quickly.

He became famous for the defence of Mafeking. His troops, 1,251 against 9,000 Boers, protected the town for 217 days before the siege ended. When he returned to Britain he was surprised to learn that his *Aids to Scouting*, which he had written for his soldiers, was being taught in schools. He rewrote it as a book for boys and in 1908 founded the Boy Scout Movement. His sister Agnes helped found the Girl Guide Movement in 1910, and later his wife, Olave, became World Chief Guide. ■

See also

Boer War
Guides

Scouts

▲ The Baden-Powells at their home in Bentley, Hampshire, in 1923. Sir Robert (he became Lord Baden-Powell in 1929) is shown giving the Scout salute, while Lady Baden-Powell gives the Guide salute. Their children Peter and Heather can be seen giving the Cub and Brownie salutes.

Baird, John Logie

Born 1888 in Helensburgh, Scotland
The 'father of television'
Died 1946 aged 57

John Logie Baird was the first person to show that it was possible to transmit visual images, and so his name will always be part of television's history.

▲ Baird looking at his first television set in 1925. The screen is at the end of the triangular paper tube. The picture is being 'drawn' by spots of light from holes in a rotating disc.

Baird's first jobs as an engineer were so miserable that when he was 26 he decided to go it alone and become an inventor. His early ideas flopped and by the time he was 35 he had lost all his money. But in 1923 he started work on a machine to transmit pictures, as well as sound, by radio. Soon he was able to send crude images by wireless transmitter to a receiver a few feet away. In January 1926 he gave a television demonstration to the public at the Royal Institution in London. This was the very first demonstration of television.

In 1929 the BBC made the first television broadcast, using Baird's equipment. Baird was also responsible for the first sight and sound broadcast and the first outside broadcast (the Derby in 1931). But he failed to make use of the cathode-ray tubes on which modern televisions depend and lost a competition against this rival system in 1933. ■

See also

Radio
Television

Balboa, Vasco Núñez de

Born about 1475 at Jerez de los Caballeros, Spain
Spanish adventurer who was the first European to see the Pacific Ocean
Executed 1519 aged about 44

Balboa was a member of a noble Spanish family. He had no money, so in 1501 when he was 26 years old he sailed to the Caribbean to make his fortune. He settled on the island of Hispaniola (now Haiti), but he was not a success as a colonist. So in 1510 he stowed away aboard a ship that was carrying an expedition to found a new settlement on the coast of Central America.

Although Balboa did not have the necessary qualities to be a good colonist, nevertheless he proved to be a born leader. Within a year he had made the little settlement at Darién a success, and the King of Spain confirmed him as Governor of Darién.

Some American Indians told Balboa that there was another ocean near by, and great wealth for the taking. Balboa reported this to the king, who created a much larger colony of Panama and appointed a cruel and ruthless soldier, Pedrarias Dávila, as its governor.

Balboa decided he would find the other ocean before the new governor arrived. With a small party of Spaniards and some hundreds of Indians, he hacked his way through the jungle until from a hilltop he could see the sea. He rushed down the hill and plunged into the waves in full armour, crying out that the sea belonged to the King of Spain. He was rewarded with the title of Governor of the South Seas.

When Pedrarias heard of Balboa's new title he became jealous of him. Just as Balboa was preparing to lead an expedition to Peru, Pedrarias falsely accused him of treason and had him beheaded. ■

◑ See also

American Indians
Conquistadores
Explorers
Spanish colonial history

▼ In 1513 Balboa led an expedition from the Spanish settlement at Darién across the narrow strip of land linking North and South America. On 25 September, from a mountain top in Panama, he became the first European to see the Pacific Ocean.

Banks, Sir Joseph

Born 1743 in London, England
Best remembered for his influence on the early settlement of Australia
Died 1820 aged 77

Joseph Banks was the son of a wealthy doctor. While still at school he became interested in botany, and when, at the age of 21, he inherited his father's fortune, he was able to explore the world looking for new plants and animals. His first expedition, in 1766, was to Labrador and Newfoundland.

In 1768 Banks set sail with Captain Cook on the *Endeavour* bound for Tahiti and the South Seas. He took with him several artists to make drawings of plants and animals on the spot. The voyage lasted for three years. In the course of it Banks had taken part in the first exploration of Australia. The beautiful Australian plants *Banksia* are named after him.

On his return, apart from an expedition to Iceland, Banks made no more long journeys. In 1788 he became President of the Royal Society, the most important British scientific society, a post he kept until his death. He was a friend of the king, George III, and

▲ The paintings above were made by artists who accompanied Banks on his travels. These Australian plants were given the botanical name *Banksia* in honour of him.

advised him on the enlargement and arrangement of the gardens at Kew and on his merino sheep, which were later to become so important in Australia. He was a friendly and hospitable person who kept open house for anybody who was interested in natural history. His collections and library were always available for other scientists to use. ■

◑ See also

Botanists
Royal Society

Biography
Cook

Barnardo, Thomas

Born 1845 in Dublin, Ireland
He founded a charity to care for children in need, which is still one of the largest of its kind.
Died 1905 aged 60

Thomas Barnardo was the son of a furrier who had emigrated from Germany to Dublin. He was a sickly child. Poor eyesight forced him to wear blue-tinted spectacles, and he never

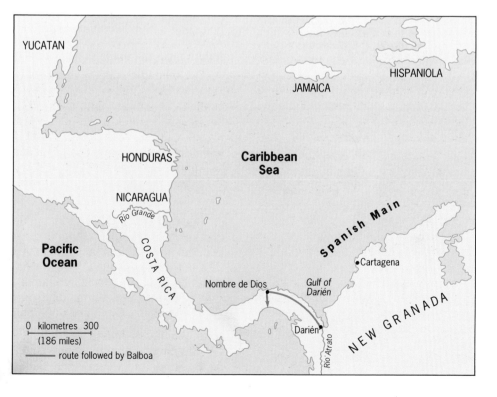

YUCATAN

JAMAICA

HISPANIOLA

HONDURAS

NICARAGUA

Río Grande

Caribbean Sea

COSTA RICA

Pacific Ocean

Spanish Main

Nombre de Dios

•Cartagena

Gulf of Darién

Darién

Río Atrato

NEW GRANADA

0 kilometres 300
(186 miles)
— route followed by Balboa

▲ This photograph shows the crowded conditions in the dining room of a Barnardo's home in the 1930s. Today Barnardo's no longer runs such large homes. The work of the charity includes arranging foster families and adoption, and supporting families where there are children with physical or mental handicaps.

grew taller than 1·60 m (5 ft 3 in), but he was always clever and high-spirited.

At 21 he moved to London to study medicine in preparation for missionary work in China. He abandoned his studies to preach and teach among the poor families of the East End.

One winter evening a 10-year-old boy begged to sleep at school because he had no home. The child showed him where other boys were sleeping rough rather than enter the workhouse. Barnardo began to raise money to provide them with a home and trained them to be wood-choppers, city messengers and boot and brush makers. When a boy he had turned away was found dead of cold and hunger, he vowed to take in any child in need.

Barnardo had lots of energy, remarkable powers of organization and a flair for fund-raising. His combination of authority and infectious gaiety won respect from the roughest children and helped him fight back against criticism and mounting debts. In his lifetime nearly 60,000 needy and handicapped children were sheltered and trained in Dr Barnardo's

Homes. His belief that no child's case is hopeless and that none should be denied help led to the state taking greater responsibility for protecting children against neglect and abuse. ■

⊙ See also

Charities
Children
Victorian Britain

▼ Captain Hook is the villain in *Peter Pan*. His hand was bitten off by a crocodile and he had it replaced with a vicious hook, from which he took his name. This production of the play made from the book was performed by the Royal Shakespeare Company in 1983.

Barrie, Sir J. M.

Born 1860 in Kirriemuir, Scotland
His play *Peter Pan* has been a favourite with children for over 80 years.
Died 1937 aged 77

James Matthew Barrie's most famous creation is Peter Pan, who does not want to grow up but wants always to be a little boy and have fun. In many ways Barrie was like Peter Pan, and his childhood memories and thoughts appear in many of his stories and plays.

He was born to a fairly poor household, the son of a handloom weaver. When he was 6 years old, his mother became seriously ill. She was ill for a long time, and while she lay in bed Barrie spent many hours with her, reading books or listening to her stories. It was then that he decided to become a writer.

He went to university, and then settled in London. His first novels were about life in his home town of Kirriemuir, which he called 'Thrums'. Then he began writing plays, and these brought him wealth and fame.

Peter Pan was first performed in 1904, and with its mixture of fairies and pirates, it was at once a roaring success in London and New York. It has been popular ever since. But many of the other plays and books that brought Barrie success are too sentimental for modern taste and are now neglected. ■

Basho

Born 1644 in Ueno city, near Kyoto, Japan
The most famous writer of the very short Japanese poems known as haiku
Died 1694 aged 50

Matsuo Basho was the fourth of seven children of a poor *samurai* (warrior). At the age of 9 he became a page and companion to the eldest son of his warrior lord, and together they studied literature, especially poetry. Later Basho studied Chinese and Japanese literature in Kyoto, where the emperor lived, and in 1672 moved to the capital city of Edo (now Tokyo), where he became well known as a poet. In the last ten years of his life Basho went on several long journeys on foot around Japan. This was an unusual thing to do, since the roads were very bad, bandits common and travel very dangerous. Basho's accounts of his journeys, particularly *The Narrow Road to the Deep North*, include many of his best and most famous poems. These and his other writings are still widely read, and Basho is regarded as the greatest master ever of the haiku, the seventeen-syllable poem. In 1694 Basho started off on another journey, this time to the south of Japan, but fell ill and died at the city of Osaka in October. ■

See also

Poems and poetry

> On this Spring morning
>
> The moon shines pale through the mist;
>
> It's a flower's face.

Becket, Saint Thomas

Born 1118 in London, England
As Archbishop of Canterbury, he became the most famous English martyr.
Murdered 1170 aged 52

'This boy will be great in the eyes of the Lord,' predicted Becket's father, a wealthy London merchant. The young Becket wanted desperately to live up to these expectations, and he went to Paris for his education, the best place in Europe. Trained as a lawyer, a priest and a knight, he entered the household of the Archbishop of Canterbury, where he soon attracted the attention of the new king, Henry II. At the age of 36, Becket became the king's chancellor. Henry loved working with Becket, and in 1162 the king decided to make his friend Archbishop of Canterbury.

To everyone's surprise, Becket at once resigned as chancellor, and started to live like a holy man, fasting, wearing a hair shirt next to his skin and even beating himself. Saying that his duty to God as archbishop now came before his duty to the king, he challenged Henry's claims to power over the Church.

Henry grew more and more angry as Becket refused to give way. The other bishops could not decide what to do. They knew that they should support

▲ Saint Thomas is seen kneeling at the altar in this stained glass window made in the 13th century for Canterbury Cathedral. His shrine at Canterbury became a place of worship for four centuries after his death, until the Reformation.

their archbishop, but also thought that he was being stubborn for the sake of it. After six years of quarrelling, including a period of exile for Becket, the two men seemed ready to make peace.

Then, in 1170, Becket excommunicated (cut off from membership of the Church) the bishops whom he felt had most betrayed him. The king flew into a temper, saying 'Will no man rid me of this turbulent priest?' Four of his knights took him at his word, went to Canterbury and slaughtered the archbishop at his cathedral altar.

This was a sensational event which shocked the whole Christian world. People even compared Becket's death with Christ's crucifixion. Nobody doubted that Becket was a great Christian martyr. In 1172 the Pope declared Becket to be a saint, and two years later he forced Henry II to make a pilgrimage to his friend's tomb in Canterbury cathedral. ■

The name is also spelt: Thomas à Becket.

See also

Saints
Stained glass

Biography
Henry II

Bede, the Venerable

Born about AD 673
Bede was the first person to write a proper history of the English people.
Died AD 735 aged about 62

At the age of 7 Bede was admitted to the monastery of St Peter at Wearmouth in the north of England to begin his education. He stayed on at the monastery and became a monk. He later moved to the new monastery which had been built near by at Jarrow. As well as carrying out all the duties of a monk, he began to write. He wrote about all sorts of subjects including astronomy and medicine.

His most famous work, which he finished in 731, was *The History of the English Church and People*. Bede tells us that he got his information from a variety of sources, such as 'local stories' and 'ancient documents', to write a history from the Roman period until his own day. Bede put his great work together by analysing the evidence, as a historian would do today. He wrote well, too, and his *History* was the most popular book of the time. Like all other monks he wrote in Latin.

About 150 years later, King Alfred the Great ordered Bede's *History* to be translated into Anglo-Saxon so that more people could read it. ■

See also

Anglo-Saxons
History

Biography
Alfred

Beethoven, Ludwig van

Born 1770 in Bonn, Germany
One of the greatest composers of all time, famous for his sonatas, quartets and concertos, and nine great symphonies
Died 1827 aged 56

Beethoven's father and grandfather were both professional musicians, so it was quite natural for him to follow in their footsteps. His family life was not always happy. His mother died when he was 17 and his father began drinking heavily. Beethoven had to take charge and act as both mother and father to his two young brothers. After a few years he decided to leave Bonn and seek his fortune in Vienna.

Everything went well at first. He made influential friends among the aristocracy and was soon much in demand as a fashionable pianist and teacher. But from about 1796 he began to go deaf. By the end of 1802 his

deafness was serious. At first he was in despair, but he pulled himself together, turned his back on the ordinary pleasures of life and began to concentrate more fiercely than ever on composition.

The music he now wrote, such as the Third and Fifth symphonies, was more powerful and dramatic than anything anyone had ever written before. It seemed to tell of a life and death struggle between titanic forces, ending always in triumph. It was also full of noble ideas. The heroine of his opera *Fidelio* defends her husband against an evil tyrant. The great choral ending of the Ninth Symphony is a celebration of liberty. The main tune is now used as a fitting 'international anthem' for the European Community. The *Missa Solemnis* (Solemn Mass) includes a prayer for deliverance from the horrors of war. In his last string quartets and piano sonatas Beethoven pushed music beyond anything anyone had yet imagined. They were considered unplayable at the time, but we can now see that they are masterpieces. Out of his own unhappiness Beethoven made music that has been an inspiration to people everywhere. ■

See also

Sonatas
Symphonies

▲ This drawing of Ludwig van Beethoven, made in 1818, was probably a study for a life-size portrait of the composer and his nephew which has now been lost.

Bell, Alexander Graham

Born 1847 in Edinburgh, Scotland
Invented the telephone, but is also remembered for teaching deaf people to speak.
Died 1922 aged 75

Bell was trained to follow in the footsteps of his family, who were all experts in teaching people to speak clearly. He went to the USA to continue this work and became convinced that he could teach totally deaf people to speak, even though they were unable to hear the sounds they were trying to imitate. But he was also interested in other kinds of science, and after he was successful in teaching two particular deaf students to speak, their fathers offered to help him with money for his other experiments. One of these experiments led to his invention of the telephone, and he set up a company to develop and make telephones for sale. This, his most famous invention, is remembered in

▲ Bell demonstrated his telephone to a group of businessmen in 1892 by sending a call from New York to Chicago. He had built his first experimental telephone sixteen years earlier in 1876.

the name of one of the great corporations of America, Bell Telephone Systems.

Bell had many other interests, one of which was to make a kite that could carry a person. His wife, Mabel Hubbard Bell, in helping him, became the first woman to provide the money for a society devoted to research, the Aerial Experiment Association.

In 1898 Bell became President of the National Geographic Society, and was so convinced that one of the best ways of teaching was through pictures that he started the National Geographic magazine, now world famous for its superb colour pictures. ■

See also

Deafness
Inventors
Patents
Telephones

Benedict, Saint

Born about AD 480 in Nursia, Italy
He wrote an important Rule for monks and founded the Benedictine order.
Died AD 547 aged about 67

Benedict's parents were wealthy and ambitious for their son. They sent him to school in Rome, but Benedict decided to devote his life to God. At the age of 14 he ran away to live on his own as a hermit in a cave, about 55 km (35 miles) outside Rome. Like Jesus in the wilderness, Benedict prayed to God and fought the temptations of the Devil.

Soon he was discovered, by a priest and some shepherds. His reputation spread, and Roman noblemen began to visit him. Many wanted him to help them lead a holy life. Benedict set up twelve small monasteries, but was forced to leave the area because a local priest was jealous of his fame. He went south to a mountain overlooking the town of Cassino. There he built the monastery of Monte Cassino.

To help all his monks, Benedict wrote a Rule which set out the way in which they should live. He explained what it meant to be a monk, and provided practical details on how the monastery should be run: for example, when to eat and sleep. Benedict stressed that monasteries should be self-sufficient, with their own farms and workshops. He encouraged study and the production of manuscripts and he urged that there should be no snobbery: monks who had been noblemen should not look down on others who had been shepherds.

During his lifetime, neither he nor his Rule were well known. Forty years after Benedict's death, Pope Gregory I wrote about his life, and over the next 300 years most of the monasteries in western Europe came to use the Rule. This is still the case today. Monks who follow Benedict's Rule are called Benedictines. ■

See also

Monasteries   **Biography**
Saints   Gregory I

Ben-Gurion, David

Born 1886 in Plonsk, Poland
Campaigned for Israel's independence and became its first prime minister.
Died 1973 aged 87

Ben-Gurion has been called 'the George Washington of Israel', because like Washington he fought for his country's independence and led it in its early years. His original name was Gruen, but he changed it to Ben-Gurion ('son of a lion-cub') after he emigrated to Palestine in 1906. He became a leader of the labour movement there.

Palestine was then part of the Turkish Ottoman empire, and Ben-Gurion was expelled as a trouble-maker by the Turks. He went to the USA and joined the Jewish Legion, a band of volunteers which fought in the British army in Palestine in World War I.

After the war Palestine came under British rule. Between the world wars Ben-Gurion was general secretary of the Histadrut (the General Confederation of Palestine Jewish Workers), and organized the defence of the Jewish settlers against hostile Arabs.

When European Jews wanted to enter Palestine and were not allowed to do so, Ben-Gurion began campaigning for an independent Jewish state there. In 1947 the United Nations decided that Palestine should be divided between Jews and Arabs, and in 1948 Ben-Gurion proudly read out the proclamation which declared Israel independent. He became prime minister, and led the new country's successful defence against an all-out attack from its Arab neighbours.

Ben-Gurion guided Israel through its early years when more than a million Jews moved into Israel. He became Israel's father-figure, called *ha-Zaken*, the 'Old Man', by his colleagues. He retired in 1953, a weary man, but was recalled in 1955 to serve as prime minister again until 1963. ■

See also

Israel
Ottoman empire
Palestine

Bernard, Saint

Born about 1090 near Dijon, France
He was the most powerful man of God in
12th-century Europe.
Died 1153 aged about 63

Bernard's mother brought up her six sons to live like holy men, giving them plain food even though their family was noble and wealthy. From an early age Bernard knew that he wanted to be a monk. When he was 20 he decided to join the newly-founded monastery at Cîteaux. He persuaded not only his five brothers to come with him, but also his uncle and 30 other people. Within two years he was abbot of another monastery at Clairvaux, a daughter house of Cîteaux.

Bernard and his companions were known as Cistercians because they followed the strict and simple way of life practised at Cîteaux. He spoke out against the lax monastic life of the previous century with its costly buildings and endless singing. Instead, he wanted to return to the example of earlier monks, like St Benedict, and built his simple monasteries in deserted and desolate places. Bernard's example made the Cistercians the most powerful monastic order in 12th-century Europe.

Bernard's influence was not limited to monasteries. He encouraged crusaders, attacked heretics (people who disagreed with the teaching of the Church), became involved in the election of bishops, and was even called on to settle a dispute between two candidates for the position of Pope. Bernard could be stern and fearless, condemning scholars and rebuking kings and emperors. Such wide-ranging activities made him many enemies, but while fully involved in the world, he remained absorbed in his worship of God. The Pope made Bernard a saint in 1174. ∎

See also

Crusades
Heretics
Middle Ages
Monasteries
Popes
Biography
Benedict

Bernstein, Leonard

Born 1918 in Lawrence, Massachusetts, USA
A composer and conductor whose work goes across all styles of music. Famous as the composer of *West Side Story*.
Died 1990 aged 72

Leonard Bernstein was born into a successful Jewish business family. He was not always a happy child. At school he was picked on because he was a Jew. He also suffered from asthma.

When he was 10, the family acquired a piano. Leonard liked it and asked for lessons. He made quick progress, and went on to study music at Harvard University and at the Curtis Institute of Music. When he was in his mid-twenties he became assistant conductor of a great symphony orchestra, the New York Philharmonic.

From the 1940s he began to be known as a composer of musical shows. The most famous and successful was *West Side Story*, which opened on Broadway, New York, in 1957 and was later made into a film. He wrote many kinds of orchestral and choral music as well as music for the stage, and was a much respected conductor and pianist. Bernstein was also a very successful teacher of conducting. ∎

See also

Musicals

Besant, Annie

Born 1847 in London, England
She fought for birth control, the rights of women workers and independence for India.
Died 1933 aged 85

Annie Besant was born Annie Wood. In 1867 she married a clergyman, Frank Besant. But her marriage was unhappy. When she was 26 she left her husband and began working as a journalist. She cared deeply about women who lived in poverty looking after large families, and she began campaigning for birth control. At that

▲ Here are some of the 'match girls' whom Annie Besant led on their march to the House of Commons in 1888. Many of these girls were as young as 13, which was the school leaving age for most children in those days.

time women were not supposed to talk about such things. When she published a book about it she was arrested and put on trial. Although she was let off, her daughter was taken away from her.

The tragedy of losing her daughter pushed Annie into fighting for more reforms, especially for the London 'match girls'. These young women worked long hours in terrible, unhealthy conditions making matches for only 4 shillings (20p) a week. In 1888, they went on strike for better pay. Annie Besant wrote about their lives in the newspapers and led a procession of match girls to the House of Commons. As a result, they won their strike, and their success helped other low-paid workers to fight for better conditions.

Annie then moved to India and, after studying eastern ideas, became a Hindu. Being very interested in education, she helped to start the Central Hindu College at Varanasi (Benares). As always, she was involved in politics. She believed that India should be an independent country, free of British rule, and she started a newspaper to support this idea. She died before this dream became a reality. ∎

See also

Indian history

Bhutto, Zulfikar Ali

Born 1928 in Larkana, Sind, now in Pakistan
He founded the Pakistan People's Party and served as President and then Prime Minister of Pakistan from 1971 to 1977.
Executed 1979 aged 51

The Bhutto family have been important in the politics of Pakistan for many years. Zulfikar Ali Bhutto was educated at the universities of California and Oxford before becoming a lawyer. At the age of 30 he joined Ayub Khan's cabinet and within five years had become Foreign Minister of Pakistan. In 1967, he started his own party, the Pakistan People's Party, which came to power in 1971. Bhutto was first president and later prime minister.

After the 1977 elections there were riots because some people thought Bhutto had rigged the vote. General Zia ul-Haq led a revolt and overthrew Bhutto's government. Bhutto himself was arrested and charged with the murder of a political opponent. In spite of protests from around the world, he was hanged in April 1979. ■

Bhutto, Benazir

Born 1953 in Larkana, Sind, Pakistan
She followed in her father's footsteps and became Prime Minister of Pakistan in 1988.

Benazir Bhutto completed her education in the USA and England. After her father's execution, she spent a total of six years either in prison or under house arrest. When her brother, Shah Nawaz, died in Paris in 1985, she was very upset and ready to give up her political life. However, the large crowds that gathered for his funeral in Larkana renewed her spirit.

The death of General Zia in an air crash in 1988 led to democratic elections in Pakistan. Benazir won the elections and became prime minister at the age of 35. She was removed from office in 1990. ■

◐ See also

Pakistan

▼ Benazir Bhutto was inspired to become a politician by her father's death. Here she is in 1988 standing proudly before his portrait, before beginning her campaign to become Prime Minister of Pakistan.

Billy the Kid

Born 1859 in New York, USA
William Bonney, or Billy the Kid, as he is more usually known, was the most famous outlaw in the Wild West.
Died 1881 aged 21

▲ This photograph of Billy the Kid was taken around 1880. His real name was originally Henry McCarty. He later used the surnames Antrim, Bonney and Wright.

By the age of 12, Bonney was already a gambler and card player, and perhaps a murderer. It is said that he was only just 12 when he knifed a man for insulting his mother. At 16, he and a partner murdered three Indians and stole the furs they were carrying. In 1877, after more murderous exploits, he became involved in a 'war' between two cattle-ranching families. As leader of one of the gangs he was in one gun battle after another. When that range war was over, Bonney went back to being a cattle thief and a murderer.

In 1880 Pat Garrett became a sheriff with the intention of catching Billy the Kid. In 1881, Bonney was captured and sentenced to hang. However, he escaped from captivity. Two months later, Garrett cornered Bonney and shot him dead.

Bonney murdered at least 21 people. His cheerful manner and his popularity with women have given him a glamorous reputation, and films have been made which show him as a hero. This sometimes happens to criminals. In reality, Bonney was a vicious murderer and a thief, with no feelings towards his unfortunate victims. ■

See also

American West

Bird, Isabella Lucy

Born 1832 in Yorkshire, England
Traveller and writer who brought to her readers vivid accounts of the Wild West of America and the Middle and Far East
Died 1904 aged 72

Isabella Bird was the daughter of a clergyman. As a child she rode with him on his horse around his parish. He taught her to look carefully at everything they passed. When she was 23 she visited friends in Canada and the United States. She began to develop her skills of describing accurately what she saw. Later she travelled to Australia, Japan, India, Tibet, Iran, Korea and China and wrote successful books about her adventures. She married her family doctor, Dr Bishop, and ceased her travels until his death five years later.

Isabella Bird was only 1·50 m (4 ft 11 in) tall. She had a quiet voice, a gentle manner and a will of iron. In England she often felt ill and depressed, but once abroad she rode great distances and lived under very hard conditions. She had 'the appetite of a tiger and the digestion of an ostrich'.

At the age of 70, stout and in pain from an injured spine, she rode a thousand miles through the Atlas Mountains in North Africa on a horse she mounted by stepladder. It was her last journey. ■

Bismarck, Otto von

Born 1815 in Schönhausen, Prussia, Germany
He served as Prime Minister of Prussia from 1862 and helped to create a united Germany in 1871.
Died 1898 aged 83

Bismarck was a member of a noble family in Prussia, which was then only one amongst many German-speaking states. He studied law at university, where he won 28 duels; then he served in the Prussian army. In 1847 he was elected to the Prussian Diet (parliament) and in 1851 represented Prussia in the German Federal Diet, a parliament of all German states. He dreamed of uniting Germany under Prussian leadership.

He was sent as ambassador to Russia and then France from 1859 to 1862, which he said was like being 'put in cold storage'. However, in 1862 King Wilhelm of Prussia called him back to be Minister President (prime minister). Bismarck declared that the great questions of the time would have to be settled by 'blood and iron', and the greatest question of all for him was the future of Germany.

In 1864 he picked a quarrel with

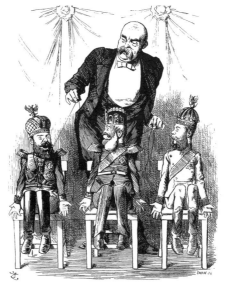

▲ This 1884 cartoon from the British magazine, *Punch*, shows the Tsar of Russia, the Kaiser of Germany and the Emperor of Austria-Hungary. Bismarck is behind them holding the strings as though they are puppets and he is controlling them.

Denmark. With Austrian help, Prussia captured the duchies of Schleswig and Holstein. Then in 1866, Prussian armies defeated Austria in the Seven Weeks War. In 1870 war broke out between France and Prussia. France was heavily defeated in 1871 and Prussia gained two border provinces, Alsace and Lorraine.

These victories persuaded other German states to join a German *Reich* (empire) with Wilhelm of Prussia as *Kaiser* (emperor) and Bismarck as chancellor. He was given the title Prince von Bismarck.

Germany gained colonies in both the Pacific and Africa and built up a fleet to compete with the British Royal Navy. Bismarck organized a congress in Berlin in 1878 which prevented a war in the Balkans, and the next year made an alliance with the Austro-Hungarian empire.

At home his government introduced the first national insurance scheme against accidents, illness and old age. Many countries later copied this idea.

The Iron Chancellor's career ended after Wilhelm died in 1888. Wilhelm's son, Frederick III, died too after only a few months. His grandson, Wilhelm II, was jealous of Bismarck's power and dismissed him in 1890. ■

See also

German history

Blake, William

Born 1757 in London, England
English poet and artist. He wrote 'The Tyger' and other inspiring poems, which he illustrated himself.
Died 1827 aged 69

Even as a boy William loved poetry and art. His father used to buy him small plaster casts of statues which he then drew. When he was 10, his father sent him to a drawing school. At the age of 14 he was apprenticed to an engraver to learn how to prepare designs and illustrations for books. When his seven-year apprenticeship

▲ These small, beautiful books of Blake's poetry, the design interwoven with the words in a unique way, are now worth thousands of pounds. Yet when Blake was alive, few people bought them.

was over, he enrolled as a student at the Royal Academy, but he hated the smooth and empty art works that he saw all around him. For the rest of his life he earned his living as an engraver. He married Catherine Boucher, whom he taught to read and write, and who was a great help and support to him in his work.

When he was in his mid-twenties, Blake began to write poetry and illustrate it with pictures of the biblical visions that he himself saw. He etched his poems on copper plates, and then printed and coloured the pages with his wife's help. Some of his finest poems appeared in a small volume called *Songs of Innocence*, which was published in 1789. They are direct and happy and full of tenderness. His later poems, including *Songs of Experience*, 1794, and *Milton*, 1804, show the anger and sadness he felt when innocent beings suffered or when his green and pleasant England was spoiled by factories that men built to make money. He protested against the cruel use of children as chimney-sweeps.

Only a fraction of Blake's poetry and paintings have survived, though that makes a large quantity. In his lifetime, few people valued his work and a lot of it was thrown away. ■

Blondin, Charles

Born Jean-Francois Gravelet, in 1824 near Calais, France
The most famous tightrope walker of all time
Died 1897 aged 72

Born into a circus family, Blondin was an 'aerobat' at 5 years of age. He did various tricks, but the tightrope, or high wire, became his speciality.

In 1859 he achieved the feat for which he will always be known. He rigged a high wire above Niagara Falls and walked across, the first person ever to do so. Having made it look easy, he repeated the walk many times, and then devised various ways of adding to it. His most fearsome trick was to call for volunteers to be carried across either piggyback or in a wheelbarrow.

After his Niagara feats he settled in England, where he performed many times and where he eventually died, in his bed. ■

▼ High-wire artistes use a long pole to help them balance as they step out on their wire. Here Blondin crosses the Niagara Falls dressed in his showy costume.

Blume, Judy

Born 1938 in New Jersey, USA
American writer of fiction for older children and young teenagers

Judy Blume was born and lived most of her life in New Jersey in America. She started her career working in education, taking a degree at New York University. Soon after, she began writing books such as *Are you there, God? It's me, Margaret* and *It's Not the End of the World*, about the problems and difficulties of growing up.

Her stories are a mixture of fiction, in the plots, and of real-life difficulties, such as being fat, or having divorcing parents. Her books draw strongly on her own memories of adolescence, and their realism struck a chord with her teenage readers. She soon became the most popular children's writer in America, receiving nearly 2,000 letters a month from children, commenting on her books and telling her about their own problems. From the money that she made from her books, she founded an organization to study children's needs and to help them. ■

Blyton, Enid

Born 1897 in London, England
Author of over 700 books for children,
including the well-known Noddy, Famous
Five and Secret Seven series
Died 1968 aged 71

Enid Blyton first started to study music, and then trained as a teacher. She did not teach for long, though, but became an educational journalist. It was then that she started to write children's books.

Her first book for children, a collection of poems called *Child Whispers*, was published in 1922. In the late 1930s, just before World War II, she started publishing the Noddy stories, for very small children, and adventure stories such as the Famous Five and the Secret Seven, for older children. It was not long before she added school story series, like Malory Towers and The Naughtiest Girl in the School, to her growing list of publications.

She had a very strong sense of the need to educate her readers, and to give them a clear picture of right and wrong behaviour. Her stories have been enjoyed by a great many children ever since they were first published, although teachers and librarians have often said that they felt the plots were too simple and the style of the writing was very flat and uninteresting. ■

Bogle, Paul

Born about 1825 in Jamaica
He is one of Jamaica's national heroes,
who gave his life in leading a protest
against unfair treatment of ex-slaves.
Executed 1865 aged about 40

Paul Bogle was born a slave. When slaves in the British colonies were freed in 1834, most wanted to move to their own small farms. The ex-owners wanted to keep them as low-paid labourers. Paul Bogle became a Baptist deacon (a church leader), and built a chapel at Stony Gut in east Jamaica where he taught that ex-slaves had the

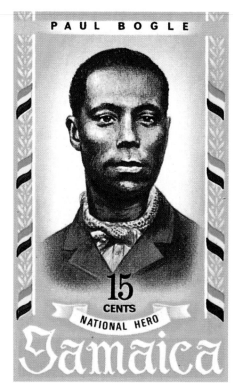

▲ One way of honouring national heroes is to put their pictures on postage stamps. Here Paul Bogle is shown on a Jamaican stamp.

right to choose their own way of life. This angered plantation owners, who were magistrates and used their power to stop blacks from getting land. They were backed by Jamaica's governor.

Paul Bogle led a 72-km (45-mile) march to the governor, but he refused to see them. Then Bogle called his followers together to discuss ways of fighting for their cause. In October 1865 they freed a man held by the police outside the courthouse in nearby Morant Bay. Police came to arrest Bogle, but men in Stony Gut forced them back. Later, Bogle and his followers gathered in Morant Bay and soldiers fired on them. Fighting followed and some magistrates were killed. It was a serious riot, but the governor decided it was more, a rebellion. He sent troops, who flogged 600 'rebels' and executed more than 400 without a proper trial. One was Paul Bogle. ■

See also

Caribbean history
Jamaica

Bohr, Niels Henrik

Born 1885 in Copenhagen, Denmark
Considered one of the great physicists
of the 20th century for his work on the
structure of atoms
Died 1962 aged 77

Bohr's father was a professor of physiology at the University of Copenhagen, where Niels himself studied physics. He not only showed his ability as a physicist but was also a really good footballer.

Bohr came to England in 1912 and worked with the great physicist Ernest Rutherford trying to discover what atoms really looked like. Bohr's work showed that atoms have a nucleus at the centre and electrons arranged in orbits a fixed distance away from the nucleus. In 1922 Bohr received a Nobel prize for this work.

During World War II Bohr worked hard to help many Jewish physicists and Danish Jews escape from the tortures that they faced under Hitler. In 1943 he left Europe for the USA, where he worked on the atom bomb project. But he was so horrified by the terrible effects that such a bomb could produce that he spent the rest of his life working for the peaceful uses of atomic energy. ■

See also

Atoms   **Biography**
Bombs   Einstein
Nuclear power   Rutherford

Bolívar, Simón

Born 1783 in Caracas, Venezuela
He was a brilliant general who led the
struggle against the Spanish rulers of
northern South America and became
known as the Liberator.
Died 1830 aged 47

Simón Bolívar's mother and father were rich, but they died when he was young. He was educated privately. As a young man, he twice travelled to Europe. There he was inspired by new ideas which claimed that all men should be free and equal. He returned

▲ Bolivar was not popular with all South Americans. Some of them, who were jealous of his fame as *el Libertador* (Liberator) and who disagreed with his plans for unification, tried to assassinate him not long before his death.

to South America in 1807, eager to free his country from Spanish rule. In 1810, he joined a group of rebels who captured Caracas, the capital city of Venezuela, but the Spaniards fought back. Bolívar became a military leader in 1811, recaptured Caracas in 1813 and was given the title of Liberator.

A year later, setbacks forced Bolívar to flee to Jamaica and Haiti. But by 1817 he was once more fighting on the mainland of South America. He scored a great victory over the Spaniards in Colombia in 1819. That same year he founded Gran Colombia (a group of states made up of present-day Colombia, Venezuela, Ecuador and Panama), and became president.

In 1822, Bolívar met the other great South American patriot and soldier, José de San Martín, who freed Argentina and Chile from Spanish rule. Bolívar later helped to defeat Spanish armies in Venezuela, Ecuador and Peru. These victories marked the end of Spanish power in South America.

In upper Peru, the people decided to form a separate republic. They named it Bolivia, in honour of their liberator, Simón Bolívar. Bolívar dreamed of uniting the whole of South America. But his dream never came true, and he died a disappointed man. ∎

See also

Bolivia
Spanish colonial history

Bonington, Christian

Born 1934 in London, England
One of Britain's best-known mountain climbers

Chris Bonington's early life was not always successful. He suffered from nerves when taking examinations and failed to get into university. Instead he went to Cranwell to train for the Royal Air Force. Unfortunately, he failed in his attempt to become a pilot, so he became an army officer instead.

When he was 16, a relation gave him a book of photographs of the Scottish mountains and that started him climbing. He carried on climbing throughout the eight years he spent in the army. Then he tried working as a management trainee selling margarine for Unilever. Nine months of that was enough. In 1962 he decided to try his luck as a full-time climber, earning money from writing, lecturing and photography. Some very successful climbs helped to make him well known, particularly the North Face of the Eiger (1962), Annapurna (1970) and Everest (1972, 1975 and 1985). ∎

See also

Mountains

Boone, Daniel

Born 1734 near Philadelphia, Pennsylvania, USA
A hero of the American Frontier who led early settlers into Indian territory in the West
Died 1820 aged 85

Daniel Boone never spent a day in a schoolhouse. Instead he hunted with the Indians who visited his father's farm. He grew up almost as skilled as they were in tracking in the wilderness. He traced their 'Warrior Path' from Pennsylvania through the Cumberland Gap in the Allegheny Mountains to the unexplored territory beyond.

On his first attempt to lead settlers to the West, his 16-year-old son was captured and tortured to death by the Indians. Two years later he completed the journey and founded Fort Boonesborough in Kentucky. For 20 years he led the defence of this settlement against Indian attack.

Boone liked to hunt alone. He seemed more at ease among the Indians than

▼ Daniel Boone soon became a hero of the American West. This painting was done by William Ranney nearly 30 years after Boone's death and shows him taking his first look at Kentucky after the long trek west.

among his own people. His simplicity in matters of law and money led to debts and misunderstandings with his neighbours. He took his family further west to Missouri and died there in his sleep, aged 85. 'I wouldn't give a hoot in Hell for a man who isn't sometimes afraid,' he once said. 'It's fear's the spice that makes it interesting to go ahead.' ■

See also

American West

Booth, Catherine and William

Together they started the Salvation Army.
William Born 1829 in Nottingham, England
Died 1912 aged 83
Catherine Born 1829 in Ashbourne, England
Died 1890 aged 61

As a young man William Booth knew poverty, because his father went bankrupt and died early. He joined the Methodist Church, but left because he wanted to preach his own ideas. In 1855 he married Catherine Mumford, a social worker. Together they started the Whitechapel Christian Mission in a poor part of London. In 1878 they changed the name to the Salvation Army, a Christian army to fight sin and poverty. William became the first General of the Salvation Army.

Catherine believed that women had as much right to preach as men. She made sure that the Salvation Army gave equal rights to all its members. She died in 1890, but William Booth continued their work. His book *In Darkest England* gave many ideas on how to help people suffering from poverty, homelessness and alcoholism. With the help of their son Bramwell and daughter Evangeline, the Salvation Army grew worldwide, and today it is still active in helping poor and homeless people everywhere. ■

See also

Salvation Army

Boru, Brian

Born about AD 926 in Ireland
The first king to rule all Ireland
Died 1014 aged about 88

When Brian was born the Irish thought of their country as five provinces: Ulster in the north, Connacht in the west, Meath in the centre, Munster in the south and Leinster in the south-east. Around the coast there were settlements of Viking traders. The provinces were often split between many chiefs. Sometimes one family would rule as kings, as the Uí Néill did in Ulster.

Brian's older brother was a chief who became king of Munster. After his brother was killed, Brian fought against the other kings. He became king of Munster, and in 1002 the Uí Néill king of Ulster came with Brian to Tara and

Boudica

Born date unknown, in East Anglia, Britain
Queen of the Iceni tribe who led a great rebellion against Roman rule in Britain
Committed suicide AD 61, age unknown

After the Romans had occupied Britain, some tribes were trusted to govern themselves. The Iceni tribe (in modern Norfolk) under their king Prasutagus was one of these. But when the king died in AD 59, the Romans decided to bring the area under full Roman rule. According to the historian Tacitus, the Romans behaved brutally. 'Roman officers plundered his kingdom. Boudica (the king's widow) was flogged and his daughters raped. The king's own relatives were treated like slaves.'

Boudica, whose name in her Celtic language meant 'Victory', was described by Tacitus as 'a very big woman, terrifying to look at, with a fierce look on her face. She wore her great mass of hair the colour of a lion's mane right down to her hips.' She gathered an army around her to fight

accepted him as high king. For a few years Brian could truly say he was king of all Ireland. In the Book of Armagh his own scribes called him Emperor of the Irish. Even the Vikings paid tribute into his treasury. But he kept power only by many battles against rivals. In 1014 he fought an army of Irish and Viking warriors at Clontarf near Dublin. His soldiers won but Brian was killed.

A Norse saga said that 'Brian died but saved his kingdom.' But his successors lost what he had gained. Later they invented legends depicting him not only as the victor over the Vikings, but as a great king who brought peace to Ireland and restored learning to her schools. ■

See also

Ireland's history
Vikings

against the Roman oppressors. At first the rebellion went well as Boudica's army destroyed the towns of Colchester, Verulamium (now St Albans) and London. They even massacred a legionary army sent out from Lincoln. In the end, the Roman governor of Britain, Suetonius Paulinus, brought a great force from North Wales and destroyed the rebel army, somewhere in Warwickshire, it is thought. Boudica took poison to avoid capture by the Romans. ■

The name is also spelt Boudicca or Boadicea.

See also

Roman Britain

Boyle, Robert

Born 1627 in Lismore Castle, Ireland
His ideas and experiments helped establish the beginning of modern chemistry.
Died 1691 aged 64

Robert Boyle was the fourteenth child, and seventh son, of the first Earl of Cork. He was a very clever boy who had an excellent memory and could speak Latin and Greek at the age of 8. In his twenties he settled in Oxford and took part in scientific experiments and discussions with a group of men who called themselves the Invisible College; they later helped to found the Royal Society. Nowadays only top scientists can become Fellows of the Royal Society and put the letters FRS after their names.

Boyle is best remembered for a law of physics named after him. Boyle's law tells us mathematically how the volume of a gas will alter if we change the pressure.

Although Boyle believed in alchemy (being sure that metals like lead could be changed into gold) he did much to establish the method and ideas of modern chemistry. He wrote a famous book called the *Sceptical Chymist*. In this and other books he helped to explain ideas about atoms and elements. But for Boyle ideas were not enough. He insisted on the importance of doing experiments to test whether scientific ideas were really true.

He remained a devout Christian all his life and gave money for missionary work abroad. In his will he founded the 'Boyle lectures' to persuade people that Christianity was the only true religion. ■

See also

Atoms
Chemists
Elements
Gases
Royal Society

Brahe, Tycho

Born 1546 in Scania, Denmark (now in south Sweden)
His observations are the most accurate ever taken without the use of a telescope; they led to a total rethink of the shape of the Solar System.
Died 1601 aged 54

Tycho was the eldest son of ten children born to the Danish nobleman, Otto Brahe, but he was brought up by his childless uncle Jörgen. Tycho had

▲ Tycho Brahe with assistants in his observatory. The instruments are for measuring the positions of the Sun, stars and planets.

a good education and was, as was the custom in those times, sent to university at the age of 13. He studied philosophy and other subjects which his uncle hoped would help him train for an important job in the government. But on 21 August 1560 something happened which changed Brahe's life. It was predicted that on that day a small eclipse of the Sun would be seen in Copenhagen. Brahe was thrilled when the eclipse took place at the predicted time. From then on, despite his uncle's disapproval, he spent his time studying astronomy and mathematics. But Brahe was not only in trouble with his uncle. He had arguments and fights with everyone, and at the age of 19, at a midnight duel, his nose was cut off; he wore a false metal nose for the rest of his life.

Brahe bought elaborate astronomical instruments for taking measurements of the position of stars and planets, but all observations had to be taken with the naked eye. Galileo's telescope was not invented until eight years after Brahe's death. Shortly before he died Brahe gave his astronomical measurements to his assistant Kepler. Kepler used them to produce, for the first time, a true description of the paths along which the planets move in our Solar System. ■

See also

Astronomers
Solar System

Biography
Copernicus
Galilei
Kepler

Brahms, Johannes

Born 1833 in Hamburg, Germany
One of Germany's greatest composers of symphonies, concertos, chamber music and songs
Died 1897 aged 63

Brahms had his first music lessons from his father, who was a double-bass player. He began to study the piano when he was 7, and gave his first recital when he was 10.

▲ Seated at his piano, Brahms poses for the camera. His style of playing the piano was deeply influenced by his friendship with the Schumanns.

Although he was a fine pianist, and later gave many recitals, Brahms really wanted to be a composer. He studied the music of the great masters and gradually found a style of his own. A great step forward came when he met the composer Robert Schumann and his pianist wife, Clara. They treated him like a brother and did everything they could to help and encourage him. A piano concerto, completed when he was 25, was his first important success, but it was not until he went to live in Vienna in 1863 that his composing career really took off.

Outside his music his life was not very exciting. He never married, though for a long time he was in love with Clara Schumann. What mattered was his music: four great symphonies, masses of chamber and piano music; songs, and choral works such as the *German Requiem*; and several fine concertos. To many people he had taken up music where Beethoven left off. ■

See also

Chamber music
Concertos
Symphonies

Biography
Beethoven

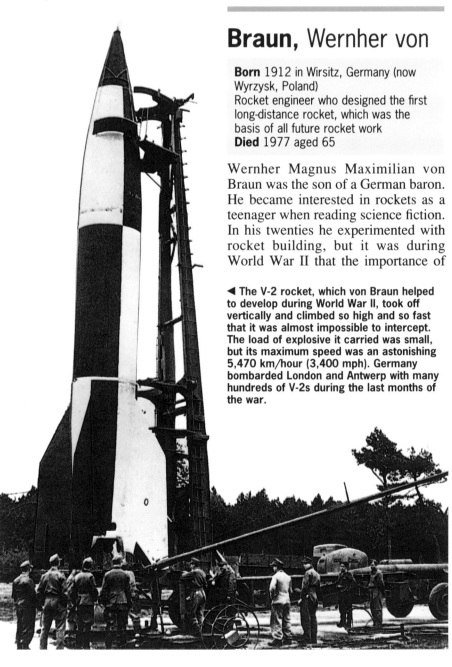

Braun, Wernher von

Born 1912 in Wirsitz, Germany (now Wyrzysk, Poland)
Rocket engineer who designed the first long-distance rocket, which was the basis of all future rocket work
Died 1977 aged 65

Wernher Magnus Maximilian von Braun was the son of a German baron. He became interested in rockets as a teenager when reading science fiction. In his twenties he experimented with rocket building, but it was during World War II that the importance of

◄ The V-2 rocket, which von Braun helped to develop during World War II, took off vertically and climbed so high and so fast that it was almost impossible to intercept. The load of explosive it carried was small, but its maximum speed was an astonishing 5,470 km/hour (3,400 mph). Germany bombarded London and Antwerp with many hundreds of V-2s during the last months of the war.

rockets was recognized; unmanned rockets would be able to carry bombs onto enemy targets. Von Braun, a member of the German Nazi party, headed a team that developed the first true missile; it was called the V-2, where the 'V' stood for *Vergeltung* which means vengeance. This rocket was fuelled with alcohol and liquid oxygen and had an explosive warhead. It could travel a distance of about 300 km (200 miles). Over a thousand of them hit London during the war.

When the war was over von Braun surrendered to the Americans. They immediately took him to the USA. There, he led a rocket-building programme which ultimately led to the building of the giant Saturn 5 rocket, used to launch America's manned missions to the Moon. Almost all rockets are still built along the same lines as von Braun's V-2s. ■

See also

Bombs
Missiles
Rockets
World War II

Britten, Benjamin

Born 1913 in Lowestoft, Suffolk, England
Perhaps the most outstanding British composer of opera and songs
Died 1976 aged 63

Benjamin Britten was a born composer. He began writing music when he was only 5. At 7 he was studying composition seriously. The *Simple Symphony* is made up of tunes he wrote as a child.

After studying at the Royal College of Music in London, Britten earned his living by writing music for documentary films. He also wrote many successful concert works. He went to live in America at the beginning of World War II, but he could not forget England. When he returned, in 1942, it was to write the work that made him world-famous: the opera *Peter Grimes*.

Many of Britten's operas were written for the world's great opera houses.

Others, such as *The Turn of the Screw* (a really chilling ghost story!), were designed for the festival he started in Aldeburgh, the Suffolk town he had made his home.

But it was not just opera that made his name. Britten wrote splendid orchestral music, including a piece especially for children: *The Young Person's Guide to the Orchestra*. His songs and choral works were also very fine, none more so, perhaps, than the great *War Requiem*. Britten was the first composer ever to be made a lord. ■

See also

Operas
Orchestras

Brontë sisters

A Yorkshire family who wrote several famous novels including *Jane Eyre*, by Charlotte, and *Wuthering Heights*, by Emily

Charlotte Born 1816 in Thornton, Yorkshire, England
Died 1855 aged 38
Emily Born 1818 in Thornton
Died 1848 aged 30
Anne Born 1820 in Thornton
Died 1849 aged 29

Charlotte, Emily and Anne were the daughters of a poor Irish clergyman. They lived in Haworth, a small town on the edge of the Yorkshire moors. Their mother died when Charlotte, the oldest child, was only 5, and after that the sisters and their brother Branwell led their own lives rather apart from their lonely father. Very soon they developed some absorbing games where they invented imaginary countries, inhabited by various pretend characters, some of whom were based on Branwell's box of wooden soldiers. The tiny letters and pretend newspapers they used to send each other in these games still survive.

Later on, the sisters went to boarding school, then became governesses to other people's children. But they hated to be away from each other and eventually all returned home and

started to write. Charlotte and Emily published a book of poems together. Then in 1847 Charlotte wrote her wonderful novel *Jane Eyre*. This describes a girl like herself who goes to a harsh school where she is cold and hungry. Later, she becomes a governess and falls in love with her employer, Mr Rochester. They are just about to marry when Jane discovers he has a wife already, locked up in the same house in a secret room, as she is quite mad. Jane runs away but returns years later to a happier ending.

Emily also wrote her only novel, *Wuthering Heights*, in the same year of 1847. Set in the bleak moors she knew so well, it describes how two boys, Edgar and Heathcliff, both adore the same girl, Catherine, while hating each other. When they grow up Catherine falls in love with Heathcliff but still marries Edgar. Both husband and wife die a few years after, leaving Heathcliff bitter and alone but still convinced that the ghost of Catherine will always be near him.

Anne had her novel *Agnes Grey* published that year too, but after writing more novels all three sisters died young. No other family of novelists have ever achieved so much as these shy, unworldly sisters whose books are read today all over the world. ■

▲ Branwell Brontë painted this picture of his three sisters in about 1835. It shows, from left to right, Anne, Emily and Charlotte. Branwell, the only son, was always in trouble with drink, debts and finally drugs. His behaviour deeply distressed his sisters.

Browning, Robert

Born 1812 in London, England
One of the most important poets of his century, and writer of *The Pied Piper of Hamelin*
Died 1889 aged 77

Robert Browning was the son of a clerk in the Bank of England. Rather than go to school he stayed at home reading books from his father's large collection. He started writing poems early on and had his first poem published when he was only 21. This was a long, rambling piece called *Pauline*, criticized at the time for being too difficult. But later Robert had more success with his shorter poems. Some of his poems seem almost like plays. Often, instead of describing his characters from the outside, Robert made them seem to speak for themselves. Because of this, it often seems, when you are reading his poems, that you are listening to the voices of real individuals from the past, some of them fine and noble, others colourful crooks.

In 1846 Robert married Elizabeth Barrett, also a poet. Her father did not approve, so the couple had to run away to Italy in order to be together. They lived there happily, although sometimes Robert missed home, once writing,

Oh, to be in England,
Now that April's there.

Sadly, after they had been married for fifteen years, Elizabeth died. For some time after, Robert avoided company, preferring instead to prepare his wife's last poems for publication. But soon he was writing again, at last becoming famous and widely read. In 1881 a Browning Society was formed by those who loved his poems and wanted to understand even the most difficult of them more fully. But many of Robert's shorter poems have always been easy to follow, unmistakable in their bouncy rhythms, brilliant rhymes and general enthusiasm for life. ∎

... Rats!

> They fought the dogs, and killed the cats,
> And bit the babies in the cradles,
> And ate the cheeses out of the vats,
> And licked the soup from the cooks' own ladles,
> Split open the kegs of salted sprats,
> Made nests inside men's Sunday hats,
> And even spoiled the women's chats,
> By drowning their speaking
> With shrieking and squeaking
> In fifty different sharps and flats ...

▲ **Extract from *The Pied Piper of Hamelin* by Robert Browning.**

Bruce, Robert

Born 1274 in Scotland
King of Scotland from 1306 to 1329, he led his country through war to independence from England.
Died 1329 aged 54

◄ **This seal of Robert Bruce dates from 1327 and shows him riding into battle wearing chain-mail armour and a cylindrical helmet, and carrying a sword in one hand and a shield bearing the royal coat of arms in the other.**

Robert Bruce came from an aristocratic and ambitious Scottish family. He grew up wanting to be king of Scotland. To gain the throne, Bruce was prepared to support the English King Edward I, even when he invaded Scotland in 1296. But he turned against Edward after the English captured William Wallace, the Scottish resistance leader, in 1305 and cruelly executed him. Bruce stabbed his main rival to the Scottish throne in a quarrel, and a month later he was crowned King Robert I at Scone.

At first things went badly for King Robert. Many of his family and supporters were captured and savagely treated by Edward I, known as 'The Hammer of the Scots'. The new Scottish king was forced to go into hiding and almost lost heart. There is a story that while Bruce was sheltering in a cave, he saw a spider struggling again and again to climb up to her web and not giving up. The spider's example inspired him to keep fighting. His guerrilla war against the English continued, wearing them down. Finally, in 1314, he overwhelmed King Edward II's forces in the battle of Bannockburn near Stirling Castle.

King Robert's victory did not end the fighting with England. But he restored order within his realm, and persuaded other countries that Scotland was an independent kingdom. King Robert I died of leprosy in 1329, recognized in Scotland then, as he has been ever since, as a national hero. ∎

See also

Scotland's history

Biography
Edward I

▲ *The Peasant Dance* by Pieter Bruegel (the elder), Kunsthistorisches Museum, Vienna, Austria. This picture shows villagers celebrating a holy day. Dancing and drinking are in full swing and a quarrel has already broken out amongst the group around the table. The peacock feather in the cap of the man beside the piper is a symbol of vanity. Bruegel's two sons were also successful painters.

Bruegel, Pieter

Born between 1525 and 1530 in The Netherlands
A painter of landscapes, moral tales and country people
Died 1569 aged about 39 to 44

There is very little evidence about Bruegel's early life. But we do know that, when he was in his twenties, he travelled to Italy to see the great works of art there. To do so, he had to cross the Alps. He fell in love with the Alpine mountain scenery; it influenced the way he painted landscapes ever after. He made religious paintings, allegorical paintings and paintings of people involved in ordinary village customs. He painted people honestly, with all their human failings, including drunk-enness and greed. Some of his pictures carried strong messages about the good and bad, foolish and sensible things in life.

In *The Blue Mantle* he has painted about 100 'proverbs' or moral messages. Every figure or shape in his crowded pictures has a special meaning. A branch growing out of a window means truth will out. A woman with fire in one hand and water in the other means deceit. His paintings are truly fascinating and need much looking into to 'read' them. ■

See also
Allegories

Brunel, Isambard Kingdom

Born 1806 in Portsmouth, England
An engineer who made great advances in railway and ship construction and built the first modern transatlantic steamship
Died 1859 aged 53

Brunel was the son of another famous engineer, Sir Marc Isambard Brunel. As a boy, he showed great skill at drawing and geometry. When he was 14, he was sent to France to finish his schooling. There he also trained with a maker of watches and scientific instruments before returning to England to work for his father. In 1826, when he was only 20, he was put in charge of a project to build a tunnel under the River Thames in London. The job almost cost him his life. He nearly drowned when water flooded into the tunnel and swept him away.

For the next few years, Brunel worked with limited success on various docks and drainage schemes. Then, in 1830, he won a competition to design a bridge to span the Avon gorge at Clifton in Bristol. But work on the bridge was delayed and it was not completed until after his death.

The turning point of Brunel's career came in 1833 when he was made chief engineer of the Great Western Railway Company. His main task was to build a railway between London and Bristol. The project took eight years and was one of the finest engineering achievements of its day.

While working on the Great Western Railway, Brunel became interested in steamships. His plan was that passengers from London to Bristol would be able to travel on to New York. Brunel's first transatlantic steamship, the *Great Western*, was launched in 1838. It had paddle wheels

▲ This famous photograph of Brunel shows him standing by the massive anchor chains of one of his great ships.

▲ The *Great Britain* being launched in Bristol in 1843. She was the first ship of her kind to cross the Atlantic.

and was built of wood using traditional methods. His second ship, the *Great Britain*, was a revolution in design. Launched in 1843, it had a screw-propeller and was built of iron. At 3,300 tonnes, it was easily the largest ship of its time and was the forerunner of all modern ocean-going vessels.

But Brunel had an even grander scheme in mind: a ship which could travel round the world without refuelling. This was the *Great Eastern*, a 19,000-tonne giant with room for 4,000 passengers. The project was plagued with problems from the start. Costs soared and the launch was a disaster. Overwork and exhaustion broke Brunel's health and he died while the ship was on its maiden voyage.

Brunel was a man of vision who believed in putting plans into action. The results of his work can still be seen today in England. They include the *Great Britain* and the Clifton Suspension Bridge (both in Bristol); the Saltash railway bridge, and Box railway tunnel near Bath. ■

See also

Engineers
Ships

Buddha (Siddhartha Gautama)

Born at Lumbini (now in Nepal)
The dates are not known but he probably lived in the 6th and 5th centuries BC from about 563 to 483 BC.
A religious teacher whose title, the Buddha, means the Enlightened One. He is also sometimes called Sakyamuni, sage of the Sakya clan.
Died aged 80 at Kusinagara, India

According to tradition, the father and mother of Siddhartha Gautama were chieftains of the Sakya tribe in northeast India, in the foothills of the Himalayas. Gautama was born at Lumbini (in modern Nepal), while his mother Maya was on her way to visit her parents. She died soon after and he was brought up by her sister, Prajapati.

There is a story which says that a wise man predicted that Gautama would either be a great world ruler, or a great religious teacher. His father, Suddhodhana, tried to turn his mind

away from the religious life, by keeping him within the pleasure gardens surrounding his home. Gautama married Yasodhara, the daughter of a neighbouring chieftain, and they had a son called Rahula.

When Gautama was about 29 he saw four signs, known to Buddhists as the 'heavenly messengers'. These changed his life. They were an old man, a sick man, a corpse, and a wandering holy man who was seeking for truth. Their message of change, suffering, death, and the possibility of understanding the meaning of life led Gautama to leave his wife and child in the care of his family and go into the forest.

For six years he learnt about meditation and strict disciplines of fasting and spiritual practice from various religious teachers. At the end of that time he was still not satisfied with what he had learnt. He decided that extreme fasting and depriving himself of sleep weakened his body too much for deep reflection. So he broke his fast and ate a little rice and drank some milk, which was offered to him by a passing villager.

Then he sat under a sacred tree, later called the Bodhi (enlightenment) tree, at Bodh Gaya in India. He meditated for a whole night and made the breakthrough to understanding truth, which

▲ A carved statue of the Buddha at Polonnaruwa, Sri Lanka.

he called the Dharma. He found out for himself the causes of suffering, the nature of impermanence, and the need to purify the heart. His final awakening to the truth is known as the Enlightenment.

The Buddha (as he was called after the Enlightenment) spent the rest of his life teaching others the way to spiritual understanding. His first sermon at Sarnath near Varanasi (Benares) outlines the Four Noble Truths and the Noble Eightfold Path which form the core of his teaching. For the next 45 years he travelled widely in northern India and taught many people. He ordained both monks and nuns and instructed them to continue to teach others.

He died peacefully at the age of 80, telling his disciples not to weep for him, but to trust in the Dharma. He had taught them that the hearts of all men and women have the potential for arriving at enlightenment, which is also called the end of suffering. ■

◔ See also

Buddhists

Buffalo Bill

Born 1846 in Scott County, Iowa, USA
William Frederick Cody, known as Buffalo Bill, was a scout for the United States Cavalry, actor and showman.
Died 1917 aged 70

Like many other people in the 'Wild West', William Cody had little schooling and could just about write his name. At the age of 11 he was working to support his family. Later, he fought in the American Civil War. After that he made his living supplying buffalo meat to railway workers. At that time great herds of buffalo (bison) roamed the American prairies, and Cody's skill at shooting them gave him his nickname.

During the 1870s, Cody was a scout with the cavalry who were fighting the Indians. His skill at this and his various adventures made him famous, and he appeared on the stage in plays about

▲ This poster, for his Wild West Show, pictures some of the things Buffalo Bill did in his life. He was particularly proud of appearing before Queen Victoria in London.

himself. From 1883, he was best known for his Wild West Show, an exhibition of horsemanship and mock battles, which toured all over the world.

Cody really was a brilliant shot, and some of his hair-raising adventures were genuine. He was also, though, a good teller of tales, and a good showman, and he always seemed larger than life with his flowing hair and beautiful costumes. ■

◔ See also

Biography
Oakley

Bunyan, John

Born 1628 in Bedfordshire, England
He was a Puritan preacher, and wrote *The Pilgrim's Progress*.
Died 1688 aged 59

John Bunyan was born into a poor family. His father was a tinker, making pots and pans, and John learnt the same craft. He also learnt to read and write, which was fairly unusual for someone as poor as he was.

By the time John was 16, the English Civil War between the king and Parliament had broken out, and he joined Parliament's army for nearly two years.

In 1649, John married. His wife was very poor too, and owned hardly anything except two religious books which had a great influence on John. He became a strict Puritan, gave up swearing and having a good time, and devoted his life to preaching. He taught that serving God was more important than anything else, and that poor people were just as important to God as the rich.

Soon after Charles II became king in 1660, strict laws were passed against Puritan preachers, and Bunyan went to prison several times. In Bedford town gaol he began to write his most famous and important book, *The Pilgrim's Progress*, which was published in 1678. *The Pilgrim's Progress* is the story of the journey through life of a man called Christian. It is an allegory, which means that the events in the story have a deeper, religious meaning. Christian faces many dangers and temptations, meets all kinds of people, and sees many different places, before he finally reaches God's Heavenly City. But what John Bunyan is really writing about is the story of how Christian learns to choose between right and wrong, and gets nearer and nearer to God. So *The Pilgrim's Progress* is an exciting and often amusing story, but it has a deeper meaning too. ■

🔵 **See also**

Allegories
English Civil War
Puritans

Burns, Robert

Born 1759 near Alloway, Scotland
The national poet of Scotland
Died 1796 aged 37

Robert Burns was one of seven children born to a struggling tenant farmer in Ayrshire. He worked in the fields from an early age, but his father gave him a decent education and he read widely for himself. Burns began writing poetry at school, and decided to make full use of the words and phrases, the rhythms and sounds of his own Scottish tongue. He wrote about life on the farm, the follies and hypocrisy of the people around him, and the pleasures of drink and women. In poems such as *To a Mouse, Holy Willie's Prayer* and *To a Louse*, Burns turned the language of Scottish peasants into great poetry.

Burns had so little success as a farmer, and caused so much trouble by his many love affairs, that he came close to leaving Scotland. He sent 34 of his best poems to a publisher in Kilmarnock, hoping to raise enough money to emigrate. But when they were published in 1786 he was recognized as a poet of genius, a 'Heaven-taught ploughman'. He decided to remain in Scotland, and began contributing to a collection of traditional Scottish songs. He gathered some from travels around the country, but he wrote many himself, including immortal and world-famous songs such as *Auld Lang Syne, My Love is like a Red, Red Rose* and *Ye Banks and Braes o' Bonnie Doon.*

For most of his life Burns had to worry about money, especially after marrying

Jean Armour in 1788 and starting a family. He returned to farming. Then in 1791 he took a full-time job as an excise-man (tax collector) in Dumfries. His last major poem, *Tam o' Shanter*, was published that same year.

Burns has been translated into more languages than any British poet apart from Shakespeare, and his birthday on 25 January is celebrated annually by Scots around the world. ■

My love is like a red, red rose
That's newly sprung in June:
My love is like a melody
That's sweetly played in tune.

As fair art thou, my bonnie lass,
So deep in love am I:
And I will love thee still, my dear,
Till a' the seas gang dry.

Till a' the seas gang dry, my dear,
And the rocks melt wi' the sun:
And I will love thee still, my dear,
While the sands o' life shall run.

And fare thee weel, my only love,
And fare thee weel a while!
And I will come again, my love,
Thou' it were ten thousand mile.

Butler, Josephine

Born 1828 in Northumberland, England
She fought for the rights of women and led a great campaign against government attacks on prostitutes.
Died 1906 aged 78

Josephine Butler was a beautiful and educated woman. When she was quite young she saw that women were not allowed by law to be equal with men, who often treated them badly. She was happily married, but when her young daughter died, Josephine decided to spend the rest of her life helping other women who suffered.

She began her work in Liverpool with prostitutes. At that time doctors and other people thought that prostitutes carried disease. Any woman suspected of being a prostitute could be arrested, examined by force and imprisoned. Josephine attacked this law and started what she called a 'Great Crusade' against it. Many people thought it was wrong for a middle-class woman to defend prostitutes, and Josephine was attacked several times. On one occasion she almost died when an angry mob set fire to a building in which she was speaking. But Josephine Butler was a brave, determined woman. She knew that women became prostitutes because they were poor, and she said it was wrong to punish prostitutes and not the men who used them. She was a religious woman and a great speaker, and she won the support of thousands of people. Through her work the laws were eventually changed. ■

Butlin, Billy

Born 1899 in Cape Town, South Africa
Billy Butlin was a fairground showman who went on to create Butlin's Holiday Camps.
Died 1980 aged 80

Billy Butlin's mother was born in a fairground caravan. When she married she went to South Africa, but soon left her husband and came back to the fairground life in England. Billy was then 8, and he was teased at school for his South African accent. He never had any real success at school, and never attended for very long. After a while he moved with his mother to Canada, and grew up there. He joined the Canadian army and served with them in World War I.

After the war he came back to England and started a hoopla stall touring fairgrounds. He became very successful, and by the twenties he owned several seaside amusement parks. At Skegness in Lincolnshire on Easter Saturday 1936 he achieved his ambition to open a cheap but comfortable holiday camp. Soon he opened others and his camps became enormously profitable and successful.

Billy Butlin was knighted by the Queen in 1964. He was a well-liked man, a great showman who did much for charity. ■

▲ In 1952, when this photograph was taken, Billy Butlin had six holiday camps in the UK.

Byron, Lord

Born 1788 in London, England
An English poet and champion of
Greek liberty
Died 1824 aged 36

George Gordon Byron was lame from birth, and rode on horseback whenever he could. When he was 10 years old he inherited his great-uncle's estate on the edge of Sherwood Forest, and became Lord Byron. As soon as he was old enough, he travelled through Europe on horseback, spending two years wandering around Greece and the islands of the Aegean Sea. On his return to London in 1812 he published a poem, *Childe Harold*, describing some of the wild landscapes he had seen. The poem was an immediate success.

Byron was a mixture of extreme good and bad. People were shocked by his

▲ This portrait of Byron shows him in Greek dress. In the last years of his life he helped the Greek struggle for independence against the Ottoman Turks.

many love affairs and he left England in bitterness. For a time he lived in Venice, where he wrote the long poem, *Don Juan*, which describes amazing adventures in extraordinary parts of the world. In 1823 he left Italy for Greece to help in the Greek struggle for independence from the Ottoman Turkish empire. He gathered together some soldiers, but before they could attack the Turkish fortifications, he caught a fever and died at Missolonghi.

After his death, a man who knew him well said, 'No man ever lived who had such devoted friends.' But 'mad, bad and dangerous' was how one of his former women friends described him. To this day people still argue about what he was really like. Byron gave his name to a new word in the English language, 'Byronic', meaning melodramatic, energetic, and romantically goodlooking. In Greece, he is remembered as a hero. ■

◎ **See also**

Greece

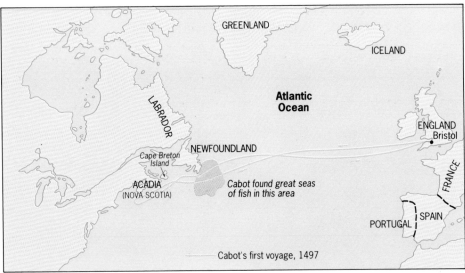

GREENLAND

ICELAND

Atlantic
Ocean

LABRADOR

NEWFOUNDLAND

ENGLAND
• Bristol

Cape Breton
Island

ACADIA
(NOVA SCOTIA)

Cabot found great seas
of fish in this area

FRANCE

PORTUGAL | SPAIN

Cabot's first voyage, 1497

▲ The map above shows the route of John Cabot's first voyage. He made a second voyage in 1498 to the coast of Greenland, sailed down to Labrador and finally returned to Bristol, where he died later that year.

Cabot, John and Sebastian

Father and son who discovered the mainland of North America for the English King Henry VII
John Born about 1450 in Genoa, Italy
Died about 1498 aged about 48
Sebastian Born about 1474 in Venice, Italy
Died 1557 aged about 83

John Cabot had an adventurous early life, during which he learned navigation and visited Mecca, in Arabia. He settled in London in 1484. In 1496 King Henry VII of England heard of the expedition of Christopher Columbus to the West Indies and realized he was missing out on a chance of wealth and colonies. So he instructed Cabot and his three sons Lewis, Sebastian and Santius to sail in search of 'all heathen islands or countries hitherto unknown to Christians' and take them for England.

The Cabots set off in 1497 in a tiny ship, the *Matthew*, with a crew of just 18 men. They reached the American coast after a voyage of 53 days, possibly at Cape Breton Island, Nova Scotia, and sailed southward along it. At first Cabot thought he had reached China.

On their return John Cabot's report was so encouraging that the king gave him £10 and a pension of £20 a year, and sent him off on another expedition

with a fleet of five ships. But Cabot found none of the gold or spices he was hoping for, and Henry and the Bristol merchants who backed the expedition were disappointed. Cabot seems to have died soon after he returned.

In 1512 the king's son Henry VIII appointed Sebastian Cabot as map-maker to the English navy. Soon afterwards Sebastian took service with the King of Spain, but returned to England and his old job as map-maker in 1548. He became governor of the Merchant Adventurers, a company which handled most of England's overseas trade. ■

👁 **See also**

Canada's history

Cadbury, George

Born 1839 in Birmingham, England
A Quaker business man who helped to change the living conditions of working people
Died 1922 aged 83

George Cadbury turned his small family firm into a great company, world-famous for cocoa and chocolate. He became a leading newspaper owner

too, but he is best remembered for his work to improve the lives of poor workers in the cities.

George got to know factory workers better than other employers did. He did not believe, as other people did, that the poor were to blame for their own poverty. He became convinced that their problems were caused by the foul conditions in the crowded and insanitary slums where they lived.

In 1879 Cadburys opened a new factory at Bournville, south of Birmingham. With his own money George built nearby a village of small, pleasant houses with gardens, and with plenty of open spaces. He meant it to be a practical example of how factory workers ought to live, and it succeeded brilliantly. Attitudes in Britain changed, and workers' housing began to improve. From all over the world people came to study and to learn from George Cadbury's experiment; more than a hundred years later, they still do. ■

👁 **See also**

Industrial Revolution
Quakers
Victorian Britain

Cadbury's cocoa
Makes strong men Stronger
The most Refreshing, Nutritious, and Sustaining of all cocoas.

▲ Advertisements for cocoa appeared on posters and in magazines. This one comes from the beginning of the 20th century.

Caesar, Gaius Julius

Born between 102 and 100 BC in Italy
Roman general and dictator
Murdered 44 BC aged about 57

Julius Caesar was born into an important Roman family and rose rapidly in his chosen career as a politician. He served his time in the army and then held various public offices. In 60 BC he was elected to the highest office in Rome, a consul. He was now in charge of the state's administration and the armed forces, although he held power jointly with another consul. After his year of office he took on the governorship of provinces in northern Italy and Gaul (part of modern France). From here he conquered a vast new area in Gaul and Germany and twice invaded Britain, in 55 and 54 BC.

He was now a very powerful leader with a huge army under his command. He decided not to disband his troops, as he should have done by law, and marched into Italy in 49 BC. He crossed the River Rubicon which formed the boundary of Italy. From here there was no turning back. He had declared war on the Roman state. We still have a saying 'crossing the Rubicon' which means that you have gone too far to turn back. This meant civil war, and Pompey the Great fought against Caesar. The war lasted until 45 BC, and the next year Caesar declared himself 'dictator for life'. He did not use the word *rex* (king) as it was hated by the Romans, but he was the sole ruler.

Not everyone wanted to be ruled by one man, and on the day called the Ides of March (15 March) in 44 BC he was stabbed to death outside the building where the senate (parliament) of Rome met.

We know a great deal about Caesar and his times because people who were there wrote about him and also because he wrote his own accounts of his adventures and battles. From his writing we can see what an intelligent and powerful man he was. At one time in his career he was the lover of Queen Cleopatra of Egypt, although he was married to Calpurnia. Cleopatra bore him a son called Caesarion who was executed by the Emperor Augustus. ∎

See also

Roman ancient history   **Biography**
Roman Britain   Cleopatra

Calvin, John

Born 1509 in Noyon, France.
He organized a Protestant Church in Geneva. His teachings influenced many other European Protestants.
Died 1564 aged 54

John Calvin grew up in France and nearly became a priest in the Catholic Church. He studied law as well as religion. He was impressed by Martin Luther's teachings, and soon began to criticize the wealth and power of the Pope and the Catholic Church.

It became too dangerous for him to stay in Catholic France, and he fled to the Protestant city of Basel in Switzerland. In 1536 he wrote a best-selling book, *The Institutes of the Christian Religion.* Calvin said Christians must use the Bible as their guide, not the Pope or the Catholic Church. He taught that people could never be good enough to deserve to go to heaven, but God chose some people specially to be his 'elect'. Christians might have a kind of vision which told them they were one of God's elect, but they should in any case live good and simple lives according to the teachings of Jesus.

Calvin was a shy, cold man, but he explained his ideas clearly and was a good organizer. In 1541, he was asked to go to Geneva to lead the Protestants. There he organized schools and a university. The sick and poor were cared for. There were all kinds of rules for everyday life. Shopkeepers were punished if they cheated or charged too much. The streets were cleaned regularly. People had to wear plain clothes and avoid bright colours. Women had to cover their hair so they would not become vain. Dancing, theatre-going and card-playing were forbidden. So were swearing and singing rude songs. Unfaithful husbands and wives were executed, and a boy was beheaded for striking his parents. Calvin became the effective ruler of Geneva.

In churches in Geneva, there were big pulpits, where the minister stood to teach the Bible in long sermons. Pictures and statues were removed, to stop people worshipping them in a superstitious way. The most important members of each church were called elders or presbyters, and they ran its affairs.

Like most religious reformers of his time, Calvin was hard on people who disagreed with him. A Spanish reformer, Servetus, went to Geneva to discuss his differences with Calvin. He was thrown into prison and then burned at the stake. Anyone accused of being a witch was burned too – about three each year.

Protestants from other parts of Europe came to Geneva to escape persecution and to learn from Calvin. By the time he died, his ideas were spreading, especially in The Netherlands, southern Scotland, the south-east of England and parts of France. ∎

See also

Christians   **Biography**
Protestants   Knox
Reformation   Luther

▲ This portrait, painted in the 1540s, shows John Calvin when he first went to Geneva to lead the Protestants there. His followers came to be known as Calvinists.

Capone, Al

Born about 1899 probably in Naples, Italy
One of the most famous criminals of all time. He ran many illegal and violent rackets in Chicago in the 1920s.
Died 1947 aged about 48

Capone claimed that he was born in New York but it is more likely that he was born in Italy and emigrated with his family to the USA when he was a small child. At that time many European families were going to America in search of a better life. As Capone grew up he realized that, partly because of his Italian background, he was not going to do so well in business as he thought.

He turned to crime very early, and was involved in New York street gangs when he was a teenager. He was a natural leader and soon had many gangsters and hoodlums following him.

In 1920 the Congress of the United States voted to ban all sales of alcoholic drinks. This ban lasted for thirteen years, and was called Prohibition. During Prohibition many criminals made fortunes, because people still wanted to drink beer and whisky, and only criminals could supply them. Capone operated in Chicago during this time, running various illegal schemes including the selling of alcoholic drink. He became rich and influential through crime, and was not arrested because he bribed many policemen and other officials. He and his gangsters were murderers and thieves, and they got away with it because of the weakness of greedy people.

Eventually, in 1932, Capone went to prison for not paying taxes, but he stayed there only for a few years. He came out a sick man and died while he was still in his forties. ■

Carnegie, Andrew

Born 1835 in Dunfermline, Scotland
A multimillionaire who gave away vast sums of money to pay for public libraries and education
Died 1919 aged 83

When he was 12, Andrew left Scotland for America with his parents and younger brother. The family settled in Pittsburgh. They were very poor, so instead of going to school, Andrew went to work in a cotton factory. He said none of his later millions 'gave me such happiness as my first week's earnings', because he was helping his family.

Whatever job Andrew did, he tried to learn more about it. As a telegraph boy, he learned exactly where every business was, going over them in his head at night, so he could deliver telegrams faster. He worked very long hours, but read as much as he could in his spare time. He used books owned by Colonel Anderson, who lent them free to 'working boys' because there were no public libraries then. Andrew was soon offered better jobs and he saved his money carefully.

The American Civil War made railways very important, because troops and ammunition could be moved much more quickly than before. Carnegie started a company in 1863 to make iron railway bridges instead of wooden ones. Ten years later his company began to produce steel too. This made Carnegie very rich. When his steel company was making 40 million dollars a year, Carnegie decided to 'stop accumulating' and began 'wise distribution'. Before he died, he had paid for 2,811 free public libraries around the world. He also established pension funds and gave financial help to universities in Scotland and the USA. ■

See also

American Civil War
Libraries

Carroll, Lewis

Born 1832 at Daresbury, Cheshire, England
Writer of the famous fantasy books, *Alice's Adventures in Wonderland* and *Through the Looking-Glass*
Died 1898 aged 65

Lewis Carroll was the name used by Charles Dodgson, a mathematics teacher at Oxford University, when he was writing children's books and poems. Charles Dodgson was the third child in a family of eleven, and as a child he and his brothers and sisters spent a lot of time playing literary games and drawing. They produced a

▲ A page from *Alice's Adventures Underground*, the first version of *Alice's Adventures in Wonderland*, which was written in Lewis Carroll's own hand and illustrated with his own drawings. He presented a bound volume of the story to Alice Liddell. It is now in the British Museum.

family magazine, with puzzles and word-games.

When he became a teacher at Oxford, he used to take the daughters of his friend, Dean Liddell, for boat-rides on the river. It was on one of these river-trips that he told the story of *Alice in Wonderland* to the young Alice

Liddell. Later he wrote the story down, and it was published in 1865.

As well as the two Alice stories, he wrote poems, including *The Hunting of the Snark,* and another children's book, *Sylvie and Bruno.* His books are adventure stories, but they do not unfold like ordinary stories. Sometimes one thing will turn into another, as they occasionally do in dreams, while at other times the people in the book seem to be moving about in a game the rules of which are never quite clear. As well as being a mathematician and a writer of story-books, he was also a very good amateur photographer, specializing in pictures of the children of his friends. ■

Cartier, Jacques

Born 1491 at St Malo, France
French navigator who explored the Gulf of St Lawrence and claimed Canada for France
Died 1557 aged 66

'Fish in appearance like horses, which go on land at night but in the daytime remain in the water.' This was how Jacques Cartier described his first sighting of walruses in the Gulf of St Lawrence. They were just some of the many wonders that Cartier had to report back to King Francis I of France, who had sent him on an expedition to search for gold.

Cartier, an experienced navigator, was 43 when he set out with two ships and 61 men on his first voyage to North America. He first explored the coast of Newfoundland, which he described as a barren place: 'the land God allocated to Cain'. Then he sailed up the Gulf of St Lawrence to the Gaspé Peninsula, where he set up a cross and claimed the land for France. He returned home, taking two Huron Indians with him.

The next year, 1535, Cartier was sent on a second expedition. On 10 August, the feast day of St Lawrence, he arrived at a river which he named after the saint. He sailed upstream as far as the place where Québec now stands. The

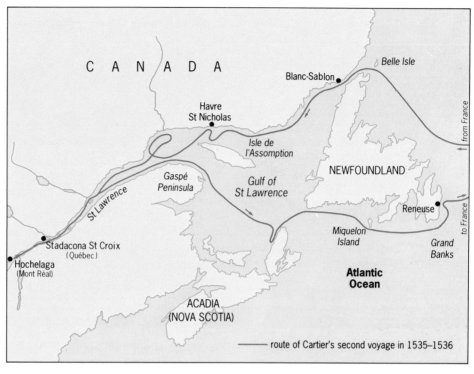

▲ In 1534 Cartier sailed from France to find a north-west passage to Asia. He reached Newfoundland and the Gaspé Peninsula and returned to France with two sons of a Huron Indian chief. Encouraged by their descriptions of Canada, King Francis I sent Cartier on a second expedition in 1535, during which he sailed up the St Lawrence River to the site of what is now the city of Montréal.

smallest of his ships sailed on as far as the Iroquois village of Hochelaga. It stood at the foot of a mountain which he named Mont Réal. The city of Montréal now stands there.

Cartier spent the winter in camp on an island off Québec before returning to France. A third voyage in 1541 in search of precious stones proved fruitless, and Cartier retired to St Malo, honoured as a great explorer. ■

See also

Canada's history

Castro, Fidel

Born 1927 in Cuba
He led a revolution that overthrew the Cuban government and turned the country into a communist state.

Fidel Castro was the son of a rich landowner. As a young man, he felt sorry for the many poor Cubans who lived in terrible conditions under the harsh rule of President Batista. In 1953 he was sentenced to fifteen years in prison for trying to overthrow the government. He was freed after two years. Soon he tried again. He trained a small group of rebels near Mexico

City. In 1956 he invaded Cuba with about 80 men. For the next three years he carried out raids against government forces from various hide-outs in the mountains and forests. He gathered more and more support until finally, early in 1959, Batista fled the country.

Castro immediately began to change the Cuban way of life. He built more schools and houses for the poor. He controlled all newspapers and radio and television services. He took over foreign-owned companies. Many of these companies were American. As a result, the United States stopped all trade with Cuba. Castro then turned to communist countries, such as the Soviet Union and China, for help. In 1961, some 1,200 Cuban exiles living in the USA tried to invade Cuba at a place called the Bay of Pigs. They had some American help, but Castro easily defeated them.

◄ Fidel Castro was always easy to recognize because of his beard and the army uniform he wore. This picture shows Castro making a speech to the Cuban people in 1963.

In 1962, the Soviet Union tried to build nuclear missile bases in Cuba, with Castro's consent. The missiles were removed after the United States had blockaded Cuba and put pressure on the Russians.

Although Castro greatly improved conditions for the poor, many other Cubans wanted more freedom, and fled to the United States. ■

⊙ See also

Cuba

Catherine the Great

Born 1729 in Stettin, Prussia (now in Poland)
Catherine II was a German princess who ruled Russia for 34 years, from 1762 to 1796.
Died 1796 aged 67

Born Princess Sophia Augusta, she came to Russia at the age of 14 and was given the name Catherine when she was received into the Russian Orthodox Church. At 15 she married Peter the Great's grandson, Peter III, a weak and stupid man. After seventeen years of marriage, Peter became tsar in 1762. Almost immediately he was replaced by Catherine and put to death by his guards.

Catherine at once set about reforming Russia and turning it into a strong power. She took a great interest in education, particularly for girls, and also did a lot to improve the care of the sick, founding a new medical college to give each town its own medical service. She loved art and literature, collecting works of art, painting, and writing histories, plays and many letters. To fit in all this work, she often rose at 5 a.m. and worked for fifteen hours.

During her rule Russia expanded eastwards towards the Pacific Ocean, westwards to take over much of Poland, and southwards to the coast of the Crimea and the Black Sea. Her own skilful diplomacy made sure that these gains became permanent.

While the landowning nobles lived well, most Russian people were serfs, little better than slaves, and badly treated. Catherine, who needed the support of the nobles, gave them even more powers over their serfs. This led to a peasants' revolt in 1773–1775 which was brutally put down. Later the French Revolution of 1789 increased Catherine's fear of revolt, and in her later years she ruled with a rod of iron. ■

⊙ See also

Russia's history

Cavell, Edith

Born 1865 in Norfolk, England
A British nurse executed by a German firing squad during World War I
Executed 1915 aged 49

Edith Cavell was the daughter of a clergyman. When she was 25 she went to Belgium as a governess, and later trained as a nurse. In 1907 she became matron of Belgium's first training college for nurses. She was a small woman with fine features and intense grey eyes. She rarely smiled, but her smile was remembered for its beauty.

In the summer of 1914, German troops marched into Brussels. Edith Cavell joined a group of people who helped British and French soldiers, trapped behind German lines, to escape to The Netherlands. During the next year hundreds of soldiers passed through the cellars of her clinic. She and her nurses tended their wounds and gave them civilian clothes. One nurse even carried messages back to London bandaged to her leg. Then, on 5 August 1915, Edith Cavell was arrested. She was condemned to death by a German military court and was shot on 12 October. She met her death calmly and bravely. 'Patriotism is not enough,' she said. 'I must have no hatred or bitterness towards anyone.' ■

⊙ See also

World War I

Caxton, William

Born about 1422 in Kent, England
Set up the first printing press in Britain.
Died 1491 aged about 69

As a young lad of about 16, Caxton began to learn the trade of buying and selling silk. He made a good living at this in France, and it is thought that he may have been a business adviser to Margaret of Burgundy, the sister of Edward IV.

Caxton liked to spend time writing, and in 1469 he started to translate into English a popular French romance called *The History of Troy*. Many people in England wanted a copy of this rather large book. Copies of books used to be handwritten and so took a very long time to complete, but by this time books could be produced by the printing process introduced by Gutenberg in Germany some years earlier. Caxton learned how to do this, then set up his own press in Bruges. Here he printed his English edition of *The History of Troy,* completing it by the end of 1473. In 1476, Caxton set up the first printing press in Britain, at Westminster in London.

During his lifetime, Caxton printed about 110 books, many of them his own translations from French. He also published Chaucer's *Canterbury Tales,* making this work available to many new readers. Before Caxton's printed editions people spelt the same words in different ways. In his printing Caxton introduced a fixed spelling for words, a very important development in the standardization of English. ■

See also

English language
Printing

Biography
Gutenberg

▲ Caxton's 'trade mark', which he used to identify the books he printed. Copies still exist of about one-third of Caxton's 110 works. When he died his pupil, Wynkyn de Worde, carried on the press.

Cayley, Sir George

Born 1773 in Brompton near Scarborough, England
His ideas led directly to the modern aeroplane.
Died 1857 aged 83

Before George Cayley, people believed that people would only fly if they flapped wings, like the birds. But by 1799, he had designed a glider with fixed wings, like those of all modern aeroplanes. In 1804, Cayley flew a model glider.

Five years later, imagining the future, he wrote that one day rigid wings would carry 'persons and goods . . . with a velocity of from 20 to 100 miles an hour'. His imaginary aeroplane might possibly be powered by steam, but since steam-engines were very heavy, he decided that one day there would be light engines powered by

Cervantes, Miguel

Born 1547 in Alcalá, Spain
The creator of Don Quixote and his squire Sancho Panza
Died 1616 aged 68

Cervantes was a great story-teller whose own life reads like a tale of adventure. He spent his childhood travelling around Spain with his father, an apothecary, who supplied medicines for the poor. At the age of 21 he went to Italy. He studied the great Italian poets, but also enlisted as a soldier. He fought the Turks in the great sea battle of Lepanto in 1571 and was wounded three times, losing the use of his left hand. Later he was captured by pirates, and imprisoned in Algiers for five years. He made several daring attempts to escape, but had to be ransomed in the end.

Back in Spain Cervantes took on various odd jobs, such as collecting grain for the Spanish Armada. Once again he got thrown into prison, this time for cheating! But in 1605 he published *Don Quixote* and his luck changed. The book was such a success

'the combustion of inflammable powders or fluids'. It would be nearly a hundred years before his prophecy became fact, and a petrol-engined aeroplane lifted a man into the air. Meanwhile, he was described as 'crazy as a tightrope-walker'.

Cayley experimented with parachutes and streamlining, and in 1800 his model helicopter rose 30 m (100 ft) on spinning discs.

In 1853, he built a man-carrying glider, and his protesting coachman flew 270 m (900 ft) in it before crash-landing. Sir George then abandoned aeroplanes as impractical until a light engine was discovered. ■

See also

Flight
Gliders
Helicopters
Parachutes

Biography
Montgolfier brothers
Wright brothers

that he could afford to spend the rest of his life writing.

In *Don Quixote* a man who reads too many stories about knights, decides to set off himself to right wrongs. He has many adventures, all caused by his own mistakes. He thinks windmills are giants, and attacks them; he thinks a flock of sheep is a great army, and attacks that too. *Don Quixote* is a long book which is funny and sad. It is sad because we feel sorry for this poor hero. His ideas come from books, but the real world is very different. ■

See also

Spain's history

Cézanne, Paul

Born 1839 in Aix-en-Provence, France
Outstanding French painter, sometimes called 'the father of modern art'
Died 1906 aged 67

Cézanne was born into an educated and wealthy family. He started studying law, but soon gave up in order to paint. His early pictures were not

▲ *Montagnes. L'Estague* by Cézanne, National Museum of Wales, Cardiff. This picture illustrates Cézanne's interest in colour and shape. The landscape has a strong 'modelled' feeling with no outlines at all. By using patches of colour and thick brush strokes, he has given a sensation of a firm, rocky structure and the hot, sun-baked countryside of southern France.

popular. People said they were crude and hopelessly unskilled.

In order to concentrate without interruption or insults, Cézanne went away from home to work quietly. He studied art for a while in Paris. Then he settled in Pontoise, a town just north of Paris, and finally, after his father died, he returned to live in Aix-en-Provence in southern France. As he had a lot of money he did not need to rely on selling his pictures to live. This gave him unusual freedom to develop his skills. He painted landscapes, still lifes, flowers and portraits. Many remained unfinished. He once made a man pose one hundred times for his portrait, and abandoned it because he was only pleased with the shirt.

Colour and shape were his two interests. He gave a feeling of immense solidity to his shapes by careful mixtures of colour and tone, making his brushstrokes 'model' a hill or a

figure without using an outline. He thought that although an 'impression' is pretty, it cannot be taken seriously without an underlying structure, in the same way as a body needs a skeleton to give it form or shape. His style of painting revealed structure and greatly influenced other artists. ■

See also

Paintings

Chadwick, Sir James

Born 1891 in Manchester, England
His discovery of the neutron was of great importance in understanding what atoms are like.
Died 1974 aged 83

In the 1920s a young scientist called James Chadwick went to work in Cambridge with the famous Ernest Rutherford, who had done very important work on atoms. Atoms are the tiny particles that everything is made of, but they are far too small to be seen even with most powerful microscopes. At this time many scientists were trying to find out what atoms are like.

In 1932 Chadwick decided to repeat some experiments done by the famous husband and wife team Irène and Frédéric Joliot-Curie. Irène was the daughter of Marie Curie. Chadwick realized that the Joliot-Curies had not correctly explained the results of these experiments. He suggested that in the nucleus, at the centre of an atom, there are not only positive particles (protons) as discovered by Rutherford, but also neutral particles, with no electrical charge. These particles were to be called neutrons.

Chadwick's discovery of the neutron became even more important when other scientists showed that neutrons can produce nuclear fission where enormous amounts of energy are released. ■

See also

Atoms
Nuclear power
Particles

Biography
Bohr
Cockcroft
Curie
Rutherford

Chagall, Marc

Born 1887 in Vitebsk, Russia
A painter of brilliantly coloured, fantastic pictures
Died 1985 aged 97

Chagall was brought up in the Jewish district of the small Russian town of Vitebsk. The people who surrounded him as a child, the stories they told, and the lively music they played, crop up again and again in his paintings.

As a young man he went to Paris at a time when there were a lot of changes going on in painting and writing and music. Excited and influenced by these changes, Chagall went back to Russia, but his painting was not popular with the authorities, and he finally returned to Paris and settled there in 1923.

His work is highly imaginative, and blends reality with fantasy. Sometimes

▲ *Bouquet with Flying Lovers* by Chagall, Tate Gallery, London. The picture combines fantasy and realism. The loving couple float in the air over the clear colours of the bouquet of flowers and are separated by them from the more menacing fantasies of the cock and the river below.

the figures in his paintings seem to be floating across the picture. He loved using clear, bright colours which shimmer on the canvas and glow in the stained-glass windows and tapestries which he designed in later life. ■

Charlemagne

Born 742 probably in Aix-la-Chapelle (Aachen), now in Germany
The king of the Franks who established the Holy Roman Empire
Died 814 aged 72

As the eldest son of Pepin, king of the Franks, Charlemagne was born into a very powerful family. The Franks were barbarians who invaded part of the Roman empire and settled in what is now France and Germany during the 5th century. When King Pepin died in 768, he divided his kingdom between his two sons, Charles and Carloman. Three years later Carloman died, and Charles became the sole ruler.

In 771 Charles's aim as king was to enlarge the kingdom that he had inherited, but at the same time to spread Christianity among the people whom he had conquered. During his long reign of over 40 years he organized about 60 military campaigns, and extended the kingdom of the Franks into an empire which stretched across what is now northern Germany, and parts of Poland, Czechoslovakia, Hungary and Yugoslavia, Italy and Spain. He led about half these campaigns himself.

His conquests earned him the name of Charles the Great (that is the meaning of 'Charlemagne'). Pope Leo III asked him to take over territory in Italy, and crowned him Emperor of the Holy Roman Empire in Rome on Christmas Day in 800.

Charlemagne's favourite place was Aix-la-Chapelle, where he built a magnificent palace and a cathedral. He also built palaces in other parts of his kingdom, such as Zürich, Boulogne, Paris and Frankfurt. Charlemagne wanted to show that the new emperor in the west could recreate some of the splendour and learning of the old Roman empire. So the courts at his palaces became centres of learning and art, and famous musicians and scholars, such as Alcuin of York, were invited to spend time at them. During his reign a number of Greek and Roman writings, including histories, poems and plays, were saved for later ages to read by being copied out by monks onto new parchments.

After his death Charlemagne's empire fell apart. Even so, during his reign, a great number of Christian peoples had been united under a single European emperor. ■

◖ See also

European history
France's history

Charles I

Born 1600 in Dunfermline Castle, Scotland
King of England and Scotland from 1625 to 1649; the only English king who was publicly beheaded
Executed 1649 aged 48

Charles I was not born to be a king. He was backward and shy, and his brilliant elder brother Henry overshadowed him. But Henry died suddenly in 1612. With great determination, Charles trained to be a good horseman, and became very dignified although he grew only about 1·50 m (5 ft) tall.

Charles was artistic, and his court was civilized and elegant. He was very religious and wanted to make Church of England services more dignified and beautiful. He dearly loved his strong-minded Catholic wife, Henrietta Maria. Puritans and other critical people were afraid she had so much influence that England would become Catholic again.

Charles believed that God had made him a king, so he did not need to consult his subjects. He managed to rule without Parliament until 1640, and tried to force his Scottish subjects to accept English church services. When this led to a war he could not afford, he promised to share some of his power with Parliament. But many people in Parliament no longer trusted him. England slid into civil war.

▲ These three views of Charles I were painted by his great court artist, Van Dyck, and were sent to a sculptor in Rome to make a head and shoulders statue of the king. It is as if we can walk round Charles, and see him from different angles.

Charles was brave in battle, but he was not a good war leader. He often put off decisions, and did not always back his best commanders.

Although he was defeated, he still believed he should not give up any of his power, and that he did not need to keep promises to his enemies. He tried to start another war in alliance with the Scots, and this led to his trial and execution. He behaved calmly and bravely on the scaffold, and said he died a martyr for his beliefs. ∎

See also

English Civil War
Puritans
Stuart Britain

Biography
Cromwell

Charles II

Born 1630 in St James's Palace, London, England
He was a king in exile for eleven years, and when he was restored to his throne in 1660, he was determined 'never to go on his travels again'.
Died 1685 aged 54

Charles II was 18 when his father Charles I was executed. He was already in exile. But in 1651 he returned to England, and spent six weeks on the run after Cromwell defeated his attempt to win back his crown at Worcester. He hid up an oak tree, and even disguised himself as a servant, and finally escaped to face nine more years of poverty and insecurity in France and The Netherlands. He had been a cheerful, outgoing boy. Exile turned him into a witty, charming man who hid his real feelings and trusted nobody.

When Charles II got back his crown in 1660 he knew that, to keep it, he must rule with Parliament and support the Church of England. So though he was probably a Catholic, he kept quiet about it, and went along with Parliament's harsh laws which punished people who did not attend Church of England services.

Charles's court was frivolous and worldly. He enjoyed the theatre, horse-racing, and gambling. He was never faithful to his shy, childless Portuguese queen, Catherine of Braganza. He had many mistresses, including the actress Nell Gwynn, and at least thirteen illegitimate children. He was easily bored by affairs of state. He would play with his spaniels in council meetings instead of making decisions.

Charles was genuinely interested in science, and founded the Royal Society to encourage research. He could be courageous and strong. When the Fire of London was raging, he stepped in personally to organize the fire-fighting. In 1678, hysterical panic about an imaginary Catholic plot threatened his Catholic brother James, the heir to the throne. Charles kept his nerve. He skilfully defeated those who wanted to stop James becoming the next king, and left the crown strong and secure when he died. ∎

See also

English Civil War
Fire of London
Royal Society
Stuart Britain

Biography
Charles I
Cromwell

Charles V

Born 1500 in Gent, in The Netherlands
Habsburg emperor who ruled over vast territories in the 16th century
Died 1558 aged 58

Charles V, a devout Catholic, ruled over the largest collection of European lands since the time of Charlemagne. He inherited the throne of Spain through his mother in 1516, and three years later became ruler of Austria and The Netherlands and was elected Holy Roman Emperor. His Spanish subjects also conquered a vast new empire for him in Central and South America. His motto was *Plus ultra* (always further). Some of his advisers had big plans for him. They wanted him to be 'God's standard-bearer', unite all the Christian nations under his rule, wage war on the Muslim Ottoman Turks, and finally become 'Ruler of the World'.

But although Charles worked hard, he was not an inspiring leader of men; a reporter from Venice wrote of 'his lower jaw long and projecting, so that his teeth do not meet, and one cannot hear the ends of his words clearly'. He always seemed to need more time, or money, to deal with the problems in his many scattered territories. By 1555 his long wars with France had led to no definite result, and he had failed to stop the Protestant ideas of Martin Luther from spreading in Germany, but he did manage to blunt the Ottoman attack on Christian Europe.

In 1556 he gave up the Empire to his brother Ferdinand, and all his other lands to his son Philip. Then he retired to a villa next to the monastery at Yuste in Spain. He spent his last years there worshipping God, eating heavily, listening to music, and dismantling and assembling mechanical clocks. ■

See also

Ottoman empire
Reformation

Biography
Philip II of Spain

▼ Charles V became king of Spain in 1516 and united the country with the lands of the Holy Roman Empire, which he inherited from his grandfather, Maximilian I, in 1519. Spain established a vast new empire in Central and South America.

Charles Edward Stuart

Born 1720 in Rome, Italy
The last serious Stuart contender for the British throne; he led the 1745 rising.
Died 1788 aged 67

Charles is usually known as Bonnie Prince Charlie. His grandfather was King James II, expelled when the English people preferred the Protestant King William of Orange and his wife Queen Mary. But, like his grandfather, Charles was a Roman Catholic, and dreamed of returning to Britain one day to claim the crown for himelf. He finally landed on the west coast of Scotland in 1745, in the reign of George II, with only twelve men. The Scottish Highlanders quickly rose to support the handsome young prince, and four days later, with over 2,000 supporters, Charles soundly beat a British army at Prestonpans, near Edinburgh.

Greatly encouraged, Charles marched into England, and got as far as Derby. But many of the Highlanders deserted on the march south, and Charles retreated again to Scotland. In 1746 his now tattered army was put down with great cruelty at Culloden Moor. For five months Charles was on the run with a price of £30,000 on his head, before escaping to France with the help of Flora Macdonald. He did little with the rest of his life, dying

overweight and addicted to alcohol. But his romantic image lived on in ballads and songs like *Charlie is my Darling.* ■

See also

Georgian Britain
Scotland's history
Stuart Britain

Biography
Macdonald, Flora

Charles, Prince of Wales

Born 1948 in London, England
Eldest son of Queen Elizabeth II and heir to the throne of the United Kingdom of Great Britain and Northern Ireland

Prince Charles was born at Buckingham Palace on 14 November 1948 and at his christening was given the names Charles Philip Arthur George. Until he was four years old his mother was the Princess Elizabeth. She became Queen in 1952. Prince Charles then became Duke of Cornwall, because the eldest son of a monarch has had that title since Edward III created it in 1337. When he was 10 the Queen gave him the title of Prince of Wales.

Charles was the first heir to the throne not to be educated at home. When he was 9 he went to Cheam School (a preparatory school for boys) and at 13 was sent to his father's old school, Gordonstoun in Scotland. Here boys had to get up at 7 o'clock every morning and go for a run, wearing only shorts and shoes, whatever the weather, and then take a cold shower before breakfast. They also had to play at least one sport every day. Prince Charles hated the school and was very lonely. He did, however, learn to play the trumpet, piano, cello and bagpipes, and enjoyed art and pottery. He also acted in school plays and once performed as Macbeth.

Prince Charles spent two terms at Geelong Grammar School in Australia, which he enjoyed. He was treated like the other boys and had to chop logs,

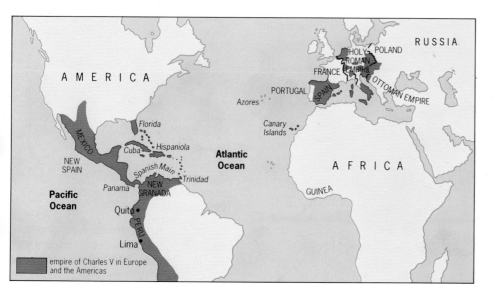
empire of Charles V in Europe and the Americas

clean lavatories, empty the dustbins, shear sheep and clean out the pigsties. Then in 1967 he went up to Trinity College, Cambridge and for the next three years studied archaeology, anthropology and history. He spent one summer term at Aberystwyth in the University of Wales and graduated from Cambridge with a BA in history.

He spent several months in the Royal Air Force, learning how to parachute and pilot a plane. He then spent five years in the Royal Navy, where he qualified as a helicopter pilot and later took command of a minehunter. His shipmates nicknamed him 'Taffy Windsor'.

In July 1981 he married Lady Diana Spencer and is now the father of Prince William and Prince Harry. Prince Charles is very concerned about the world in which we live and has a keen interest in architecture, town planning, conservation, the problem of pollution of the environment, and also in farming, industry and trade. In 1976 he set up the Prince's Trust which advises young people on setting up and developing small businesses. ■

See also

Biography
British Royal Family

Chaucer, Geoffrey

Born about 1340 in London, England
He wrote *The Canterbury Tales*, the first important book written in English.
Died 1400 aged about 60

When Chaucer was a small child, he was a page in the household of the Countess of Ulster, the wife of Lionel, son of the king, Edward III. When he grew older, he became one of the king's 'squires', which meant he did everything from making beds to serving at the royal table. In the war between England and France Chaucer was taken prisoner, but in 1360 the king paid a ransom to get him back. Later he became a diplomat, travelling to France and Italy on missions for the

king. In Italy he read books by the Italian writers Boccaccio, Petrarch and Dante. He later used some of their stories in his own writing, which probably began at about this time.

In 1374 he was made Controller of Customs in the Port of London. He left that post in 1386, and began writing *The Canterbury Tales* shortly afterwards. By that time he had also written many other long poems. These were mainly about love and included *The Parliament of Fowls* and the poem that many people consider to be his greatest work, *Troilus and Criseyde*, a very sad love story.

In 1386 Chaucer was made Member of Parliament for Kent and then became Clerk of the King's Works, which involved looking after royal estates and building grandstands for tournaments. He died in 1400 and is buried in Westminster Abbey. ■

See also

Canterbury Tales   **Biography**
English language   Dante

Daysies

Now have I thereto this condicioun

That, of alle the flowers in the mede,

Than love I most these flowres whyte
  and rede,

Swiche as men callen daysies in our toun.

To hem have I so greet affeccioun,

As I seyde erst, when comen is the May,

That in my bed ther daweth me no day

That I nam up, and walking in the mede

To seen these floures agein the sonne
  sprede,

Whan it up-riseth by the morwe shene,

The longe day, thus walking in the grene,

And whan the sonne ginneth for to weste,

Than closeth hit, and draweth hit to reste.

Chiang Kai-Shek

See Jiang Jieshi

Chopin, Frederick

Born 1810 in Zelazowa Wola, Poland
One of the greatest of all pianist-composers
Died 1849 aged 39

It was always clear that Chopin would become a great pianist and composer. One of his compositions was published when he was 7, and he gave his first public concert a week before his eighth birthday.

Chopin loved his native land, but he realized that he would have to travel if his career was to prosper. Eventually he settled in Paris, but he never forgot Poland. The music he wrote – the brilliant polonaises and mazurkas, the powerful ballades – were Polish through and through. They were an inspiration to his fellow countrymen in their struggle for independence from domination by Russia, Prussia and Austria. Equally inspiring were his sparkling waltzes and romantic nocturnes. Chopin could make the piano talk. He could make it sing.

He never married. Among his great loves was a famous woman who wrote novels under the name 'George Sand'. ■

Christie, Dame Agatha

Born 1890 in Torquay, England
Immensely popular author of detective stories, and creator of the two famous figures, Miss Marple and Hercule Poirot
Died 1976 aged 85

Agatha Christie was born and brought up in Torquay. She did not go to school at all. During World War I she worked in a hospital dispensary, where she learned some of the details of chemicals and poisons which proved so useful to her in her later career of detective-story writer.

She was married twice, once to Colonel Archibald Christie, from whom she was divorced in 1928, and then to the archaeologist Max Mallowan. His care with fragments of evidence and her detective skills combined well together when she helped him in his excavation of sites in Syria and Iraq.

She wrote several plays and over 70 detective novels. Her books are excellent stories which hook the reader into longing to know what will happen next. Since her death, several of her books have been successfully turned into films and television series. ■

▼ Dame Agatha Christie at the age of 60, framed by copies of her own books.

Churchill, Sir Winston

Born 1874 at Blenheim Palace, Oxfordshire, England
Statesman, soldier, orator and writer who led Britain during World War II
Died 1965 aged 90

Winston Leonard Spencer Churchill was the grandson of the Duke of Marlborough. He did not do well at school, but joined the army and had many adventures in Cuba, India and the Sudan. In the Sudan he took part in a cavalry charge at the battle of Omdurman in 1898. The next year Churchill left the army and went to

▲ Churchill as a war correspondent in South Africa, 1899.

▲ As Secretary for War and Air, 1919.

▲ Churchill as Prime Minister, 1940.

▲ In the uniform of the Royal Yacht Squadron, 1942.

South Africa as a newspaper reporter during the Boer War. He was captured by the Boers, and escaped with a price on his head: £25, dead or alive.

In 1900 he was elected to Parliament as a Conservative, but in 1904 fell out with his party and joined the Liberals.

He held several government posts, including President of the Board of Trade (1908–1910), when he introduced labour exchanges (which were later called Job Centres), and Home Secretary (1910–1911). Before and during World War I he served as head of the Admiralty, and then resigned from government to command troops in France for a time. After serving again as a Liberal minister after the war he returned to the Conservative Party, and was Chancellor of the Exchequer from 1924 to 1929.

During the 1930s Churchill was not a government minister. He warned that there was a danger of another world war, but many people ignored him. However, when World War II came the prime minister, Neville Chamberlain, put him in charge of the Admiralty once again. And when German armies were overrunning Europe in May 1940, King George VI asked him to be prime minister and lead a coalition government of all parties. His courage and his speeches inspired the people to withstand air raids and military defeats, and carry on to victory. His speeches were a triumph over difficulties, for in his early years Churchill had a stutter, and he had to fight hard to cure it.

Churchill remained prime minister until a general election in 1945 brought Labour to power, just before the war ended. He was prime minister again from 1951 to 1955, and finally gave up politics in 1964.

In his younger days, Churchill wrote newspaper articles and books to add to his army pay and later to earn a living. In 1953 he was awarded the Nobel prize for literature, especially for books such as *The Second World War*. He took up painting in later life as a hobby, and became an accomplished artist. ■

◑ See also

British history 1919–1989
World War II

Clemens, Samuel

See Twain, Mark

▶ On the wall of the great temple of Dendera in Egypt this relief shows Cleopatra standing behind her son Caesarion. He is portrayed as pharaoh and she is offering incense to him.

Cleopatra

Born about 69 BC in Egypt
Queen of Egypt, remembered for her influence on two of Rome's most powerful men, Julius Caesar and Mark Antony
Committed suicide 30 BC aged about 39

Egypt was an ancient civilization established long before the Roman period. Alexander the Great conquered Egypt in 332 BC. After Alexander's death a Macedonian general called Ptolemy established himself as king of Egypt. All kings of Egypt after this were called Ptolemy.

Cleopatra was the daughter of Ptolemy XII. It was the custom for brother and sister to be married and to rule jointly. On her father's death, Cleopatra ruled Egypt with her younger brother Ptolemy XIII. However, Cleopatra's father had appointed Rome the guardians of his children. Egypt was no longer independent of the Roman empire.

Cleopatra was forced out of Egypt, but was restored to power by Julius Caesar, who allowed her to rule with another of her brothers. One of the reasons for Caesar's decision must have been that he had fallen in love with her. She lived openly with Caesar in Rome and bore him a son who she called Caesarion. She stayed with

Caesar until he was assassinated in 44 BC. She then returned to Egypt with her son and ruled jointly with him.

A civil war soon followed in the Roman world, and Cleopatra became an ally and then the mistress of Mark Antony. She was 28 years old and, some said, the most beautiful woman in the world. Antony had his base in the capital of Egypt, Alexandria. He permitted Cleopatra and Caesarion to be proclaimed joint rulers of Egypt and Cyprus. Cleopatra had three children by Antony, each of whom was proclaimed ruler of a part of the Roman empire with Antony as 'king' in the east.

In the civil war Antony and Cleopatra were defeated at the battle of Actium by Octavius (later the Emperor Augustus). They both committed suicide rather than be taken prisoner. Antony stabbed himself and died in the arms of Cleopatra, and later she let a poisonous snake bite her. ■

◑ See also

Egyptian ancient history
Biography
Augustus
Caesar

Clive, Robert

Born 1725 in Shropshire, England
Soldier and founder of British rule in India
Committed suicide 1774 aged 49

As a schoolboy Clive was described as 'addicted to fighting' and it was as a soldier that he first became famous. He had been sent to India as a clerk in the East India Company. He fell overboard on the voyage to India and was rescued by the captain of his ship who threw him a bucket on a rope.

In India, he hated his work as a clerk and lost no time in joining the Company's army. Clive distinguished himself in the fighting against the French and their Indian allies in south India. In 1756, Clive commanded the Company's army which defeated the Indian ruler of Bengal. Bengal was still a province of the Mughal empire and it was also one of India's richest areas. After the victory at Plassey, the Mughal emperor granted the Company the right to collect the revenues of Bengal. In effect, the Company became the masters of Bengal and Clive had laid the foundations for British rule in India. In later years, as governor of Bengal, Clive did much to cut out corruption and provide firm government, though he himself accepted large gifts and became very wealthy. He was bitterly attacked for this when he came back to England and in 1774, sick and depressed, he killed himself. ■

👁 **See also**

British empire
Indian history

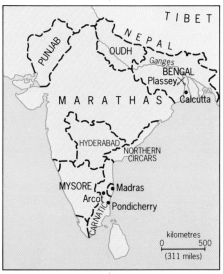

▲ Clive served in India in 1744–48; 1750–53; 1756–60 and 1764–66 as Governor of Bengal. His greatest victory was at Plassey in 1757. The map shows the parts of India controlled by the East India Company as a result of Clive's victories.

Cnut

Born about 994 in Denmark
King of both England and Denmark in the early 11th century
Died 1035 aged about 41

Cnut was the son of Swein I, King of Denmark. He came with his father on his invasion of England in 1013. Swein's Danish army had conquered

the whole of England by the time he died, and Cnut was declared king in February 1014. His reign in England nearly came to an end quickly, as the English king Ethelred (who had fled to Normandy when Swein invaded) returned. Cnut went back to Denmark, but returned with an invasion force in 1015. By the end of the next year he really was the king of all England.

Cnut became King of Denmark in 1018 and King of Norway in 1030. ■

The name is also spelt Canute.

Cobbett, William

Born 1763 in Surrey, England
A fearless 19th-century journalist and writer who attacked corruption
Died 1835 aged 72

William Cobbett's first job was as a ploughman, and he always loved the countryside. He became a soldier and served abroad in the war against France, rising to the rank of sergeant-major.

After the army, he became a journalist in America. Cobbett was a man of strong feelings. With his pen he attacked what he thought was wrong with American democracy, writing enough to fill twelve volumes. He made many enemies and earned the nickname 'Peter Porcupine'.

He returned to England, and in 1802 started his own weekly publication, the *Political Register*. He spent two years in prison because he attacked the flogging of some soldiers. Cobbett attacked unjust laws, low wages, and all corruption. Everyone wanted to read what he had to say, and he brought out a cheap edition of the *Register*. 'Two-penny trash' his enemies called it. His words alarmed the government, which feared that they might stir up the peasants to rise against their rulers, as had already happened in France in the revolution of 1789. Cobbett had to go to America for a while to avoid arrest.

Safe in England again, he toured the countryside he loved on horseback. He

published descriptions of these journeys in a book called *Rural Rides*. Cobbett wanted England to be a nation of peaceful country dwellers all living in harmony together, far from factories. ■

👁 **See also**

Industrial Revolution

Cockcroft, Sir John

Born 1897 in Yorkshire, England
He invented a machine which could make protons, which are found in the centre of atoms, move very fast. The results of this work were an important step towards the development of the H-bomb.
Died 1967 aged 70

In the 1930s John Douglas Cockcroft was working in the Cavendish Laboratory in Cambridge University, where many famous physicists were studying atoms, the tiny particles which make up everything in the world. Cockcroft had not always been interested in atoms. He was the son of a textile manufacturer and had studied electrical engineering. He fought in World War I, and then went to the Cavendish Laboratory to apply his knowledge of electrical engineering to building a machine which could provide enormous voltages and make protons (positive particles from the centre of atoms) go very fast. These tiny bullets were fired at a target. They combined with protons in the atoms of the target and produced the gas helium. This was the process that years later was of great importance in developing the hydrogen bomb. It is called nuclear fusion and is the way the Sun produces all its energy. Cockcroft had been helped in his work by Ernest Walton, and in 1951 they received a joint Nobel prize for physics. ■

👁 **See also**

Atoms
Particles
Sun
Biography
Bohr
Chadwick
Rutherford

Cockerell, Sir Christopher

Born 1910 in Cambridge, England
He designed the first practical hovercraft, which could travel over land and water.

Christopher Cockerell trained as an engineer and in electronics. He was fascinated by the idea of a hovercraft, a machine travelling on a cushion of air.

Other scientists had already shown that a machine like an upside-down tea-tray would float on a cushion of air pumped down from above, but the air quickly escaped round the edges. Cockerell showed that a 'wall' of air was much better at trapping the air cushion. In his first experiments, he fitted a cat-food tin inside a coffee tin and blew air from a vacuum cleaner down between them.

His first hovercraft tests in 1959 created a great sensation. His experimental hovercraft travelled along the Solent on England's south coast at 30 knots (55 km/h), then climbed the beach and settled down in the dunes.

SR-N1, built by Saunders-Roe, could cross the English Channel in two hours. The bigger SR-N4s were used to take cars and passengers to France. But Cockerell's invention is of greatest use in countries with poor road and rail systems, where it can travel up rivers and across deserts. ■

◉ See also

Hovercraft

▼ The SR-N1 hovercraft, designed by Sir Christopher Cockerell, arriving at Dover having crossed the English Channel from Calais in 1959.

Columbus, Christopher

Born 1451 in Genoa, Italy
Rediscovered the Americas while trying to find a westward route to Japan and India.
Died 1506 aged 54

Columbus was a man with a dream. European navigators were trying to find a way to reach China, Japan and India by sea. Columbus knew that the Earth was round, and thought the easiest way to Japan was to sail west round the globe. The distance, he believed, was about 5,000 km (3,000 miles) from the Canary Islands.

Columbus, a skilled sailor, tried to sell his idea to the King of Portugal, who turned him down. England's king, Henry VII, would not risk the money needed for the venture. So Columbus decided to try his luck in Spain.

For four years he was kept waiting at court by the Spanish rulers, King Ferdinand and Queen Isabella. Finally he left the court in despair – to be overtaken by a messenger from the queen saying she would put up the money after all.

Columbus sailed with three small ships, *Santa Maria, Niña* and *Pinta*, and about 90 men. After leaving the Canaries they sailed west for three weeks, until the men were ready to mutiny with terror. But Columbus, a tall, forceful man with red hair, said 'Sail on!' and calmed their fears. And early in the morning of 12 October 1492, a look-out sighted land in the moonlight.

The land was one of the Bahamas islands. Columbus was convinced it was the Indies and that he was very near Japan. He cruised around from one island to another, seeing people whom he thought were 'Indians', which is why American Indians are so called.

The *Santa Maria* was wrecked off the island Columbus named Hispaniola. He decided to leave 40 men there to form a colony, and returned to Spain with the other two ships. He was hailed

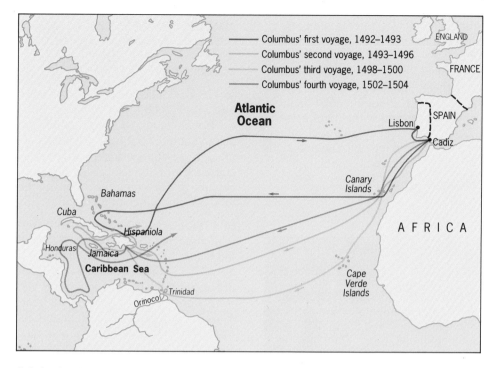

Columbus' first voyage, 1492–1493
Columbus' second voyage, 1493–1496
Columbus' third voyage, 1498–1500
Columbus' fourth voyage, 1502–1504

▲ Columbus believed that by sailing west across the Atlantic Ocean he would reach China. Instead, he came upon America, which was unknown to Europeans at the time. His first two voyages took him around the islands of the Caribbean. On his third and fourth voyages he reached the mainland of South America and Central America.

as a hero. He was given the titles of Admiral of the Ocean Sea and Viceroy of the Indies, and set off again in 1493 with a fleet of 17 ships and 1,200 men.

On his second arrival at Hispaniola Columbus found that all 40 of the men had been murdered. He founded another colony, and also visited Jamaica. Some Spaniards who had returned to Spain complained about his harsh rule as viceroy, but in spite of this he was allowed to go on a third expedition in 1498. This time he reached Trinidad and set foot on the mainland of South America.

However good an explorer he was, Columbus was not a good governor. Nor were his two brothers, who were working with him. So many complaints about their rule reached Spain that a new governor, Francisco de Bobadilla, was sent to take over. He promptly arrested Columbus and his brothers and sent them back to Spain in chains.

They were all pardoned. In 1502

Columbus was allowed to make one more voyage. During this he became convinced he was near the mouth of the Ganges in India, and claimed that he saw visions. He returned to Spain, a sick man, and he died still believing he had reached the Orient. ■

See also

Caribbean history
Explorers
Sailing ships

Confucius

See Kongzi

Constable, John

Born 1776 in Suffolk, England
One of the most familiar and beloved of all British artists
Died 1837 aged 60

John Constable's family were well-to-do country people. His father was a corn merchant who owned Flatford Mill in East Anglia and expected his son to continue the successful family business. John did try but could not settle to it. Luckily his father understood and gave his son an allowance which enabled him to train as an artist. At the age of 23 he began at the Royal Academy School in London.

Constable devoted himself almost entirely to landscape painting. Unlike most earlier landscape painters, who

▼ *The Haywain* by Constable, National Gallery, London. This painting of a wagon crossing the River Stour, near Flatford Mill in Suffolk, was at first called *Landscape: Noon*. This shows Constable's interest in the precise time of day, and the direction of light on one particular spot at that time.

were content with depicting pleasant but rather placid imaginary scenes, Constable showed real places under differing conditions of light and weather. He caught the lushness of meadows, the scudding movement of clouds, and the drama of storms, painting with vigorous strokes of the brush. Most of all he enjoyed painting the places he knew and loved best, particularly the Suffolk countryside and Hampstead Heath in London. Although he never went abroad, at first he was more popular in France than in England. His most famous painting, *The Haywain*, won a gold medal in Paris in 1824. It was only after his death that he became recognized as a truly great artist in England too. ∎

Constantine the Great

Born AD 274 in the Roman province of Moesia, now Serbia (Yugoslavia)
Roman emperor who accepted Christianity and who moved the capital of the empire to Constantinople
Died AD 337 aged about 63

Emperors had ruled Rome for over 300 years when Constantine came to power. The empire had become so huge that arguments about who should be in charge had led to the formation of an eastern and a western empire.

Flavius Valerius Constantinus was with his father, the emperor of the western empire, when he died in York in AD 306. The troops proclaimed the young Constantine as the new emperor of the west. For the next few years he fought many battles to win the whole empire. By 312 he had invaded and taken over Italy and by 324 he held total power over both east and west.

Once he had reunited the Roman empire under a single emperor he set about building a new capital at Byzantium on the entrance to the Black Sea. He completed the task in 330 and called the city Constantinopolis, the City of Constantine. He was known throughout his huge empire as Constantine the Great.

Although he was not brought up as a Christian, he did not persecute Christians as several emperors had done. In 313 he issued an edict (order) allowing Christianity to be a recognized religion. He tried to unite the various groups within the Christian Church who argued with each other. He was baptized into the Christian faith on his death-bed. ∎

See also

Byzantine empire
Roman ancient history

▲ This 13th-century wall-painting shows Constantine the Great (centre) leading the mounted Pope Sylvester I into Rome. Constantine's contribution to the spread of Christianity was so great that the early Christian Church thought of him as a 'thirteenth Apostle' of Jesus.

Cook, James

Born 1728 in Marton, Yorkshire, England
Daring navigator who explored and mapped the Pacific Ocean and its islands
Killed 1779 aged 50

People laughed when James Cook said he wanted to go to sea. He was a farm labourer's son and had worked selling groceries and haberdashery (sewing materials). At 18 he was considered old to start a career afloat. But go to sea he did, in small ships carrying coal and other goods.

In 1755, with England on the brink of war with France, Cook volunteered for the Royal Navy as a seaman. His skill in navigation won him promotion to master, a non-commissioned rank entrusted with the navigation of a ship. He also displayed skill in charting the St Lawrence River in Canada.

In 1768 a scientific voyage to Tahiti was organized to observe the transit of the planet Venus across the face of the Sun. The Admiralty made Cook an officer with the rank of lieutenant and gave him the command of the ship *Endeavour*, carrying the scientists including the famous natural scientist, Joseph Banks. The Admiralty also gave him secret orders to search for the Great Southern Continent which people believed existed.

On that voyage around the world from 1768 to 1771, Cook explored and charted the coast of New Zealand and the eastern coast of Australia. Cook's high opinion of Botany Bay led to English criminals later being transported to settle there. He named it Botany Bay because of its many plants.

Cook proved to be a natural leader. He was tall and sturdy, a calm man of few, if sometimes forceful, words.

In 1772 the Admiralty sent Cook off again, this time with two ships and the rank of commander. He sailed south of the Antarctic Circle, the point at which the Sun does not set for several days every summer. He proved that no large continent existed where it had been expected. He then cruised about the Pacific, charting it accurately and visiting many islands. Back in the Atlantic he discovered South Georgia.

When he returned to Britain he was promoted to captain. Soon he was off again. This time the Admiralty ordered him to explore the possible sea route north of Canada from the Pacific end. He discovered Hawaii, passed through the Bering Strait between Alaska and

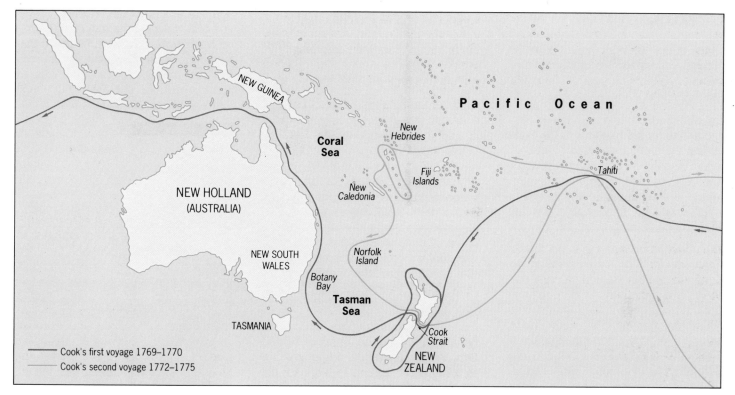

▲ James Cook made three voyages to the Pacific Ocean. He declared that his aim was 'not only to go farther than anyone had done before but as far as possible for man to go'. He set out on his last voyage in 1776, but was killed during a fight on the island of Hawaii in 1779.

Siberia into the Arctic Ocean, and returned to Hawaii to pick up food and water. There he was murdered in a scuffle on shore. ■

See also

Australia
Australia's history
Explorers
New Zealand
Oceania

Biography
Banks

Copernicus, Nicolas

Born 1473 in Poland
Before Copernicus's work the planet Earth was believed to be in the centre of the Universe. He showed that the Sun was in the centre, with the planets orbiting around it.
Died 1543 aged 70

Copernicus was the son of a wealthy merchant. When he was 10 his father died and he was brought up by his uncle, a bishop in the Catholic Church.

Copernicus was well educated and he considered becoming a priest, but soon changed his mind and began studying astronomy. He also studied mathematics, law and medicine, but astronomy remained his favourite subject.

At that time everyone believed that the Earth was at the centre of the Universe. But Copernicus realized that this picture did not agree with astronomical observations. He worked out that the Sun was at the centre with all the planets moving round it. He said that our Earth takes a year to travel round the Sun, and also revolves once every 24 hours. Copernicus believed the planets moved round the Sun in perfect circles. Fifty years later Kepler used the extremely accurate measurements of Tycho Brahe to show that they do not.

Copernicus wrote his theory in a famous book, *De revolutionibus*. It was printed a few weeks before he died. At first the bishops and senior priests of the Roman Catholic Church were not upset by the shift in the position of the Earth, but their view changed. In 1616 Copernicus's book was regarded as a source of evil ideas and put on the 'Index', a list of books that Roman Catholics were not allowed to read. The Copernican system was the subject of a famous trial when the great Galileo was forced to confess that the Earth did not move at all. It was not until 1835 that Copernicus's book was removed from the Index. ■

See also

Astronomers
Solar System

Biography
Brahe
Galilei
Kepler

▲ This drawing of Copernicus shows a kindly man. He divided his time in later life between his astronomical studies and an administrative post at Frauenberg Cathedral. He also gave medical help to the poor.

Cortés, Hernán

Born 1485 at Medellín, western Spain
Spanish conquistador who conquered
Mexico
Died 1547 aged 62

Cortés studied law in Spain, but decided to try his fortunes in the West Indies. He settled at Santo Domingo, where he combined farming with some law work. In 1511 he became a soldier, joined an expedition to Cuba, and in 1519 was sent to Yucatán, on the Mexican coast, to explore the country.

He marched inland to Tenochtitlán (now Mexico City), the capital of the Aztec rulers of Mexico. Cortés had about 600 Spaniards with him, and several thousand Amerindians who hated the Aztecs. The Aztec ruler, Moctezuma, at first gave the Spaniards a friendly welcome. But Moctezuma was killed in a riot and Cortés and his men had to escape.

The Spaniards returned and besieged the city, bringing with them guns, steel armour and weapons, and horses, all new to the Aztecs. They also had an invisible ally: smallpox. This disease, along with the war, killed thousands of Aztecs, and by 1521 Cortés had conquered the country. For nine years he ruled it as governor. An expedition to explore Baja California ended in disaster, and Cortés returned to Spain, where he was received coldly. ■

See also

Aztecs
Conquistadores
Mexico
Spanish colonial history

Biography
Moctezuma

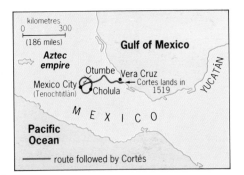

▲ Cortés's fleet of 11 ships sailed from Cuba to Mexico in 1519 and by 1521 the Spaniards had conquered the Aztec empire.

Cousteau, Jacques

Born 1910 in Saint-André-de-Cubzac, France
The best-known underwater explorer

As a French naval officer, Jacques Cousteau was always keenly interested in exploring the oceans. In 1943 he helped invent the aqualung. This is a breathing device which allows divers to spend long periods under water. Later on he also developed both the first underwater diving station and an observation vessel known as the diving saucer. Cousteau used the pictures he shot this way to make some amazing films and television programmes.

In 1960 Cousteau led a campaign to stop the dumping of nuclear waste in the Mediterranean Sea. His fame helped swing public opinion behind him, and the plans were dropped. Since then he has continued to work for the conservation of the sea-bed, writing books and making more fascinating films about what goes on in the depths of the ocean. ■

See also

Divers
Oceans and seas

Cranmer, Thomas

Born 1489 in Aslockton, Nottinghamshire, England
He was Henry VIII's Archbishop of Canterbury, and arranged the king's divorce from Catherine of Aragon; in Mary I's reign he was burnt for his Protestant faith.
Executed 1556 aged 66

Thomas Cranmer was a quiet Protestant scholar who kept his beliefs to himself. He was the only one of Henry VIII's close advisers who avoided the king's wrath. Cranmer's Protestant faith strengthened as time went on. He served the young Edward VI loyally, and wrote the Book of Common Prayer. This was used in parish churches in Edward's reign, and is still used sometimes today.

When Catholic Mary became queen, she put him in prison. He was lonely and old, and signed a statement giving up his beliefs. But when he heard that he would be burnt anyway, he realized he was wrong. As the fire was lit around him, he put the hand which had signed into the flames first. ■

See also

Protestants
Reformation
Tudor England

Biography
Edward VI
Henry VIII
Mary I

▲ Cranmer was burnt at the stake in Oxford. Before he went to his death he said, 'as my hand offended in writing contrary to my heart, it shall be first burned,' and held his hand into the flames.

Crick and Watson

Discovered the structure of DNA, a large, complicated chemical that controls the way we look and how our bodies work.
Crick, Francis Harry Compton
Born 1916 in Northampton, England
Watson, James Dewey
Born 1928 in Chicago, USA

During World War II, Crick was a physicist working on the development of radar. After the war his interest turned to a new science called molecular biology. Physicists and chemists were working together to try to unlock the secrets of chemicals found in the body. There was special interest in the chemicals we inherit from our parents that make us look like them. This information is contained in tiny structures called chromosomes which are found in all the cells of our body. These chromosomes are made of a complicated chemical called DNA.

You cannot see the detailed structure of DNA under a microscope. Several scientists including Maurice Wilkins and Rosalind Franklin in London investigated DNA by firing X-rays at it. The X-rays produced patterns as they passed through the DNA, but they were difficult to understand.

A young man called Watson came to Cambridge and joined Crick in the difficult task of sorting out what those X-ray patterns meant. With a sudden flash of inspiration, Watson realized that a so-called double helix (a spiral within a spiral) could describe the structure of DNA. This led to an understanding of how DNA can make copies of itself. It was the key to all sorts of research on what animals and plants inherit from their parents, and in 1962 Crick, Watson and Wilkins shared a Nobel prize. ∎

See also

Cells
DNA
Genetics
X-rays

Biography
Darwin
Franklin, Rosalind
Mendel

Crockett, Davy

Born 1786 in Greene County, Tennessee, USA
A hunter and politician who was seen as the typical 'backwoodsman' of the expanding West
Killed 1836 at the battle of the Alamo, aged 49

Davy Crockett was the son of poor settlers. His grandparents had been massacred by Indians. From the age of 12 he earned money by driving cattle. He often played truant from school, and ran away from home for so long that when he returned at 16 only his sister recognized him.

Davy grew up a gentle humorous man with 'the face of a woman, and the manner of a girl'. Many tales are told of his adventures as a bear hunter. He married and settled in Tennessee. There he became a colonel in the militia and a magistrate, 'using my natural born sense . . . for I never read a page in a law book in my life'.

In 1827 he was elected to the Congress of the United States, where he defended the land rights of poor farmers in the west of Tennessee. When they failed to re-elect him in 1835, he set out for Texas, taking only his rifle, shot-pouch and powder horn. Texas was fighting for independence from Mexican rule. He arrived in Fort Alamo and died there in its heroic defence against the Mexicans. ∎

See also

American West

Cromwell, Oliver

Born 1599 in Huntingdon, England
In the English Civil War, this middle-aged Puritan country gentleman became a brilliant soldier, and later the ruler of England and Wales.
Died 1658 aged 59

Oliver Cromwell was a boisterous schoolboy, but his stern Puritan schoolmaster, Thomas Beard, had a great influence on him. Like many Puritans, Cromwell became convinced God had specially chosen him to do His will.

▼ Cromwell had strong, heavy features, and was not a vain man. He is said to have told one of his portrait painters to put in all his 'ruffnesses, warts and pimples' or he would not pay him. This portrait was painted in about 1649, four years before he became Lord Protector. He was about 50 years old at the time.

Cromwell's chance came when he was 41. He sat in the Long Parliament of 1640, and was a strong supporter of Parliament's powers. When civil war began, he trained his own cavalry, nicknamed 'Ironsides' because they were such good fighters. They joined Parliament's victorious 'New Model Army', which Cromwell later commanded. He and his men never lost a battle.

After the war, Cromwell and other army leaders tried to make a deal with Charles I. But the king broke his promises. Cromwell was clear what to do, though many others were terrified. Charles was put on trial for bringing war to his people, and beheaded. It is said that after the execution, Cromwell came alone at night to look at the corpse of the dead king, and muttered sadly: 'Cruel necessity'.

Cromwell was determined to defend the new 'Commonwealth' of England. He was not usually a cruel man, but he distrusted the Irish, and they have never forgotten his ruthless conquest of Ireland. When the Scots tried to help the young Charles II, he defeated them too.

Cromwell's victories made him the most powerful man in England. He became 'Lord Protector' in 1653. He tried to rule with Parliament, though he also used his army to enforce what he thought right. He allowed more religious freedom than usual (except in Catholic Ireland), and gave Jews permission to live in England. He won a high reputation abroad too.

Parliament offered him the crown in the end: he refused it. He probably did not want to be 'King Oliver', but his old soldiers felt betrayed because he had even considered it. When he died, his funeral was like a king's, and no one was sure what to do next. ■

See also

English Civil War
Ireland's history
Puritans
Roundheads
Stuart Britain

Biography
Charles I
Charles II

Curie, Marie

Born 1867 in Warsaw, Poland
Marie Curie with her husband Pierre did important work with radioactive substances.
Died 1934 aged 66

Marie Curie was born Marya Sklodowska in Poland's capital. Her father taught physics and her mother was the headmistress of a girls' school. But her father lost his job because of his opposition to the Russian rule of Poland, and when Marya was 11 years old her mother died. Women were not allowed to go to university in Poland at this time, so Marya worked hard as a governess and saved some money so that she could go to study at the Sorbonne University in Paris. Now living in France she changed her name to the French 'Marie'. She was so poor that she sometimes fainted with hunger during her classes. But she still managed to come top of the class in the exams.

In 1894 Marie met a successful chemist called Pierre Curie, and in a year they were married. Pierre soon realized that Marie was a really great scientist and he happily worked as her assistant. In the year of their marriage Röntgen discovered X-rays, and soon afterwards the French scientist Becquerel found that a substance containing uranium produced similar types of rays.

Marie Curie was to spend her whole life studying these radioactive substances. She invented an instrument

▼ Marie Curie at work in her laboratory. She and her husband Pierre shared a Nobel prize for their discovery of the element radium. Her exposure to this radioactive material eventually killed her.

to measure radioactivity, and found that a substance called pitchblende (the ore from which uranium is extracted) was a thousand times more radioactive than the uranium itself. But what was making the pitchblende so radioactive?

Marie and Pierre arranged for tonnes and tonnes of pitchblende to be sent to Paris from a mine in Austria. They worked non-stop in an unheated, damp shed, trying to separate out the tiny quantity of unknown radioactive material. After several years work they ended up with a pinch of the highly radioactive element, which they called radium. They received a Nobel prize for this work.

Sadly, in 1906 Pierre was killed when he carelessly crossed a road in front of a horse-drawn cart. Marie carried on with her work and received a second Nobel prize in 1911.

The dangers of radioactivity were not properly understood at that time, and Marie Curie suffered throughout her life from radiation burns on her skin and eventually died from a type of cancer called leukaemia. ■

See also

Nuclear power
Radiation
X-rays

Biography
Röntgen
Rutherford

Custer, General George

Born 1839 in New Rumley, Ohio, USA
American general who fought in the Civil War and was later killed in battle against Indians
Killed 1876 aged 36

George Custer grew up in a large, boisterous family. He decided to be an army officer, but was almost expelled from the US Military Academy at West Point. A friend wrote, 'He is always connected with all the mischief that is going on, and never studies more than he can help.'

After West Point, Custer fought in the American Civil War from 1861 to 1865. His commanding officer called him 'gallant' but 'reckless'. The newspapers called him the 'Boy General' because he was only 23 when he was promoted. His long, golden hair streaming, he raced his cavalry to victory after victory and became a legendary hero for his courage.

After the Civil War, Custer was sent to fight the Indians who still roamed the Great Plains. He often fought rashly and did not treat his men well, but the newspapers praised him for his success.

▲ You can see Custer's long hair flowing down from his general's hat. The stars on his hat and on his shoulders show that he was then a major general, a rank which he achieved by the age of 26.

Then in 1876, Custer and all 266 of his troops were killed at Little Bighorn, South Dakota, by a larger force of over 3,000 Sioux Indians led by Chief Sitting Bull. The only survivor was one horse, which was found wandering by itself at the scene of the massacre. ■

See also

American Civil War
American Indians

da Gama

See Gama

Daguerre, Louis

Born 1789 in France
He invented the first practical camera and produced photographs known as 'daguerreotypes'.
Died 1851 aged 61

As a young man Daguerre worked as a tax collector. He then became an artist, painting large pictures of wide views and including real objects as part of the display. These pictures were on permanent exhibition in Paris and London and were very popular. But what Daguerre really wanted to do was to produce an exact copy on paper of the world around him.

Daguerre was familiar with the camera obscura, where sunlight entered a dark box through a pin-hole and produced on a screen an image, or picture, of what was outside the box. In the same way, light entering our eyes through our pupils forms a picture on the retina (the screen at the back of the eye). Remove the light and the picture is gone.

In the 1830s Daguerre designed a box in which the image fell on a flat metal plate; the plate was coated with a chemical called silver iodide, which turned black in sunlight. The bright part of the picture became dark and the darker parts of the picture were left lighter. It took a long time to produce a picture, and it was a bit fuzzy, but this was how the first photographs were taken. Only one print could be made from each shot.

A few years later the Englishman W. Fox Talbot invented a process for getting any number of prints from the same negative. ■

See also
Cameras
Photography
Biography
Talbot

Dahl, Roald

Born 1916 in Llandaff, Wales
An outstandingly popular author of books for children
Died 1990 aged 74

Roald Dahl's early life was almost as adventurous as any of his novels. He did not always enjoy boarding school, finding the teachers there too strict. So it was a relief to leave in order to go out to Africa as a young business man working for Shell Oil. After some extraordinary adventures, some involving wild animals, Dahl volunteered for the Royal Air Force when Britain declared war on Germany in 1939. After flying in East Africa, he crashed his plane in flames in the middle of the Western Desert. Despite dreadful injuries Dahl was soon flying again in Greece and Syria, before transferring to the USA in 1943.

After World War II he started writing stories, at first for adults and later for children. His third book for children, *Charlie and the Chocolate Factory*, is still one of the best-selling children's books of all time. Other favourites include *The BFG*, *Revolting Rhymes* and *The Witches*. He often used magic in his stories, but in a new and bold way. Sometimes Dahl's stories may seem cruel, at other times even rather rude. But many would say he got closer to what children are interested in than do other more restrained authors writing for the young. Some adults do not like everything he wrote, but young readers themselves seem to. During the 1980s he was the most popular children's author in the world. ■

▲ The author Roald Dahl with the cover of his third book. Charlie is being shown around the Chocolate Factory by Mr Willy Wonka who is demonstrating the process to Charlie and Grandpa Joe.

Dalai Lama

Born 1935 in Takster, Tibet
A Buddhist monk who is the spiritual and political leader of the Tibetan people

Tenzin Gyatso was born in a cowshed to a poor farming family who lived in a very remote region of north-east Tibet. When he was only 2½ a group of Buddhist leaders came to his house looking for the reincarnation of the previous Dalai Lama who had died in 1933. They had been led to the house by signs and visions seen in a mystical lake. They gave the little boy tests to see if he could recognize objects belonging to the previous Dalai Lama, and when he succeeded they hailed him as their new leader, whom they believed was the Buddha of Compassion come down to Earth.

When he was 4 years old he went on the long journey to Lhasa, the capital

▲ Tibetans still look upon the Dalai Lama as the rightful ruler of their country and as a spiritual leader, even though he has been forced to live in exile in India since 1959.

of Tibet, carried in a golden palanquin, and was placed on a peacock throne in a huge, magnificent palace called the Potala. Thousands of people greeted him and wept with joy that their Dalai Lama had been found. Although he was so young, he seemed to know exactly what to do during the long ceremony of enthronement and spontaneously blessed many of the people.

Life in the Potala was quite strict and lonely for the Dalai Lama. He had to study extremely hard and take many exams in Buddhist philosophy, which he passed with flying colours.

When he was 16 he faced his greatest crisis. The Chinese invaded Tibet, killing many people and destroying the great Buddhist monasteries. For nine years he tried to coexist peacefully with the Chinese, but in 1959, when his life was threatened, he made a daring escape, disguised in layman's clothes, over the Himalayan mountain passes to India.

The Dalai Lama now lives in the small Himalayan hamlet of McLeod Ganj in north-east India, taking care of the 120,000 Tibetan refugees who had followed him into exile and trying to

get the world to help his people in Tibet. He is a very humble man who wears the robes of a Buddhist monk. He wakes at 4 a.m. every day to pray and meditate. He also likes gardening and mending clocks and watches.

He has become known and respected worldwide for his message of universal peace. He believes that it is only by each individual developing a kind heart and seeing everyone as a member of the same human family that this can be achieved. Because of his desire to unite all people through non-violent means he was awarded the Nobel Peace Prize in 1989. ■

See also

Buddhists
Reincarnation
Tibet

Dalton, John

Born 1766 in Eaglesfield, Cumbria, England
His ideas about atoms changed the way scientists think.
Died 1844, aged 77

When John was only 10 he went to work for a man called Elihu who was very interested in science. Elihu soon realized that John was very bright and

started to teach him mathematics. He did so well that when he was only 12 he became the head of a small country school. He used to teach children of all ages with the tiny ones sitting on his knee to learn to read. Later John Dalton became a lecturer at New College in Manchester and later still went to London to lecture at the Royal Institution.

In his early twenties he began to keep a diary which was mainly notes about the weather. When he died there were 200,000 entries. He was interested in how the dew is formed, found that it was a sudden lowering of temperature that made it rain, and suggested (correctly) that the aurora, of which there was an especially brilliant display in 1787, was electrical in origin.

His most important work was his atomic theory. The Greeks of the ancient world had some ideas about atoms but John Dalton was the first modern scientist to suggest that atoms of different elements had different weights. ■

See also

Atoms
Auroras
Dew

Elements
Physicists

Dante Alighieri

Born 1265 in Florence, Tuscany, Italy
He wrote one of the world's greatest poems, *The Divine Comedy*.
Died 1321 aged 56

Dante grew up at a time when children in Tuscany were taught that their first duty was to take revenge on those who harmed their family. This meant that the people of Florence, where he lived, were constantly fighting one another. When Dante was 9 years old, he met a girl who was younger than himself, and she changed his life for ever. Years later, when he had already written much beautiful poetry about her, he described their meeting: 'Her dress on that day was of a most noble colour, a soft and beautiful crimson, tied together and decorated in a way that

▲ This is an illustration by Gustave Doré of Hell as Dante had described it in his poem. Doré, a French painter, who lived from 1832 to 1883, was just one of the many artists inspired by Dante's poem.

best suited her youth . . . it is my hope that I may write about her in a way that no one has ever written about a woman before.'

Dante called her Beatrice. We know very little about her except that she married another man and died quite young. Dante saw her occasionally when he was a young man, but only among a group of friends. In 1302 he quarrelled with the supporters of the Pope in Florence and spent the rest of his life in exile in other cities of northern Italy. His great poem, *The Divine Comedy*, describes his journey through Hell, Purgatory and Paradise. Throughout, he feels that the love of Beatrice directs him, and at last she herself guides him among the blessed souls in Paradise.

Dante was one of the first great poets to write in the ordinary language of the people, and not in Latin. He used his local Tuscan dialect to create one of the most beautiful poems that the world has ever known. ■

See also

Italy's history

Darius I

Born about 558 BC
Ruler of the ancient kingdom of Persia. He was most famous for his invasion of Greece.
Died 486 BC aged about 72

Darius I took the throne of Persia in 521 BC. Persia was then a very large empire which controlled the countries along the eastern edge of the Mediterranean (now Turkey, Syria, Lebanon, Israel, Egypt and Libya) and beyond to the east (now Iraq, Iran,

▲ On this enlarged cylinder seal impression the Great King is shown hunting lions from a chariot.

Afghanistan and Pakistan). As soon as Darius became king, he had to deal with revolts against him all over the empire. He established peace by military might and then divided his empire into 20 provinces. He appointed a governor, called a *satrap*, to each. These satraps were like kings in their own territory but had to provide tribute (taxes) and loyalty to the 'Great King'.

The Greeks on the mainland had helped the Greek cities in Asia Minor (now Turkey) in their revolt against the Persians. So Darius decided to punish them. The first fleet sent by Darius was destroyed in 492 BC off the north coast of the Greek mainland. In 490 King Darius sent an army of perhaps 25,000 across to the Greek mainland. This ended in a disastrous defeat for the Persians. The battle was fought at Marathon. It was said that a messenger ran the 42 km (26 miles) to Athens with news of the victory of the 10,000 Greek warriors. About 6,400 Persian soldiers died and only 192 Greeks.

Darius I died a few years after the battle of Marathon. His son Xerxes succeeded him. ■

See also

Greek ancient history
Persians

Biography
Xerxes

Darling, Grace

Born 1815 in Bamburgh, Northumberland, England
Her part in a brave sea rescue made her a national heroine.
Died 1842 aged 26

Grace Horsley Darling was one of nine children. She grew up on the Farne Islands, off the coast of Northumberland, where her father, William Darling, worked as a lighthouse keeper.

On 7 September 1838 Grace, aged 22, was alone with her father and mother in the Longstone lighthouse, when a paddle-steamer called the *Forfarshire* was wrecked in a storm. Most of the people on board were drowned, but a few of them managed to scramble onto a rock. Grace and her father could see the survivors, so they set out in their small rowing boat to rescue them. As a result of their bravery, nine people were saved.

When newspapers reported the rescue, Grace became a national heroine and she and her father were awarded gold medals by the Humane Society. Grace coped sensibly with her fame, but four years later she died of tuberculosis. ■

See also

Lifeboats

Darwin, Charles

Born 1809 in Shrewsbury, England
Best known for his theory of evolution by natural selection, Darwin was a great biologist who studied many other things including coral reefs, barnacles, earthworms and orchids.
Died 1882 aged 73

Charles Robert Darwin was born into a famous family. His grandfather, Erasmus Darwin, was a doctor who also wrote poetry and philosophy. His mother was the daughter of Josiah Wedgwood, the pottery manufacturer.

As a boy, Charles Darwin did not care much for school. Instead he enjoyed gardening and looking at plants and animals. His father, a doctor, decided that Charles should study medicine. But Charles found that he could not stand the sight of blood and hated the brutality of the treatments given in those days before anaesthetics. After two years he went to Cambridge to study classics instead but was more interested in geology and botany.

He became the friend of the professor of botany, who suggested, after Darwin had only just scraped through his final exams, that he would be a suitable person to go as the naturalist and companion to the captain of a naval survey ship, HMS *Beagle*. Charles set sail on 27 December 1831 for what was to be a five-year journey.

▲ While on the Galapagos Islands, Darwin observed several species of finch, each with a different shape of bill to suit its method of feeding.

▲ This newspaper cartoon appeared soon after Darwin had published his theory of evolution. Many people thought, wrongly, that Darwin was claiming that humans had descended directly from apes.

He suffered terribly from seasickness throughout the voyage, but when the weather was good he made notes on everything seen from the ship and collected small sea creatures in a towing net. When the *Beagle* spent time in ports, Darwin was able to get ashore. He saw something of the Amazon rainforests and the deserts of Patagonia. In Chile he journeyed up into the Andes and observed the changes in the countryside made by a recent large earthquake.

But the most important part of the voyage turned out to be the few weeks that the *Beagle* spent in the Galapagos Islands, which lie on the Equator, about 1,000 km (600 miles) from the coast of South America. They have plants and animals that are found nowhere else. Darwin was struck one day when a resident of the Galapagos said that he could say, without being told, which island a particular tortoise came from, as each island had its own sort. Why, wondered Darwin, should this be?

When he got home, Darwin realized that some of the birds from the Galapagos were like the tortoises in being closely related to each other but different in the shapes of their beaks. Yet the birds from any one island were similar. They were all rather like some small birds that live on the South American mainland, and Darwin decided that some of these must have reached the Galapagos accidentally, perhaps by being blown off course during a storm, and had evolved (changed) in their new home.

Darwin began to investigate all the animals he could. After many years he eventually came to a conclusion based on four observations.

1 All individual animals and plants are different from all of the rest.

2 In spite of the differences between individuals, children tend to look like their parents.

3 All living things produce very large numbers of young.

4 In spite of this, the numbers of all living things stay much the same from one year to the next.

These four observations led him to one conclusion: most of the young animals must die, and the ones that survived were those best fitted to their way of life. If, every now and again, an animal was born which had some feature that gave it an advantage it would survive, and so would its offspring that were like it. Selection would work, rather like a farmer selecting the animals that he wished to breed from, but in this case it would be natural selection that would cause a population to evolve.

Darwin hesitated to publish his ideas, possibly because he knew they would upset many people. But in 1859 his book called *The Origin of Species* came out. It caused an uproar, as it contradicted the ideas found in the Bible. But few people nowadays doubt the basic truth of Darwin's arguments.

A year or so after his return from the *Beagle* voyage Darwin's health declined until eventually he was an almost permanent invalid. In spite of this, he seems to have retained his good temper and kind disposition. He had married his cousin Emma in 1839, and they lived in Downe in Kent where they had ten children. ■

See also

Evolution of living things
Evolution of people
Galapagos Islands

Biography
Huxley
Wedgwood

David, King of Israel

Born date unknown, probably near Bethlehem, Palestine
Jewish king who united the tribes of Judah and Israel into a strong nation
Died about 970 BC, age unknown

David was the son of Jesse. According to the story in the Bible, as a boy he watched over his father's sheep and he killed the Philistine giant, Goliath, with a stone from his sling. He was invited to the court of King Saul of Judah to play his harp when the king was worried or depressed. Jonathan, the king's son, became his great friend,

and Saul's daughter Michal was his first wife.

After Saul and Jonathan had been killed in a battle against the Philistines, David was made King of Judah. In seven years of warfare he defeated the Philistines and other enemies, captured Jerusalem and took the Ark of the Lord containing the Ten Commandments to the city. David became king over all the tribes of Israel as well as of Judah. He ruled for over 30 years, and before he died he had Solomon, his son, anointed as king in order to leave Israel secure.

The Jews regarded David as the ideal king and hoped that there would be another king, descended from him, called the Messiah, the anointed one.

The history of his reign is told in the First and Second Books of Samuel, and in the First Book of Kings, chapters 1 and 2, in the Old Testament of the Bible. There is a tradition that the Psalms were composed by David, but in fact many of the Psalms were written centuries after he lived. ■

See also

Bible

Biography
Solomon

David, Saint

Born in the 6th century in Wales
A Christian monk and bishop, who became the patron saint of Wales
Died 589 or 601, age unknown

We know almost nothing about the life of this saint. His monastery was at 'Menevia', which is now called St Davids, in Dyfed, south-west Wales. Later writers nicknamed him 'the Waterdrinker'. This was because he led a very simple life, and refused to drink wine or beer. In medieval times it was said that he founded ten monasteries, including the one at Glastonbury in England. The monks in all of them were made to lead lives of great hardship. Ever since the 12th century he has been the patron saint of Wales. His feast day is 1 March, when

the Welsh wear leeks or daffodils. Shakespeare called this 'an ancient tradition', but no one knows for sure how it started. ■

See also

Welsh history

Davy, Sir Humphry

Born 1778 in Penzance, England
A brilliant chemist who discovered many chemical elements and invented the miner's safety lamp
Died 1829 aged 50

As a boy Humphry had an extremely good memory and was quite a showman. He used to stand on a cart in the market place and tell Cornish folk-stories to crowds of children. He was later apprenticed to a surgeon, and while he worked making up medicines and pills he became interested in chemistry. When he was 21 he began to study a gas called nitrous oxide, which is sometimes called laughing gas. It was later used to put people to sleep while they had their teeth pulled out. He took many risks, and once nearly died because he had been too long without oxygen to breathe.

Count Rumford, the American-born scientist who founded the Royal Institution in London, heard about Davy's work and invited him to be an assistant lecturer there at a salary of £100 a year. He was a very popular lecturer and people used to flock to his lectures at the Royal Institution. It is said that Albemarle Street, off Piccadilly in London, was probably one of the first one-way streets in the world. Carriage drivers bringing people to his lectures were all asked to come in from the same end to avoid traffic jams! Davy did so well that only one year later, when he was 24, he became professor of chemistry.

Scientists today remember him particularly because he discovered so many new chemical elements. But he is generally remembered for his invention of the miner's safety lamp. In 1813 a dreadful gas explosion

▲ This 1802 cartoon by James Gilray shows Humphry Davy during one of his lectures at the Royal Institution. Davy is holding the bellows. A member of the audience is being given a whiff of nitrous oxide (laughing gas).

occurred in a mine near Newcastle-upon-Tyne and more than 90 miners were killed. Davy was asked to help to prevent such accidents in the future. The safety lamp he then invented must have saved thousands of lives all over the world. He made many scientific discoveries, but he always said that his greatest discovery was a young man who came to work for him who also became a great scientist. He was Michael Faraday. ■

See also

Anaesthetics
Chemists
Elements
Mining

Biography
Faraday
Rumford

Debussy, Claude

Born 1862 in St-Germain-en-Laye, France
France's most revolutionary 20th-century composer
Died 1918 aged 55

Claude Achille Debussy began studying at the Paris Conservatory of Music when he was 10. At first he hoped to become a great pianist, but he found that he was not quite good enough, so he turned to composition instead.

As a composer he soon proved that he had genius. Such works as the *Prélude à l'après-midi d'un faune* startled everyone. Instead of treating harmony according to the old rules, he used it freely, choosing chords for the sake of their effect, just as a painter chooses his colours. Indeed, many people said that his music was the equivalent of the French Impressionist painters.

Debussy's ideas set music free and opened up all sorts of possibilities for other composers to follow. He is therefore one of the most important composers of his day. Among his other works there are the opera *Pelléas et Mélisande* and two important collections of piano *Préludes*. ■

Defoe, Daniel

Born 1660 near London, England
He wrote the first real English novel, *Robinson Crusoe*.
Died 1731 aged 71

Daniel Defoe, a butcher's son, led an exciting and adventurous life. In 1685 he took part in the rebellion against King James II and was lucky to avoid execution. He was later put in prison for publishing opinions against the government, and even spent time as a secret agent.

He is best known as the writer of *Robinson Crusoe*, which he published in 1719. Many people think of this as the first successful English novel. It tells how the hero survives after being shipwrecked on an island. Defoe based it partly on the real-life adventures of a traveller called Alexander Selkirk. Another novel, *Moll Flanders,* tells the story of a woman who became a thief.

Defoe published his own newspaper, and all his writing is vivid and realistic, like that of a good journalist. *A Journal of the Plague Year*, for example, tells exactly what it was like in London during the plague; and many people think that *A Tour through the whole Island of Great Britain* is the liveliest guide-book ever written. He also wrote hundreds of pamphlets and articles on everything from politics to pirates. In all his writing Defoe showed an interest in people and the difficulties facing them in the society of his time. ■

See also

Robinson Crusoe

▲ Daniel Defoe being punished in the pillory for his writings which encouraged people to rebel against the King.

Degas, Edgar

Born 1834 in Paris, France
One of the greatest French artists of the
19th century
Died 1917 aged 83

Edgar Degas was born into a wealthy Paris banking family. From early on he wanted to be an artist, and his family had no objection to such an insecure life. His school studies were poor, his books filled with drawings of dreamy heads and figures. Soon enough he was introduced to the art world by his artistic and educated family.

After studying at art school he was able to spend his time painting without the misery of poverty, simply because his family's money could keep him going until he was well known and established. Degas exhibited with the Impressionists, but was always an individualist rather than a member of a group. Although he was skilled at drawing and planning pictures in a traditional way, he realized that picture designs could break all the usual rules. In particular he realized that the artist need not place the main subject in the middle of the picture or show it complete. A picture showing just parts of people could look just as lifelike, if not more true to life, like a photographic snapshot. He loved to paint scenes from unexpected angles,

▲ *The Dancing Class* by Degas, **Metropolitan Museum, New York, USA. This painting of a ballet class shows a busy scene of bodies caught at unusual angles as if in a photograph. In the middle of the figures stands one isolated dancer with a mirror behind her. She gives a calm centre to all the activity going on around her.**

particularly ballet-dancers, their bodies making exciting and unusual shapes.

He experimented with different sorts of paints and inks, using every type and mixture to make new textures.

Finally he enjoyed pastels most of all, especially in his old age, when his dim eyesight coped best with free strokes of pure colour. He was also a fine sculptor. He made figures in wax, which were then cast in bronze. His sculptures portrayed moving figures, mainly ballet-dancers. ■

 See also

Paintings
Sculpture

de Gaulle, Charles

Born 1890 in Lille, France
A lifelong patriot and soldier who
became one of France's greatest leaders
Died 1970 aged 79

As a child, Charles de Gaulle enjoyed playing war games. Once his brother tried to persuade Charles to let him be the King of France for a change. 'Never!' replied Charles. 'France belongs to me.' Later he went to St

◄ **In 1944, when Paris was freed from the Germans, de Gaulle insisted on walking along the Champs-Élysées to the Arc de Triomphe. He liked to do the same sort of 'walkabout' years later when he was President of France, as this photograph shows.**

Cyr Military Academy. When he left in 1912 his reports said that he was 'average in everything except height'.

He was wounded and captured during World War I, and remained a soldier after the war. In 1934 he wrote a book on the use of tanks and aircraft. At the start of World War II he commanded a tank division. When France was invaded by the Germans in 1940, he escaped to England. From there he became the leader of all the French troops who had also escaped from occupied France. The Free French forces, with de Gaulle at their head, returned victorious to Paris in 1944 alongside the British and American troops.

De Gaulle was elected president in 1945, but resigned after only ten weeks. It was not until 1958 that he returned to power when France was going through a political crisis. He survived a number of assassination attempts to become one of the most powerful presidents in French history. He insisted that France should be able to defend itself with its own nuclear weapons, and often argued with other leaders in Europe and the West.

When he was defeated in a referendum (national vote) in 1969, he retired to his home village of Colombey-les-deux-Églises, where he died the following year. ■

See also

France's history
World War II

Deng Xiaoping

Born 1904 in China
He took part in the struggles of the Chinese Communist Party and became China's most important leader after 1978.

Deng Xiaoping came from a rich family, but in 1920, when he went to study in France, he became a communist. He helped to bring about the revolution in China in 1949.

By 1956 he was one of the leading people in the communist government,

▲ Deng Xiaoping with his grandchildren. This photograph was taken in 1988.

but the next 20 years were difficult as he did not support Mao Zedong's extreme ideas. When Mao turned against those who disagreed with him during the Cultural Revolution, Deng lost all his power.

But after Mao died in 1976, Deng became important again, and from 1978 he was the most powerful leader in China. He used his power to improve the standard of living. More food was grown, and factories began to produce goods such as clothing, sewing machines, bicycles and television sets. Peasants were allowed to leave the communes (shared farms), and factories no longer had to work to the orders of communist officials. Deng allowed small private businesses to grow up, and ended the most severe government censorship of television and newspapers.

However, many people began to demand democracy in China, wanting the right to control their own lives. When these protests became so huge in 1989 that Deng thought the communist government was under threat, he ordered troops to put down the demonstrators and thousands of people were killed. ■

See also

China's history   **Biography**
Communists   Mao Zedong

Descartes, René

Born 1596 in La Haye, Touraine, France
A famous philosopher
Died 1650 aged 53

Descartes was a very intelligent child who showed a great talent for mathematics. As 20 he took a degree in law. Then he spent time in the armies first of Holland, then of Bavaria. In 1619 he had an unforgettable dream where he imagined he was at last able to understand everything through possessing one simple, central explanation. He later moved to Holland, where he lived a quiet life, always seeking for this single explanation, and in so doing writing the books that were to make him famous.

The most important of these was called *Discourse on Method*. In this Descartes advised all students: first, never to accept anything as necessarily true until they have proof; second, always to attack problems bit by bit rather than in a rush; third, always to try to solve the simple questions before getting on to the hard ones; and lastly, always to check their answers to make sure nothing has been left out.

Descartes also discussed the problem of how we can ever be sure about anything. For example, how do we know we are not dreaming at any moment, with everything around us actually quite unreal? But as Descartes explained, even if we are all dreaming we still have our own thoughts at the time, and no one can ever say that these do not exist. Or as he puts it, 'I think, therefore I am'; perhaps the best-known sentence ever written by a philosopher, and still often quoted today. ■

See also

Philosophers

de Valera, Eamon

Born 1882 in New York, USA
A leader of the Irish struggles against British rule who became Prime Minister of Ireland
Died 1975 aged 92

Eamon de Valera was born in America, but at the age of 3 he was sent to live with his mother's family in Ireland. After he became a mathematics teacher, he joined the Volunteers who were preparing to fight against the British. In Easter week 1916, he was one of the commanders of a rebellion in Dublin. The rebels had to surrender to the British, who shot most of their leaders.

De Valera was reprieved and so he lived to become leader of Sinn Féin (Ourselves Alone), which fought a guerrilla war against British rule from 1919 to 1921. Sinn Féin and the British then signed a treaty to set up an Irish Free State, but de Valera would not agree to it because Ireland was to be partitioned. He supported the anti-Treatyites who fought a civil war from 1921 to 1923 against those who signed.

In 1926 he started a new party, Fianna Fáil (Warriors of Ireland). It won the 1932 general election, and Eamon de Valera was prime minister until 1948. During World War II he kept Ireland

▲ In 1921 de Valera was on the run from the British troops, but he still came out of hiding to inspect these men of the Irish Republican Army.

as a neutral country. He broke nearly all the links with Britain, so it was easy for Ireland to become a fully independent republic in 1949.

For five years between 1951 and 1959 he was Taoiseach (prime minister) of the republic, and between 1959 and 1973 he was president. ■

See also

Ireland's history
Irish Republic

de Valois, Ninette

Born 1898 in Batiboys, County Wicklow, Ireland
A great British ballet-dancer and teacher, who founded The Royal Ballet

She grew up in Ireland as Edris Stannus, but became famous as Ninette de Valois, dancing as a principal ballerina in England and Europe. By 1926 she was running her own ballet school, and in 1931 she formed the Vic-Wells Ballet. She was a brilliant organizer and teacher, and helped to shape the careers of such dancers as Margot Fonteyn. Under her direction, the Vic-Wells Ballet became the Sadlers Wells Ballet, moved to Covent

Garden, and was recognized in 1956 as The Royal Ballet.

Ninette de Valois created many famous ballets for her company, to scores by such modern composers as Stravinsky and Vaughan Williams. She wanted Britain to have a great national ballet company. She worked hard to achieve her aims and expected others to put in as much effort. Her achievement was recognized when she was made a Dame of the British Empire in 1951. Ninette de Valois retired as director of The Royal Ballet in 1961, but is still actively involved in the work of its ballet school. ■

See also

Ballet
Biography
Fonteyn
Stravinsky

▲ Dame Ninette de Valois rehearses a young dancer in the ballet *The Rake's Progress*.

Dias, Bartolomeu

Born about 1450 in Portugal
The first European navigator to discover
the Cape of Good Hope
Died 1500 aged about 50, at sea

Nothing is known of the early life of Bartolomeu Dias except that he was an experienced sea captain, and was a knight at the court of the Portuguese king, João II. In 1487 João sent him on an expedition to sail as far south as possible along the west coast of Africa, looking for a sea route to India.

A storm blew Dias and the three little ships under his command out to sea, until his crews feared they would fall off the edge of the Earth. When the storm subsided Dias turned east, then north, and reached the African coast at Mossel Bay. After sailing as far as the Great Fish River on the south-east African coast, his men then insisted on going home. But Dias had seen that the coast of Africa turned northwards leaving the passage to India clear. Dias named the south-western point of Africa the 'Cape of Storms', but King João changed the name to 'Cape of Good Hope'.

Dias joined Vasco da Gama on a voyage to the Cape Verde Islands, but did not go with him on the expedition that finally reached India. Instead he was sent to Brazil, but was lost at sea in a great storm off the cape he had discovered. ■

See also

Explorers

Biography
Gama (map)

Dickens, Charles

Born 1812 in Portsmouth, England
One of the greatest novelists of Victorian
England
Died 1870 aged 58

Charles Dickens was the son of a naval clerk, a pleasant but ineffective man who frequently got into debt. When this led to his imprisonment, the young Charles, then aged 12, was taken out

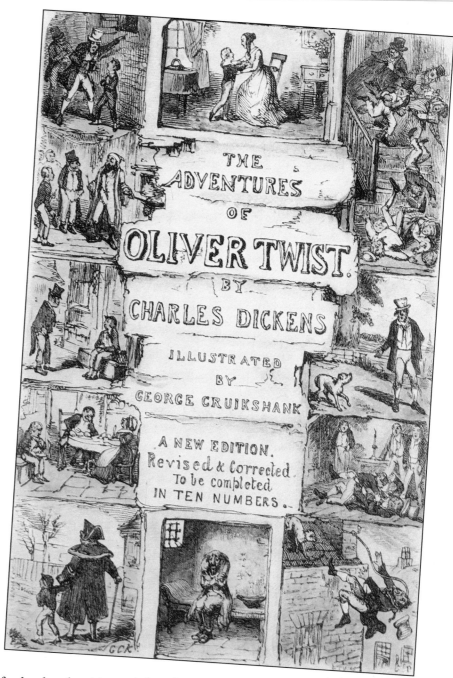

▲ The title page from an edition of *Oliver Twist*, which describes the adventures of an orphan boy and was famous for its description of London's criminal world. The illustrations are by the artist George Cruikshank (1792–1878). Many of Dickens's novels first appeared as instalments in weekly or monthly periodicals before being published as complete books.

of school and put to work in a factory pasting labels onto bottles of shoe polish. This proved a bitter experience. He never forgave his mother for wanting him to continue at the factory even after his father was released from prison and the family's fortunes had improved.

He went to school again, and left at 15 to become a reporter covering debates in the House of Commons. His genius for describing comic characters and his anger about social injustice were soon noted. In 1836 he began *The*

Pickwick Papers, which describes the ridiculous adventures of a wealthy group of friends who never seem able to keep out of trouble. It was so popular that by the age of 24 Charles was famous in Britain and America.

Charles Dickens never lost his fame nor his passion for work. He had ten children, numerous friends, and loved putting on amateur theatrical productions. He wrote stories of such power that Parliament sometimes passed laws to stop the various scandals he described so vividly. After his book *Nicholas Nickleby*, some of the cruel boarding-schools he described were forced to close down following such bad publicity. In *Oliver Twist* he attacked the way that poor orphans were mistreated, and in *A Christmas Carol* he criticized mean employers who thought only of themselves.

Dickens also had a wonderful gift for creating larger-than-life characters in his novels: the villainous Fagin in *Oliver Twist*, the bitter Miss Havisham in *Great Expectations*, the drunken nurse Mrs Gamp in *Martin Chuzzlewit*, and the optimistic, unreliable Mr Micawber in *David Copperfield*, a character based on his own father. When Dickens died of a stroke, he was mourned all over the world, and his books have remained popular ever since. ∎

Diesel, Rudolf

Born 1858 in Paris, France
Invented a new type of engine for motor vehicles, now known as the diesel engine, which uses cheap diesel fuel.
Died 1913 aged 55, drowned in the English Channel

Born in Paris of German parents, Diesel trained as an engineer in Munich. In the 1890s he began experiments on the internal combustion engine used to power cars. By 1897 he had perfected a simpler type of engine that did not need spark plugs and used a cheaper form of petrol, now called diesel. Diesel engines have been widely used in lorries and are increasingly fitted into family cars. They are very economical to run, because they travel further per litre of fuel than ordinary cars with internal combustion engines.

Diesel was a difficult man to work with; he always suffered with bad headaches and was often extremely miserable and depressed. He died when he fell overboard crossing the English Channel. Some people think he may have committed suicide. ∎

See also

Engines
Fuel
Internal combustion engines

Disraeli, Benjamin

Born 1804 in London, England
Conservative prime minister in 1868 and again from 1874 to 1880
Died 1881 aged 76

When Disraeli became prime minister in 1874, he said 'I have climbed to the top of the greasy pole.' Disraeli was Jewish, and did not go to a well-known school. It was difficult for someone like him to get to the top in Victorian Britain.

As a young man, he dressed in flashy clothes, and wore his black hair in long ringlets. He wrote successful novels, but when he got into Parliament nobody thought much of him. That did not stop him. He married a rich widow, probably for her money. It became a very happy marriage, and Disraeli was grief-stricken when Mary Anne died, just before he finally gained power. He was nearly 70, in bad health, and lonely, but he achieved a great deal as prime minister.

He believed that the Conservative Party should improve the lives of ordinary people, especially now so many had the vote. In 1867 as Chancellor of the Exchequer he had introduced an important Reform Act which had given the vote to working men living in towns and cities. While he was prime minister from 1874 to 1880 his government encouraged better housing and cleaner conditions in towns.

Disraeli wanted to see the British empire grow stronger than ever. Through him, Britain took control of the newly built Suez Canal, the shortest route to India. He had great support from Queen Victoria, whom he charmed and flattered. He persuaded Parliament to give her the title of 'Empress of India'. In 1876, she made him Lord Beaconsfield.

Disraeli was a clever speaker and very witty. When he lay dying, someone asked him if he would like the Queen to visit him. 'Better not,' he said. 'She would only want me to take a message to Albert.' ∎

See also

British empire
Victorian Britain
Biography
Gladstone
Victoria

Dodgson, Charles

See Carroll, Lewis

Dominic, Saint

Born about 1170 in Caleruega, Spain
He founded an order of friars, named the Dominicans after him.
Died 1221 aged about 51

Dominic was born in a small village in northern Spain, but his parents soon sent him away to be educated, first by a priest in the next parish, then at university. For ten years he studied theology, and was such an excellent scholar that the Bishop of Osma made him a canon in his cathedral.

With the bishop, Dominic travelled on a diplomatic mission to Denmark. As they passed through the south of France, they met a heretic, a member of a group called the Albigensians who did not follow the teachings of the Church leaders. Dominic argued with the Albigensian all night until the man agreed that his beliefs were mistaken. There were many heretics in the area, and Dominic felt called to stay and preach the true faith to them.

At first the French bishops took no notice of Dominic and his small band of followers, because the bishops were trying to stop heresy by force. But eventually they came to realize that Dominic's tactics of persuasion were in fact more effective. In 1216 the Pope gave him permission to found the Order of Friar Preachers.

Like Francis of Assisi, who had founded his own order six years earlier, Dominic insisted that his friars should own nothing and be totally obedient to the rules of the order. But while the early Franciscans had to give up their books, the Dominicans were encouraged to study.

Within a year, enough people had joined the order for Dominic to be able to send his Dominicans out beyond the south of France. At the same time, the Franciscans were leaving Italy and starting to travel. Gradually Dominic and Francis of Assisi filled Europe with friars. In 1221 Dominic helped to draw up a clear set of rules for the Dominicans. He died soon afterwards, worn out by his labours. ■

See also

Christians
Heretics
Monasteries

Biography
Francis of Assisi

▼ A poster advertising the film *The Hound of the Baskervilles*, produced in 1939 and starring Basil Rathbone as Sherlock Holmes.

Doyle, Arthur Conan

Born 1859 in Edinburgh, Scotland
Writer and inventor of the famous detective, Sherlock Holmes
Died 1930 aged 71

Conan Doyle was trained as a doctor, but he was never very successful in this profession. After he had tried to make a living in medicine for nine years, he found that he could earn more money by writing than by doctoring, so when he was 32 he gladly stopped practising medicine and took up writing full time.

He wrote all sorts of books, historical romances, books of adventure and a large number of short stories, but it

was the detective stories which he wrote with the brilliant Sherlock Holmes as their hero which brought him money and fame. After the two first long Holmes books, *A Study in Scarlet* and *The Sign of Four*, which were only fairly successful, Doyle wrote the short stories which make up *The Adventures of Sherlock Holmes*, and these established his reputation. Later Conan Doyle became tired of writing about Sherlock Holmes and tried to kill him off, in a struggle to the death with the arch-villain Moriarty. But his readers complained so much that he had to write another story in which Holmes miraculously reappears and tells of his amazing escape. ■

Drake, Sir Francis

Born about 1543 near Tavistock, England
Elizabethan sea captain who was the first Englishman to sail round the world
Died 1596 aged about 53

A short man with a commanding air and a merry nature: that is how people who knew him described Francis Drake. He learned seamanship from his cousin, Sir John Hawkins, who took him on two expeditions to carry slaves

from Africa to America. A surprise attack by Spaniards made Drake a lifelong enemy of Spain.

Queen Elizabeth I granted Drake a privateering commission. That was a kind of pirate's licence, which meant that Drake could plunder the Spaniards as long as he was doing it unofficially. After several successful voyages plundering the Spaniards in the West Indies and on the Spanish Main, he set out in 1577 to explore the South Pacific and raid Spanish colonies in South America.

Drake had five ships. Two were burned; one sank in a fearful storm and another turned for home. In the remaining ship, the *Pelican*, which he renamed the *Golden Hind*, Drake sailed up the west coast of South America, capturing treasure ships. Then he sailed right across the Pacific, and so home around Africa. For this deed Elizabeth knighted Drake on the *Golden Hind* at Deptford on the River Thames.

Drake raided Spanish settlements in the Caribbean Sea in 1585. Two years later, hearing that the Spaniards were building a fleet to attack England, he

▼ A replica of Drake's original *Golden Hind* was built in 1974 and, like its predecessor, sailed around the world.

raided the harbour at Cádiz and burned the fleet. By this time the Spaniards hated and feared Drake, and thought he was in league with the Devil.

The Spaniards equipped a new invasion fleet, which they called the Invincible Armada (fleet). When it sailed in 1588 Drake helped defeat it. Seven years later he died at sea off Portobelo, Panama, during another raid on Spanish colonies in America. ■

See also

Armada
Explorers
Spanish colonial history

Biography
Elizabeth I
Frobisher
Hawkins

Dunlop, John Boyd

Born 1840 in Ayrshire, Scotland
Remembered as the inventor of the pneumatic (pump-up) tyre
Died 1921 aged 81

John Dunlop was born into a farming family. His parents wanted him to continue in the family tradition, but instead he went to college and became a veterinary surgeon. He moved to Belfast, in Ireland, when he was 27, and ran a big and successful vet's practice.

During the 1880s, bicycles were becoming very fashionable, helped by the invention of the 'safety' bicycle which was more or less the same shape as a modern one. Bicycles usually had solid rubber tyres, but Dunlop had the idea of a hollow tyre with air pressure inside it after his son had asked for something which would help him to go faster on the cobbled streets of Belfast.

He patented his 'pneumatic' tyre in 1888. He never made a fortune out of it, though, for two reasons. One was that someone else, William Thompson, had patented an exactly similar idea in 1845, although it had not been made then because bicycles were much rarer. Another problem was that his pneumatic tyres were stuck to their wheels with glue, making it very difficult to mend punctures. Not until

later inventors came up with other methods of keeping pneumatic tyres fixed to wheels did they become really popular.

Dunlop went on to run a group of drapery shops (selling cloth and clothes), and he died quite well off, but not as rich as might be expected for someone whose name is so well remembered. ■

See also

Bicycles
Tyres

▼ An early advertisement for John Dunlop's air-filled tyres. The first tyres which Dunlop sold had to be stuck to their wheels with glue.

Dürer, Albrecht

Born 1471 in Nürnberg, Germany
The greatest Renaissance artist of northern Europe
Died 1528 aged 56

Dürer's father was a goldsmith, and Albrecht was one of eighteen children; only three survived to adulthood. His artistic talent developed early. At the age of 13 he made a brilliant self-portrait, and at 15 he was apprenticed to a painter and book illustrator in Nürnberg. Four years later, when he had completed his apprenticeship, he took off on his travels to find out what other European artists were doing.

Armed with new knowledge, he was able to take refreshingly modern ideas to the north from Italy. Although he made many paintings, including water-colour landscapes, portraits, and studies of nature, his main achievement is in the difficult technique of print-making. He is one of the greatest ever masters of engraving and wood block prints.

The skill and beauty of his prints made him famous, and his work was often copied. He was a thoughtful, religious and learned man, a 'whole' man, knowledgeable in many subjects, including religious philosophy, mathematics, geometry, Latin and literature. ■

See also

Renaissance

Dvorak, Antonin

Born 1841 in Nelahozeves, Bohemia (now part of Czechoslovakia)
The most important Czech composer of his day
Died 1904 aged 62

The Czechs are a very musical nation. So it was quite natural for the young Dvorak to play the violin and join in the village music-making. When he was 12 he began to learn how to be a butcher, like his father and grandfather. But he could not forget music, and eventually an uncle agreed to pay for proper lessons.

When his studies were complete, Dvorak earned his living by playing the violin. He also wrote music, but it was not until he was nearly 40 that people began to recognize his importance.

Dvorak wrote many colourful operas, concertos, chamber music pieces, and nine symphonies, one of which, *From the New World,* was composed when he went to teach in America. His music is full of splendid, dance-like tunes that seem to have sprung out of the Czech countryside. Dvorak put Czech music on the map. ■

See also

Chamber music   Symphonies
Concertos

▲ Amelia Earhart beside one of the aircraft she flew. In 1932 she became the first woman to fly across the Atlantic Ocean alone, completing the journey in 15 hours and 18 minutes.

Earhart, Amelia

Born 1897 in Kansas City, USA
Famous American woman pilot
Disappeared 1937 aged 40

Amelia Earhart was always keen on aeroplanes, and as a young woman she took various odd jobs to pay for flying lessons. She was first noticed by the public when she flew the Atlantic with two men in 1928. She was slightly embarrassed by all the attention she got for this, because she had really only been a passenger. However, she went on to make long-distance flights on her own. She married George Putnam, who acted as her manager and promoter.

In 1932 she flew the Atlantic again, this time alone. She became known as the 'Winged Legend'.

In 1937 she embarked on her biggest journey, a trip around the world with Fred Noonan as navigator. All the stops on the route were carefully planned, but one of them was at a small island in the Pacific Ocean. Her friends and advisers were worried about whether she and Noonan would be able to find it, even though they would be in radio contact. Their fears were justified. Although Amelia could be heard on the radio, she failed to find the island and disappeared in the sea. ∎

Edison, Thomas Alva

Born 1847 in Ohio, USA
One of the greatest inventors of all time. Of his thousands of inventions the phonograph and the electric lamp are the best known.
Died 1931 aged 84

When Thomas was only 7 he was expelled from his school because the headmaster thought he was too slow to learn. But his mother taught him at home and encouraged his interest in science. By the time he was 10 he had made his own laboratory. At the age of 12 he began to sell newspapers and sweets in the carriages of the new railway trains. He set up a laboratory in the luggage van so that he could do experiments while the train was in the station.

Edison set up his own company, which he called his 'invention factory', and he used to boast that they made a small invention every ten days and a big one every six months. All the inventions were patented, but his greatest invention was the world's first machine for recording sounds, the phonograph. The whole of our modern recording industry, for both pop and classical music, really developed from this invention.

Edison also invented the electric lamp. It consisted of a wire inside a glass bulb from which all the air had been taken out to create a vacuum. When an electric current was passed through the wire, called a filament, it glowed white hot and so gave out light. While he was experimenting Edison found that a current could also flow across the vacuum to a plate inside the bulb. He did not understand why, but this fact, that we now know to be due to electrons escaping from the filament, is named after him, the Edison effect. This discovery led to the invention of electronic valves and was really the beginning of the whole of our modern electronics industry. ∎

See also

Electricity
Electronics
Inventors
Light
Patents
Recording
Valves

▲ This light bulb, made by Thomas Edison, can be seen in the Science Museum, London. Modern bulbs work in the same basic way, though they have a much finer, coiled filament.

Edward I

Born 1239 in London, England
King of England from 1272 to 1307; he
conquered Wales but could not subdue
the Scots.
Died 1307 aged 68

As a boy, Edward was tall, strong and
agile. When he was 12, he started to
help his father, Henry III, in ruling the
kingdom, and by the time he was 16
he was married. He first showed his
strength in battle by defeating a group
of barons who were rebelling against
his father, and then proved himself a
courageous knight on crusade to the
Holy Land.

After Edward became king in 1272,
he was faced with rebellion by a
powerful Welsh prince, Llywelyn.
Edward invaded Wales and within five
years, Llywelyn was dead, and all
Wales was under his control. Edward
built a string of fortresses in Wales to
demonstrate English strength. But
when he tried to conquer Scotland he
was not so successful.

Edward was determined to keep
fighting, whatever the expense, and he
died leading an army north. His last
request was that his body should be
boiled until the flesh fell off the bones,
and his skeleton carried on every
expedition against the Scots. ■

See also

Castles   **Biography**
Scotland's history   Bruce
Welsh history   Llywelyn ap Gruffudd

Edward III

Born 1312 in Windsor, England
King of England from 1327 to 1377, he
began the Hundred Years War and
revived the ideal of chivalry.
Died 1377 aged 64

During his childhood, Edward's
parents, Queen Isabella and Edward
II, quarrelled bitterly with each other.
They both wanted Edward on their
side, and his mother took him to France
where she was plotting with her lover,
Roger Mortimer. When Prince Edward

▲ This picture of Edward III is taken from a
15th-century manuscript.

was 14, they murdered his father and
had him crowned king. Three years
later, King Edward had Mortimer put
to death as a traitor and began to act
for himself.

Edward wanted to be a true chivalrous
knight, fighting for fame and glory like
his grandfather Edward I. He saw
himself as the new King Arthur, and
his men as the Knights of the Round
Table. In 1339 he invaded France,
starting a war that was to continue for
100 years. Under Edward and his son,
nicknamed the Black Prince, the
English won many battles. The greatest
was at Crécy in 1346. They were so
successful that Edward came to control
almost as much territory in France as
Henry II had done a century before.

In his last years, Edward began to lose

his grip. By 1370, most of the fighting
companions of his youth were dead,
as was his wife Philippa of Hainaut. In
his loneliness, Edward turned to a
lover, Alice Perrers. Her ambition for
power at court made the nobles jealous.
At the same time in France, a strong
king was taking back the lands that
Edward and the Black Prince had won.
Edward lost his reputation as a true
knight, and died a broken man, with
his mistress, Alice, waiting to strip the
rings from his fingers. ■

See also

Arthur and his knights   **Biography**
Chivalry   Edward I
France's history
Hundred Years War
Weapons

Edward VI

Born 1537 at Hampton Court, London, England
The son that Henry VIII had wanted for so long. He was only 9 when he became king, and ruled from 1547 to 1553.
Died 1553 aged 15

Edward was a serious, clever boy. He was carefully educated to be king and could even talk to important foreign visitors in Latin. He was a strong Protestant. The English Church became Protestant in his reign.

Edward could not of course rule himself, because he was so young. First his ambitious uncle made himself Duke of Somerset, and Protector. Then Somerset was pushed out by the efficient, ruthless Duke of Northumberland. But when he was only 14 Edward became seriously ill with tuberculosis. He and the Duke of Northumberland probably decided together that Edward's Protestant cousin Lady Jane Grey should become queen instead of Catholic Mary, the real heir. But it was all in vain. None of the doctors' extraordinary cures saved Edward from death. Jane was queen for only nine days. Mary won the support of most people and took the crown. ■

See also

Reformation   **Biography**
Tudor England   Henry VIII

◄ In this portrait of the boy King Edward VI, he is holding the Tudor rose, his family's badge.

Edward VII

Born 1841 in London, England
King of the United Kingdom from 1901 to 1910; a popular king who tried hard to improve Britain's relationships with other countries
Died 1910 aged 68

Edward was the eldest son of Queen Victoria and Prince Albert. As a child he was a disappointment to his demanding parents since he would rather enjoy himself than work. During his time at university, he served with the army in Ireland. When news of his wild behaviour there got back to England, his father was most upset. Shortly afterwards, Prince Albert died of typhoid, but Queen Victoria was convinced that his death was hastened by worry about their son. On the queen's command, Edward was shut out from important government business until he was over 50.

In 1863 he married Alexandra, daughter of the King of Denmark. They had five children, but Edward was not close to his family. He preferred racing, shooting, yachting and playing cards. He did, however, take politics seriously. He made an important visit to India in 1875–1876 and worked with the royal commission on housing.

When Queen Victoria died in 1901, Edward became king. He was 59. When he visited France he was so popular that a new spirit of friendship grew up between the two countries. He was also the first British monarch to visit Russia. At home he gave his full backing to the reform of the army and navy. When he died many people missed his pleasure-loving personality, but some welcomed a return to the sober values of his son, George V. ■

See also

Edwardian Britain   **Biography**
British Royal Family
Victoria

Edward VIII

Born 1894 in Richmond, Surrey, England
King of the United Kingdom in 1936, but never crowned; uncle of Queen Elizabeth II
Died 1972 aged 77

Edward suffered from having, in George V and Queen Mary, a strict father and mother. He first trained for the Royal Navy and then served as an officer in the army during World War I. Afterwards he travelled to Canada, the USA, Africa, India and Australia, and always impressed people with his friendly approach. He was popular in Britain because of his concern for the unemployed. He would often visit working men's clubs, and supported schemes to create new jobs.

When George V died in 1936, he became king. However, he had fallen in love with Wallis Simpson, an American lady already in her second marriage. Edward wanted to marry her once she got her divorce, but Parliament believed that most people would never accept her as queen. When Edward insisted on the marriage, he was forced to abdicate (resign from the throne) and then leave Britain itself. He was created Duke of Windsor, but spent the rest of his life abroad, bitter to the end at the unfair way he felt he and his wife had been treated. ■

See also

British history 1919–1989

Biography
George VI
British Royal Family (family tree)

Einstein, Albert

Born 1879 in Württemberg, Germany
One of the world's greatest physicists, who was also deeply concerned about world peace
Died 1955 aged 76

As a boy Albert was very unhappy at school, and the schoolmasters treated him badly because they thought that he was not very clever. At 15 he had

▲ Albert Einstein was one of the greatest scientists of all time. Although his ideas were later used in developing nuclear weapons, he himself was a prominent campaigner for world peace.

very bad results in many of his school subjects but was good at music, and especially at playing the violin. After spending some time in Italy he eventually went to Zürich in Switzerland, and there his skill as a scientist was recognized.

In one year, when he was only 26, he published several scientific papers that completely changed the way scientists think. He became a Swiss citizen and began to work in the Patent Office, examining applications made by other people. In 1914 his family moved back to Berlin. He remembered how harsh his schoolteachers had been, and he thought that the whole German system of government was also harsh, and said so quite openly. He thought the army was given too much power. When World War I ended in 1918 he hoped that would be the end of the army's power. Unfortunately he was wrong. In 1921 he was awarded the top prize in science, the Nobel prize. It is typical of his modesty that he travelled third class with his violin under his arm when he went to Stockholm to receive the prize!

He hated to see the Nazis gaining military power, and although he was now world-famous, he suffered a lot of abuse because he was Jewish. The Nazis even wrecked his summer cottage and stole his boat. Eventually

he had had enough, and in 1933 he went to America. Although he did not believe in war he was so horrified by what the Nazis were doing that he urged America to build up its army to be ready to prevent the spread of Nazi ideas.

He lived the rest of his life in the USA, and after World War II he spent much of his time trying to persuade world leaders to abandon nuclear weapons.

His ideas in science were so new and strange that for many years ordinary people used to say that no one else could possibly understand them. But now his theories about time and space (relativity), about how the very tiny particles like electrons and protons behave (quantum theory), and many others, are important parts of the courses that all physics students learn at their universities.

Not many people really deserve the title 'genius' but Einstein must be one of them. Nearly all branches of physics were changed by his theories, and without them lasers, television, computers, space travel and many other things that are familiar today would never have been developed. ■

◉ **See also**

Atoms	Particles
Energy	Patents
Nazis	Physicists
Nuclear power	Relativity

Eisenhower, Dwight David

Born 1890 in Denison, Texas, USA
Commanded the Allied invasions of North Africa, Italy and France in World War II; President of the USA 1953–1961
Died 1969 aged 78

From his childhood everybody called Eisenhower 'Ike', and his cheerful grin made him friends everywhere. He became a soldier during World War I. When World War II came he had never been in action, though he had risen to the rank of brigadier-general. However, his organizing ability led to his promotion to command US forces in Europe in 1942. British and American generals were often jealous of each other, but as commander-in-chief of the Allied armies, Eisenhower turned them into a winning team.

Eisenhower held two more important army posts; he was chief of staff of the US Army, and in 1951 he was invited to be supreme commander of the NATO forces in Europe. In 1952 the Republican Party persuaded him to be its presidential candidate. He left the

▼ At a meeting of the heads of the Allied Expeditionary Force before their landings in Normandy in 1944, during World War II, Eisenhower (on the left) is sitting with Montgomery, the British army chief.

army, and his supporters swept him to power in the election with the slogan 'I like Ike'.

He served for two terms, winning a second election in 1956. During his presidency he brought the Korean War to an end; saw two new states, Alaska and Hawaii, join the United States; and began the US space programme. He made goodwill visits to more than 20 countries. ∎

See also

NATO
USA: history
World War II

El Cid

Born around 1043 in Burgos, Spain
Spanish soldier and national hero
Died 1099 aged about 56

When El Cid (whose real name was Rodrigo Díaz de Vivar) lived, Spain was divided into many small kingdoms. Most of these were ruled by Muslim invaders from North Africa; a few were governed by Christian Spanish kings. It was a tough time, and people were very cruel.

Rodrigo collected an army of brave men around him, who were very loyal to him. Sometimes they fought for a Christian lord, sometimes for a Muslim king. Rodrigo was very cruel and bloodthirsty, but he was such a successful leader that the Muslims nicknamed him *El Cid* (the lord).

Poets began making up stories about him, and 50 years after his death one of the greatest poems of Spain, the *Cantar de mío Cid*, was written. In the poem El Cid is described as the perfect knight, the bravest soldier and (because he fought the Muslim invaders) the best of Christians. The beautiful words of the unknown poet turned the real Rodrigo into a national hero, and have kept his name alive until today. ∎

See also

Spain's history

Elgar, Sir Edward

Born 1857 in Broadheath, near Worcester, England
England's first great composer of symphonies and oratorios, and famous for a set of five marches, *Pomp and Circumstance*
Died 1934 aged 76

Elgar's father ran a music shop in Worcester, so although Edward could never afford to study at a college or university he was surrounded by music. He therefore decided to teach himself. He played the violin in local orchestras and was happy to write music for anyone who needed it.

But he was a sensitive man and easily discouraged. It was only when he married, in 1889, that he found someone who really believed in him. Once this had happened his music began to blossom, until finally, in 1899, the *Enigma Variations* for orchestra proved to the entire world that he was a musical genius. Oratorios, such as *The Dream of Gerontius*, two great symphonies, concertos for violin and cello, and a symphonic poem *Falstaff* were further proof.

Suddenly, in 1920, his wife died. Elgar was broken-hearted, and for the rest of his life wrote almost nothing. ∎

See also

Concertos
Symphonies

El Greco

Born 1541 in Candia, on the island of Crete, Greece
The first great painter in the history of Spanish art
Died 1614 aged 73

El Greco's real name was Domenikos Theotokopoulos. The name by which he is now famous is a mixture of Italian and Spanish meaning 'the Greek'. This curious mixture reflects his career. His birthplace, Crete, was Greek speaking, but at that time was part of the Venetian empire. He worked in Italy when he was in his twenties and thirties, but

settled in Toledo in Spain in 1577 and spent the rest of his life there.

In Crete he had trained as a painter of icons, but in Spain he painted religious pictures on a much bigger scale, many of them for church altars. Spain was a fervently religious country and El Greco's paintings often convey a sense of spiritual rapture. He elongated his figures into forms resembling flickering flames and they seem free of earthly restrictions. Few other painters have depicted so convincingly the awesomeness of great religious events. El Greco painted magnificent portraits as well as religious scenes. ∎

See also

Icons

Eliot, George

Born 1819 in Chilvers Coton, Warwickshire, England
One of the greatest novelists of Victorian England
Died 1880 aged 61

George Eliot was the name adopted by Mary Ann Evans, the daughter of a Warwickshire estate manager. After a good education she returned to keep house for her father, following the death of her mother. When her father died too, Mary became an editor and journalist and worked with some of the most brilliant minds of the time. Finally she started writing her own books under the name 'George Eliot'. She believed that novelists thought to be male were always likely to be treated more seriously by critics.

Her first novel, *Adam Bede*, was set in the countryside she remembered so well. It is rich both in detail and in her understanding of country people. She then wrote *The Mill on the Floss*, drawing on her own childhood for its descriptions of the growing tension between the lively and intelligent heroine, Maggie Tulliver, and her family. But her masterpiece was still to come: *Middlemarch*, written in 1871 and describing a small town society from rich landowners and clergymen to shopkeepers, farmers and labourers. To read it is still to feel part of a community that has long since disappeared.

During this time, Mary shared her life with Henry Lewes, another brilliant writer. He was already married but long separated from his wife. At that time it was a very daring thing for a couple who were not married to live together. Mary's family was deeply shocked, but she still believed she was doing the right thing and stayed with Henry Lewes until he died. After that Mary married a much younger man, only to die herself later in the same year. ■

▲ This portrait of George Eliot, drawn in 1865 when she was 46, shows an interesting and highly intelligent individual.

Eliot, Thomas Stearns

Born 1888 in St Louis, Missouri, USA
One of the most important 20th-century poets
Died 1965 aged 76

Although T. S. Eliot was born in the USA, he spent most of his life in England, first at Oxford University, then in London, where he worked as a bank clerk and later as a publisher. His first important poem was *The Love Song of J. Alfred Prufrock*. Using language that is an intriguing mixture of the ordinary and the poetic, it describes the thoughts and feelings of a middle-aged man. In 1922 Eliot published an even more extraordinary poem for his time, *The Waste Land*. This again combined everyday speech with highly unusual images in its description of what the poet saw as the empty, worthless aspects of life in his own century. Traditional critics hated his modern approach to writing, but younger ones saw it as an important break from the past.

Later on Eliot became more religious and less daring in outlook. He turned to writing plays, the most famous being *Murder in the Cathedral* (about the death of Thomas Becket). In 1939 he also wrote the very jolly *Old Possum's Book of Practical Cats*. Later this was the basis for the popular musical *Cats*, first performed in 1981. ■

▼ Extract from *Macavity: The Mystery Cat* by T. S. Eliot.

... Macavity's a ginger cat, he's very tall and thin;
You would know him if you saw him, for his eyes are sunken in.
His brow is deeply lined with thought, his head is highly domed;
His coat is dusty from neglect, his whiskers are uncombed.
He sways his head from side to side, with movements like a snake;
And when you think he's half asleep, he's always wide awake.

Macavity, Macavity, there's no one like Macavity,
For he's a fiend in feline shape, a monster of depravity.
You may meet him in a by-street, you may see him in the square –
But when a crime's discovered, then *Macavity's not there!* ...

Elizabeth I

Born 1533 in Greenwich Palace, London, England
Tudor Queen of England and Wales who ruled from 1558 to 1603
Died 1603 aged 69

There was not much rejoicing when Elizabeth was born. Henry VIII wanted a son. When she was 2, her mother, Anne Boleyn, was executed. Then Elizabeth had four different stepmothers. Later, she was in great danger in her Catholic sister Mary's reign because she was Protestant. Not surprisingly, the 25-year-old woman who became queen in 1558 had learnt to hide her feelings. She was cautious, clever and quick-witted, and, unlike most girls of her time, she was very well educated.

Queen Elizabeth I was a woman in a world of men. She cleverly controlled her powerful courtiers by being charming, or witty, or angry. Everyone expected her to marry, but we do not know what Elizabeth herself felt. She may have been in love with her favourite, the Earl of Leicester. She almost married various foreign princes, when she needed their country's friendship. Once she promised Parliament she would marry 'as soon as I can conveniently' – but it never was convenient.

Elizabeth could be very stubborn. She refused to change the Church of England set up in 1559, though at first neither Catholics nor Protestants were really satisfied. She often put off difficult decisions. Though Mary Queen of Scots was a great danger, Elizabeth took seventeen years to agree to her execution. Even then she pretended she had allowed it by mistake.

Elizabeth hated spending money. She avoided an expensive war with Philip II of Spain as long as possible, though she secretly encouraged sailors like Drake to attack Spanish treasure ships, and took some of the silver and gold they captured. When the Spanish Armada set out to invade England, Elizabeth became an inspiring war

▲ Elizabeth I was slim, with pale skin and red hair. When she was older she wore thick white makeup and a red wig; she may have lost her hair when she had smallpox. She kept careful control of her portraits. They had to show her as an impressive queen. This one was painted to celebrate the victory over the Armada in 1588. The battle is in the top left corner. The crown reminds us of Elizabeth's power, and her hand rests on the globe. Her magnificent dress is covered in jewels.

leader. But after the victory, she did not pay the sick and starving English sailors who had done the fighting.

Elizabeth's greatest talent was the way she could win people's affection wherever she went, from the grandest noblemen to the ordinary people who happened to see her as she passed. ■

See also

Armada
Puritans
Reformation
Tudor England

Biography
Drake
Henry VIII
Mary, Queen of Scots
Philip II of Spain
Ralegh

Elizabeth II

Born 1926 in London, England
Queen of the United Kingdom and
Northern Ireland and Head of the
Commonwealth from 1952

Queen Elizabeth II is the 42nd ruler of England since William the Conqueror. Until she was 10 years old she did not expect to be Queen. When her uncle King Edward VIII abdicated in 1936, her father became King George VI and Elizabeth his heir. Unable to pronounce her own name as a child, she called herself 'Lilibet', a name that her family still use today. Her full names are Elizabeth Alexandra Mary.

Elizabeth had a sheltered upbringing and never went to school. Instead she was taught by a governess and other tutors at Buckingham Palace and at Windsor, where she and her sister Princess Margaret lived during World War II. She continued to study history and constitutional law until she was 19 when she enrolled in the ATS.

From an early age her hobbies were riding and swimming. She was given a pony on her fourth birthday and won the Children's Challenge Shield for swimming when she was 13. Both she and her sister were Girl Guides.

Just before the outbreak of war in 1939, Elizabeth had accompanied her parents on an engagement to the Royal Naval College where she met a young sailor who was a distant relation. He was Prince Philip. Years later he became her first and only boyfriend. They married in Westminster Abbey when she was 21 and had four children: Prince Charles, Princess Anne, Prince Andrew and Prince Edward.

When her father King George VI died suddenly in 1952 Elizabeth was well equipped to be Queen. She had been taught much about the history of the United Kingdom and Commonwealth and had travelled all over Britain attending official duties, at first with her parents and then on her own.

As Queen she undertakes more than 400 public engagements a year. In 1967 she introduced the 'walkabout' so that she could meet more people. She has visited nearly every Commonwealth country at least once, and has more experience of state affairs than some prime ministers.

▲ In 1945 Princess Elizabeth joined the Auxiliary Territorial Service (ATS), drove heavy lorries and was taught to be a motor mechanic.

Queen Elizabeth is keenly interested in horses, enjoys going to the races and is happiest in the country, riding or walking with her dogs. ∎

See also

Queens
Royal families

Biography
Charles, Prince of Wales
George VI
British Royal Family

Ellington, 'Duke'

Born 1899 in Washington DC, USA
He was perhaps the world's greatest jazz band leader and jazz pianist and composer.
Died 1974 aged 75

Edward Kennedy Ellington's stylish clothes as a teenager gained him the nickname Duke. He won a scholarship to art college, but was too busy learning jazz piano to attend.

In New York in 1927 he formed a ten-piece band, grandly calling it an orchestra, and became famous playing in Harlem's Cotton Club. Unlike most jazz musicians, Ellington also wrote fully orchestrated works, like his *Black,*

▼ Although he was always a brilliant jazz pianist, Duke Ellington was particularly proud to be praised as a serious modern composer.

Brown and Beige suite, which allowed no room for improvisation. Many hit records, including 'Don't Get Around Much Anymore' and 'It Don't Mean a Thing', spread his fame worldwide. Even the modern composer Stravinsky counted Ellington as an influence.

He was the first black composer commissioned to write major film sound-tracks, including *Anatomy of a Murder* (1959), and TV show themes. After 1965, he played many religious concerts in cathedrals, and continued working until his death from cancer. ∎

See also

Jazz

Erasmus, Desiderius

Born about 1466 in The Netherlands
A Renaissance scholar, and a great friend of Sir Thomas More
Died 1536 aged about 70

Erasmus was an orphan, and grew up in a monastery which he loathed. He was allowed to leave, and spent the rest of his life in the universities of Paris, Cambridge and Basel.

He thought the wealthy Catholic Church of his day had forgotten the teachings of Jesus. He made a new,

accurate Latin translation of the New Testament. He also wrote a best-selling book poking fun at worldly, lazy monks. But he never wanted to leave the Church, and disagreed strongly with the Protestant ideas of Martin Luther.

Erasmus often stayed with Thomas More in England, and they shared many interests. He was an old man when his friend was executed in 1535. He wrote: 'In More's death I seem to have died myself. We had but one soul between us.' ∎

See also

Reformation
Renaissance

Biography
Luther
More

Euclid

Lived about 300 BC in Alexandria, Egypt
A Greek mathematician who wrote the most famous textbook ever written

When Alexander the Great captured Egypt he set up a new city called Alexandria. A wonderful library was built there and a university. It became the most important place in the world for people to go and study. Clever mathematicians like Euclid went from Greece to Alexandria to work.

Euclid was especially interested in geometry and wrote a textbook called *Elements of Geometry.* It has been described as 'the most studied book apart from the Bible'. For over 2,000 years Euclid's textbook was the book all schoolchildren used as an intro-duction to geometry. Even the books you use today are based on the way Euclid taught geometry.

Euclid wrote other books, but many have been lost. Surprisingly, we know nothing about Euclid's life, not even when he was born or died, but his name remains one of the most famous in mathematics. ∎

See also

Geometry
Greek ancient history
Mathematics

Faraday, Michael

Born 1791 in London, England
One of the greatest of the 19th-century scientists, remembered especially for his invention of the dynamo and for his skill in explaining science to the public
Died 1867 aged 75

At the age of 12 Michael became an errand boy to a bookseller, and he was such a good worker that he was taken on as an apprentice to learn bookbinding without having to pay the usual fee. A customer noticed his interest in science and gave him a ticket to attend one of Sir Humphry Davy's lectures. He made careful notes, bound them, and sent them to Davy, who was so impressed that he offered him a job. So, aged 22, Michael became an assistant in the laboratories of the Royal Institution. He was given two rooms in the attic, free candles and twenty-five shillings a week pay. In 1825 he succeeded Davy as Director of the laboratory.

Faraday's researches covered many subjects in both chemistry and physics and especially in a new science that was in between the two. It concerned the effect of electric currents on chemicals and the way electric currents were produced from chemicals in cells (batteries). He studied how gases turned liquid at low temperatures, and how to make new kinds of glass for the lenses of microscopes.

He had heard of the experiments by Ampère, a French physicist, to show that electricity flowing in a coil made it behave like a magnet, and he thought that if electricity could produce a magnet then a magnet could produce electricity. He wound a coil of wire on a piece of iron, and when electricity was passed through the coil the iron became a magnet. Then he wound another, separate coil on the same piece of iron. When he switched on the current in the first coil he found that a current flowed in the second. So his idea was right: when a piece of iron inside a coil becomes magnetic an electric current flows in the coil. He had, in fact, discovered the transformer, which now plays a vital part in most electrical equipment. Then he found that if he took a hollow coil and moved a magnet in and out, a current flowed in the coil. He had invented the dynamo. How astonished he would be if he could come back and see the great power-stations of the modern world!

▼ Faraday at work in his laboratory at the Royal Institution in London. The laboratory and much of Faraday's equipment have been carefully preserved to this day.

Apart from making many discoveries, he also had the knack of explaining what he was doing in a simple way, so that ordinary people could understand. He started the famous Royal Institution Christmas Lectures in 1826, and they have been held every year since except for three years during World War I. Nowadays they are seen by millions on television. ■

See also

Dynamos
Electricity
Electricity supply
Experiments
Magnets

Transformers

Biography
Davy

Fawkes, Guy

Born 1570 in York, England
One of the conspirators who planned to blow up the Houses of Parliament in the Gunpowder Plot
Executed 1606 aged 35

Guy Fawkes was the son of a lawyer. He was brought up as a Protestant. But his father died when he was only 9, and after his mother remarried he became a Catholic. In 1593, when he was 23, he left England to join the Spanish army. He fought in Flanders and won the respect of his fellow soldiers.

When James I became king in 1603, Guy Fawkes and other English Catholics hoped for better treatment than they had received during Elizabeth I's reign. But it quickly became obvious that James I intended to allow the persecution of Catholics to continue. In 1604, a small group of Catholics, led by Robert Catesby, formed a conspiracy and plotted to kill the king. They invited Guy Fawkes to join them.

The plan was to blow up the House of Lords, when the king came to open Parliament. So they hired a cellar and filled it with gunpowder. Guy Fawkes undertook to look after the cellar and to light the fuse that would set off the explosion, when Parliament met on 5 November 1605. But the plot was discovered and on 4 November Guy

▲ A contemporary print shows the conspirators in the Gunpowder Plot. Guy (Guido) Fawkes is third from the right; beside him is Robert Catesby.

Fawkes was arrested. Although he was tortured, at first he bravely refused to give the names of the other conspirators. Eventually he signed a confession, and in January 1606 he was tried and executed.

Many people think that Guy Fawkes was a ruffian. In fact, he was a brave man, with strong religious beliefs, who paid the penalty for his part in a treacherous plot. ■

👁 **See also**

Gunpowder Plot

Biography
James I

fission and this would eventually produce atom bombs and nuclear power.

During World War II Fermi worked in the USA developing the first nuclear reactor. It was built in a squash court at the University of Chicago and was called the Fermi atomic pile. It led directly to the development of the atom bombs that were dropped on Hiroshima and Nagasaki. Fermi died two years before the first nuclear reactor was built for the peaceful use of providing electricity. ■

👁 **See also**

Atoms   **Biography**
Hiroshima   Chadwick
Nuclear power   Rutherford
Particles

New York's Jazz at the Philharmonic concerts in the 1950s. A master of scat-singing, she uses her voice like an instrument to improvise fast and furious nonsense sounds round the song's melody. Her crystal-clear tones and perfect diction are unrivalled for singing popular songs. Indeed, Fitzgerald's finest achievement is her series of 'songbook' albums recorded in the late 1950s, each containing the work of one popular writer, such as Cole Porter or George Gershwin. These are widely regarded as the best possible versions of the songs they contain, which include 'Manhattan' and 'Ev'ry Time we Say Goodbye'. ■

👁 **See also**

Jazz

▲ Ella Fitzgerald did not mind whether she sang in front of a big orchestra or a small group; she just loved to sing the songs that she liked best.

Fermi, Enrico

Born 1901 in Rome, Italy
Discovered nuclear fission without realizing it, and developed the first nuclear reactor.
Died 1954 aged 53

Enrico Fermi was a professor of physics at the University of Rome in 1932, when news reached him about James Chadwick's discovery of the neutron, a particle in the centre of atoms. He decided to do some experiments with neutrons himself. He set up a target made of uranium and bombarded it with neutrons, hoping to make a new substance. He did not realize that he had discovered nuclear

Fitzgerald, Ella

Born 1918 in Virginia, USA
One of the most influential of popular jazz singers; her style is still much copied.

Ella Fitzgerald was brought up in a New York orphanage, and became a singer because of a teenage dare. At 16, she was dared to sing in the Amateur Hour at Harlem's Apollo Theatre, and won $25. Then, invited to sing with Chick Webb's band, she found success with novelty hits like 'A-Tisket A-Tasket'. Her status improved along with her voice, which became a rich contralto. She brought jazz to new audiences as star singer of

Fleming, Sir Alexander

Born 1881 in Ayrshire, Scotland
Discovered penicillin.
Died 1955 aged 73

Fleming's family moved to London and he trained as a doctor at St Mary's Medical School near Paddington Station. Here he spent his entire

▲ This stained glass window in St James's Church, Paddington, London, shows Sir Alexander Fleming at work in his laboratory. The church is close to the hospital where Sir Alexander carried out his research.

working life. Fleming became interested in the infections caused by bacteria that resulted in so much death and disease. He joined researchers looking for vaccines that would kill such bacteria.

One day in 1928 when Fleming was working as usual in his laboratory, he noticed that a mould had formed on one of his experimental dishes containing live bacteria. The bacteria next to the mould were dying. Fleming realized that the mould was producing a substance which killed the bacteria. The mould was called *Penicillium notatum*, so Fleming called this substance penicillin.

Fleming showed that penicillin could kill many dangerous bacteria, but he was slow to see that it could be used as a medical treatment and, in any case, he found it very hard to produce except in very small quantities. So there was little interest in penicillin until 1941, when Howard Florey, Ernst Chain and other scientists in Oxford found a way of making enough penicillin to begin treating patients with serious infections. The results were spectacularly successful, and there was enormous public interest. The enthusiastic but ignorant press gave Fleming too large a share of the credit for this medical revolution, and he became a world legend. He accepted

the honours that showered upon him, but remained modest about his discovery. In 1945 Fleming, Florey and Chain shared a Nobel prize for their work. ■

See also

Antibiotics
Bacteria
Penicillin

Fonteyn, Margot

Born 1919 in Reigate, England
One of the world's greatest classical ballerinas
Died 1991 aged 72

Born Peggy Hookham, she grew up in Hong Kong where she studied dance. When she came back to England, she rapidly made her name as Margot Fonteyn, dancing from 1934 onwards with Sadlers Wells Ballet, later to become The Royal Ballet. For nearly 30 years, Fonteyn was the company's leading ballerina under the guidance of Ninette de Valois. While still in her teens, she took on some of the great classic roles, especially Odette-Odile in *Swan Lake*. Her remarkable technique and her warm personality made her very popular.

▲ In 1950 Margot Fonteyn danced the lead part in the ballet of *Cinderella*.

Fonteyn had two great partnerships. One was with the choreographer Frederick Ashton, who created many outstanding roles for her. The second, from 1962, was with the Russian dancer Rudolf Nureyev. He proved to be a perfect match.

Fonteyn continued to dance, create new roles, and teach until she was well into her 50s. In 1979 she broke new ground by writing and presenting a television series, 'The Magic of Dance'. ■

See also

Ballet
Biography
de Valois
Nureyev

Ford, Henry

Born 1863 near Dearborn, Michigan, USA
An early car-maker, and the inventor of the factory assembly line for making cars quickly and cheaply
Died 1947 aged 83

Henry Ford was born on his family's farm, but he did not like farming. He thought the work was dull. When he was 12 years old, he saw a steam tractor. 'Why shouldn't machines do all the boring work?' he thought.

At 15, he became an apprentice in a machine shop. At night he worked repairing watches. He tried to build a cheap, light tractor, using steam and petrol engines.

In 1893, Ford built his first car. It had two cylinders, two forward gears, and reverse. He drove it for a thousand miles, then sold it and built two bigger cars. In 1903, he started the Ford Motor Company. He hired a racing driver, Barney Oldfield, to race Ford cars.

Using light, strong vanadium steel, he built cheap, light cars for everyone to buy. In 1908, he built the first Ford 'Model T', the 'Tin Lizzie', which sold for $825. By June, he was selling a hundred cars a day. By 1927, 15 million Model Ts had been made, and the Ford Motor Company was worth 700 million dollars.

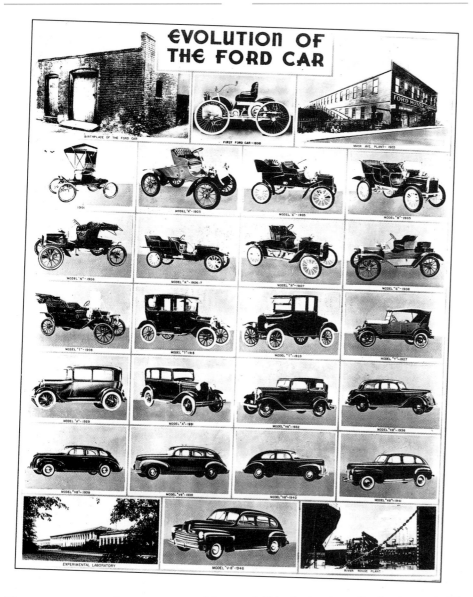

EVOLUTION OF THE FORD CAR

The cars were made on an assembly line: as they slowly moved the 300 m (one-fifth of a mile) through the factory, workers completed simple single tasks on them. It was boring work, but Ford paid the highest wages in the industry, and once, when he advertised for more workers, the police had to control the crowd looking for jobs.

During World War II, Ford returned to his first dream and produced a successful tractor.

Ford went on to produce many fine cars, in America and in Europe; the V8 Pilot, the Mustang and the Cortina among them. Although Ford has not been the world's biggest car manufacturer since 1927, the company still

▲ This picture shows the development of the Ford motor car from 1901 to 1946. At first the company produced only expensive cars, but the simple, sturdy Model T which first appeared in 1908 was cheap enough for large numbers of people to afford.

aims at the best product at the lowest possible price. Early Fords were simple, cheap and reliable; 'Anyone can drive a Ford' was one slogan, and later 'You can afford a Ford'. But keeping things simple sometimes meant less choice. 'You can have any colour you like,' said Henry Ford of his Tin Lizzie, 'so long as it's black.' ■

See also

Mass production
Motor cars

Biography
Nuffield

Fox, George

Born 1624 in Fenny Drayton, Leicestershire, England
He founded the Society of Friends, the Quakers.
Died 1691 aged 66

George Fox was the son of a Puritan weaver and grew up a strong Christian. But he became confused and unhappy about the best way to worship God. Gradually George came to believe that there is an 'inner light' in everyone which helps them to understand Christ's teachings. People should meet together to worship God quietly as equal friends, without priests and set services. He began to win enthusiastic followers, who became the 'Society of Friends'.

He travelled around preaching, wearing plain leather working men's clothes. He ignored the manners of the time. He spoke as an equal to upper-class people, and never took his hat off to show respect. His independence soon got him into trouble. Once when he was on trial, he told the magistrate that he should quake before the Lord. So the magistrate called him and his followers 'Quakers'.

He was imprisoned eight times for his beliefs, but he kept the Friends together in spite of persecution. His teachings have lived on in the Quaker movement today. ■

See also

Puritans
Quakers

Francis of Assisi, Saint

Born 1182 in Assisi, Italy
An inspired holy man, he founded an order of wandering friars, named the Franciscans after him.
Died 1226 aged about 44

Francis was the son of Pietro Bernadone, a rich cloth merchant of Assisi. He had all the makings of a successful man of the world, such as good looks, talent and drive. He took part in military campaigns and started learning the cloth trade.

Around the age of 22, he suffered a serious illness and began to feel that helping the poor was more important than making money. Two years later, he secretly left home. When his father found him and tried to make him come back, Francis stripped off his clothes and stood naked in the town square, as if to say, 'I am no longer your son, I am a new Francis starting again.'

The new Francis seemed to behave like a madman. He worked for no money. He let robbers beat him up. He kissed lepers. But he still searched for a pattern to follow in his life. He found it in the instructions given by Christ to his disciples: 'Go to the lost sheep . . . Heal the sick . . . cleanse lepers . . . Provide no gold, silver or copper to fill your purse, no pack for the road, no second coat, no shoes, no stick: the worker earns his keep.' (Gospel of Matthew, chapter 10, verses 6–10).

Francis became a travelling preacher, owning nothing but his coat and living on the food that people gave him. He loved the whole of creation, and preached in simple language to the animals and birds as well as to the men and women he met on his journeys.

Francis made people want to live like him, and in 1210, with the permission of the Pope, he set up a new order of 'friars' (meaning brothers). At this point there were just twelve of them, living around Assisi and committed to a life of poverty, obedience and prayer. Within nine years there were Franciscans all over Europe, but Francis himself was not interested in running such a large organization, and refused to be their leader. He travelled to Egypt in 1219 to preach to the Muslims and made other missionary journeys. But for most of his life he stayed near Assisi with a small group of followers, praying and preaching until his death in 1226. ■

See also
Christians
Middle Ages
Monasteries

Biography
Dominic

▲ Franco watching a battle during the Spanish Civil War. The war lasted from 1936 to 1939, causing great distress and loss of life.

Franco, General Francisco

Born 1892 in El Ferrol, Spain
He overturned Spain's republican government and ruled as dictator for 36 years.
Died 1975 aged 82

Francisco Franco was born into a navy family, but he decided to be a soldier. He became an officer at 18 and was gradually promoted until he was one of Spain's top generals. Then, in 1931, King Alfonso XIII left the country and Spain became a republic. Franco often criticized this republican government for the disorder in Spain.

In 1936 there was a military uprising against the republican government. Franco joined the rebels and soon became their leader. Civil war began between the two sides, and Franco was given military aid by Mussolini and Hitler. One million people died before Franco won the war in 1939.

He then became *caudillo* (dictator) and ruled Spain, without allowing any opposition or criticism, for 36 years. Before he died, he named Juan Carlos, grandson of Alfonso XIII, to be king after his death. ■

See also
Dictators
Republics
Spain's history

Biography
Hitler
Mussolini

Frank, Anne

Born 1929 in Frankfurt, Germany
A brave Jewish girl who wrote a diary when in hiding during World War II
Died 1945 aged 15

After the rise of Hitler and the Nazi party in Germany, Anne's father Otto Frank moved his young family to Amsterdam in The Netherlands. There Anne and her sister lived happily until 1942, when the Germans invaded. When, in 1942, the family heard of plans to take them back to Germany to a concentration camp they all went into hiding. With four other Jews they concealed themselves in a hidden room in Otto Frank's former warehouse. Kindly Dutch friends smuggled them tiny rations of food.

Meanwhile Anne was keeping a lively diary of all this, noting down daily events in these cramped quarters in such a good-humoured way it is difficult to remember how hard her life had become. Sometimes she describes the little quarrels that spring up between people living too closely together, but more often she dreams of being outside in the sun and fresh air once again.

All this is done without self-pity; indeed, Anne always seemed to remain hopeful. In spite of everything she could still write sentences like 'I still believe that people are really good at heart.' Towards the end of her diary she writes about her growing feelings for the teenage son of the other family imprisoned in the little room.

After two years in hiding they were given away to the Germans by a Dutch informer. On 4 August 1944, the secret room was broken into and the families dispersed to concentration camps.

Anne's mother died first, then Anne and her sister. Their father Otto survived and published Anne's diary in 1947. Since then it has been translated into over 30 languages, and the Franks' hiding place in Amsterdam has been converted into a museum. ■

See also

Concentration camps   World War II
Nazis

▼ Like many girls, Anne Frank dreamt of becoming a film star. On this photograph, she wrote, 'This is a photo as I would wish myself to look all the time. Then I would maybe have a chance to come to Hollywood.' Less than three years later, she was dead.

Franklin, Benjamin

Born 1706 in Boston, Massachusetts, USA
Statesman and scientist remembered by most people for his dangerous experiment of flying a kite in a thunderstorm
Died 1790 aged 84

As a young man Benjamin Franklin tried a number of jobs in America and England. He even thought about teaching swimming. Then, back in America, he set up his own business, and by the age of 23 was printing all the money for Pennsylvania. In 1753 he became the postmaster for that colony.

He was always interested in science, and wanted to prove that lightning was just a giant electrical spark. He took the risk of flying a kite up into a thundercloud and showed that an electrical spark would jump from a key tied to the wet string.

In 1757 he became the representative of Pennsylvania in London. Later he spoke in Parliament against the British government's tax policies towards the American colonies. Then, after helping

Thomas Jefferson to write the Declaration of Independence in 1776, he served in Paris where he persuaded France to support the rebels in the American Revolution. He was very popular in France, and when he died a French writer said 'He snatched the lightning from the skies and the sceptre from tyrants.' ■

See also

American Revolution

Biography
Jefferson

Franklin, Rosalind

Born 1920 in London, England
Worked on the structure of DNA
Died 1958 aged 37

Rosalind went to St Paul's Girls' School and then to Cambridge University. Her scientific work was first on the structure of coal and then on DNA, and she made very important discoveries about both.

She was a brilliant scientist, very clever at doing experiments and making apparatus. Some books describe her as awkward and difficult to work with, but people who knew her well thought that she was a very likeable and human person. At one place she decided that her white laboratory coat was dull so she sewed on brightly coloured pockets. And once when staying with friends the cat carried her new family of kittens and put them in Rosalind's bed. She said that she thought it was a great honour for her!

Sadly Rosalind Franklin died of cancer when she was still young, but her work was so important that if she had lived a few years longer she might well have shared in the Nobel prize, the greatest achievement possible for any scientist. ■

See also

DNA

Biography
Crick and Watson

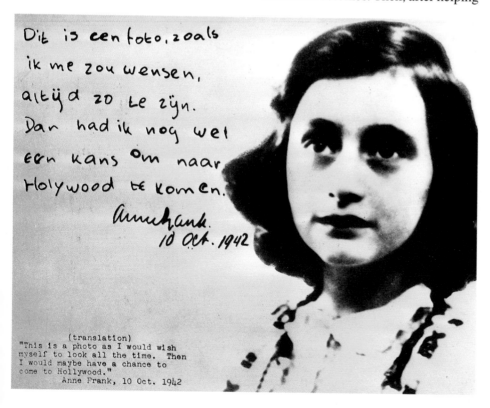

Dit is een foto, zoals ik me zou wensen, altijd zo te zijn. Dan had ik nog wel een kans om naar Holywood te komen.
Anne Frank.
10 Oct. 1942

(translation)
"This is a photo as I would wish myself to look all the time. Then I would maybe have a chance to come to Hollywood."
Anne Frank, 10 Oct. 1942

Freud, Sigmund

Born 1856 in Freiberg, then in Austria (now Príbor in Czechoslovakia)
A psychologist who looked deeper into the human mind than anyone before
Died 1939 aged 83

Sigmund Freud was an Austrian Jew who changed the way we think about ourselves. As a doctor he worked with patients who were very depressed or else given to strange ways of behaving that made other people think them extremely odd. The usual sort of treatment for mental trouble at that time was lots of rest in the hope that things would gradually get better on their own. Freud decided instead to talk to such people at great length, particularly about their childhood. He believed their present strange behaviour was often linked to past worries, which often reappeared in dreams and nightmares.

Although patients could not at first remember what it was that had once made them so unhappy, Freud found that, given time, troubled memories always came back. Some patients remembered how they had once been so angry with their parents or with their brothers and sisters that they had sometimes wished they were all dead. Later on they often felt shocked at themselves and tried to blot out the memory of such feelings altogether. But trying to hide something in the mind sometimes causes different types of strange behaviour instead. After talking to Freud openly about such things, many patients felt much better, at last able to shed problems that had been poisoning their lives without their knowing it.

By the time of Freud's death many other doctors were treating patients in similar ways, listening carefully to all they had to say and so helping them to cure themselves. ■

See also

Psychologists

Biography
Jung

Frobisher, Sir Martin

Born about 1539 in Yorkshire, England
He made three voyages in search of the North-West Passage to China round the north of America.
Died 1594 aged about 55

Frobisher's father died when he was very young and he was brought up in London by an uncle, who decided to send him to sea. As a sailor, he became interested in trying to discover the sea route from Europe to Asia round North America, known as the North-West Passage.

Between 1576 and 1578 he made three voyages of exploration. On the first voyage, Frobisher reached Baffin Island and sailed into the long narrow inlet which is now named Frobisher Bay. He mistakenly thought he had found the passage to Asia. He also brought back rock samples which were believed to contain gold. Amid great excitement two further voyages were made, but they achieved little. His cargoes of rock were found to be worthless, and the search for the North-West Passage was abandoned. In 1585 Frobisher sailed in Sir Francis Drake's expedition to the West Indies as vice-admiral, and in 1588 he was knighted

for his part in the defeat of the Spanish Armada. He died from wounds received when leading his men in an attack on a fort near Brest in France. ■

See also

Armada
Explorers

Biography
Drake
Elizabeth I
Hudson (map)

Froebel, Friedrich

Born 1798 in Oberweissbach, Germany
He developed a system for teaching young children which is still influential today.
Died 1852 aged 70

Friedrich Froebel was the son of a Lutheran pastor (a Protestant minister), an 'earnest and severe' man so absorbed in his parish that Froebel always considered him a stranger. His mother died when he was nine months old, and a stepmother treated him harshly. Throughout his schooldays Froebel had great difficulty in learning.

▼ Children in a Froebel demonstration school in the 1890s. The children are surrounded by objects designed to catch their imagination and stimulate creative abilities.

He always wanted to 'investigate and understand' things by taking them apart. His teachers did not understand him. At 15 he was apprenticed to a forester and surveyor. He took a number of jobs, and served for a time in the Prussian army fighting Napoleon. He struggled constantly to repair the gaps in his education. He was tall and lean with a sensitive, excitable temperament and had difficulty in explaining his beliefs. He made few friends, but he inspired a lasting devotion in those he had.

He began to teach, devising ways in which the playful, creative energies of young children could be released to help them learn. He studied their traditional games. He twice visited the famous teacher Pestalozzi, but was not fully satisfied with his methods. Froebel believed that children, like all living things, have a natural pattern of development. The teacher's task is to encourage and defend this inborn power, just as a gardener cultivates a plant. His first kindergarten, 'children's garden', was opened in Blankenburg in 1837. There children were encouraged to learn through play, handicrafts and exercise. After his death his friends started the spread of these methods around the world. ∎

Fry, Elizabeth

Born 1780 in Norwich, England
A brave prison reformer
Died 1845 aged 65

Elizabeth Gurney was the daughter of a wealthy Quaker banker. In 1800 she married Joseph Fry, a London merchant. Although she had a large family, she still found time to work amongst the poor. She soon became particularly interested in prison conditions, believing firmly that prisoners should always be helped to become better citizens.

Prisons then were often very violent places and full of disease, but Elizabeth insisted on visiting some of the worst in Britain and Europe. It was she who was responsible for making sure that

women prisoners were always looked after by women staff. She also managed to get prisons to start educating or training some of their prisoners, so that it was sometimes possible for them to get jobs when they were released. Near her own home, Elizabeth opened a free school and began the first proper training course for nurses. When she died she was mourned by thousands, including many of the very poorest people among whom she had always worked. ∎

▲ In the 19th century many women prisoners had their children in prison with them. This painting shows Elizabeth Fry reading the Bible to prisoners and their children in Newgate Prison in 1816.

See also

Prisons
Quakers

Fukuzawa, Yukichi

Born 1835 in south-west Japan
Well known for his writings, and for work in education and journalism, he introduced Western ideas to 19th-century Japan.
Died 1901 aged 66

Fukuzawa came from a poor *samurai* (warrior) family. He studied Western languages, ideas and science in the 1850s and 1860s, when most Japanese knew nothing of other countries. Japan had been shut off from the outside world for over 200 years. He was one of the first Japanese to visit America and Europe, and in 1866 published the first volume of his most famous book, *Conditions in the West*, in which he described everyday life in Western countries. It was a best-seller.

In 1868 Fukuzawa set up a school in Tokyo (then called Edo). He had many students, and the school later on became Keio University, which is still one of Japan's most famous universities. In 1868 there was a revolution in Japan. A new government came to power, very keen to learn more about the West and spread new ideas. For the rest of the 19th century Fukuzawa was the most influential commentator on Western ideas. His school trained many of Japan's leaders, and his books and other writings in journals and newspapers were read by thousands of Japanese. He never joined the government, but is known as one of the founders of modern Japan. ∎

See also

Japan
Japan's history

Gagarin, Yuri

Born 1934 in Gzhatsk, Russia (then in the USSR)
The first cosmonaut or spaceman.
Died 1968 aged 34

Yuri Gagarin was born into a poor farmer's family in a village, now renamed Gagarin, near Smolensk. As a teenager Yuri learned a steelworker's trade, intending to work in a foundry. While at college, he joined an aero club near Moscow and learned to fly in his spare time. Soon he preferred flying to foundry work, joined the air force and began to fly fighter planes.

His daring and skill led to him being singled out for space training. Being tiny also helped, as the first spacecraft did not have enough room inside for big people.

His spaceship, *Vostok*, was launched from the Baykonur site in the Kazakh desert on 12 April 1961. Although his flight round the Earth took only 1 hour 48 minutes, it has gone down as the first human journey into space.

Only seven years later he was killed while testing a new plane. He was buried with honours alongside the Kremlin wall in Moscow's Red Square. ■

See also

Astronauts
Explorers
Space exploration

Galilei, Galileo

Born 1564 in Pisa, Italy
The first person to use a telescope to look at the Sun, Moon and planets, Galileo dramatically changed the science of astronomy. He is also remembered for his contributions to physics.
Died 1642 aged 77

Galileo is nearly always called just by his first name. He was the eldest of seven children, whose father was a musician and scholar from one of the noble families of Florence. Galileo himself became a good organist and

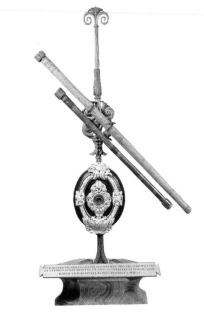

▲ Two of Galileo's telescopes can still be seen today in the Science Museum in Florence, Italy. The longer telescope has a magnification of x 20.

enjoyed playing the lute, but it was his contributions to science that made him famous.

At first, young Galileo had a tutor at home in Pisa. Then he went to school at a monastery when the family moved to Florence. As his family were not wealthy, Galileo had to be educated to earn a living. His father sent him to the University of Pisa to study medicine, but he was much more interested in mathematics and physics. Galileo left Pisa without finishing the medical course, but in 1589, at the age of 25, he became professor of mathematics.

In 1609, Galileo made a small telescope, having heard about this new invention in The Netherlands. When he turned his telescope on the sky, he gradually discovered four moons circling the planet Jupiter, craters on the Moon, spots on the Sun and rings around Saturn. He also observed that the planet Venus has phases like the Moon's. This could only mean that Venus travelled around the Sun. Galileo became convinced that the Earth and all the other planets orbit the Sun.

At that time, the Christian Church thought any idea that the Earth was not the centre of the Universe went against the Scriptures. The book published by the astronomer Copernicus in 1543, setting out such a theory, was officially banned by the Church.

Galileo's views on the subject and the books he wrote were to get him into serious trouble with the Church. As the Church was very powerful in those days Galileo was forced to say publicly that he did not agree with Copernicus in order to avoid torture or even execution. Although he made this declaration, he never changed his real belief.

Galileo also did other important scientific experiments. One of them showed that objects fall at the same rate, whatever their weight. There is a story that he experimented by dropping weights from the Leaning Tower of Pisa to demonstrate this, but this is probably not true. Galileo continued to work even when he was very old and almost blind. ■

See also

Astronomers
Motion
Planets
Renaissance
Solar System

Telescopes
Weight

Biography
Copernicus
Torricelli

Gama, Vasco da

Born about 1460 at Sines, southern Portugal
The first European to complete the sea route to India
Died 1524 aged about 64

Vasco da Gama had already distinguished himself in the service of the King of Portugal when he was chosen to lead a voyage to India around the Cape of Good Hope. Since Christopher Columbus had failed to find a westward sea route to India, the Portuguese were determined to find the eastward route.

Da Gama sailed in 1497 with four small ships and 170 men. Unlike earlier navigators he did not hug the African coast, but sailed boldly into the Atlantic before turning east to round the Cape. The little fleet ran into a storm, and many men mutinied, but da Gama had the ringleaders arrested.

The fleet reached the coast north of the Cape of Good Hope after three months without seeing land. There at Mossel Bay, da Gama abandoned his largest ship, which had carried stores. With the rest he cruised along the coast, stopping at various places. To their astonishment, the Portuguese found flourishing Arab towns with stone houses on the coast of what is now Mozambique. Da Gama found a friend in the Sultan of Malindi, who supplied two Arab pilots to guide him to India.

With their aid he made a peaceful voyage across the Indian Ocean to Calicut, in south-west India, where he was received by its ruler, the Zamorin. Gama's simple trade goods, cloth, hats and wash-basins, were coldly received by the wealthy Zamorin, who wore ruby and diamond rings. But da Gama persuaded the Zamorin that Portugal did have valuable goods to offer, and made a trade agreement with him. He

returned to Portugal with a rich cargo of spices, two years after he set out. He had lost two-thirds of his men and half his ships, but he had done what he set out to do.

Gama made two more voyages to India. In 1502 he took nineteen ships to help the Portuguese settlers in Goa. After this voyage he retired, but he was recalled 21 years later in 1524 to go as viceroy to India, where the Portuguese colonial government was in a mess. Da Gama died of fever on Christmas Eve soon after reaching India. ■

See also

Explorers

Biography
Columbus
Dias

▼ Vasco da Gama's voyage round the coast of Africa to India in 1497 and 1498 opened up an important new trade route by sea between Europe and Asia. Dias had reached the Cape of Good Hope in 1487 and realized that a great ocean lay to the east of the Cape.

Gandhi, Indira

Born 1917 in Allahabad, India
Prime minister of India from 1966 to 1977 and again from 1980 till her death
Assassinated 1984 aged 66

Indira Priyadarshani was the only child of Jawaharlal Nehru, India's first prime minister. After her mother died she became the companion and confidante of her father. She married a journalist, Feroze Gandhi, who died in 1960. They had two sons: Rajiv and Sanjay. The younger son, Sanjay, died in a plane crash when he was only 33.

Indira Gandhi followed her father's interest in politics and was elected president of the Indian National Congress, the country's main political party, in 1959. She became Minister for Information and Broadcasting in 1964. Two years later she became prime minister.

For several years she was successful and popular. But opponents in the Congress party thought she had too much power. In 1975, faced with the growing opposition threat, she declared a state of emergency. Opponents of her policies were even sent to prison.

This made her very unpopular and in the general elections of 1977 she and her party were defeated by a united opposition. Mrs Gandhi even lost her own seat in parliament.

She came back to power with a large majority in 1980. Soon after this she was faced with unrest in the Punjab where a section of Sikhs began to agitate for an autonomous state. A group of armed Sikhs occupied the Golden Temple, the holiest Sikh shrine, in Amritsar. In June 1984, Mrs Gandhi ordered the troops to storm the Golden Temple and a large number of people were killed. A few months later, Mrs Gandhi was shot dead by one of her Sikh bodyguards in revenge for the attack on the Golden Temple. ■

See also

Indian history
Sikhs

Biography
Nehru

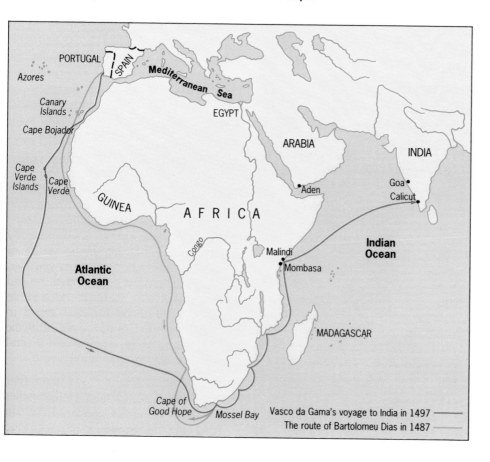

Vasco da Gama's voyage to India in 1497 ——
The route of Bartolomeu Dias in 1487 ——

Gandhi, Mahatma

Born 1869 in Porbandar, India
Gandhi was revered by the Indian people as their leader in the struggle for independence from British rule. Mahatma means 'great soul'.
Assassinated 1948 aged 78

Mohandas Karamchand Gandhi was born in the small princely state of Porbandar in western India. He was a shy, nervous boy who often ran home from school to avoid speaking to other children in case they made fun of him. He was married at the age of 14, and at 18 he travelled alone to London to study law. Here he was lonely and unhappy at first. He tried to come to terms with his new surroundings by living the life of an Edwardian English gentleman. He bought an evening suit and a top hat, took dancing lessons and spent £3 on a violin. The expense became too much and he settled for a simpler lifestyle.

▼ This photograph of Mahatma Gandhi with his two granddaughters was taken in New Delhi not long before he was killed.

When Gandhi returned to India in 1890, he struggled to make a living as a lawyer. In 1893 he accepted an offer to represent a firm of Indian merchants in a court case in South Africa.

South Africa was the making of Gandhi. He went there as a shy young man with little self-confidence. He returned to India 21 years later with a reputation as a political leader.

Soon after his arrival in South Africa, Gandhi was thrown out of a first-class railway carriage because of the colour of his skin. Realizing that his fellow-countrymen in South Africa suffered much worse humiliations, Gandhi decided to stay on to help them. Most Indians in South Africa were labourers who worked on the plantations or in the mines. Gandhi represented them in court and he became quite wealthy. But in time he rejected his wealth and decided to live more simply.

He established a number of settlements which became experiments in community living. Everyone shared in the most basic and the dirty chores. Gandhi also developed his strategy of non-

violence. The idea was to oppose unjust laws by non-violent protest. He knew that he would be sent to prison but by imposing hardship upon himself and also showing no sign of anger or hatred, Gandhi believed that he could persuade his opponents that his cause was just. Gandhi was arrested three times and in prison he was set to work breaking stones.

When he returned to India in 1915, Gandhi was not at first opposed to British rule there. But in April 1919, General Dyer, a British officer in the Indian Army, ordered his soldiers to open fire on a crowd of unarmed Indians at Amritsar, a city in the Punjab in northern India. Nearly 400 people were killed and over 1,000 wounded. The massacre, and the manner in which some British people defended General Dyer, led Gandhi to declare that he could 'no longer retain affection for a government so evilly manned as it is nowadays'.

Over the next 20 years, Gandhi led the Indian National Congress party in three major campaigns against British rule. His campaigns began in 1920 with the co-operation movement. In 1930 he launched a civil disobedience movement by walking 240 miles to the coast to break the government's salt laws. In 1942 he led Congress in the Quit India movement. On each occasion Gandhi was arrested and sent to prison.

During these years Gandhi campaigned to improve the status of the un-touchables, the lowest group in Hindu social order. He also believed that people and nations should be self-sufficient. He set an example, by devoting part of each day to spinning home-made cloth. The spinning wheel which he used represented the simplicity of life in an Indian village. It was a way of life he wanted to preserve and improve. In his eyes, indus-trialization, as in Europe and North America, led to exploitation, greed and squalor.

When Gandhi was released from prison in 1944 he struggled in vain to overcome the growing gap between the Hindu and Muslim populations which led in 1947 to the creation of the separate Muslim state of Pakistan. When India and Pakistan became independent in 1947 there was an explosion of violence between the different communities. Gandhi appealed for peace and fasting. He also defended the rights of those Muslims who were left behind in India. He was assassinated by a Hindu extremist in January 1948.

His belief in peace and non-violence has greatly influenced other civil rights leaders such as Martin Luther King. ■

See also

India
Indian history

Garibaldi, Giuseppe

Born 1807 in Nice, France
A famous guerrilla fighter, he helped to unite Italy.
Died 1882 aged 74

Coming from a family of fishermen, it was natural for the young Garibaldi to work as a sailor. In 1832 he was made a sea captain, but he had become interested in the idea of uniting the separate states of Italy into one country. After taking part in an unsuccessful mutiny in 1834, he escaped first to France and then to South America. There he led an adventurous life, sometimes driving cattle, but mostly fighting in rebel armies. He also eloped with a married woman, whom he married after her husband died.

Well known now as a brave, but sometimes reckless, fighter, Garibaldi led a group of Italians back to northern Italy in 1848 to help in the war against Austria. Next year he helped to defend Rome against the French armies, before being forced to retreat into exile in 1849. He did not return to Italy until 1854, when he retired on the island of Caprera.

He came out of retirement to fight for Victor Emmanuel II, the King of Piedmont. In 1860 he led 'the

▲ Garibaldi's army conquered Sicily, marched through southern Italy and defeated the troops of the king of Naples at the battle of Volturno. The army of King Victor Emmanuel II of Piedmont marched south and Garibaldi handed over the territory he had won to the king.

Thousand' (*i Mille*) guerrilla volunteers in red shirts in a successful revolt in Sicily and then defeated the army of the King of Naples. This made sure that the whole of southern Italy became united under the rule of Victor Emmanuel. Garibaldi then returned to Caprera, refusing any reward for his efforts. Garibaldi's name is still famous in Italy. Almost every town has a square or street named after him. ■

See also

Guerrillas
Italy's history

Garrett Anderson, Elizabeth

Born 1836 in London, England
Britain's first woman doctor, and a champion of women's rights
Died 1917 aged 81

Elizabeth Garrett was sent to a girls' boarding school with a most unusual headmistress. At a time when all girls expected to stay at home to be wives and mothers, Elizabeth was taught to lead a fuller life and to want a career.

At 22, she decided that she wanted to be Britain's first woman doctor. At that time, only men were allowed to be doctors. Her parents were against her idea, but when they saw that she

▲ This photograph shows the pioneer woman doctor, Elizabeth Garrett Anderson, absorbed in a book. The picture was taken in 1889, when she was in her fifties.

was determined they promised her every possible help. She first trained as a nurse at the Middlesex Hospital in London. With the help of her professors, and despite the protests of the male students, she studied in her spare time and was allowed to 'practise' or perform as the first woman medical practitioner at the age of 29. But she was still not a full doctor.

Elizabeth Garrett opened the St Mary's Dispensary for poor women and children, but she was still refused permission to study and become a doctor solely because she was a woman. So she went to the university in Paris, studied there and passed her examinations, all in French, with six distinctions, becoming a qualified doctor.

Elizabeth Garrett married James Anderson, a shipowner, and added his name to her own. She fought for the rights of women, especially women wanting to be doctors. She saw the first women medical students accepted after the government passed the Medical Act of 1876. Elizabeth Garrett Anderson was also the first woman mayor in England when she became mayor of Aldeburgh, Suffolk.

After her death, the St Mary's Dispensary became the Elizabeth Garrett Anderson Hospital. It still serves women and children, and was enlarged in 1984. ■

See also

Doctors
Women's movement

Garvey, Marcus

Born 1887 near St Ann's Bay, Jamaica
He taught the black people of the West Indies and America to have a pride in their race and their history.
Died 1940 aged 52

Marcus Mosiah Garvey was born to poor parents in Jamaica. As a young man he was a printer, but no one would give him work after he led a strike. He took jobs in Central America, where he was shocked by the discrimination against West Indians working there. In 1912 he visited London and met leaders of the Pan-African movement, who taught him about the rich history which all Africans shared, whether they lived in Africa or were the descendants of slaves.

In 1914 he returned to Jamaica and started the Universal Negro Improvement Association to build self-

▲ At the time this photograph of Marcus Garvey riding through New York was taken in 1921, he had about 2 million followers who believed, as he did, that black people should return to Africa to fulfil their destiny.

pride in its black people. He said their struggle for fair treatment was the same as the fight to free African countries from rule by Europeans. In 1917 he moved to America to start more branches of the UNIA. It printed newspapers, ran its own Black Star shipping line, and opened black community centres, called Liberty Halls.

Garvey was leader of a great movement which soon had branches all over the world. Then the UNIA was banned in African countries, and in the USA Garvey was accused of fraud and deported to Jamaica. In 1935 he moved to London, where he died in 1940. His life was full of disappointment, but his ideas inspired many others to work to win respect for black people. ■

See also

Caribbean history
Rastafarians

Biography
Marley

Gauguin, Paul

Born 1848 in Paris, France
A French artist who searched for a natural and straightforward way of painting
Died 1903 aged 54

Paul's mother was Peruvian and he spent his childhood in Lima. Later he joined the merchant navy and eventually settled in France. He became a successful businessman, with quite a lot of money, and a wife and family. When he was 35 years old, he decided to give up his job and devote his time to painting. Although he had been very interested in art and had painted as a hobby in his spare time, he had never really had any training. The next ten years were very hard for him.

As he worked and developed his own style, Gauguin came more and more to feel that European artists had become too clever, too contrived and insincere. In perfecting slick skills, artists had forgotten about true feelings

▲ *Nafea faaipoipo* by Gauguin, Rudolph Staechelin Family Foundation, Basle, Switzerland. The title of this picture means 'when will you marry' in a Polynesian language. The flower in the girl's hair shows that she is looking for a husband. Gauguin painted the Tahitians and their island in bright, strong colours over and over again.

expressed in simple direct ways. At first he tried to get away from that kind of artificial painting by studying peasant art in Brittany, but finally he felt that he must escape from Europe altogether if he was to find his own way of painting.

He went to Tahiti, an island in the South Pacific Ocean. There he painted the local people going about their daily tasks in the forests and by the seashore. His pictures often showed the works of art created by the islanders themselves. He quite happily ignored centuries of European ideas about painting, such as perspective, and developed a strong personal style of his own. When his paintings were shown in Paris, many people were shocked and called Gauguin a 'barbarian'. He was proud of that!

Gauguin remained a lonely man. At the age of 54 he died in the Marquesas Islands in the Pacific, after years of ill health, disappointment and poverty. ■

🔵 **See also**

Biography
Van Gogh

Geldof, Bob

Born 1954 in Dublin, Ireland
A pop musician who is famous for working to raise money for the hungry people of the world

Bob Geldof did not have a happy childhood. His mother died when he was at junior school, and his father was away working much of the time. Although he loved reading, he did not do well at school and was often beaten.

When he left school he lived for a while in England, and in Vancouver in Canada, where he wrote about pop music for a magazine. Soon, though, he was back in Dublin, and in 1975 he and some friends formed the group which they called 'The Boomtown Rats'. By 1978 the Rats were very successful and the single 'Rat Trap' reached number one.

In 1984 Geldof saw a film of a famine that was devastating Ethiopia, and wondered whether he could do something about it. He had the idea of a record, made by lots of stars, with the proceeds going to Ethiopia. The song 'Do They Know It's Christmas?' came out in time for Christmas 1984 and raised £5 million for what was now called 'Band Aid'. Geldof travelled the world, publicizing the problem of famine and badgering famous people into supporting him.

Then on 13 July 1985 Geldof mounted a huge televised charity pop concert called 'Live Aid'. Eighty thousand people saw it live at Wembley in London, and many millions more on

▲ Bob Geldof is often seen unshaven and in casual clothes. He is much more concerned to give his time and energy to the children of Ethiopia like those he is seen with here.

TV across the world. 'Live Aid' raised about £70 million to help the starving people of the Third World.

'I think this must be the greatest day of my life,' said Bob Geldof from the platform that day. ■

Genghis Khan

Born 1162 in Dulun-Boldaq, Mongolia
He created the Mongol empire, the largest ever known in history.
Died 1227 aged 65

It is said that Genghis came out of his mother's womb holding a blood clot in his fist. This was interpreted as a sign of victory. His father, chief of a Mongol tribe, called him Temujin, the name of a Tartar enemy he had just defeated.

Temujin was married when he was 9, as was the custom in his tribe. But in the same year his father was poisoned by the Tartars. Temujin was not old enough to lead his father's men, and they deserted him. Temujin and his mother were left to live on roots and fish, not the usual mutton and mare's milk. Then another tribe raped Temujin's wife, because of an old feud with his father.

As soon as he could, Temujin begged 20,000 soldiers from a friendly chief,

▲ In this Persian miniature, Genghis Khan is surrounded by his Mongol followers who are paying homage to him.

punished the men who had raped his wife, and set about making himself leader of all the Mongol tribes. His methods were brutally efficient: to make sure there was no rebellion from defeated tribes, he killed everyone taller than a cart axle — all the adult warriors — while everyone shorter had to swear loyalty to him.

By 1206 Temujin was recognized as lord of all the Mongols. He took the title 'Genghis Khan', which probably means 'Ocean-like Ruler'. Now he led his armies against the Chinese empire. His aim originally was to conquer land and turn it into grazing pasture for Mongol sheep and horses, but Genghis soon learnt better ways of holding power, such as taxing the conquered people.

Genghis Khan lost none of his energy for revenge. When the Shah of Khwarizm killed his envoys, Genghis turned west, and in two years destroyed the Shah's empire, leaving its cities in rubble.

In the 1220s he turned back to China, but died before he could complete the conquest. Genghis left his son Ogodei and three others to share in ruling his empire, which stretched from the Pacific Ocean to the Black Sea. His death had to be kept a secret until Ogodei was proclaimed his successor, so the members of the funeral procession killed everyone that they met on the way. ■

See also

Mongolia   **Biography**
                            Kublai Khan

George I

Born 1660 in Osnabrück, Germany
The first king of Great Britain to come from Germany; he ruled from 1714 to 1727.
Died 1727 aged 67

When Queen Anne died in 1714 she had no children, so the crown was passed to George of Hanover. He was the great-grandson of James I of England, and as a German prince had

fought with the British against the French. Once in Britain George was rather shy and lazy. He had never learned to speak English, and so was forced to talk to his ministers in French. He was also disliked because of the way he had treated his first wife Sophia in Germany, whom he divorced and then locked up for 32 years. Even so, his reign provided stability in Britain. The king was happy to leave all important decisions to Parliament and his ministers, especially Walpole. He missed Germany, however, and on one of his visits to Hanover he died there of a stroke. ■

See also

Georgian Britain

Biography
Walpole

George III

Born 1738 in London, England
King of Great Britain from 1760 to 1820; his obstinacy helped cause the final break with Britain's American colonies.
Died 1820 aged 81

George was known as one of the most scientific botanists in Europe. He made the agricultural shows in Windsor Great Park into important occasions for encouraging better stock-breeding among farmers. Unfortunately he was not such a success as king. Proud of his position, he always wanted others to be proud of him too. This led him to interfere in politics, but because he was awkward with people this meant that George lost rather than gained friends.

When the American colonies objected to the taxes the British made them pay, George was firmly against giving in to them. This led to the American Revolution in 1775, and George became even more unpopular when Britain was driven out of America in 1781 after a long and bitter conflict.

In his own family George was a loving but very jealous father. When his sons broke away from him he became so upset he gave way to periods of mental illness. Doctors now suspect he was really suffering from porphyria, a disease which produces some of the symptoms of madness. From 1811 until his death, his son ruled as Prince Regent in his place. ■

See also

American Revolution
Georgian Britain

George VI

Born 1895 in Sandringham, Norfolk, England
King of the United Kingdom 1936–1952; father of Queen Elizabeth II
Died 1952 aged 56

George was younger brother to Edward VIII, and when young was always rather in his shadow. While Edward was confident and sociable, George was quiet, with a bad stammer. He studied briefly at university and Naval College, but was happiest working with children. In 1921 he organized camps where boys from different backgrounds could meet each other, all at his own expense. In 1923 he married Lady Elizabeth Bowes-Lyon (later the Queen Mother), and was a devoted father to their two daughters, the princesses Elizabeth and Margaret.

His whole world was turned upside-down when his brother Edward VIII unexpectedly abdicated (gave up the throne) in 1936 after Parliament had forbidden his marriage to Mrs Simpson, a divorced American lady. George had to become king instead, and although he felt he was too shy a person for this demanding job, he gradually got used to it.

In the war against Germany between 1939 and 1945, he set an example of bravery, staying in Buckingham Palace as the bombs rained down, and visiting

▼ George VI when Duke of York, with the Duchess and their children, Princess Elizabeth (standing, now Queen Elizabeth II) and Princess Margaret Rose at their country home in 1936.

the ruined streets of London the day after particularly bad air raids.

After the war he continued to play his part in the rebuilding of Britain, but sadly his heavy smoking led to an early death from lung cancer. He was succeeded by his daughter Elizabeth, who became Queen Elizabeth II. ■

See also

British history
1919–1989

Biography
Edward VIII
Elizabeth II
British Royal Family

George, Saint

Born some time in the 3rd century AD, probably in the Middle East
A Christian martyr who became the patron saint of England
Died about 303 AD

We know very little for sure about this saint and martyr. He was probably a soldier, who was killed in Palestine for his Christian faith by the Romans. But centuries later, a famous story grew up about him.

It told of a dragon which was terrorizing a whole country. Every day the people gave it two sheep to keep it satisfied. But the number of sheep ran low, and a human being had to be offered instead. The first victim was to be the king's own daughter. She went to her fate dressed as a bride. But George attacked the dragon, pierced its side with his lance and led it away. Then he told the people that if they became Christian, he would rid them of this monster. Fifteen thousand men agreed to be baptized, and George killed the dragon.

This saint was most popular during the medieval age of chivalry. At that time he seemed like the perfect Christian knight. Venice, Genoa, Portugal and Catalonia, as well as England, took him as their patron. His feast day is celebrated on 23 April. ■

See also

Chivalry
Dragons
Knights

Gershwin, George

Born 1898 in New York, USA
A composer, mainly of musical shows.
To some people he was the greatest of
all composers of popular music.
Died 1937 aged 38

George Gershwin was the son of Jewish parents who had emigrated from Russia to New York. He did badly at school, and showed no interest in music until one day when he was 10 he heard another schoolboy playing the violin. He started having piano lessons and made very quick progress.

As a young man he started writing songs for shows. During the 1920s and 1930s he turned out a stream of music, much of which is still sung and played: songs such as 'Somebody Loves Me', 'Fascinating Rhythm' and 'A Foggy Day'. Many of the words of his songs were written by his elder brother Ira.

Gershwin always wanted to be a more serious composer, and he wrote orchestral and piano music and an opera, *Porgy and Bess*. This music is admired today, but he is best remembered for his tuneful and clever songs.

He died of a brain tumour at the age of 38. ∎

▲ **George Gershwin was always influenced by the jazz and blues music of black Americans. His most famous work,** *Porgy and Bess*, **was composed as a black 'folk opera'.**

Gielgud, John

Born 1904 in London, England
A famous English actor with a long and
wide-ranging career

John Gielgud's mother came from a stage family. From an early age he loved the theatre, and by the age of 12 was saving his pocket money to go to theatres in the West End of London. At 17 he went to a stage school, and began to appear in small parts. From there his career was a gradual climb to the top. All through the 1930s he appeared in theatres in London and New York, making a particular reputation for parts in Shakespeare's plays. He was very impressive as Hamlet.

John Gielgud as a young man was handsome, fair-haired, with very sensitive looks. His face was particularly expressive. Later in life he showed that he could act powerfully in older parts, and continued to give impressive performances well into old age. He was very versatile, excellent in modern plays as well as in Shakespeare, and he also appeared in films and television. He was knighted in 1953. ∎

Giotto

Born about 1267 in Italy, probably near
Florence
A medieval painter who worked out a
way of making painted figures look solid
instead of flat
Died 1337 aged about 70

Giotto lived in Florence with a wife and eight children, and painted frescos (wall paintings) of religious subjects. Perhaps the most splendid are those which tell stories from the lives of Jesus Christ and the Virgin Mary in the Arena Chapel in Padua. There is a famous series of frescos in Assisi which show scenes from the life of St Francis, but it is not certain whether Giotto actually painted these himself.

Giotto developed skills that had never been seen in painting before. He used

▲ *Lamentation over the Dead Christ* by Giotto, Cappella Scrovegni, Padua, Italy. This scene is one of a series of frescos which cover the walls of the Arena Chapel in Padua. It expresses the grief felt at the death of Christ in the contorted facial expressions and agonized gestures. The solid quality of the forms is stressed by the heavy draped bodies in the front of the picture.

paint to give the impression that people are solid objects, and not merely flat shapes. He discovered ways of making figures stand out of the painting, as if they were sculptures and not simply outlines. For the first time, figures looked like real people, showing human emotions, and not just stiff, cold, unbending models.

Because of his fame and success, Giotto was given the job of designing a bell tower for Florence Cathedral, but the building was not completed until after his death. ∎

◉ See also

Frescos

prime minister for the last time aged 84. He began as a Conservative but later created the modern Liberal Party. He believed that people should have the chance to help themselves. In 1870, when he was prime minister, schools were provided for every child under ten, however poor. In 1884, ordinary people in the countryside got the vote.

Gladstone's reforms upset many richer people, but he never minded being unpopular if he felt he was right. Unlike his great rival, Disraeli, he did not believe the British empire should be bigger than it already was. Many disagreed with him, including Queen Victoria, who never liked him much.

Gladstone wanted above all to bring peace to Ireland. He fought hard to give Home Rule (the right to run their own home affairs) to the Irish. Many people in the British Parliament and in Ulster bitterly opposed him, and in the end he failed. In 1894 he was in poor health and resigned from being prime minister. He died four years later. ■

◐ See also

Ireland's history
Schools
Victorian Britain
Biography
Disraeli
Victoria

Glyndwr, Owain

Born about 1354 in Montgomeryshire, Wales
He led the last Welsh revolt against English rule.
Died about 1416 aged about 62

Glyndwr was a northern Welsh land-owner who claimed to be descended from the great leader, Llywelyn ap Gruffudd. As a young man he studied law in London, and marched with Henry Bolingbroke's army against King Richard II. When he returned to Wales, he found his countrymen crippled by English taxes. In 1400, a local quarrel between Glyndwr and an English lord flared up into a national uprising. Glyndwr proclaimed himself Prince of Wales and summoned his first independent Welsh parliament at Machynlleth in 1404. He even persuaded the French to support his cause.

Henry IV, the King of England, saw his castles burned and his leaders captured, but could do little to stop the revolt. Worse still, Glyndwr was a natural ally for English lords plotting against the king, and in 1403 he lent his support to the rebellion of the Percy family, in the north of England.

Gladstone, William Ewart

Born 1809 in Liverpool, England
Liberal prime minister four times in Queen Victoria's reign: 1868–1874; 1880–1885; 1886; 1892–1894
Died 1898 aged 88

William Gladstone's father was a rich Scottish business man who educated his son at Eton and Christ Church, Oxford. William was clever and deeply religious; he believed he must give his whole life to God. He was very energetic. He liked long walks and tree-felling and worked a sixteen-hour day even when he was an old man. He was devoted to his wife Catherine, who supported him in all he did.

Gladstone was 23 when he first became a Member of Parliament, and was

▼ A sketch of Gladstone aged 83 listening to a debate in Parliament. Gladstone was a great speaker, and looked very impressive, especially in old age. He had bright eyes and hawk-like features.

In 1405 the tide turned against Glyndwr, especially after Prince Henry, later to become Henry V, took over the English campaign. Within three years Glyndwr had lost his main strongholds. But even when his supporters abandoned him, he still fought on as an outlaw. Centuries after his death, he remained an inspiring legend for many Welsh nationalists. ■

See also

Welsh history

Biography
Henry V
Llywelyn ap Gruffudd
Richard II

Gobind Singh

Born 1666 in Patna, Bihar, India
Guru Gobind Singh was the tenth and last Sikh Guru. The word 'guru' means teacher.
Assassinated 1708 aged 41

Gobind Singh was the son of the ninth Guru, whose name was Tegh Bahadur. Guru Gobind Singh was very well educated, a good horseman and trained to fight in self-defence. He also had a very generous and kind nature and for Sikhs is something of an ideal human being.

In 1699 when the Sikhs came together for the festival of Baisakhi at Anandpur, Guru Gobind Singh asked for five Sikhs who were prepared to give their lives for their faith. These five went through a new form of initiation into the order of the Khalsa (the order of Sikhs dedicated to following the Guru in all respects), and many more followed them. This involved being sprinkled with and drinking *amrit*, a mixture of sugar and water stirred with a two-edged sword. They also began to wear the 'the Five Ks' which are the outward signs of being a member of the Khalsa.

All the men added Singh (lion) to their names and the women added Kaur (princess), to show their equality and unity, like brothers and sisters.

He was killed by an assassin. The reason is a mystery, but the killer may have been someone working for a man whom the Guru had fought in the Punjab. As he lay dying from the wounds, Guru Gobind Singh said that the Sikh holy book, the *Adi Granth*, was to succeed him in guiding the community rather than another human being. The book was then called the *Guru Granth Sahib*. ■

See also

Sikhs

Biography
Nanak

Goethe, Johann von

Born 1749 at Frankfurt am Main, Germany
Germany's greatest poet
Died 1832 aged 82

Goethe lived an extremely full life: he was without doubt the most gifted man of his day. His parents lived comfortably, but out of their seven children only he and his sister survived. When he was 10, Goethe watched with interest the French soldiers occupying his home town during the Seven Years War. His writings show that he was influenced by many people, by great philosophers, Shakespeare, folk singers, Byron, and, not least, by the characters of the many women he fell in love with. Goethe was amazingly versatile: he made important discoveries in science; he was a good actor, and a theatre director. But he is best remembered for his great plays, his novel *The Sorrows of Werther*, published in 1774, his many songs, and above all the poetic drama *Faust*, in which the hero sells his soul to the devil in exchange for enjoying all that the world can offer. ■

Gogh

See Van Gogh

Goodall, Jane

Born 1934 in London, England
Has carried out a long-term study of chimpanzees, and made the first observations of wild chimpanzees using implements, proving that human beings are not the only tool users.

Even as a very small child Jane Goodall was interested in animals, and at the age of about 8 she decided that she wanted to go to Africa to see the wildlife. After leaving school and taking a secretarial course, she had the chance to stay with a friend in Kenya. Soon after this she met Louis Leakey, and became his secretary and assistant. With the Leakeys she visited the Olduvai Gorge and dug for fossils.

In 1960, with Leakey's encouragement and help in raising funds for the venture, she started work in the Gombe Stream Reserve in Tanzania, watching the troops of chimpanzees that live in the area. After a few months the animals began to accept her presence, so she was able to see and record their behaviour. Some of her most important observations were of chimpanzees making and using tools to get water out of holes and using twigs to catch

▲ By behaving in a very calm and non-threatening fashion, Jane Goodall won the trust of the chimpanzees she was observing in the Gombe Stream Reserve in Tanzania.

termites. Although chimpanzees in captivity had been known to use tools, people thought that they had been taught to do this. The fact that chimpanzees in the wild could adapt and alter things around them to use as tools led Louis Leakey to say 'We must now redefine the word tool, or the word human', for until this time, humans were thought to be the only tool makers.

Jane Goodall's studies showed how little we know about chimpanzees in the wild, and the Gombe Stream Research Centre was set up with her as director. Many students have worked there, and the family histories of the chimpanzees of the area are now well known. The University of Cambridge awarded Goodall a Ph.D. for her original work, and she has written many scientific papers and several books on the behaviour of chimpanzees. ∎

See also

Animal behaviour
Chimpanzees

Biography
Leakey family

Gorbachev, Mikhail

Born 1931 in Privolnoye, Russia, USSR
Leader of the USSR from 1985 to 1991

Mikhail Gorbachev was born on a farm in the Stavropol region of Russia between the Black and Caspian seas. His father, Sergei, was a tractor driver and Communist Party official who died in World War II. His mother, Maria, was a farm hand and a regular church-goer. After the war, at the age of 14, Mikhail began work on tractors and also studied hard at school, gaining a place at Moscow University to study law. A bright, popular and open-minded student, he joined the Communist Party in his second year.

At the early age of 39, he became Party leader of the Stavropol region. In 1985, at the age of 54, he became General Secretary of the Communist Party and so took over the leadership of the whole of the USSR.

▲ Mikhail Gorbachev's policy of *glasnost* made him more willing than previous Soviet communist leaders to listen to the views of ordinary men and women in the street. This photograph was taken in Yugoslavia in 1988. His wife, Raisa, is standing beside him. He married her while still at university. She was a sociology student and later became a university lecturer.

For the first time in 60 years, the USSR had a relatively young and reforming leader. He launched three new policies: *perestroika*, meaning 'restructuring', to make the economy more efficient; *glasnost*, to make the country more open and honest; and *demokratizatsiya*, to give people initiative. His policies were popular abroad: he withdrew Soviet troops from Afghanistan so ending a long war there, and he signed an agreement with the USA to reduce short range nuclear missiles.

But problems grew at home. The economy was in trouble. The nationalities (Latvians, Ukrainians, Moldavians and others) began to demand more independence. He allowed the countries of Eastern Europe to throw off communist rule, but sent troops in to suppress demands for independence in the Baltic states. His reforms displeased the conservatives who tried to overthrow him in 1991. Even though he survived that coup, he was much weakened. When Russia and the other states formed a new Commonwealth of Independent States, Gorbachev resigned. He had introduced sweeping reforms but could not hold the Soviet Union together. ∎

See also

Russia's history
USSR 1922–1991

Goya, Francisco de

Born 1746 in Fuentedetodos, Spain
A great Spanish painter, famous for the emotional power of his work
Died 1828 aged 82

Goya was born in a village, but he spent most of his career in the capital, Madrid. There he worked mainly for the court, and in 1799 he was appointed the king's principal painter. He painted many portraits of the royal family and courtiers, designed tapestries for the royal palaces, and also did religious pictures for churches.

His most original works, however, are of a much more unusual kind. When he was 46 he suffered a mysterious illness that temporarily paralysed him and left him stone deaf for the rest of his life. This traumatic experience made him think deeply about human suffering and inspired him to paint imaginative scenes, often involving terror or the supernatural.

▲ *Third of May 1808* by Goya, Prado Museum, Madrid, Spain. The use of shadow and light in this picture underlines its horror: the dark line of figures with their rifles pointed at a single man in a white shirt, surrounded by light. The cruelty of this scene shows Goya's feelings about war and suffering.

After Spain was invaded by the French armies of Napoleon in 1808, Goya also produced a number of horrifying anti-war paintings and prints. ■

Graham, Billy

Born 1918 in Charlotte, North Carolina, USA
He has travelled the world, converting many thousands of people to Christianity.

Billy Graham became a minister in 1939. He was working for a church in Illinois in 1943 when he decided to travel the country preaching to people. Soon hundreds of thousands of people were attending his meetings, and by 1949 he was being invited to the White House to lead prayer meetings for the President of the USA.

In 1954 he began his first tour outside the USA. One million people attended his meeting in Glasgow, and he drew large crowds throughout Great Britain and Europe.

He built up a business organization to run his Christian crusades, which made some people worry that money was becoming more important than his religious message.

After his first visits to the White House, Billy Graham became a friend of many US presidents including Truman, Eisenhower, Johnson, Nixon and Reagan. His broadcasts on radio and TV were carried by hundreds of stations throughout the USA. ■

See also
Christians

Graham, Martha

Born 1896 in Pittsburgh, USA
A famous modern dancer and choreographer
Died 1991 aged 95

When Martha Graham was 8, her family moved from Pittsburgh to California. Even as a very small child she loved dancing, and as soon as she had completed her formal schooling she devoted her life to dance. She studied dance in Los Angeles and when she was 25 she became a professional dancer. At first she toured the United States with a dance company, but eventually appeared in New York dancing on her own.

From that time Martha Graham developed her own style of ballet, dancing to classical and modern music. She also made up her own very unusual, modern and imaginative dances. When she was 35 she formed her own dance company, training her dancers to follow her colourful and modern style of ballet. She employed modern artists and composers to design colourful sets, costumes and music for her ballets. Her dances were based on many unusual themes, including ancient Greek legends and the lives of North American Indians. When Martha Graham was 75 she stopped performing, but continued to teach and to make up ballets. ■

See also
Dance

▲ Martha Graham used her entire body in her dance movements to express the inner feelings of the characters she portrayed. In the early part of her career, some audiences were shocked by the unusual poses and jerky actions which she used to express emotions such as fear, anger and hatred.

Grant, Ulysses S.

Born 1822 in Point Pleasant, Ohio
Commanded Union armies in the
American Civil War; he was President of
the USA from 1869 to 1877.
Died 1885 aged 63

Grant was named Hiram Ulysses Grant, but did not use his first name. The S. crept into his name through a mistake when he enrolled at the US Military Academy, West Point, New York. He never corrected it.

After eleven years in the army Grant, then a captain, resigned and tried farming. He failed, and eventually got a job in his father's business. When the American Civil War broke out in 1861 he volunteered for the Union Army of the northern states. Within four months his skill as a commander had earned him promotion to brigadier-general.

A series of victories led President Abraham Lincoln to appoint Grant commander-in-chief of all the Union armies. Grant's drive and ruthlessness forced the Confederates of the southern states to surrender in April 1865.

Three years later, in 1868, Grant won

▲ Ulysses S. Grant is shown here sitting next to his wife and surrounded by the family he loved. The signs of strain from his long, hard life can be clearly seen on his face.

the presidential election for the Republicans with the slogan 'Let us have peace'. He was honest himself, but many members of his administration were not. Scandals about bribes rocked the government. However, he won re-election in 1872. That year he helped set up the first national park in the USA, Yellowstone.

Grant refused to run for a third term, and retired in 1877. He invested his considerable savings in a firm which went bankrupt in 1884, leaving him with heavy debts. To make money he wrote his memoirs. It was a race against time, for he knew he was dying of cancer. Almost as soon as he finished the work he died, but it earned his family $450,000. ■

⊙ **See also**

American Civil War

Greco, El

See El Greco

Greene, Graham

Born 1904 in Berkhamsted, England
A novelist who tackled some of the most important questions facing the world this century.
Died 1991 aged 87

Graham Greene was the son of a headmaster and he attended his father's school as a pupil. From early on he was very aware of the difficult position this put him in; he owed loyalty both to his fellow pupils and also to his headmaster father. This may be why novels like *The Honorary Consul* or *Our Man in Havana* often contain characters who are also split between conflicting duties.

Finally he ran away from school, later becoming a journalist, then an author. Some of his novels, such as *A Gun for Sale* or *The Ministry of Fear*, can be read like detective stories. Others, like *Brighton Rock* or *The Power and the Glory*, take on important issues like belief in God or how far the poor and oppressed should rebel against their own, often corrupt political leaders.

Many of these novels have been made into films. But however successful these are, they could never equal Greene's skill as a writer, particularly when it comes to describing the ordinary, sometimes rather shabby detail often found in everyday life. ■

Gregory I

Born about 540 in Rome, Italy
He was the first monk to become Pope.
Died 604 aged about 64

Gregory came from a rich and noble Christian family. His great-great-grandfather had been Pope, three of his aunts lived as nuns, and his father was a government official in Rome.

Gregory himself was made chief magistrate of Rome, but in 574 he gave up everything to become a monk. With a group of friends, he turned the family house into a monastery named after St Andrew, and together they led a life of prayer and Bible study.

This peaceful life was frequently interrupted. First, Gregory was sent to Constantinople to represent the Pope and to try to stop the barbarian invasions of the Roman empire. Then he became papal secretary. In 590, the Pope died of the plague and the people of Rome chose Gregory to succeed him.

Gregory was sad to leave the quiet of his monastery, but this did not stop him from becoming a very active Pope. His main aim was to bring the word of God to as many people as possible. He taught his monks how to preach, and then made them abbots and bishops all over Italy. In 596 he sent a group of monks, led by Augustine, to Britain to preach to the Anglo-Saxons.

Pope Gregory was a great leader and organizer. He reformed the way in which the Church carried out its business and how its services were presented and sung. He collected stories about holy preachers in Italy, especially about St Benedict, and through his own life and his writings changed the way Church leaders behaved. Gregory showed how it was possible to combine a monk's existence of reading and prayer with a Pope's life of action and power. ■

See also

Christians
Monasteries
Popes

Biography
Augustine of Canterbury
Benedict

Grimm brothers

They recorded and published some of the best-loved fairy tales in the world.
Jakob Born 1785 in Hanau, Germany
Died 1863 aged 78
Wilhelm Born 1786 in Hanau
Died 1859 aged 73

Sons of a German lawyer, the Grimm brothers both went to university with the intention of becoming civil servants. But once there they became more interested in folk tales. Later they spent their lives hearing and studying the stories, songs and poems that people had told and sung long before the invention of printing. The brothers busily wrote down the stories in case one day they might be forgotten altogether. Between 1812 and 1815 they published around 200 of the best examples in two volumes. These soon became very popular with children; they included *Snow White*, *Hansel and Gretel*, *Cinderella* and *Little Red Riding-hood*.

At the time the brothers said that they wrote down the tales exactly as they heard them from story-tellers. But in reality both brothers rewrote most of the stories in order to make them longer and more satisfying to readers. Their collection was soon translated into other languages, appearing in English in 1823.

Other people have also written down popular fairy tales. But the Grimm brothers were the first major collectors, very important in the effort to keep fairy tales alive, so that children can still read them today long after the older spoken versions have been forgotten. ■

See also

Folk tales and fairy tales

Gropius, Walter

Born 1883 in Berlin, Germany
A modern architect of enormous influence
Died 1969 aged 86

Gropius was the son of an architect. From early on he designed buildings that used only modern materials. In 1914 he built some factories constructed only from glass and steel. He also borrowed ideas from modern art, sometimes making his buildings look like abstract paintings. In 1919 he founded the 'Bauhaus' in Germany, a school of design that used the most outstanding artists, sculptors and architects of the day. Gropius himself created the new building for the school. Its white walls, flat roof and expanses of glass helped create a constantly

▲ This is the Bauhaus which means 'building house' in German. It was designed by Gropius and built in 1925–1926 at Dessau in Germany. The large areas of flat glass and the severe geometric shapes of the construction became typical of the Bauhaus style of architecture.

changing impression as it reflected the different angles of the Sun. Students there were taught how to use smooth surfaces, bright colours and three-dimensional design in their buildings.

In 1933 the Bauhaus was closed down by the Nazis. Gropius, who had left the Bauhaus five years before that, moved to England in 1934 because of the growing power of the Nazi government. After designing more striking modern buildings in Britain he finally settled in America. There he collaborated in designing the Pan Am Building in New York as well as many other famous projects. He continued to work closely with designers in his search for truly modern architecture fitting for life in the 20th century. ■

See also

Architects
Designers

Gutenberg, Johann

Born about 1398 in Mainz, Germany
Traditionally known as the inventor of
printing in Europe
Died about 1468 aged about 70

Before Gutenberg found a way to print
them, most books were handwritten,
with a few produced by using carved
wooden blocks. By either method it
took a long time to complete a single
copy of a book, which meant that there
were few books available and these
were very expensive. Only wealthy
people, monasteries and universities
could afford books, and they were so
valuable that they were often chained
to the desk where they were read, so
that no one could steal them.
Gutenberg's printing method changed
all that.

All that we know about Gutenberg's
childhood is that his family were quite
well off and had the name Gensfleisch.
But Gutenberg chose to use his

mother's surname. He was skilled at
working with metals, and invented a
mould with which he was able to cast
a lot of identical copies of each letter
of the alphabet on metal stamps. These
could be put together to form words
and arranged as whole pages of a book.
After ink had been applied to the metal
stamps, any number of copies could
be made on paper, using a specially
constructed press.

Gutenberg printed many other things
besides books, but his best-known
work, and the only one we know for
sure must have come from his press,
is what is called the 42-line Bible or
Gutenberg Bible. He began to print
pages of this Latin Bible in 1452 and
it took him until 1456 to finish the
whole work. By that time he had
printed only 300 copies. The Bible was
over 1,200 pages long and cost
Gutenberg a lot of money and effort.
He gave up printing altogether in 1460.
He had made little money out of it,
and died a poor man. ■

See also

Printing

Biography
Caxton

▲ A page from Gutenberg's 42-line Bible,
printed at Mainz in Germany about 1454.

Halley, Edmond

Born 1656 in London, England
An astronomer remembered for his
work on the comet named after him
Died 1742 aged 85

Edmond Halley was the son of a well-
to-do London business man. By the
age of 16 he had decided to be an
astronomer. When he went to Oxford
University he took astronomical
instruments with him, and soon became
a good observer and mathematician.
He was so keen to do astronomy that
he left Oxford before getting his degree
to spend two years on the island of St
Helena in the South Atlantic, making
charts of the southern sky.

As well as doing astronomy, Halley
made important studies of the Earth's
magetism, tides, weather, statistics
and many other subjects. From 1696
to 1698 he was deputy controller of
the mint (where coins are made) at
Chester, and after that he commanded
a Royal Navy ship for two years. In
1703 he became a professor at Oxford,
and Astronomer Royal in 1720.

Halley worked out that a bright comet
seen in 1682 was the same one that
had appeared in 1531 and 1607. He
correctly predicted that it would be
seen again in 1758, though he did not
live to see it. ■

See also

Astronomers
Comets

Handel, George Frederick

Born 1685 in Halle, Germany
German composer who wrote the
Messiah and other famous works
Died 1759 aged 74

Handel's father wanted him to become
a lawyer. He was very unhappy when
the boy insisted on studying music.
When he was 18 Handel went to
Hamburg to work as an orchestral
player and learn all he could about
opera. He wrote two operas. One of

▲ In this picture, painted in 1756, Handel is shown seated in front of a copy of his famous oratorio *Messiah*.

them, *Almira*, was a great success and he was invited to Italy, the home of opera in the 18th century.

He stayed in Italy for nearly three years and wrote many successful works. But he was still restless. In 1710 he visited London and was so happy there that he decided to make it his home, even though he had already accepted an appointment in Hanover. Fortunately the Elector of Hanover was about to become King George I, so he was able to make London his home after all.

At first the operas he wrote for London audiences were enormously successful. But later he began to lose money. To save himself from ruin he turned to oratorios, a kind of opera without scenery or costumes. The British liked them because they had plenty of choral singing and were often based on familiar stories from the Bible. The most famous oratorio writen by Handel is *Messiah*, first performed in 1742.

Handel wrote vast quantities of music of all kinds, including orchestral works, such as the *Music for the Royal Fireworks* and the *Water Music* suite, and many fine concertos. His music is bold and vigorous, full of splendid tunes and very dramatic. ■

See also

Choirs   Operas

Hannibal

Born 247 BC in North Africa
Carthaginian general who crossed the Alps with war elephants to attack Rome in 218 BC
Committed suicide 183 BC aged 64

Carthage, a colony founded by the Phoenicians in North Africa, became a powerful nation through the wealth created by its trading by sea. In 264 BC it clashed with the other great power, Rome. Hannibal's father, Hamilcar, was the general in charge of Carthaginian forces in this first war. The Romans defeated Carthage and made them pay huge fines.

At the age of 9, Hannibal was taken to Spain by his father on campaign. His father made him swear to be a lifelong enemy of Rome.

In 221 BC, at the age of 25, Hannibal took over command of the forces in Spain. He attacked the town of Saguntum in northern Spain, and war broke out again. Although the Romans sent an army against him, Hannibal outwitted them by marching right across the Alps into Italy. He started with about 40,000 soldiers and 37 elephants (mainly to frighten the Roman troops) but, after the crossing, only 26,000 men and 12 elephants were left.

Hannibal raised a new army and defeated the Romans in several major battles. One Roman historian, Livy, said that 'he was the best among the foot and horse soldiers – first into battle and the last to leave.' The Romans were in despair of ever defeating Hannibal, until they appointed a new general, Cornelius Scipio.

Scipio finally drew Hannibal away from Italy by attacking Carthage, and he defeated Hannibal's army at Zama in North Africa in 202. Hannibal returned to Carthage, but eventually committed suicide to avoid being captured by the Romans. ■

See also

Phoenicians
Roman ancient history

Hardie, James Keir

Born 1856 in Legbrannock, Scotland
He did more than anyone to create the modern British Labour Party, and is still one of its heroes.
Died 1915 aged 59

Keir Hardie was born in a one-roomed house, and was the eldest of nine children. By the age of 10 he was working down a pit, where he saw miners risking appalling injuries and death in return for very low wages. He thought that trade unions could improve conditions for working people, and by 1886 he was a full-time union organizer in Ayrshire.

At first he thought that the Liberal Party would speak up for working people in Parliament, but he gradually lost confidence in them and decided that a new party was needed. In 1892 he stood for Parliament in West Ham, Essex, and became the first independent Labour Member of Parliament. He wore a soft tweed cap, which angered the other, smartly dressed MPs, but 'the man in the cloth cap' became a working class hero.

▲ Keir Hardie appears in this photograph, signed by him in 1899, as he did when he first entered the House of Commons in 1892. It was a cap like the one he wears in the picture which caused such an outcry from other MPs.

Hardie spoke out in Parliament against unemployment and poverty. He also attacked the Boer War and demanded votes for women. At first he was a lone voice, but by 1906 the number of Labour MPs had grown to 29, and Hardie became the first leader of the new Labour Party. He gave the rest of his life to the Party, speaking at countless meetings and writing thousands of articles. His colourful personality and strong views were disliked by many political opponents, but he inspired great love and affection amongst supporters.

He was strongly in favour of international co-operation, and made many journeys abroad. He was a pacifist, and when World War I broke out in 1914 he hoped that a great international strike would stop it. He was bitterly upset when most of his Labour and socialist colleagues supported the war. He died, a disappointed man, in 1915. ■

See also

Boer War
Edwardian Britain
Political parties
Trade unions

Hardy, Thomas

Born 1840 in Upper Bockhampton, Dorset, England
A great English novelist
Died 1928 aged 87

Thomas Hardy was the son of a builder. A bright boy at school, he later worked as an architect and church-restorer in London. But he so missed the Dorset countryside that he returned there in 1867, and also began writing novels and poetry.

In 1872 he published *Under the Greenwood Tree*, the first of many novels describing the ups and downs of country life in the West Country. But the good humour running through his early work began to disappear in favour of a sadder approach to life. Hardy increasingly saw his characters

as victims of a cruel and uncaring world. In *The Mayor of Casterbridge*, the main character, Michael Henchard, is brought down by his inability to change and by the fact that as a young man he had once sold his wife to someone else at a fair. *Tess of the D'Urbervilles*, written five years later, describes an innocent girl destroyed by a villainous lover and a series of dreadfully unlucky mishaps.

In 1874 Hardy married, but the relationship was never easy. He described the type of difficulties he and his wife had in his novel *Jude the Obscure*. But readers were not ready for this sort of honesty about marriage, and the outcry against him caused Hardy to abandon novels for the writing of poetry. The death of his wife in 1912 led to some beautiful poems where Hardy regrets their past unhappiness together. In 1914 he married again and lived quietly until his death. Today many visitors to Dorset go there especially to see the sights that he described so vividly in his writings. ■

Harvey, William

Born 1578 in Folkestone, England
Discovered how blood travels round the body.
Died 1657 aged 79

William Harvey was the eldest of seven sons of a wealthy farming family. His brothers all did very well as merchants in London. But William went off to study medicine. He was a very successful doctor, and became court physician to King James I and then to King Charles I.

Harvey made a careful study of the heart and blood vessels (veins and arteries) in the dozens of different animals which he cut up. King Charles even supplied him with royal deer on which to experiment. He saw valves in the blood vessels which allowed the blood to move in only one direction.

For more than 1,500 years doctors had

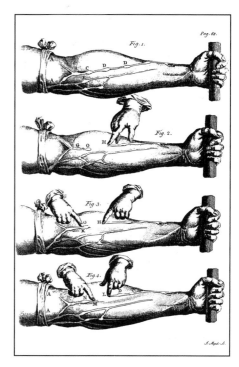

▲ The method used by Harvey to demonstrate that blood flows in one direction only. By applying finger pressure to different points on an arm, he could work out which way the blood was flowing through the veins.

followed the writings of the ancient Greek physician Galen, who taught that blood moved backwards and forwards in the vessels which carried it. It was also believed that blood was constantly being destroyed in the body and replaced from the food we eat. But Harvey showed that the heart pumped an enormous amount of blood in just one hour: three times the weight of a man. Nobody could eat enough to replace blood at that rate!

Harvey showed that blood was pumped from the heart all the way round the body and back to the heart, where it began its journey again. He was the first person to describe the circulation of the blood accurately. At first most doctors preferred to carry on believing Galen's ideas, but by the end of Harvey's life doctors and scientists had accepted his ideas on the circulation of the blood. ■

See also

Blood
Hearts
Human body

Hawkins, Sir John

Born 1532 at Plymouth, England
A naval commander who took part in the defeat of the Spanish Armada
Died 1595 aged 63

Hawkins came from a seafaring family, and as a young man he learned of the profits to be made from slave trading. In 1562 and 1565 he made two voyages, carrying slaves from West Africa to the West Indies; these made his fortune and established his reputation as a sea captain.

His third voyage in 1567 was a disastrous failure, but in 1572 Hawkins became treasurer of the navy. He used his experience to improve ship design, and built ships with a longer hull and a smaller forecastle (forward part), which were faster and more manœuvrable. In 1588, Hawkins commanded one of these new galleons against the Spanish Armada, and was knighted for his part in the battle. Although Hawkins was suspected of using his position as treasurer to enrich himself, no charges against him were ever proved. In 1595, aged 63, he joined an expedition against the Spaniards in the West Indies led by Sir Francis Drake. But off Puerto Rico he died and was buried at sea. ■

See also

Armada   **Biography**
Slave trade   Drake

Haydn, Joseph

Born 1732 in Rohrau, Austria
A composer, sometimes called the 'father of the symphony'
Died 1809 aged 77

Haydn's father was a poor wheelwright who could do little to help a son who wanted to become a musician. Fortunately a relative agreed to pay for his education. Even more fortunately the organist of Vienna's great cathedral took him into the choir, where he remained until he was 17.

He learned all he could, and taught himself to compose by studying the

▲ Haydn's last public appearance was at a performance of his oratorio, *The Creation*, on 27 March 1808. Beethoven was among the audience.

music he most admired. In 1759 he obtained his first official appointment, as musician to Count Morzin. The job did not last long, but in 1761 he found a post that was to last a lifetime. He went to work for Prince Esterházy, at his splendid palace at Eisenstadt.

Haydn served the Esterházy family for 30 years. He wrote operas for their private opera house, and church music for their private chapel. He wrote symphonies and quartets, concertos, songs and piano music for their day-to-day entertainment.

His fame spread far beyond the walls of Eisenstadt. When the time came for him to retire, his music was known and loved throughout Europe. He visited England twice, first in 1791 to 1792, and again in 1794 to 1795. Both visits were a great success, and prompted him to write the twelve 'London' symphonies. Haydn's music is ingenious and inventive. Without him, the symphony and string quartet might never have become such important musical forms. ■

See also

Chamber music
Choirs
Concertos
Symphonies

Henry I

Born 1068 in Selby, England
King of England from 1100 to 1135; he managed to keep together under his rule the English kingdom and the duchy of Normandy.
Died 1135 aged 67

Henry was the youngest son of William I. When Henry was 9, his father died and his two elder brothers took power, Robert succeeding as Duke of Normandy and William Rufus as King of England. Henry had nothing. But in 1100 he got his chance, after William II's sudden death. He seized the royal treasure and within three days had himself crowned as Henry I of England. Once he was king, he started to fight Robert for control of Normandy. After six years, he finally defeated his brother and shut him up in prison for the rest of his life.

It was not easy for Henry to hold onto both England and Normandy. Nearly every year of his reign, he had to raise money in England to go and fight in France. He ruled his subjects by fear, and lived in fear himself. It is said that he kept moving his bed around, because he was afraid of being murdered in his sleep.

In 1120, Henry's only legitimate son was drowned when the *White Ship* sank in crossing the English Channel. Henry promptly remarried, but had no more children. Now there was no clear heir to the throne, and all Henry's work seemed wasted. He lived for another fifteen years, but, according to a writer of the time, he never smiled again.

Although ruthless in his struggle for power, Henry was a just ruler who made some major and popular reforms. After his death he was known as the 'Lion of Justice', and as Henry 'Beauclerc' because of his love of learning. ■

See also

Normans

Biography
William I

▼ In this picture, painted on a manuscript a few years after his death, Henry I dreams that the peasants come to him to appeal against the taxes. In his dream he agrees not to collect the land tax for seven years.

Henry II

Born 1133 in Le Mans, France
King of England from 1154 to 1189, he was the most powerful ruler in 12th-century Europe.
Died 1189 aged 56

Henry's father was count of Anjou in France and his mother, the Empress Matilda, was the daughter of Henry I. His mother fought for her claim to the English throne throughout Henry's childhood. Henry joined in the fighting as soon as he could, so that by the time he was 21 he was lord of Anjou and king of England. Through his wife, Eleanor of Aquitaine, he ruled also in southern France. Henry's power stretched from Ireland to the Pyrenees.

Henry's subjects knew and feared him as a man of immense energy; often he would go out hunting at dawn, come back in the evening, and not sit down except to eat.

At first, everything went right for Henry. He kept succeeding in war, especially against his main enemy, the king of France, and in his own lands he maintained peace and justice. Then,

in 1170, his bitter quarrel with Thomas Becket, Archbishop of Canterbury, ended with Becket's murder by Henry's men. This was an outrage and Henry had to pay for it.

Now Henry's good luck ran out. In 1173 his wife and two eldest sons, Henry and Richard, rebelled against him, with the support of the French king. In England people criticized his unfair methods of raising money to fight his wars, and his delays in dealing out justice. When judging a case, Henry would deliberately keep both sides waiting as long as possible for the outcome, as a way of showing his power.

Henry died with his strength and his heart broken. All his sons were in revolt against him, even his youngest and favourite, John. ■

 See also

France's history
Middle Ages

Biography
Becket
John, King
Richard I

Henry V

Born 1387 in Monmouth, Wales
King of England for only nine years, from 1413 to 1422, he was a war hero who died in his prime.
Died 1422 aged 35

As a boy, Henry could not have known that he would ever be king. After all, his father, Henry Bolingbroke, was a trusted counsellor of King Richard II. But then the king banished his father, and the young Henry was left in the king's care. The next year (1399) his father came back, seized the English throne from Richard, ruled as Henry IV and created young Henry Prince of Wales and heir to the kingdom of England.

During his father's reign, Prince Henry spent his time with 'wild company', but when Henry IV died in 1413 and the young Henry succeeded as king,

▲ This painting of Henry V was made in France soon after he married the French king's daughter, Catherine.

he became serious and determined, abandoned his old friends and turned his attention to France.

King Charles VI of France did not take the new English king seriously, and Henry vowed to make him regret this. He made careful preparations for war, and invaded France in 1415. Within two months, Henry had destroyed the French army at Agincourt, while the English had lost no more than 300 men. Henry kept up the military pressure for the next five years, until the French king had to agree to let Henry marry his daughter, and so become his heir.

Henry was now the most powerful ruler in Europe, and he even started making plans to go on crusade to the Holy Land. But seven years of fighting had exhausted him. During another long French siege, he caught camp fever and died, leaving a nine-month-old baby as his successor. Henry's last wish was that he might live to 'build again the walls of Jerusalem' and win it back from the Muslims. ■

◉ See also

Hundred Years War

Biography
Richard II

Henry VII

Born 1457 in Pembroke Castle, Wales
The first Tudor king; he ruled from 1485 to 1509 and brought peace to England after the turbulent Wars of the Roses.
Died 1509 aged 52

Henry Tudor was the son of a Welsh gentleman and of Margaret Beaufort, one of the royal family of Lancaster. After the death of the last Lancastrian king, Henry VI, Henry Tudor had a claim to the the throne. The Yorkists ruled next, but King Richard III was so unpopular that Henry took the risk of invading from France where he had been in exile. At the battle of Bosworth his supporters defeated Richard and killed him. He then married Elizabeth of York, Richard's niece. But it is dangerous to win a crown by battle, and Henry VII spent the first part of his reign fending off challenges.

Henry was very practical. He built up riches for the crown in many ways, including punishing disobedient nobles with heavy fines. This made sure the nobles obeyed him, too. Henry was also lucky when he died; his son was just old enough to take over as Henry VIII, and the rule of the Tudors was secure. ■

◉ See also

Tudor England
Wars of the Roses

Biography
Henry VIII
Richard III

Henry VIII

Born 1491 in Greenwich Palace, London
King of England and Wales from 1509 to 1547. His divorce of his first wife led to the Reformation of the English Church.
Died 1547 aged 55

When Henry VIII came to the throne in 1509, he seemed to have everything. He was tall, handsome, and good at hunting and jousting. He was religious, well educated and musical. He was devoted to his new wife Catherine of Aragon. And he soon found an energetic and loyal minister in Thomas Wolsey, whom he made Lord Chancellor.

But Henry wanted a son to follow him, and was prepared to stop at nothing to get his own way. He grew tired of Catherine, who had given him a daughter, Mary. He wanted to marry a lively lady of the court, Anne Boleyn. Wolsey failed to persuade the Pope to give the king a divorce, and so he was dismissed from the post of minister.

Henry with his new minister, Thomas Cromwell, and the Archbishop of Canterbury, Thomas Cranmer, found a more ruthless solution. Henry broke with the Pope. He married Anne Boleyn (and divorced Catherine afterwards), became Supreme Head of the English Church, and destroyed the monasteries because he wanted their wealth. This was the beginning of the English Reformation. Henry dealt ruthlessly with those who opposed him. Few people close to him, especially his wives, escaped trouble.

The old Henry was a terrifying figure. He had a painful ulcer on his leg, and was so overweight that a machine had to haul him upstairs. But to his people he was a real king. When he died, his councillors did not dare announce the news for three days. ∎

See also

Monasteries	**Biography**
Reformation	Cranmer
Tudor England	More
	Wolsey

◀ **The six wives of Henry VIII: Catherine of Aragon (divorced), Anne Boleyn (beheaded), Jane Seymour (died), Anne of Cleves (divorced), Catherine Howard (beheaded the portrait may not be of Catherine), and Katherine Parr (survived). See the article on Tudor England for a family tree.**

Hepworth, Barbara

Born 1903 in Yorkshire, England
One of the first abstract sculptors
Died 1975 aged 72

Barbara Hepworth was the eldest of four children. Her father, a surveyor, took her on his trips to inspect buildings in the remote and wild landscape of the Yorkshire Dales. She became interested in sculpture at the age of 7.

Like her friend, Henry Moore, Barbara Hepworth went to Leeds School of Art and then to the Royal College of Art in London. Later a scholarship took her to Italy, where she took marble carving lessons in Rome. Nearly all her early work is direct carving into stone or wood. Later she used bronze, sometimes curving metal into shapes joined by thin metal rods, giving the appearance of strings as in musical instruments. Her work soon became entirely abstract. Her pieces of sculpture do not look like or even suggest anything in particular. They are concerned with shape, texture, size and weight, inside and outside surfaces. Her forms seem to grow out of stone or wood. Her shapes are often split open or hollowed out or completely pierced, making even more complex rhythms of spaces and surfaces. After World War II she gained an international reputation as one of the greatest modern sculptors, and carried out many commissions for public places. She died tragically in a fire in her studio in St Ives, Cornwall. ∎

See also

Sculpture   **Biography**
                             Moore

▲ **The sculptor Barbara Hepworth at work in her garden in 1964. Her large, abstract but strangely beautiful sculptures won her a reputation as one of the foremost sculptors of her day. Collections of her work can be seen in galleries and museums all over the world.**

Hereward the Wake

> **Born** date unknown, in Lincolnshire,
> England
> He led Anglo-Saxon resistance in the
> 11th century against King William the
> Conqueror.
> **Died** age unknown

Hereward is a figure of legend: very little is known about his life. He was a tenant of the abbey of Peterborough, farming land in Lincolnshire. In 1070 a Norman abbot, Turold, got control of that abbey, and Hereward, with other Anglo-Saxon tenants, decided to rebel against him. They burnt and plundered the abbey, and made off with its treasure to the Isle of Ely, a marshy area that Hereward could easily defend.

Anglo-Saxons from other parts of the country, who were resisting the Normans, came to Ely to join Hereward. In 1071 King William decided to take action, and attacked the rebel stronghold. There is a story that Hereward was betrayed by one of his own men, who showed the Norman soldiers a secret way through the marshes. In fact, Hereward may have escaped, because the Hereward mentioned in 1086 in the Domesday Book as a landowner may be Hereward the Wake. In any case, Hereward lived on in people's imaginations, as Robin Hood did later, as an outlaw hero who defied the power of the Normans. ■

See also

Normans

Biography
William I

Hero of Alexandria

> Lived about 60 AD in the Greek city of
> Alexandria in Egypt
> Invented many clever devices, including
> a toy which used the first steam-engine.

We know nothing of Hero's life, but we do know about his marvellous inventions because copies of the books he wrote have been passed down through the centuries. His books contain descriptions of mechanical playthings he invented. The most famous was a small ball which whizzed round by the force of steam. This was the very first steam-engine, but it was to be another 1,700 years before anyone thought of using steam to drive machines other than toys.

Hero also invented some very useful devices, such as his 'dioptra'. This instrument could measure the distance between far-off points and could give their height. It was similar to the modern theodolite used by surveyors today, when examining a piece of land before plans can be made for building houses or roads.

Hero produced several toys using water; they have been given such names as 'Hero's magic fountain' and 'Hero's magic jug'. He also developed a water-clock. He was obviously a very clever inventor with a good sense of humour! ■

See also

Steam-engines
Surveyors

Herod

> **Born** about 73 BC
> King of the Jews who ordered the
> massacre of children in Bethlehem when
> he heard of the birth of Jesus
> **Died** 4 BC aged about 69

Herod was appointed King of the Jews by the Roman Mark Antony in 40 BC. This Herod (there were several) was called 'the Great' because of the forceful way he ruled the kingdom of Judaea (now modern Israel). It is doubtful whether any of the Jewish population would have agreed with this title, since he ruthlessly put down rebellions.

Although he was given the province of Judaea by the Romans he had to fight for it to make it his kingdom. His first job was to besiege Jerusalem, and eventually he took control there. Throughout his life he was a suspicious man, always thinking that there were plots against him. He executed his own son and those of his sister, Salome. He also executed his wife and her mother and the High Priest.

It must have been on his death bed that he ordered the 'Massacre of the Innocents', as it came to be called. Herod found out about the birth of Jesus, whom people were calling the future king of the Jews. He ordered all children under the age of two in Bethlehem to be put to death. Jesus and his family escaped to Egypt, and Herod died the same year. The story of the flight of Mary, Joseph and Jesus to Egypt is told in the Gospel of St Matthew, chapter 2. ■

See also

Roman ancient history

Biography
Jesus

Herschel, Sir William and Caroline

> As an astronomer, Herschel is often
> described as one of the greatest
> observers ever, an achievement made
> possible with the help of his sister
> Caroline.
> **William Born** 1738 in Hanover,
> Germany
> **Died** 1822 aged 83
> **Caroline Born** 1750 in Hanover
> **Died** 1848 aged 97

William Herschel started his working life following in his father's footsteps as an oboist in a German military band. In 1757, he came to England and worked as a musician, eventually settling in Bath. His sister Caroline joined him there in 1772. Gradually his interest in astronomy grew and he started to build his own telescopes.

In 1781, he discovered the planet Uranus, the first planet to be found with the help of a telescope. This discovery changed his life. King George III paid him so he could devote himself completely to astronomy.

Herschel directed his tremendous energy towards making far more observations of a much higher quality than anyone had done before. He made catalogues of nebulas and double stars, and discovered moons around Uranus and Saturn.

He married in 1788, and his son John, born in 1792, also became a famous astronomer.

Caroline Herschel started as William's housekeeper, but soon became his expert and devoted assistant. She went on to do research of her own. She discovered new comets and nebulas, and was awarded the Gold Medal of the Royal Astronomical Society for making a huge catalogue of her brother's observations. After William's death, she returned to Germany. ■

◉ See also

Astronomers
Nebulas
Planets
Telescopes

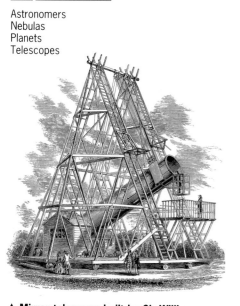

▲ Mirror telescope built by Sir William Herschel. The curved mirror was at the bottom end of the tube, which could be raised or lowered by pulleys. There were rollers under the platform so that the telescope could be turned.

Heyerdahl, Thor

Born 1914 in Larvik, Norway
A famous explorer and author, he led the 'Kon-Tiki' and 'Ra' expeditions.

Thor Heyerdahl always had very definite ideas about how human civilization might have spread during the world's early history. Most scholars believe that people lived in widely separated communities and usually had to discover important new techniques,

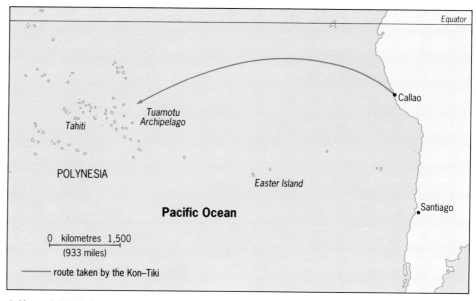

▲ Heyerdahl's balsa-wood raft, *Kon-Tiki*, sailed from Callao (Peru) in April 1947. Using both wind and ocean currents it moved in an arc, coming closer to the equator and then drifting south-west to reach the Tuamotu Ridge in August.

such as the wheel, for themselves. But Thor was convinced that early progress was often spread by those from advanced communities travelling to other parts of the world carrying their new knowledge with them.

To prove that this might have been so, Thor and five companions built themselves a simple balsa-wood raft they called the *Kon-Tiki*. In 1947 they sailed it from Peru to Eastern Polynesia to prove that Indians from South America could once have made this journey. Their journey involved great danger from sharks, lack of water and the possibility of becoming hopelessly lost. But to everyone's delight the Kon-Tiki expedition landed safely on an island in the Tuamotu Archipelago.

Thor's next important project was to cross the Atlantic from Morocco to the Caribbean, this time in *Ra*, a reproduction of an ancient Egyptian boat made of papyrus. His idea was to suggest that South America could once have been influenced by ideas from Egyptian civilization. His first voyage ended in the Leeward Islands in the Caribbean. The following year, 1970, he sailed again and reached Central America.

While many scholars are still not convinced that people in ancient times would have done such daring feats themselves, they all admire Thor's bravery and skill. He has also become a leading fighter for the conservation of the world's natural resources. ■

Hill, Octavia

Born 1838 in Wisbech, England
She devised a simple but effective way of improving poor housing conditions in London, and became a leading social reformer.
Died 1912 aged 73

When Octavia Hill was 5, her father, a wealthy business man, had a mental breakdown and was unable to support his large family. But Octavia was a vigorous child and grew up happily under the care of her grandfather. Once she wished for 'a field so large I could run in it for ever'. At 14 she was paid by a charity to run a workshop where poor children made toy furniture. Later, with her mother and sister Miranda, she ran a school in their own home.

In 1864 the artist and writer, John Ruskin, gave her the money to buy three houses occupied by poor families. Octavia was against giving charity. She collected the rents herself in order to get to know the occupants. She tried to be a good landlady, and encouraged tenants to take care of their homes and

▲ Octavia Hill is shown here towards the end of her life, when she said that she had only 'done so simply and at no great cost, just what lay before me'.

pay their rent on time. She was so successful that other wealthy friends bought similar houses and put them under her management. She also worked to protect open spaces and provide city parks as 'open air sitting rooms for the poor'. She helped to start the National Trust.

A friend described her as a 'lady of great force and energy with a wide-open, well-stored brain'. At the same time she was 'gentle and womanly and possessed of a wonderful tact'. ■

Hill, Rowland

Born 1795 in Kidderminster, England
A schoolmaster who put his skills to reforming the postal system; he invented the postage stamp.
Died 1879 aged 83

At 12, Rowland Hill began to teach mathematics at his father's school. At 16 he took over the running of its finances, which were in a mess, and freed his family from 'the terrible inconvenience of being poor'. Their

new school became famous because the pupils made their own rules and enforced them without corporal punishment.

In 1837, Hill published a pamphlet suggesting that instead of making very expensive charges, all letters weighing up to half an ounce should be delivered anywhere in the country for one penny. He also recommended the use of 'a bit of paper just large enough to bear the stamp and covered at the back with a glutinous wash' – in other words, an adhesive postage stamp.

Post Office officials opposed it, but most people thought it was an excellent idea, and the 'Penny Post' came into use in 1840. Later Hill was knighted for his achievement in giving Britain the first proper postal service. ■

See also

Postal services

Hillary, Sir Edmund

Born 1919 in Auckland, New Zealand
With his friend Tenzing Norgay, he was the first man to climb Everest.

Edmund Hillary started adult life as a bee-keeper before taking up mountain climbing. After climbing in the New Zealand Alps and the Himalayas, he became a member of the British Everest expedition in 1953. Almost at the summit, it was left to Edmund and Tenzing, a Sherpa tribesman from Nepal, to make the final climb. This they did on 29 May. News of their success reached Britain on the day of Queen Elizabeth's coronation. Edmund was knighted by the new Queen in July 1953.

Since then he has made other trips to Everest, becoming a good friend to the Sherpa people. With them he has worked on schemes for building new schools and hospitals.

In 1958 he was a member of the British Commonwealth Trans-Antarctic expedition, travelling to the South Pole

NEWS CHRONICLE

No. 33,381   TUESDAY, JUNE 2, 1953   PRICE 1½d.

THE CROWNING GLORY: EVEREST IS CLIMBED

THE QUEEN'S DRESS TODAY *Back Page*

Tremendous news for the Queen

The new Elizabethan

Here the forecast is rain—hail—sun—storm, BUT the crowds are singing in the rain SO—

WHO CARES NOW

▲ **2 June 1953 was the day of Elizabeth II's coronation and the British newspapers were delighted to link that to the news of Edmund Hillary's successful conquest of Everest.**

in a tractor. Other trips have involved more climbing and an unsuccessful search for the abominable snowman in the Himalayas. ■

See also

Climbing
Himalayas

Biography
Tenzing

Hippocrates of Cos

Born about 460 BC on the Greek island of Cos
Sometimes called the 'father of medicine' because of his sensible treatment of his patients
Died about 377 BC aged about 80

Unfortunately we do not know much about Hippocrates, but the little we do know shows him to have been a kind and sensible doctor. In those days most people believed that illnesses were caused by evil spirits or bad magic, but Hippocrates taught that disease was caused by not eating good food or by living in a dirty place. He kept careful records of people's illnesses and how they responded to treatment. He was a good surgeon and could set broken bones straight. He taught his methods to other doctors, including his own two sons.

Doctors today, 2,400 years after Hippocrates' death, still remember him with respect: they all promise to keep the 'Hippocratic Oath' and look after their patients with every care and kindness. ■

See also

Doctors
Medicine

Hirohito, Emperor

Born 1901 in Tokyo, Japan
He was emperor from 1926 to 1989, and announced Japan's surrender at the end of World War II.
Died 1989 aged 87

Hirohito was the eldest son of Emperor Taisho of Japan. At school he became very interested in the study of sea life, and later wrote books about this subject. He visited Europe in 1921, the first crown prince of Japan to travel abroad. When he returned, his father retired because of mental illness and Hirohito became prince regent, ruling in his place.

He became emperor in 1926 and was known as Tenno Heika (Son of Heaven). By Japanese tradition, he was the 124th direct descendant of Jimmu, the first emperor. Although his reign was supposed to be one of Showa ('bright peace'), Japan soon became involved in war. First Japan invaded China and then joined World War II on the side of Germany and Italy.

Hirohito did not want war against the USA, but he could not stop his military leaders from attacking Pearl Harbor. Only at the end of the war, when atom bombs had been dropped on Hiroshima and Nagasaki, did Hirohito overrule his generals. For the first time ever, he spoke on the radio to announce Japan's surrender. ■

After the war, he stayed on as emperor, but real power was given to the people and their elected politicians. Hirohito tried to be more popular by making personal appearances and allowing stories and pictures of his family to go in the newspapers. Japan also became friendly with its old enemies in the West, but even when Hirohito died many could not forgive him for the things his armies had done in World War II. ■

See also

Hiroshima
Japan's history
World War II

Hitler, Adolf

Born 1889 in Braunau-am-Inn, Austria
As dictator of Nazi Germany, he started World War II in 1939.
Committed suicide 1945 aged 56

After leaving school at 16, Adolf Hitler tried to get into art college in Vienna, but he failed twice. Instead he earned a miserable living painting postcards and advertisements. In World War I he fought as a corporal in the German army and was awarded the Iron Cross for bravery.

▲ At the height of his power, Adolf Hitler was admired by millions of Germans who thought that he had made their country great again. Here the crowds can be seen giving him the Nazi 'Heil Hitler' salute in 1938 as he toured Sudetenland, which he had seized from Czechoslovakia and annexed to Germany.

When Germany lost the war, Hitler was so angry about the terms of the peace treaty that he turned to politics. He joined a small party which became the National Socialist (Nazi) Party in 1920, and soon became its leader. Many joined the Nazi Party, and in 1923 they tried to seize power in Munich. This attempt failed and Hitler went to prison.

There he wrote *Mein Kampf* (My Struggle) which set out his ideas: that all Germany's problems were caused by Jews and communists and that Germany needed a strong *Führer* (leader) to be great again. Times were hard in Germany at this time, and his ideas caught on. Although he got only 37 per cent of the votes in the presidential election, Hitler was invited by President Hindenburg to become chancellor (chief minister) in 1933.

When Hindenburg died in 1934, Hitler became president, chancellor and supreme commander of the armed forces. All opposition to his rule was crushed. Millions of people were sent to concentration camps, and Jews gradually lost all their rights. Abroad Hitler became an ally of Fascist Italy and began to push Germany's boundaries outwards. In 1938 he invaded Austria and in 1939 occupied Czechoslovakia and finally attacked Poland too.

This started World War II. Hitler took personal command of Germany's war plans. He became angry and wild when things went against him. Finally, having ordered the deaths of 6 million Jews and others in extermination camps, he was defeated by the Allied powers and shot himself in his bunker (underground shelter). ∎

◉ See also

Concentration camps
German history
Nazis
World War II

Ho Chi Minh

Born 1890 in Kim Lien, Vietnam
He was the founder of the Vietnamese Communist Party which drove the French from Indo-China, and he became President of North Vietnam.
Died 1969 aged 79

Ho Chi Minh (meaning 'He who shines') was born Nguyen That Thanh in Vietnam when it was part of Indo-China, a colony ruled by France. After secondary school he worked as a cook in London and Paris. There he met French communists who thought it was wrong for France to rule over colonies. They helped him go to the Soviet Union, where he was trained as a communist organizer. Then he lived just outside Vietnam so he could organize a Communist Party inside the country without being arrested.

In 1941 Japan entered Indo-China and Ho set up an underground movement, the Vietminh, to fight them. He hoped to take over when the Japanese left in 1945, but the French came back. In 1946 Ho declared war on the French, and his Vietminh forces fought them and finally won the battle of Dien Bien Phu in 1954.

Vietnam was then divided at the Geneva Conference. Ho Chi Minh became President of North Vietnam. Non-communist South Vietnam was supported by the USA, but Ho was determined to reunite the two. He backed the South Vietnam communists, called the Vietcong, who were fighting their government and the Americans. Peasants carried supplies to them from North Vietnam along the Ho Chi Minh trail.

In 1965 the USA began to bomb North Vietnam. Its farmers and city people spent much of their lives in shelters, but the bombing made them even more loyal to Ho Chi Minh. Six years after he died, the two Vietnams were united under the rule of the Communist Party that Ho had founded in 1930. ∎

◉ See also

Vietnam

▲ After North and South Vietnam were united to become one country again in 1975, the capital of the old South Vietnam, Saigon, was renamed Ho Chi Minh City in honour of the dead leader.

In 1964 she became only the third woman ever to be awarded the Nobel prize for chemistry (the other two were Marie Curie and Irène Joliot-Curie). She received it for finding out how the atoms are arranged in penicillin and vitamin B_{12}. The following year she became only the second woman to be awarded the very special distinction of the Order of Merit (Florence Nightingale was the other). ■

⊙ See also

Atoms
Crystals
Penicillin
Vitamins
X-rays

Holiday, Billie

Born 1915 in Baltimore, USA
She became the best-known black female jazz singer of the 1940s and 1950s.
Died 1959 aged 44

Billie's father played banjo and guitar in a jazz band, and at 15 she was in New York singing in jazz clubs. Her very distinctive voice and emotional appeal brought her rapid success. All through the 1940s and 1950s she toured and recorded, making two trips to Europe, in 1954 and 1958. Her best-known records are probably 'Strange Fruit', 'Fine and Mellow', 'Lover Man' and 'Violets for my Furs'.

At the time when she was touring, there was still deep prejudice against blacks in the American South, and as a black singer, Billie Holiday (nicknamed 'Lady Day') often suffered humiliation, such as not being allowed to eat or stay in the same places as her white band.

Her life was filled with personal problems. The biggest one was her drug addiction. This eventually brought about her early death, at a time when she should have been reaching her artistic peak. ■

⊙ See also

Jazz (photograph)

▲ This portrait of Dorothy Hodgkin was painted by Maggi Hambling in 1985. It hangs in the National Portrait Gallery, London.

Hodgkin, Dorothy

Born 1910 in Cairo, Egypt
One of the world's greatest chemists, who discovered how atoms are put together to make complicated substances like penicillin and vitamin B_{12}.

Dorothy Hodgkin was born Dorothy Mary Crowfoot in Cairo, and though she has travelled to most countries of the world, most of her time has been spent in her chemistry laboratory in Oxford.

Everything in the world is made of atoms, but they are much too small to see even with a powerful microscope. But if a chemist wants to make a new drug or to copy a chemical that occurs naturally, it is necessary to know just what sort of atoms it contains and how they are fitted together. In other words a plan or design is needed, just as you would need one to build a house or a model car. Scientists found that, if a beam of X-rays is passed through a crystal of some chemical, a pattern of spots is produced on a photographic film placed near it and the pattern of spots is different for each different material. But trying to sort out exactly which arrangement of atoms gives any particular pattern of spots is rather like solving a very difficult code. Professor Hodgkin is the world's leading expert in solving this kind of problem.

Homer

Dates of birth and death unknown. He may have lived in Greece in the 8th or 7th century BC.
Homer is traditionally the author of two very long poems about the gods and heroes of ancient Greece, the *Iliad* about the capture of Troy (Ilium), and the *Odyssey*, an account of the adventures of one hero (Odysseus) going home to Greece from Troy.

We know almost nothing about the poet Homer. In fact some people thought he did not exist at all but that his poems were collections of verses which were recited in royal courts by wandering story tellers. Most experts of this early Greek period and its literature now think that there was a man called Homer who composed these long, epic poems. They think that Homer did not write the poems down but took famous stories (some recited by others) and put them all together. His poems were probably not actually written down for another hundred years.

Later Greek and Roman writers said that Homer was blind. It is also thought that he came from one of the cities in Asia Minor (now Turkey). There is a legend that he died and was buried on the Greek island of Ios. ■

See also

Odysseus
Trojan War

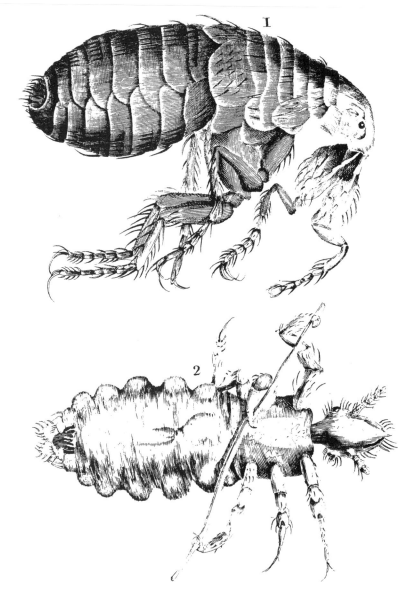

▲ Robert Hooke was particularly skilled at devising new scientific instruments. His compound microscope enabled him to make the first detailed observations of such objects as the flea (top) and the louse (bottom). Hooke illustrated his book *Micrographia* with many such drawings.

Hooke, Robert

Born 1635 in the Isle of Wight, England
Invented the compound microscope, and worked out how metals behave when stretched.
Died 1703 aged 67

Robert was a very bright boy, who was said to have mastered the whole of a geometry course and learned to play 20 lessons on the organ in one week! Unfortunately when he grew up he was very bad-tempered and was always having rows with other scientists. He was so worried that someone else might steal his discoveries that he sometimes left proof of what he had done in code. He almost discovered the law of gravity and its effect on the planets before Newton, but his mathematics was not good enough. The result of all his secrecy and grumpiness was that he did not get the credit for all his discoveries.

He studied the way metals behave when they are stretched and described it in a way that we still call 'Hooke's Law'. A Dutch scientist called Leeuwenhoek had shown how useful microscopes could be in many branches of science, but he only had a microscope with one lens. Hooke invented a much more powerful microscope with several lenses, called the compound microscope. He described his invention and many other ingenious pieces of apparatus in his book *Micrographia*. ■

See also

Microscopes

Biography
Leeuwenhoek
Newton

Houdini, Harry

Born 1874 in Budapest, Hungary
A magician and entertainer who specialized in performing miraculous escapes
Died 1926 aged 52

Houdini was the stage name of Ehrich Weiss. His family had emigrated to America from Hungary when he was a child but he later claimed to have been born there. He began his career as a trapeze artist, but it was as a magician who could perform amazing escapes that he became famous.

Houdini taught himself how to escape from all kinds of chains and bindings. He toured America and Europe, attracting publicity for his show by performing stunts, such as escaping from a strait-jacket or a prison cell. He even escaped from an airtight tank that was full up with water.

His most famous trick was the 'Chinese Torture Cell' into which he was locked, hanging upside-down with his ankles held by stocks. During his career, he invented many new acts, which included making a live elephant disappear and walking through a brick wall.

All Houdini's acts were tricks, which depended only on his skill and his physical strength and fitness. He was annoyed whenever it was suggested that he had special powers, and he would expose others, who claimed that they had supernatural powers, by performing their tricks himself. ■

▶ The English navigators Frobisher and Hudson each made several attempts to find a northern route between Europe and Asia through America. Although Frobisher's three trips and Hudson's four increased European knowledge of the continent, neither succeeded in finding the 'North-West Passage'.

Hudson, Henry

Born about 1570, place not known
Explored Hudson River, New York and discovered Hudson Bay while seeking a route to China.
Died 1611 aged about 41

The early life of Henry Hudson is a mystery. The earliest news of him is on 1 May 1607, when he sailed from London as captain of the tiny ship *Hopewell*, with a crew of ten men and a boy, his own son John. He was looking for a sea route to China to the north of Europe and Asia.

This and a second voyage the next year proved unsuccessful. Hudson then took a job with the Dutch East India Company. In the slightly larger ship *Half Moon* he explored the east coast of North America, and in particular the Hudson River, later named after him.

In 1610 Hudson set sail in an English ship, *Discoverie,* hoping to reach China by way of the North Pole. He discovered Hudson Bay, where he had to spend the winter. Next summer the crew mutinied and set Hudson, his son and seven (some accounts say six) others adrift in a small boat. They were never seen again. ■

◉ See also

Arctic Ocean
Explorers

Biography
Frobisher

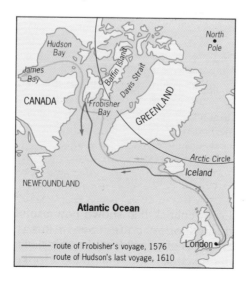

— route of Frobisher's voyage, 1576
— route of Hudson's last voyage, 1610

Hughes, Ted

Born 1930 in Mytholmroyd, Yorkshire, England
One of Britain's leading poets

Ted Hughes was brought up near the moors of the West Riding of Yorkshire. At Cambridge University he started to write poetry, and soon became well known. Many of his poems feature the countryside of his childhood. Hughes describes the beauty and also the occasional cruelty of life in the wild. In his series of poems *Crow*, the bird is portrayed as both savage and brave, a menace to other small animals but also a strong force in itself, determined to survive whatever the cost.

In 1956 he married the American poet Sylvia Plath (1932–1963). He edited her collected poems which won the Pulitzer prize for poetry in 1982.

▲ The cover of *The Iron Man*, first published in 1968 and published in America as *The Iron Giant*. This is one of the many books which Ted Hughes has written for children.

Hughes's later poems are less violent, especially those gathered together in a book called *Moortown*, published in 1980. He has also written warmly about his childhood in *Remains of Elmet*, and has produced an excellent short novel for children called *The Iron Man*. This describes how a young boy called Hogarth manages to make friends with a huge iron robot that comes out of the sea. Eventually Hogarth persuades this Iron Man to save the world from an even greater danger threatening from outer space. As well as telling a good story, Hughes also shows here how even the most frightening things in life can be put to a useful purpose, given the will.

In 1984 Hughes was made Poet Laureate. This is an award given to a poet, in return for which he or she agrees to write about royal events such as weddings and christenings, themes that make a real change from the more sinister subjects of Hughes's earlier poems. ■

Humboldt, Baron von

Born 1769 in Berlin, Germany
German scientist who explored the rivers of South America and founded the science of geography
Died 1859 aged 89

Alexander von Humboldt was a member of a noble German family, and a man of many talents. He studied biology, geology, metallurgy, mining and politics at university. From 1799 to 1804 he and a companion explored the rainforests surrounding the Amazon and Orinoco rivers, travelling nearly 10,000 km (6,000 miles). He studied the Peru Current, sometimes called the Humboldt Current, a flow of cool water along the coast of Peru, and reported that guano would make good fertilizer. He also identified the cause of mountain sickness.

For over 20 years he lived in Paris, doing scientific experiments and writing up the results of his explorations, before returning to Berlin. In 1829 he spent six months in Siberia, studying its weather and geology. He then organized the setting up of a chain of weather stations around the world. For a time he was sent on diplomatic missions by the government of Prussia. Humboldt spent the rest of his long life writing a five-volume book, titled *Kosmos*, about the universe. ■

Huxley, Thomas

Born 1825 near London, England
A popular science writer best remembered as a strong supporter of Charles Darwin's theory of evolution
Died 1895 aged 70

Thomas Henry Huxley was a doctor who spent much of his life studying animals and fossils. He is best remembered for the enthusiastic support he gave to Charles Darwin's ideas. In 1859 Darwin published a book called *The Origin of Species* in which he described how animals and plants continually struggle to survive. Huxley was one of the first to be convinced by Darwin's ideas that if there are slight differences among some animals then those who are fitter will survive and pass on their characteristics, and so the appearance of animals will slowly change. At that time most people believed in the story of creation as told in the Bible. They thought it wrong to suggest that animals evolved over millions of years rather than having been created by God, exactly as they are. Darwin was not popular.

Huxley took every opportunity of speaking up for Darwin's ideas. In a famous meeting in Oxford in 1860 Bishop Wilberforce asked Huxley whether his ape ancestors belonged to his mother's or father's family. Huxley replied that he would rather have an ape than the bishop as a distant relative! ■

See also

Evolution of living things
Evolution of people

Biography
Darwin

Huygens, Christian

Born 1629 in The Hague in The Netherlands
A great mathematician, who also improved the telescope, made the first accurate clock and produced important ideas about how light travels
Died 1695 aged 66

Christian's parents realized he was a brilliant mathematician when he was very young. Fortunately his father was an important official in the Dutch government and so could afford to give Christian a good education.

Huygens was not only a really great mathematician but he was also good at making things. He made big improvements to the telescope (invented by Galileo in 1609) and for the first time a ring round Saturn could be seen. No one had ever seen anything like that before. Huygens also built the first pendulum clock, which was much more accurate than any other clock at that time.

He studied light, and thought that it moved along in waves spreading out in just the same way as the circles of ripples on a pond travel outwards when a stone is dropped into the water. But scientists preferred Newton's ideas that light was a stream of tiny particles. Huygens's 'wave theory' was ignored for 150 years until Thomas Young showed that light does behave like a wave. ■

See also

Clocks and watches
Light
Telescopes

Biography
Galilei
Newton
Young

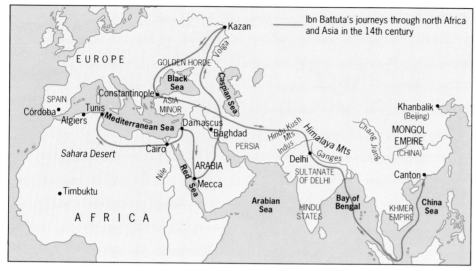

Ibn Battuta's journeys through north Africa and Asia in the 14th century

◀ The map shows some of the many journeys made by Ibn Battuta. He recorded his travels in the book *Rihla* (Journey), which has for a long time been highly valued by historians because of the information it gives us about the time in which he lived.

Ibn Battuta

Born 1304 in Tangier, Morocco
A remarkable traveller who left a vivid account of the Muslim world in the late Middle Ages
Died 1378 aged 74

When he was a boy, Ibn Battuta studied the Koran (Qur'an) very thoroughly. By the age of 21, he was an expert in Muslim theology and law, and he set out on the pilgrimage to Mecca. At first he was homesick. At Tunis, he said, 'There was no salutation for me. I knew no soul there. I burst into a flood of tears.' But he was to go on to travel more than 120,000 km (75,000 miles) over the course of the next 28 years, even further than Marco Polo who lived at about the same time.

He was prevented from crossing the Red Sea when the pilgrims' ships were sunk by pagan tribesmen. Instead he journeyed to Damascus through cities ruined by the crusaders, and joined the pilgrimage there. At Mecca he joined the caravan returning to Persia (now Iran).

He continued to travel in Asia Minor (now Turkey), observing and keeping records, relating tales and wonders.

Curious to see the different length of night and day, he travelled north to Kazan on the River Volga (the same latitude as Moscow). From there he accompanied one of the sultan's wives to Constantinople, to visit her father the emperor. There he was irritated by the din of Christian bells.

He crossed the Hindu Kush mountains and remained eight years in the service of the Sultan of Northern India. He was sent to accompany a returning Chinese embassy, but a storm destroyed the fleet of junks before he embarked. He was left with only his prayer mat and ten pieces of gold. He reached China in 1344, where he approved of paper money but not of eating dog meat. At last he returned home through Damascus and Cairo, both stricken by the Black Death. Later he travelled throughout Spain and crossed the Sahara to Timbuktu before dictating his reminiscences. ■

See also

Explorers
Muslims

Issigonis, Alec

Born 1906 in Smyrna (Izmir), Turkey
Issigonis was an engineer, best known as the designer of the Mini.
Died 1988 aged 82

Issigonis had Turkish parents, but his father was a naturalized British citizen. His mother took him to London after World War I and he went to Battersea Technical College at the age of 15.

In 1936 Issigonis joined Morris Motors. After World War II he set about designing an inexpensive small

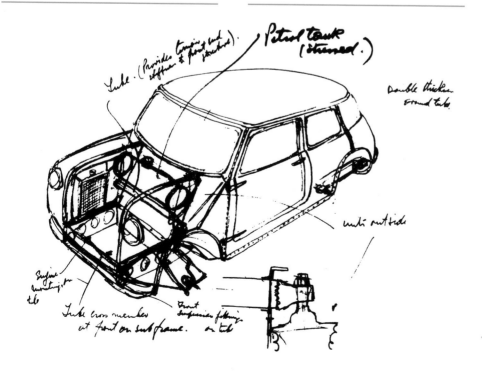

◀ One of Alec Issigonis's first sketch designs of the Mini car. The Mini was a very economical car and it soon became extremely popular. Issigonis reduced the engine space to a minimum to leave more room for the passengers.

car which would have four seats and good performance. The result, in 1948, was the Morris Minor. This became the first British car to sell a million.

After a period with Alvis, in Coventry, Issigonis went to the British Motor Corporation in 1956, and set about designing a new small car. He aimed to make the smallest vehicle which would provide proper accommodation for four adults. His 'Mini' had small wheels, rubber suspension, front-wheel drive and an engine mounted across the car with the gearbox underneath. Launched in 1959, it was a tremendous success. By 1965 sales reached 1 million, and by 1976 2 million. After 30 years, the Mini was still in production and selling strongly. ■

See also

Designers
Motor cars

Biography
Nuffield

Ivan the Terrible

Born 1530 in Moscow, Russia
Emperor of Russia from 1547 to 1584, he unified and greatly strengthened the Russian state.
Died 1584 aged 53

Ivan became Grand Prince of Moscow at the age of 3. At 16 he had himself crowned 'tsar and grand prince of all Russia'. Tsar is Russian for 'Caesar', meaning emperor. Ivan IV possessed useful qualities as a ruler: energy, common sense and understanding of the needs of his backward country. He chose advisers to help him rule and created an assembly (*Zemsky sobor*) as a sort of parliament.

His rule marked a turning point for Russia in foreign affairs. In 1552 he defeated the Mongol-Tartars at Kazan, so ending their 300 years of domination. His kingdom now stretched to the Urals and the Caspian Sea; the eastern road across Siberia to the Pacific was open. Russia also tried to expand westwards towards the Baltic

▲ A woodcut of Ivan the Terrible, who by the age of 22 was undisputed ruler of Russia. Russia expanded into Siberia under his rule and conquered the land along the River Volga. He made Moscow the capital of Russia.

Sea, but even after 20 years of war, Ivan failed to keep the land he had gained. He did, though, make trade links with England after the arrival in Moscow of Richard Chancellor and English sailors in 1553.

Ivan really was 'Terrible': he killed in an orgy of terror not only his enemies but also his friends, and even his own son in 1581. He married no fewer than seven times. After his son's death he knew no peace of mind, his mad howls ringing nightly through the Kremlin. To the relief of many, he died in a sudden fit in 1584. ■

See also

Russia's history

Jackson, Andrew

Born 1767 in Waxhaw, South Carolina, USA
President of the USA from 1829 to 1837
Died 1845 aged 78

Andrew Jackson was born two months after his father died. A slave on his uncle's plantation remembered him as 'the most mischievous of youngsters thereabouts'. Andrew ignored school, and loved fighting and racing horses. As a 14-year-old soldier in the American Revolution, he was captured by the British. When he refused to clean a British officer's boots, the officer slashed his shoulder deeply with a sword. In prison Andrew caught smallpox, and while he was ill, his mother died.

▲ Andrew Jackson, who is shown here during his military career, was the seventh American president and the first one not to be born into a wealthy family.

Jackson lived, and gambled away the money he was left. Then he apprenticed himself to a lawyer in North Carolina, but his wild ways won him few clients. Moving west, he caused a scandal by marrying his landlady's daughter before her divorce was final. But his new family helped him to become a politician, a judge, and a major-general.

In 1812 the US declared war on Britain, because Britain was opposed to the westward expansion of the US and was also trying to limit US trade with Europe. Jackson attacked the Creek Indians, who had joined the British. Nicknamed 'Old Hickory' because of his toughness, he caused 'dreadful carnage' in an Indian battle that won him fame on the western frontier. In 1815 he slaughtered British troops at New Orleans. This made him an American hero.

Elected president in 1828, and again in 1832, Jackson was the first president to represent the western frontier people. These people wanted to farm land that Indians hunted on, to pay low taxes, and to look after themselves. President Jackson tried to move all Indians to the west of the Mississippi River, a policy that caused great suffering to the Indians. However, he was a firm believer in democracy and encouraged the introduction of the vote for all adult males. ■

See also

American Indians
USA: history

Jackson, Jesse

Born 1941 in Greenville, South Carolina, USA
One of the most famous spokesmen for black Americans

Jesse Jackson was illegitimate. His stepfather adopted him in 1957. At school he was clever and a star football player. While he was growing up, black people in the southern states of America could not by law go to school with whites, eat in the same restaurants as whites or use the same facilities as whites. Most black people did not even have the right to vote.

Jackson went to university in North Carolina and then trained to be a Baptist minister in Chicago. He worked with Martin Luther King to change the laws that discriminated against black people. His tremendous energy, and his gift of swaying people's emotions, helped him become a leader of the blacks after King was shot dead.

He taught everyone to say 'I am somebody'. Wanting to do more than change laws, he founded PUSH (People United to Save Humanity) in 1971 to help blacks get better schools and jobs.

Although he had never been elected to office, Jackson won almost enough votes in 1988 to become the Democratic presidential candidate. ■

See also

Afro-Americans
Biography
King, Martin Luther

Jacob

Dates of birth and death not known. He may have lived about 1700 BC in Canaan (Palestine).
A Hebrew; ancestor of the Jews and father of Joseph

Jacob and his brother Esau were the twin sons of Isaac and Rebekah and the grandsons of Abraham and Sarah. According to the Bible he persuaded his elder twin to give up his birthright (rights and possessions as the eldest son) in exchange for a mess of pottage (bowl of food). He then tricked his father into giving him the elder son's blessing. He had to escape from his

▲ The Bible story of Jacob's dream of a ladder stretching between Earth and heaven inspired pictures from many artists. This one is a German-made 17th-century stained glass roundel in Wragby Church, Lincolnshire.

brother's revenge, and for fourteen years worked for his uncle Laban and married Laban's daughters, Leah and Rachel.

Another story about Jacob describes a dream in which he saw a ladder stretching between heaven and Earth. On it were angels and, from above, God told Jacob that He would always be with him and that his descendants would have a special land and history. God later gave Jacob the name of Israel, meaning 'one who struggles with God'. Jacob had twelve sons who became the ancestors of the twelve tribes of the people of Israel. His favourite son was Joseph.

The stories of Jacob are told in the Book of Genesis, chapters 25 to 49, in the Old Testament of the Bible. ∎

See also

Bible
Hebrews
Palestine

Biography
Joseph

James I

Born 1566 in Edinburgh Castle, Scotland
King James VI of Scotland (from 1567) became James I, the first Stuart king of England, in 1603.
Died 1625 aged 58

James I did not have a happy childhood. His father, Lord Darnley, was murdered, and his mother, Mary, Queen of Scots, was executed. James became King of Scotland when he was a baby. He was brought up strictly but none too safely by Scottish nobles. He was even kidnapped twice. But when he grew up, he made a good job of ruling Scotland.

James was a highly intelligent man. He wrote several books, including one against smoking. He loved peace, and did not want to persecute people for their religion. But he was also rather lazy, and extravagant. He was undignified: he walked clumsily, and dribbled a lot. He had favourites, and

gave them too much power, especially after he got to England.

When James became King of England he hoped for an easier life. But in 1605 some Catholics nearly blew him and his Parliament sky high in the Gunpowder Plot. Puritans were disappointed that he did not change the Church of England as they wanted, and later some of them, the Pilgrim Fathers, emigrated to America. But in his reign a fine new English translation of the Bible was made, now called the 'King James Bible', or the 'Authorized Version'.

Like all kings of that time, James believed his power came from God, and he often told Parliament so. This did not stop Parliament criticizing the way he spent his money, and the power he gave to his favourites. There were bitter arguments, but James was sensible enough to avoid real trouble. ∎

See also

Bible
Gunpowder Plot
Pilgrim Fathers
Puritans
Scotland's history
Stuart Britain

Biography
Fawkes
Mary, Queen of Scots

James, Jesse

Born 1847 in Clay County, Missouri, USA
He led a vicious gang of outlaws, who held up stage-coaches and trains and robbed banks.
Died 1882 aged 34

Jesse James's father was a farmer and a Baptist preacher, who died when Jesse was only 3. At the age of 15, Jesse joined a group of southern guerrillas and fought against the Unionists in the American Civil War.

When the war ended in 1865, Jesse and his elder brother Frank formed a gang and turned to crime. During the next ten years the gang carried out a series of daring hold-ups, until in 1876

they tried to rob the bank at Northfield, Minnesota. The robbery went wrong. Most of the gang were killed or captured, but Jesse and Frank escaped and formed another gang. There was now a price on their heads, and in 1882 a gang member called Bob Ford shot Jesse and claimed the reward.

Legend has turned Jesse James into a hero, but many of the stories about him are not based on historical fact. He was really the leader of a ruthless gang who murdered at least ten people. ∎

See also

American Civil War
Guerrillas

Jefferson, Thomas

Born 1743 in Shadwell, Virginia, USA
Wrote the American Declaration of Independence and was President of the USA from 1801 to 1809.
Died 1826 aged 83

When Thomas Jefferson was born, Virginia was still a colony, ruled by Britain. After going to college, Jefferson became a lawyer and in 1769 was elected to the House of Burgesses, a parliament with very little power. Many Virginians felt that Britain should allow the colonists to rule themselves. Jefferson agreed. He wrote that the Parliament in London had no right to make laws for people who had left England. Many people read and discussed his ideas.

Then, during the American Revolution, he wrote the Declaration of Independence, which became the basis of America's constitution. He wrote 'all men are created equal and independent', and therefore they have rights which no one can take away. These rights include 'the preservation of life and liberty, and the pursuit of happiness'. Jefferson always believed it was the job of the government to give people these rights.

In 1801 Jefferson became the third President of the USA. During his

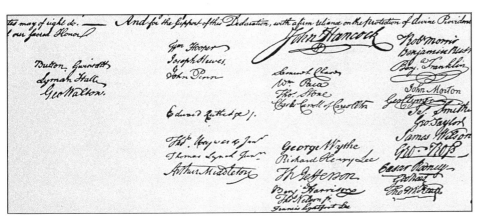

▲ Thomas Jefferson's signature ('T H Jefferson') appears here with many others at the bottom of the Declaration of Independence which he wrote, with only small changes being made by others.

presidency, the size of the USA doubled. In 1803 America bought a vast area of land from France, whose colony it had been. Jefferson sent an expedition, led by Lewis and Clark, to explore this 'Louisiana Purchase'. After a two-year journey from St Louis across the Rocky Mountains to the Pacific and back, Lewis and Clark returned with a wealth of notebooks and specimens of plants and rocks and with valuable information about Indian nations in the West.

But Jefferson was perhaps most proud of his last great achievement, the foundation of the University of Virginia in 1819. ∎

See also

American Constitution
American Revolution
USA: history

Jenner, Edward

Born 1749 in Berkeley, Gloucestershire, England
He discovered vaccination and prevented the spread of smallpox.
Died 1823 aged 73

Edward Jenner was the son of a vicar. Both his parents died when he was only 5 years old. After going to grammar school he was apprenticed to a local surgeon, and then, at the age of 21, he went to study medicine in London. Three years later he returned to his home town of Berkeley and began working as a doctor. He loved the surrounding countryside and wrote poems about birds. He discovered that a cuckoo, newly hatched in another bird's nest, threw the other eggs out of the nest.

At Jenner's time there were regular outbreaks of a deadly disease called smallpox and it claimed tens of thousands of lives in England alone. He heard stories that milkmaids claimed that they could get protection from smallpox if they caught cowpox, a mild disease which affected cows' teats.

In 1796 Jenner extracted the contents of a blistering pustule from the arm of a milkmaid suffering from cowpox and injected it into an eight-year-old boy. The boy became ill with cowpox but soon recovered from this mild infection. Jenner then inoculated him with smallpox. The boy did not become ill; his first injection had made him immune to smallpox.

In 1798 Jenner published the results of his work, and within three years people as far away as America and India were receiving the new protection from smallpox. Jenner's discovery made him rich; he was rewarded by Parliament with sums totalling £30,000, an enormous sum in those days. ∎

See also

Immunity
Vaccinations

Biography
Montagu
Pasteur

Jesus

Born about *4 BC, in Palestine
A Jewish prophet and teacher who became the founder of Christianity
Crucified probably AD 28 or 29 aged about 32 or 33

There are four written lives of Jesus, called the gospels of Matthew, Mark, Luke and John. They are found in the New Testament section of the Bible. The gospels gather together many stories about Jesus. According to these stories, Jesus' mother was Mary but his father was God, instead of Mary's husband, Joseph.

One story tells us that Jesus' birthplace was Bethlehem. The Romans were ruling the lands now called Israel. They told all Jewish people to go to their family towns for a census, in which everyone would be registered. Mary had to go to Bethlehem although she was expecting her baby, and he was born there in a stable because there was no room in the inn. This story is remembered each Christmas, when the birthday of Jesus is celebrated.

There is a story that, at the age of 12, Jesus went missing for three days. Finally Mary and Joseph found him in the city of Jerusalem, in the temple (the major place of worship for Jews). He was talking with the teachers of religion. He said to Mary and Joseph, 'Did you not know that I must be in my Father's house?'

At about the age of 30, Jesus was baptized by John the Baptist, a prophet (someone who feels an inner call to preach to people about God). After this Jesus began to preach and to heal the sick and disabled. Large crowds gathered to be cured and to listen.

Jesus taught them to love God and their neighbours, particularly those in

*At the time when Jesus was born, the Romans dated years from the legendary foundation of Rome. About 500 years after the lifetime of Jesus, Christian scholars worked out a new system, counting from what they thought was the year of his birth. Historians now know that he was born a few years earlier than this, in about 4 BC.
BC stands for Before Christ.
AD stands for *Anno Domini*, 'in the year of Our Lord'.

This painting by Barna da Siena, who lived in the 14th century, shows Jesus crucified on the cross. According to the Gospel of John, the wound in his side was made by a Roman soldier, to check that Jesus was dead. At the foot of the picture, the body of Jesus has been taken down and his friends and followers mourn his death.

crowds, who were talking about a new kingdom. A large crowd even greeted Jesus as a king when he rode into Jerusalem one day on a donkey.

Knowing that he was about to be killed, Jesus made a special occasion of his Last Supper with his followers. He took bread and gave it to them to eat, saying 'This is my body', and gave them wine to drink, saying 'This is my blood'. He told them to go on celebrating this meal in his memory. Today this special meal is called the eucharist, Holy Communion, or the mass, and it is celebrated in church.

Later that night, Jesus was arrested, after Judas, one of the apostles, had shown the Jewish religious authorities where to find him. The next morning he was put on trial before the Roman governor, Pontius Pilate. Those who were accusing him said he claimed to be a king, but Jesus replied that his kingdom was not of this world. Then he was led outside the walls of Jerusalem to be put to death by crucifixion (nailing to a cross).

The third day after Jesus' death news spread that he had risen, and those who believed in him would share in his victory over death. Easter is the day when Jesus' resurrection from the dead is celebrated. Jesus' followers became known as Christians, and soon there were many non-Jewish as well as Jewish Christians, thanks to early preachers like Paul, who travelled widely through the Roman empire.

Muslims also think Jesus was a prophet, but they do not believe, as Christians do, that he was God himself, who had become a human being to save the world from sin and death. ∎

See also

Apostles
Bible
Christians
Christmas
Easter
Parables

Biography
John the Baptist
Paul, Saint
Peter, Saint

need. He explained that God cares more about what goes on in our hearts than about just keeping rules. He called people to be sorry for their sins, in preparation for the 'kingdom' of God. He told them that God is a father who looks after us and forgives us, and he taught them the Lord's Prayer, which begins 'Our Father . . .' He used parables (stories with a deeper, hidden meaning) as a teaching method.

Jesus' followers came to believe that he was the Messiah or Christ (a king

whom the Jewish people were waiting for, to come and save them). Jesus chose twelve from among his followers to carry on his work of preaching. They were called 'apostles', meaning 'those who are sent out'.

The official religious authorities were alarmed by what Jesus was doing, as he criticized them, and spoke with tremendous confidence about God as though he was God's equal. There also seemed a danger to Roman government because Jesus was gathering big

Jiang Jieshi

Born 1887 in Zhejiang, China
A soldier who became ruler of China
from 1928 to 1949, when he was driven
to Taiwan by the communists
Died 1975 aged 87

The parents of Jiang Jieshi (Chiang
Kai-Shek) were wealthy farmers and
merchants, and he was trained as an
army officer. In 1911 he helped in a
rebellion to overthrow the dishonest
and inefficient rulers of the Chinese
empire. China became a republic,
which was soon divided among
warlords who kept power with their
private armies.

Jiang joined the Nationalist Party
(Guomindang) started by Sun Yixian,
who believed in a single government
to modernize China and end poverty.
Jiang was commander of the
Nationalist armies. He used them to
put down the warlords, and became
President of China in 1928. By then
he had turned against Nationalists who
believed in improving life for the
peasants and poor workers. Jiang's
friends were Chinese business men and
foreign merchants. He married Song
Meiling in order to gain the support of
her wealthy family. In 1927 he had
many trade unionists and communists
killed. Mao Zedong became leader of
those who were left. Jiang used his
armies to try to crush the communists
but failed.

When Japan invaded China in 1937,
Jiang relocated the capital city from
the fallen Nanking to Chungking.
Meanwhile both Nationalists and
communists fought the Japanese occu-
piers. In 1945 the communists started
a civil war against Jiang. In 1949 he
had to flee to the island of Taiwan,
which became known as the Republic
of China (or Nationalist China). Jiang
was its president until he died. ■

See also

China's history
Communists
Taiwan

Biography
Mao Zedong
Sun Yixian
Zhou Enlai

Jinnah,
Mohammed Ali

Born 1876 in Karachi, Pakistan
He was the founding father of the state
of Pakistan.
Died 1948 aged 71

When he was a young man,
Mohammed Ali Jinnah went to
London where he trained as a lawyer.
He qualified at the age of 20, and then
returned to India. Later, he became
involved in politics, and joined the
Indian National Congress, an organization which wanted India to become
an independent country, free of
British rule. Jinnah believed that
unity between Hindus and Muslims
was the best way to bring this about.
However, his growing concern that
Congress was interested only in the
Hindu population of India led him to
join the Muslim League which represented Muslim interests.

Under his leadership, the Muslim
League grew in importance, and in
1940 it adopted a resolution for a
new state – Pakistan. In the 1945 election, the Muslim League won nearly
all the seats in the Muslim areas. This
greatly strengthened Jinnah's demand
for Pakistan, which was opposed by
the Hindu leadership. Tragically,
many people, both Muslims and
Hindus, died in the struggle that led to
independence for India and Pakistan
in August 1947. Jinnah became
Governor-General of Pakistan, but he
only lived for another thirteen months.

He is called *Quaid-i-Azam* ('the great
leader') in Pakistan. ■

See also

Indian history
Pakistan

Joan of Arc, Saint

Born 1412 in Domrémy, France
Inspired by God, she led the French
against the English in the Hundred
Years War.
Burnt at the stake 1431 aged 18

Joan was the daughter of a French
peasant who lived in the village of
Domrémy in the north-east of France.
She grew up helping her father and
three brothers with farm work. The
neighbours knew her as a devout and
intelligent child who could read and
write.

As Joan later remembered: 'I was in
my thirteenth year when God sent
voices to guide me. At first I was very
frightened. The voices came towards
the hour of noon, in summer in my
father's garden.' The voices kept
returning and she stopped being afraid.
She recognized them as St Michael, St
Catherine and St Margaret, the patron
saints of France. They spoke about the
sufferings of France at the hands of
the English, who had invaded under
Henry V. The true heir to the French
throne, Charles the Dauphin, was a
refugee and had not yet been crowned
king. The saints told Joan to put on
man's clothes to lead the fight against
the English, and promised to help her.

Joan obeyed; she went to court to
persuade Charles of her mission. Some
courtiers scoffed at this peasant girl,
but Charles believed her. He sent her
with troops to Orléans, the last city in
northern France still resisting the
English. Within a week of her arrival
in May 1429, the siege of Orléans was
over. Within two months, the English
had been defeated in battle and Charles
had been crowned King of France in
Reims cathedral.

Now known as 'the maid of Orléans',
Joan carried on the fight. Her fame
spread before her. At some fortresses
she had only to appear, and the place
would surrender. But after a year she
was captured by the Duke of
Burgundy, an ally of the English. King
Charles of France made no attempt to
rescue Joan. Although she had broken
the English power, he was afraid that
she would go too far.

The English decided to have Joan put
on trial as a witch and a heretic (a

▲ Joan of Arc directing archers and other soldiers beseiging Paris in 1429. The picture was painted in an illuminated manuscript made about 60 years later.

person who disagrees with the teaching of the church). Her accusers insisted that it was the Devil who had inspired her to wear man's clothes and to claim such power for herself. After three months' trial, Joan was found guilty and threatened with death. For a moment, Joan gave in, but then her voices returned to give her strength.

Joan was burnt at the stake in Rouen in May 1431. She died clasping a rough cross of sticks given to her by an English soldier. When her ashes were thrown into the river, her executioner said that her heart had not burnt. Twenty-five years later, the French king proclaimed her innocent, and nearly 500 years after her death the Pope declared her a saint. ■

See also

France's history
Heretics
Hundred Years War
Biography
Henry V

John, King of England

Born 1167 in Oxford, England
As king of England from 1199 to 1216 he lost Normandy and had to accept Magna Carta.
Died 1216 aged 48

John was the youngest son of Henry II and Eleanor of Aquitaine. From an early age he was nicknamed 'Lackland' because, while his older brothers were all given some of Henry's lands to look after, he had nothing. When Richard succeeded Henry as king in 1189, John was still kept out of power. But Richard named John as his heir on his deathbed.

As king of England, John went too far in attacking his enemies, and he did not respect his friends enough. His supporters began to lose trust in him, and let the French king invade Normandy. In the fight to win the land back, John used every means he could to raise money in England. Finally his subjects refused to pay any more because the king was acting illegally. In 1215 they made a great list of their rights called Magna Carta (the Great Charter), and John had to agree to respect it. He died the next year, a humiliated king. ■

See also

Feudal system
Magna Carta
Biography
Henry II
Richard I

John Paul II, Pope

Born 1920 at Wadowice near Kraków, Poland
The first non-Italian Pope (head of the Roman Catholic Church) since 1523

His own name was Karol Wojtyla (pronounced Voy-ti-wa). His father was a soldier, his mother a teacher. When he was only 9 his mother died and four years later an older brother died. 'Lolek' (as he was known) was good at studies and sports, especially football and skiing.

By the time his father died in 1941, Poland had been occupied by Nazi Germany and the Soviet Union. Many Polish people were set to work for the Nazis during World War II. Karol worked in a stone quarry and wrote poems about it. His first ambition was to be an actor, and six of his plays

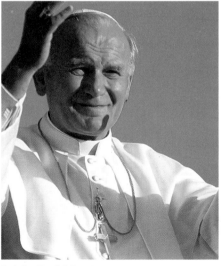

▲ John Paul II has been seen by more people than any other Pope in history, and on TV by countless millions.

were later published. But he thought the Polish people needed priests more urgently, so in 1946 he became a priest and went to study in Rome. When he returned to Poland he became a university teacher as well as parish priest, and in 1964 he was made Archbishop of Kraków and three years later a cardinal.

His election as Pope in 1978 was a complete surprise. The Pope before him, the smiling John Paul I, had died after only 33 days in office. Wojtyla was chosen because he was only 58, which was young by papal standards, and a strong Pope was needed. He is very strict on sexual morality, wants priests to stay out of politics, and is opposed to women priests. He has carried this and the message of the gospels to Roman Catholics all over the world and has made many international journeys. He always kisses the ground on arrival in a country as a sign of love and respect. ■

See also

Poland
Popes
Vatican

Johnson, Amy

Born 1903 in Hull, England
A daring woman pilot who caught everyone's imagination with her exploits
Died 1941 aged 37

As a schoolgirl Amy was good at hockey and at cricket. As a young woman she became interested in flying and she joined the London Aeroplane Club. As well as learning to fly, she wanted to know about engines, and she became the first Englishwoman to be a qualified ground engineer for servicing planes.

While still quite a new pilot, she shocked her friends by planning a flight to Australia. She wanted to beat Jim Mollison's record for the journey. In 1930 she made the journey, with lots of adventures and mishaps on the way. She was the first woman to fly to Australia, but she was disappointed

▲ Amy Johnson became world famous and appeared on the front page of many magazines and newspapers when she completed her flight to Australia in 1930.

that she just failed to beat the existing record. Shortly afterwards she and Mollison were married.

In the early 1930s she made a number of long-distance flights: to Japan, to Capetown, to America. Some of these were made with Jim Mollison, some of them alone. She became very popular, and a song was written about her: 'Amy, wonderful Amy!' Her aircraft plunged into the sea in 1941 in mysterious circumstances. ■

John the Baptist

Born about 4 BC in Palestine
A Jewish prophet who lived at the same time as Jesus
Beheaded about AD 28 aged about 32

According to the Bible, John was the son of a priest, Zacharias, and his wife Elizabeth, who was the cousin of Mary, the mother of Jesus. We do not know anything about his early life. In about AD 27 John began preaching on the banks of the River Jordan. He was living in the wilderness, wearing rough clothing made from camel's hair and eating wild honey and locusts (insects).

He asked people to be sorry for the wrong they had done and to lead a new life. To show that they had repented and that their sins were washed away, John immersed them in the River Jordan. This sign of cleansing is called baptism and gives John his title. When Jesus came to be baptized to show that he approved of John's work, John was at first unwilling and pointed out to the people that Jesus was far greater than he was.

Later, John criticized the Jewish ruler, Herod Antipas, for marrying his brother's wife, Herodias. So she had a grudge against John, who was arrested and put in prison. At a banquet, Herodias persuaded her daughter Salome to dance for the king and his guests and to ask for the head of John the Baptist as her reward. Herod knew that John was a holy man and did not want him killed. But he had promised Salome that she could have whatever she wished. So John was beheaded. The severed head was carried in on a dish and presented to Salome, who gave it to her mother.

The story of John the Baptist is told in the gospel of St Matthew, chapter 3; Luke, chapters 1 and 3; Mark, chapters 1 and 6. ■

See also

Baptism
Prophets

Biography
Jesus

John XXIII, Pope

Born 1881 in Sotto il Monte, near Bergamo, northern Italy
Pope (head of the Roman Catholic Church) from 1958 to 1963
Died 1963 aged 81

Angelo Roncalli came from a farming family that had lived in the same place for over 300 years. He had many brothers and sisters. They were so poor he sometimes had to carry his shoes to school to save the leather. At the age of 12 he went to the seminary (school for priests) in Bergamo and

from there to Rome. In World War I he was a hospital chaplain. After the war the Pope sent him to various countries as his ambassador, including Bulgaria, Turkey and France. In 1953 he became Bishop of Venice, which was not far from his home. He thought it would be his last job.

But he was unexpectedly elected Pope in 1958. He was nearly 77, already an old man. People said he would do nothing of importance. But he came out of his home in the Vatican City in Rome, visited children in hospital and prisoners in jail. He was especially concerned with the need to give more help to the poor and was involved with movements for international peace. He asked the Catholic bishops from all over the world to travel to Rome to meet and help him solve the problems of the Roman Catholic Church and make much-needed changes. More than 2,000 bishops met in Rome between 1962 and 1965 at the Second Vatican Council. But 'good Pope John' died before the council ended. He once said: 'The Church may have enemies, but she is no one's enemy.' By his friendliness with Christians who belonged to the Protestant and Orthodox churches and with Jews he changed the image of the Pope. ■

See also

Popes
Vatican

Joseph

Dates of birth and death not known. He may have lived about 1700 BC.
A Hebrew, born in Canaan (Palestine), who became adviser to the Pharaoh of Egypt

According to the Bible, Joseph was the son of Jacob and Rachel and the youngest but one of Jacob's whole family. There is a story that Jacob gave Joseph a coat of many colours and that Joseph dreamed that he would be a great man. His half-brothers were so jealous that they sold him to merchants travelling to Egypt and told their father that his favourite son was dead.

In Egypt Joseph was sold as a slave. He was sent to prison because he had offended his master's wife. While in prison he told people the meaning of their dreams; and when Pharaoh, the ruler of Egypt, had some dreams that no one could interpret, Joseph was sent for. He said that the dreams foretold a famine. Pharaoh then ordered Joseph to oversee the building of granaries so that, when the famine came, there was plenty of corn stored in Egypt.

Because there was a shortage of grain in Canaan, Joseph's brothers travelled to Egypt to buy corn. After so many years they did not recognize their half-brother. But he knew who they were, and first his younger brother, Benjamin, and then his old father joined him and lived in Egypt.

The stories of Joseph are found in the Book of Genesis, chapters 37 to 50, in the Old Testament of the Bible. There is a chapter named after him in the Koran too. ■

See also

Bible
Hebrews
Palestine

Biography
Jacob
Lloyd Webber

▲ This picture shows a scene from the musical *Joseph and the Amazing Technicolor Dreamcoat* by Tim Rice and Andrew Lloyd Webber, which is based on the Bible story of Joseph's life.

Joule, James

Born 1818 in Salford, England
He did lots of very careful experiments measuring heat.
Died 1889 aged 70

James Prescott Joule's father was a wealthy brewer, and when he retired his son, then in his twenties, helped run the brewery. But Joule always found time for doing experiments. He had not had a proper education, but taught himself whatever he needed to know.

Joule was fascinated by heat, and as a teenager he performed experiments measuring the amount of heat produced by electric motors. On his honeymoon Joule took careful measurements of the temperature of the water at the top and bottom of waterfalls.

He measured the amount of heat produced by every process he could think of. He pumped water through small holes and measured how much heat was produced by the friction of the water's movement. He noticed that work always produces heat. The work could be done by a drill boring a hole in a piece of metal, or it could be done by water pushing a wheel round. He found that a certain amount of work always produced a certain amount of heat.

Joule wrote about something we call 'energy', and explained that energy is never destroyed; it is just changed into different forms. When you jump up and down you use lots of energy; when you stop jumping where has the energy gone? The ground you were jumping on will have got hot, and so will you. Your jumping energy has become heat energy. This is a very important rule in science and became known as the 'law of the conservation of energy'. ∎

See also

Cold
Energy
Heat
Temperature

Jung, Carl

Born 1875 in Basel, Switzerland
A psychologist who helped people understand their dreams, and ultimately themselves
Died 1961 aged 85

Carl Jung was for some time a close friend of Freud. He believed as Freud did that people with mental troubles could be helped by talking about them at length with a doctor. But unlike Freud, Jung did not believe that most mental problems began with the very strong feelings sometimes felt in the family. Instead, he thought we are all born with certain problems which have to do with how we are made.

Some people, for example, will always feel better in company; Jung called these 'extroverts'. Others dislike social life and are happier on their own; in Jung's terms, 'introverts'. In fact, Jung believed it was important for us to feel at home with both types of behaviour, otherwise we can sometimes become rather unbalanced.

Talking to patients, Jung discovered that, at times, their dreams could give them a good idea where they were going wrong in their lives. If someone always dreamt about fierce, wild animals, Jung might suggest this was because they were refusing to face up to their own occasionally angry feelings. Why not, he would go on, try to turn all this energy into something creative like painting, writing or carving, just as many other humans seem to have done in the past?

This interest led Jung to study art and myths from all over the world. The strong similarities he found within them, wherever he looked, proved to him that all human beings are much the same at heart. ∎

See also

Psychologists
Biography
Freud

Kandinsky, Wassily

Born 1866 in Moscow, Russia
The first artist to paint totally abstract paintings
Died 1944 aged 77

At the age of 30 Kandinsky gave up a promising career teaching law and went to art school in Munich. Since childhood he had been fascinated by colour and later on by science and music. Once he became an experienced artist he began to make experimental pictures in which colour was all important.

Kandinsky is famous as the first artist to paint pictures that did not look like something, such as a house, a person or a landscape. He was the first abstract artist. He described how he came into his studio one day in twilight and saw a glowing and beautiful painting of shapes and colours. The next day, in clear daylight, he was disappointed to recognize all the objects in the picture. The reason he had seen it as colour and shape was that it had been turned on its side.

He decided that painting recognizable objects harmed his pictures. In future he would try to make his pictures seem somehow like music: they did not mean anything in particular but they had a deep effect on the viewer. Just as musical sounds affect people deeply, Kandinsky believed colours and forms could also express emotions. These 'colour music' pictures astonished the world. No one had dreamt that a great work of art might not easily be recognizable as something real. These pictures were more to do with what goes on in the mind.

Kandinsky was always strongly influenced by his Russian background, although he wandered Europe, becoming first a German and later a French citizen. He was a courageous man. His thoughts, his teachings; his writings and his artwork caused an artistic revolution. ∎

See also

Paintings (for reproduction of a painting)

Keats, John

Born 1795 in London, England
A wonderful romantic poet
Died 1821 aged 25

John Keats was the son of a stable-manager who died in a riding accident when John was only 8. Six years later his mother died of tuberculosis. John, with his two brothers and sister Fanny, was left in the charge of a guardian. At 16 he started to train as a doctor and later studied medicine at Guy's Hospital, London. But by this time he was determined to be a poet, and in 1817 published his first book of poems.

Not many people read his verses, but a few influential figures spotted Keats's genius and backed him from that moment. His next publication was a long story in verse called *Endymion.* This was severely attacked by critics because they disliked John's new friends, so they made fun of him as a young cockney medical student trying to be a poet. One critic wrote that it would be 'a better and a wiser thing to be a starved apothecary (chemist) than a starved poet, so back to the shop, Mr John'.

While Keats never doubted his own talents, these bad reviews meant that he could never earn enough money from writing alone. Even so he wrote some of his finest poems during this period, including *Ode to a Nightingale, The Eve of St Agnes* and the mysterious *La Belle Dame Sans Merci* with its menacing opening lines:

Oh what can ail thee, knight at arms,
Alone and palely loitering?
The sedge has withered from the lake,
And no birds sing.

In these poems, Keats's genius for the music of words is backed by his strong feelings for what he is describing. But he became seriously ill after a walking tour in Scotland where he tramped 20 miles a day in the cold and wet. His brother Tom had already died of tuberculosis and John probably caught the disease while nursing him. Keats's friends paid for him to go to Rome in Italy for its warmer climate. This meant leaving behind the great love of his life, Fanny Brawne, the girl to whom he was engaged to be married. Keats died in Rome and is buried in the English cemetery there. ■

There was a naughty boy,
And a naughty boy was he,
He ran away to Scotland
The people for to see –
There he found
That the ground
Was as hard,
That a yard
Was as long,
That a song
Was as merry,
That a cherry
Was as red –
That lead
Was as weighty,
That fourscore
Was as eighty,
That a door
Was as wooden
As in England –
So he stood in his shoes
And he wondered,
He stood in his shoes
And he wondered.

▲ Extract from 'A Song about Myself' by John Keats.

Keller, Helen

Born 1880 in Alabama, USA
A writer and scholar who achieved success despite being deaf, blind and virtually mute.
Died 1968 aged 87

Helen Keller had a severe illness when she was a baby, which made her deaf and blind. Young Helen could not make recognizable sounds. Unable to make herself understood, she stopped making any sounds at all and became mute. Her parents were desperate to help her but did not know what to do. Eventually they sought advice from an expert who had been successful in teaching speech to the deaf. His name was Alexander Graham Bell, the inventor of the telephone.

On his advice they employed a teacher, 20-year-old Anne Sullivan. She had herself once been blind and proved to be a brilliant teacher. Patiently, Anne taught Helen the names of objects by pressing letters into her hand. She taught her to speak by letting her feel the vibrations in her own throat. Helen soon showed that she was an intelligent student. With the help of special schools in New York and Boston, she learned to read and write in braille. Anne eventually helped her to obtain a university degree.

If you imagine how difficult it must be to speak without hearing, you will understand why the sounds Helen made were difficult to understand. A translator was needed when she spoke in public. But in spite of the problems, Helen tried to help as many people like herself as she could. Her own amazing success was a great inspiration, and she toured the world giving lectures.

▲ Helen Keller (on the left) is 'reading' the sign language of her interpreter through the palm of her right hand. Deaf-blind people throughout the world communicate in this way.

She wrote many books, including *The Story of My Life*, published in 1902. This was made into a prize-winning play, *The Miracle Worker* by William Gibson, and a film in 1962. ■

See also

Braille

Biography
Bell

▼ Ned Kelly's suit of armour, in which he tried to escape from the police, was put on display after his execution. He must have found it difficult to move with such a weight of iron on him.

Kelly, Ned

Born 1855 in Beveridge, Victoria, Australia
He became Australia's most famous bushranger, an outlaw who ranged the country robbing and killing.
Hanged 1880 aged 25

Ned Kelly's father was transported as a criminal from Belfast to Tasmania and hated the police. Ned soon showed that he had the same attitude, and from the age of 15 was constantly in trouble.

Between 1878 and 1880, Ned operated in a gang known as the Kelly Gang with his brother and two others. They were famous for holding up and killing three policemen in 1878. They became outlaws with a price of up to £2,000 each on their heads.

They then made several daring hold-ups and robberies of banks and police stations. The police seemed powerless against them. Many were outraged by these crimes, but to others, Ned became a hero. He claimed to be fighting for justice for the poor against the rich and powerful.

The gang hid for sixteen months, helped by sympathizers. In 1880 came the final shoot-out with police after an attempted train ambush. Ned tried to escape in a suit of armour, but was shot in the legs. He was tried for murder and hanged in Melbourne gaol. ■

Kennedy, John Fitzgerald

Born 1917 in Brookline, Massachusetts, USA
President of the USA from 1961 until 1963, when he became the fourth US president to be killed in office
Assassinated 1963 aged 46

John Kennedy was one of nine children. He did well at college, but hurt his back playing football. It gave him great pain all his life. During World War II, he commanded a small ship. The Japanese sank it, but Kennedy swam with his men three miles to safety. Then his elder brother Joe was killed in 1944. Kennedy's father, who had made himself rich, had decided Joe would be president one day. Now John took Joe's place.

The whole family helped Kennedy win his first election as a Democrat member of the House of Representatives in 1946. His father spent money and everyone else talked to voters. One opponent said, 'It's that family of his. They're all over the state.' The same thing happened when Kennedy became senator for Massachusetts in 1952.

In 1960 he was elected President of the USA. Handsome and inspiring, in

▲ John Kennedy out on the campaign trail in 1960 when he narrowly defeated his Republican opponent, Richard Nixon, to become President of the USA.

his first speech he said, 'My fellow Americans, ask not what your country can do for you, but what you can do for your country.'

Although he was energetic and intelligent, Kennedy soon faced problems. He gave American help to Cuban refugees trying to invade communist Cuba. They failed, making the US look foolish. Nevertheless, Kennedy did stop the USSR from building nuclear missile bases on Cuba in 1962. He also sent military advisers and troops to Vietnam, which led, after his death, to American involvement in the Vietnam War. At home, he proposed laws to give black Americans their rights, but Congress did not pass these laws in his lifetime.

In November 1963, Kennedy travelled to Dallas, Texas, to gather support in the American South. He was shot and killed by a sniper while travelling in an open car. The world mourned Kennedy not only for what he did, but for the good he could have done had he lived. ■

See also

Cuba
USA: history
Vietnam

Kenyatta, Jomo

Born about 1897 at Ngenda, Kenya
After many years in prison, he became Kenya's first president.
Died 1978 aged about 81

Kamau wa Ngengi was born into the Kikuyu tribe at a village on the Thiririka river in Kenya. He was baptized Johnstone Kamau and educated by Scottish missionaries before getting a job in Nairobi.

Jomo Kenyatta, as he became known, joined the Kikuyu Central Association and visited London on their behalf. He lived in Britain during the 1930s and studied anthropology. He married an English woman, and during World War II worked on a farm.

Back in Kenya, Kenyatta became president of the Kenya African Union in 1947. At this time many Kikuyu formed a secret group called 'Mau Mau' which used violence to drive white farmers from Kikuyu lands. Although he denied it, Kenyatta was suspected by the British rulers of Kenya of leading Mau Mau. In 1953 he was sentenced to seven years' hard labour. Even when he was released from prison in 1959 he was kept under close watch and was not completely free until 1961. Then, when Kenya became independent of Britain in 1963, Kenyatta was the first prime minister.

▲ When Kenya became independent in 1963, Jomo Kenyatta celebrated in front of a statue of himself describing him as 'father of the nation'. In his hand he waves the fly whisk which he often carried.

In the following year he was made President of the Republic of Kenya, and became famous as a spokesman for the newly independent African nations. His fifteen years in power brought stability and prosperity to the people of Kenya. ■

See also

Kenya

Kepler, Johannes

Born 1571 in Weil, Germany
Kepler was one of the great astronomers of his time, and is remembered especially for his three laws of planetary motion.
Died 1630 aged 58

Johannes Kepler was the son of a soldier. He was not a strong child, and an attack of smallpox left him with poor eyesight. His early intention was to be a Lutheran Church minister and he studied theology at university. But it turned out that he had a flair for mathematics, and his interest in astronomy grew.

In 1594 he became a professor of mathematics at Graz, where he settled and married. Four years later, the family was forced to flee because of religious persecution and he went to work as assistant to the Danish astronomer Tycho Brahe. When Brahe died in 1601, Kepler got his job. He also inherited a huge number of astronomical observations, which he eventually got published.

Using Brahe's observations of Mars, Kepler proved that the planet's orbit round the Sun is an oval shape and not a circle. Later he found two more important laws about the orbits of the planets.

Kepler's whole life was afflicted by bad luck, war, religious persecution and ill health. Yet he is remembered as one of the greatest astronomers of his age. ■

See also

Astronomers   **Biography**
Planets   Brahe

◀ **Martin Luther King (front row, centre) leads the march on Washington in 1963.**

King, Martin Luther

Born 1929 in Atlanta, Georgia, USA
He led the black civil rights movement in the USA in the 1950s and 1960s.
Assassinated 1968 aged 39

At the age of 15 Martin Luther King went to college on a special programme for gifted students. He gained his degree in divinity in 1948 and then trained to be a Baptist minister. In 1953 he married Coretta Scott, a fellow student.

He became a pastor in Montgomery, Alabama, two years later. Straight away he joined the struggle for black people's rights. The buses in Montgomery had separate seats for blacks and whites, and black people were supposed to stand to let white people sit. Led by King, the blacks boycotted the buses. They shared cars or walked to work until the bus company gave in and allowed all passengers to sit anywhere.

This victory convinced King that the best way for black people to win their rights was to break laws in a non-violent way. In Atlanta and Birmingham, he led 'sit-ins' by blacks in 'whites only' eating places. In spite of being attacked, arrested and imprisoned, King and his followers kept up their campaign. They gained so much support that in August 1963, 200,000 people joined their march on Washington. It was at the rally after this march that he gave his famous 'I have a dream' speech which inspired millions of people throughout the world to campaign for civil rights. Here is an extract:

'I have a dream that one day this nation will rise up and live out the true meaning of its creed: "We hold these truths to be self-evident; that all men are created equal." I have a dream that one day on the red hills of Georgia the sons of former slaves and the sons of former slave-owners will be able to sit down together at the table of brotherhood. I have a dream that my four little children will one day live in a nation where they will not be judged by the color of their skin but by the content of their character.'

The next year the Civil Rights Bill was made law and King was given the Nobel Peace Prize for his work. However, he then began to be opposed by other black leaders who believed that blacks should fight violence with violence. He also became unpopular with some people, especially the government, because he opposed the war in Vietnam.

Then in 1968 he visited Memphis, Tennessee and was killed by a sniper. Only the night before his death, King told his audience: 'I may not get to the promised land with you, but I want you to know tonight that we as a people will.' ■

See also

Afro-Americans
Civil rights
USA: history

Biography
Jackson, Jesse

King, William Lyon Mackenzie

Born 1874 in Kitchener (then called Berlin), Ontario, Canada
He held the office of prime minister of Canada for 21 years, longer than anyone else.
Died 1950 aged 75

Mackenzie King was named after his grandfather, William Lyon Mackenzie. His mother told him a great deal about his grandfather, who had been the first mayor of Toronto and had led a rebellion in Upper Canada in 1837 demanding a better deal for the hard-working pioneer farmers. Mackenzie King grew up wanting to help ordinary people too.

He began his career in politics in 1900, and as minister of labour for the Liberal Party drafted a law to help people settle strikes. He became leader of the Liberal Party in 1919 and was elected prime minister in 1921. King's government introduced the first old-age pension in Canada and developed a Canadian foreign policy independent of Great Britain.

In 1929 there was a major economic crisis in the world. King did not manage to protect people from the problems that it caused, and he lost an election to the Conservatives in 1930. He returned to power in 1935 and led his nation through the war years 1939–1945. After the war he provided free training for returning soldiers. He introduced family allowances and unemployment insurance to protect people from hardship. ■

See also
Canada's history

Kingsley, Charles

Born 1819 in Holne, England
English priest and writer, best known for his children's book, *The Water-Babies*
Died 1875 aged 55

As a boy Charles was very shy. He had a bad stammer which stayed with him all his life. When he was 12, he was accidentally present when a crowd of angry and poor people set fire to buildings in Bristol because they felt it was unjust that they had no say in the government of the country. That made a deep impression on him, and he resolved to make the world a fairer place.

He wrote two novels and many pamphlets about the terrible conditions in which working people lived. His most famous book is *The Water-Babies*, published in 1863. The story describes the short life of Tom, a chimney sweep. The people who read it were shocked at the terrible hardships that children like Tom suffered. The books that Charles wrote and the speeches that he made in public helped to persuade people to improve living and working conditions for poor children. ■

See also
Victorian Britain

Kingsley, Mary Henrietta

Born 1862 in London, England
One of the most famous explorers and travellers in Africa in the 19th century
Died 1900 aged 37

Mary Kingsley was the niece of Charles Kingsley who wrote *The Water-Babies*. Her father was a doctor who spent most of his time travelling abroad. Her mother, who had been his servant, was constantly ill. Throughout her childhood Mary looked after her mother and her little brother and ran their household on very little money. She was never given any schooling, but she learned to read and taught herself Latin, physics, chemistry, mathematics and engineering from her father's library. From his letters and books she learnt that there were bright, warm countries beyond the sea with strange plants and animals.

She grew up tall, fair-haired and very shy. She spoke with her mother's cockney accent, had a lively sense of humour and an impressive vocabulary of swear words. When she was 30 her parents died. She was poor and alone, but she never let anything frighten her. Now she was determined to visit the places she had read about.

During 1893 and 1894 she travelled in West Africa to collect specimens of fish for the Natural History Museum in London, and information about African religions. She explored the forests north of the River Zaïre (Congo) on foot and by paddling expertly in a dug-out canoe. She had come to observe and learn and became very interested in the customs and culture of the African people she met.

When she returned to England she wrote two successful books and became popular as a lecturer. In 1900 she went to South Africa to nurse the soldiers in the Boer War. She died there of fever. ■

See also
Boer War

Biography
Kingsley, Charles

BULDEO LAY STILL, EXPECTING EVEF

Kipling, Rudyard

Born 1865 in Bombay, India
A famous writer for adults and children
Died 1936 aged 70

When Rudyard Kipling was only 6, he was sent by his British parents from their home in India back to England. There he spent five miserable years staying with a foster-mother he hated. But things looked up when he went to boarding school, where he was quickly noticed as a budding young writer.

At 16 he returned to India and began writing short stories and poems describing the lives of the British and Indian people. In 1894 he wrote *The Jungle Book,* which includes stories about an Indian child, Mowgli, brought up by wolves. These stories made such an impact that junior Boy Scouts were called 'Wolf Cubs' from then on.

Kipling next wrote *The Just So Stories*: a series of fables describing how the leopard got his spots, the camel his hump and others. His finest novel, *Kim,* appeared in 1901. Kim is an orphan boy who survives various exciting adventures in India through his mastery of disguise. Kipling was the first English writer to win the Nobel prize for literature. ■

MOWGLI TURN INTO A TIGER, TOO.

▲ This illustration from *The Jungle Book* shows Mowgli beside the dead body of the tiger Shere Khan, while Akela the wolf pins Buldeo, the village head-man, to the ground.

Knox, John

Born 1505 in Haddington, Scotland
Religious reformer who set up the Protestant Kirk of Scotland
Died 1572 aged 67

John Knox became a strong Protestant as a young man, when Scotland was still a Catholic country, ruled with French help. During a Protestant rebellion in 1547, Knox was captured by the French, and spent two terrible years as a prisoner in a huge rowing boat called a galley.

He went to England, and became a chaplain to Edward VI, but when Catholic Mary I came to the throne he and many other Protestants had to escape. He spent most of his exile in Geneva, where he was much influenced by John Calvin. He called Geneva 'the most perfect school of Christ'.

In 1559 he returned to Scotland, determined to set up a Protestant Kirk (Church) like Calvin's at Geneva. His preaching helped to begin a rebellion, which forced out the Catholics. He drew up the 'Scottish Confession', a statement of Protestant beliefs. No one was supposed to go to Catholic services, nor obey the Pope.

Although the Catholic Mary Queen of Scots arrived in Scotland in 1561, the Protestant Kirk grew stronger, and Knox wrote a Protestant prayer book called the Book of Common Order. He wrote a history of the Reformation in Scotland, and several pamphlets disapproving violently of women rulers, especially Catholic ones. He made things very difficult for Mary Queen of Scots, who lost her throne in 1567, partly because of him.

▲ This portrait of John Knox was first published in 1602. The H in the top right hand corner is the signature of the artist who 'made it'.

Knox was a hard and determined man, and he faced danger and hardship fearlessly. His fiery preaching and writing played an important part in the Reformation in Scotland. Protestants there who followed him were afterwards called Presbyterians. ■

◕ **See also**

Catholics
Protestants
Reformation
Scotland's history

Biography
Calvin
Mary, Queen of Scots

Kongzi (Confucius)

Born about 551 BC in north China
Kongzi was a travelling teacher of young noblemen in ancient China. His ideas and writings have been valued by Chinese ever since.
Died 479 BC aged about 70

Kongzi was the son of a poor nobleman in Lu, which was one of the states in China at that time. At the age of 15 he began work as an official in charge of public grain stores and pastures. When his mother died he followed the custom and returned to mourn for three years at home. There he gave up all pleasures and studied the ancient history and literature of the people of China. Afterwards he spent his life, apart from six years when he was a senior official, as a travelling teacher of young noblemen and officials.

Kongzi's teaching was about what made an orderly society with contented people. He showed why the ancient books stressed the importance of polite behaviour and ceremonies. Noblemen and court officials should not plot to gain more power, but study music, poetry and the history of their

▲ This painting of Kongzi, by the artist Kano Tan'yu, dates from the 17th century AD, more than two thousand years after Kongzi died.

ancestors. Ceremonies were a way of showing respect to ancestors, just as people should bow to their living rulers or to older people as a sign of obedience. In the last years of Kongzi's life, many of his sayings were written down in a collection called the *Analects*. The best known is the golden rule: 'Do not do to others what you would not have them do to you.'

The *Analects* and other collections of Kongzi's ideas have always been respected by the Chinese. Until the 20th century all students training to be officials had to study them. ∎

See also

China's history
Confucians

Kruger, Paul

Born 1825 near Middelburg, now in Cape Province, South Africa
President of the first South African Republic and leader of the Boers in the Boer War
Died 1904 aged 78

Paul Kruger's parents were Boer farmers in southern Africa. The Boers were the descendants of Dutch settlers who did not like the power that the British had in southern Africa, so in 1835 when Paul was 10 years old his parents, along with many other Boers, decided to travel north in order to form their own independent country. They eventually settled across the Vaal River in territory they called Transvaal. There Paul made a name for himself as a bold hunter. He also joined in the frequent battles against the black African nations surrounding his new country.

In 1877 Britain decided that Transvaal should also come under its rule. Paul, by this time a respected politician, led the opposition to this. First he visited Britain to plead the cause of Transvaal. Later he became general in a rebel army against British troops in Transvaal. In 1883, having at last won some sort of independence, Paul was elected first president of the new South

African Republic he had helped to form in Transvaal.

But more trouble was to come. When gold was discovered, prospectors from all over the world rushed out to South Africa to try their luck. Those who decided to stay on were not popular with the Boers, who preferred their own people. Paul himself did his best to exclude these newcomers from Transvaal, banning them from full citizenship until they had been in the country for at least seven years. The British government objected to this, and the Boer War followed.

Paul was eventually driven out of his country to Switzerland, where he died. But by uniting the Boers under his leadership he made sure that one day South Africa would become an independent nation. ∎

See also

Boer War
South Africa

Kublai Khan

Born 1215 somewhere in central Asia or northern China
Mongolian general and ruler who founded the Yuan (Mongol) dynasty in China
Died 1294 aged 79

Kublai Khan was the grandson of Genghis Khan, one of the most terrifying soldiers in history, who had begun life as an obscure chief of a wandering tribe and ended it as ruler of a huge empire in central Asia. When Kublai was 10 years old, he fought on horseback in his grandfather's last campaign.

When Kublai grew up he conquered all of China and established his capital at Khanbalik (now Beijing). He added Korea and Burma to his empire, which stretched from the Black Sea to the China Sea. Like his grandfather, he was greedy and very cruel, and neither he nor his descendants left behind any lasting contribution to civilization. But he invited Marco Polo, a Venetian explorer, to work for him, and it is

thanks to Marco's praise of the wonderful civilization that he found in China that the name of Kublai Khan became known in Europe. ∎

See also

China's history
Biography
Genghis Khan
Polo

▲ Wearing a luxurious black and white full cape, Kublai Khan leads his Mongol followers through the desert. This painting was made on silk in the 14th century.

Laurier, Sir Wilfrid

Born 1841 in St-Lin, Québec, Canada
Canada's first French-speaking prime minister
Died 1919 aged 77

Wilfrid's mother died when he was only 7, and three years later his father sent him to live in a nearby town. He stayed with a Scottish family so that he could learn English. At the age of 13 he entered a very strict school run by French-speaking Catholic priests. Later he studied law in Montréal and became a lawyer.

He began his career in politics in the provincial government of Québec in 1871, but in 1874 he was elected to the national government in Ottawa and remained a politician for the remaining 45 years of his life. He became leader of the Liberal Party in 1887 and in 1896 was elected prime minister.

The most successful period of his career came after 1900. His government offered free land to immigrants willing to start wheat farms in the west. Other immigrants came to work in factories, supplying the needs of the farmers. Between 1901 and 1911 Canada's population increased by 2 million. Two new provinces, Saskatchewan and Alberta, were created. However, Laurier disappointed some people by not providing for those in the west who wanted a Catholic education for their children. They had hoped he would support them, as he had a Catholic background.

In 1910 he lost French-Canadian support when he set up the Royal Canadian Navy and promised to help Great Britain in any European war. In 1911 English Canadians criticized his new plan to increase trade with the United States of America. He lost the election and spent the remaining years of his life in the opposition. ■

See also

Canada's history

Lavoisier, Antoine Laurent

Born 1743 in Paris, France
The 'father of modern chemistry'
Executed 1794 aged 50, by the guillotine

In Lavoisier's day chemists had discovered quite a lot about the way chemical substances change when heated and when mixed together, but they had an odd assortment of strange ideas about what was really happening. Lavoisier changed all that.

As a young man Lavoisier became interested in improving street lighting and studied how different fuels burnt in lamps. Burning became a subject that interested him for the rest of his life. His careful experiments of burning substances in air, and those of the English chemist Joseph Priestley, made Lavoisier realize that air contains two gases; he called one 'oxygen' and the other 'azote', which we now know as nitrogen.

He proved that when a substance is burnt it combines with oxygen in the air. This really moved chemistry into the modern age, because it explained for the first time what really happens during the important chemical process of burning.

▲ Apparatus used by Lavoisier to investigate burning. There is a furnace on the left. The material to be burnt was placed inside the curved flask. By looking at the water level in the bell jar, Lavoisier could work out how much of the air had been used up during burning.

Lavoisier went on to tidy up chemistry. He gave chemicals many of the names we now use and arranged them into family groups.

Lavoisier came from a wealthy family and was never short of money to do his experiments. He increased his wealth by investing half a million francs in a business called tax-farming. The tax-farmers were paid by the government to collect all the taxes. Their profits provided Lavoisier, and other investors, with a great deal of money each year. But many of the people were very poor and hated the tax-farmers. During the French Revolution they rebelled, and by 1794 France was ruled by a violent group who hated the king, the aristocracy and tax-farmers. Lavoisier was found guilty of being a tax-farmer and his head was chopped off by the guillotine. ■

See also

Air
Chemists
France's history
Oxygen

Biography
Priestley

Lawrence, D. H.

Born 1885 in Eastwood, Nottinghamshire, England
A powerful novelist who always tried to be absolutely true to his basic feelings
Died 1930 aged 44

David Herbert Lawrence was the son of a coal-miner and a schoolteacher. A clever child, he later went to Nottingham University and trained as a teacher. By this time he had started writing, and in 1913 produced his greatest novel, *Sons and Lovers*. This describes his childhood and the various strong relationships he had both with his mother and with friends outside the home. The hero of the story, Paul Morel, is constantly torn by his desire both to love and be loved while also remaining free to go his own way.

In other novels, such as *The Rainbow*, he got deeper into his characters' secret feelings than any previous novelist.

Later on Lawrence felt that British industrial society was too cut off from nature and genuine feelings for his own particular needs. With his wife, Frieda, he roamed first through Europe, then to Australia, America and Mexico in the search for the ideal surroundings for his restless spirit. His already poor health gradually got worse, and he finally died in the south of France of tuberculosis. ■

Lawrence, T. E.

Born 1888 at Tremadog, Wales
Known as Lawrence of Arabia and famous for his book *The Seven Pillars of Wisdom*, which describes his experiences in the Arabs' struggle for independence
Died 1935 aged 46

Thomas Edward Lawrence was the son of an Irish landowner, Sir Thomas Chapman, and the family governess, Sara Maden. As a young man he enjoyed exploring castles, and following the routes of the crusaders in Palestine which was then part of the Ottoman empire. He learnt Arabic and travelled around North Africa, wearing Arab clothes and eating Arab food.

In 1914, at the beginning of World War I, he was sent to Cairo as a British intelligence officer and was attached to the Arab leader, Feisal (later King of Iraq), to help in leading Arab troops to free their country from the rule of the Turkish Ottoman empire. Lawrence himself led dashing surprise raids on camel back, dynamiting railway lines and forcing the Turks to keep back troops which were urgently needed elsewhere. The Turks offered a high price to anyone who could capture 'al-

▲ **T. E. Lawrence felt comfortable wearing Arab clothes in the hot climate of North Africa and the Middle East. He became skilled at riding on camels and directing military operations from camel back.**

Urans, destroyer of engines'. In 1917 he was captured and tortured. Eventually the Turks were defeated, and Lawrence became a legendary and romantic hero. But he refused all honours and retired to write *The Seven Pillars of Wisdom*.

Lawrence was bitterly disappointed when Britain and France did not give the Arabs their complete independence.

He felt that his friends had been betrayed. In 1923 he enlisted as a private under the name of Shaw, in the British army. In 1925 he joined the air force and served in it as a mechanic. One day he swerved on his motor bike to avoid two boys riding abreast on a country road, and was killed. A brilliant writer and an extraordinary person, his character continues to puzzle and fascinate people. ■

◉ **See also**

Arabs
Ottoman empire
Palestine
World War I

Leakey family

Famous for their finds of fossil humans in East Africa
Louis Born 1903 in Kabete, near Nairobi, Kenya
Died 1972 aged 69
Mary Born 1913 in England
Richard Born 1944 in Kenya

Louis Leakey had a great love for everything African. A chief of the Kikuyu tribe called him 'the black man with the white face'. Leakey is best remembered for his archaeological work in East Africa. He made his first discoveries between 1925 and 1936, when he married Mary Nicol. In 1945 he was made the curator of the Coryndon Museum in Nairobi, one of the most important museums in Africa.

He and Mary concentrated their explorations for fossils in the Olduvai Gorge in Tanzania. There, in 1959, Mary discovered a skull which belonged to a large 'southern ape', *Zinjanthropus* (later called *Australopithecus*) *boisei,* which dated back about 1·7 million years. They also discovered the remains of *Homo habilis*, at that time the earliest human known, and *Homo erectus*, the maker of many beautiful implements found throughout Africa.

The Leakeys' care of African things extended to wildlife, and their home and garden often contained animals that had been brought to them. They also loved dogs, and Louis was president of the Kenya Kennel Club. His Dalmatian dogs always went with them on expeditions into the bush.

Louis Leakey was explosively enthusiastic about his work and encouraged many young students to begin research. Perhaps the most famous of these is Jane Goodall, whose work on chimpanzees has enabled us to understand both apes and humans better.

Mary Leakey continued to excavate at Olduvai Gorge, uncovering living places and implements of the earliest inhabitants of East Africa, after Louis's death and until 1984.

If all of the excavations that she did, examining and recording every pebble and bone, could be joined together, they would make a trench 4 m wide, 4 m deep and 1 km long (or 10 ft by 10 ft by 1 mile).

Mary also worked in other areas. Some of her most important finds have been at Laetoli, in Tanzania. Here she discovered the footprints of our ape-like ancestors who lived more than 3½ million years ago. These prove that they walked upright, as we do, long before they looked much like us.

Richard Leakey did not at first wish to follow the same career as his parents, but before Louis died, Richard had made important discoveries of human fossils in the Lake Turkana area in Kenya. He has since made others at many places in East Africa and Ethiopia, including the discovery of an almost complete *Homo erectus* skeleton in 1984 at Lake Turkana. Like his father, he became the curator of the Coryndon Museum, but has now returned to his first love, which is wildlife, and is in charge of Kenya's game parks. ■

See also

Archaeologists
Evolution of people
Biography
Goodall

▼ Mary Leakey beside the ancient footprints she found in Tanzania in 1978. The footprints had been preserved by volcanic ash.

Lear, Edward

Born 1812 in Highgate, London, England
A poet famous as the popularizer of limerick verse
Died 1888 aged 75

Edward was the 20th child of a wealthy stockbroker and his wife. From the age of 7 he suffered from epilepsy. He was unhappy and felt a failure for much of his life. When he was 13 his father lost all his money, his house and his possessions and was taken to a debtor's prison. The children had to find work. When he was 19 Edward got work making drawings of birds and produced a book of drawings of the parrots at the London Zoo. The Earl of Derby then invited him to his estate to draw his animals too. While he was there, Edward made up limericks and illustrated them for the earl's grandchildren. He published them in the *Book of Nonsense* in 1846, and they were an immediate success.

He spent most of his life travelling abroad, painting, and writing 'nonsense' verse in which nutcrackers, chairs, birds, and creatures like the Dong with the Luminous Nose, the Pobble and the Jumblies were given human feelings and character. Lear invented words such as the 'runcible' spoon and the 'scroobious' bird, and his lines often have a great beauty of sound. His way of describing his deepest feelings was to make fun of them; many of his funny poems have an echo of sadness. His cat Foss, who lived with him for nearly seventeen years, is famous because he appears in so many of Lear's drawings and letters. ■

See also

Poems and poetry

There was an Old Man with a nose,
Who said, " If you choose to suppose
That my nose is too long,
You are certainly wrong ! "
That remarkable man with a nose.

▲ Edward Lear not only wrote nonsense rhymes but also illustrated them with nonsense pictures, like this one for his limerick about an 'Old Man with a nose'.

Le Corbusier

Born 1887 in La Chaux-de-Fonds, Switzerland
An important architect and town planner
Died 1965 aged 77

Le Corbusier was the name later adopted by Charles-Édouard Jeanneret, who was born in a small town in the Jura mountains. He left school at 13 to learn the family job of enamelling and engraving watches, but was soon more interested in architecture, painting and writing. He became famous for his campaign for entirely new ways of building. Houses should be on columns, so freeing the ground underneath, and should have flat roofs with terraces and gardens. Individual flats should make the most of limited space by mixing large, open-plan, sometimes split-level rooms, with much smaller rooms simply for sleeping. Furniture must be slim and modern, and windows long and horizontal, so letting in as much light as possible. These new living quarters should be in planned new developments with gardens at the foot of each cluster of high buildings.

In this way, Le Corbusier believed that modern towns could house big populations while also offering decent living conditions to all. In 1925 he had the chance to put his ideas into practice when he designed a workers' city of 40 houses in France. But local people were suspicious of his colourful, modern designs, and he had more success planning individual houses, many of which quickly became famous. In 1947 he was given another opportunity to design a large housing complex in Marseille for 1,800 people. The plan for this *Unité d'Habitation* included two 'streets' running through the buildings so that all shopping could be done indoors, a school, a hotel and, on the roof, a nursery, open-air theatre and gymnasium. After this Le Corbusier was invited to plan an entire new city at Chandigarh as the capital of one of the states of India. This was also a triumph for fresh modern ideas in planning, although some still preferred more traditional ideas in building – an argument that continues to this day. ■

See also

Architects (photograph of *L'Unité d'Habitation*)
Churches (photograph of chapel at Ronchamp)

Lee, Robert E.

Born 1807 in Stratford, Virginia, USA
He commanded the Confederate troops of the southern states during the American Civil War.
Died 1870 aged 63

Robert grew up to love the state where he was born. Later he did extremely well at the US Military Academy at West Point, before becoming an army officer. In the US war with Mexico (1846–1848), his bravery made him famous.

Many years later, when the Civil War broke out, Lee decided to return to Virginia to 'share the miseries of my people'. So in April 1861, he resigned from the US army. He trained the Confederate army of the South and won major victories. But the South could not provide the guns, or even the food, his men needed.

At the battle of Gettysburg in 1863 his forces were outnumbered and defeated. For the next year and a half he was forced back on the defensive until his ragged and hungry army had to surrender at Appomattox Courthouse.

He spent the last five years of his life as president of Washington College, Virginia, and did what he could to heal the split between North and South. ■

See also

American Civil War

Leeuwenhoek, Anton van

Born 1632 in Delft, The Netherlands
He was the first to realize just how useful the microscope could be in science.
Died 1723 aged 90

Anton was apprenticed to a linen draper in Amsterdam. When he was 22 he went home to Delft, opened his own shop and stayed there for 70 years.

He was always interested in scientific things and made a simple microscope with just one lens. Many people claimed to have invented the microscope up to 50 years before Leeuwenhoek was even born, but they treated it more like a toy than a useful scientific instrument. Leeuwenhoek's microscope was made of brass and the things to be studied were held on the point of a needle. The lens was only half a millimetre across, but what amazing things it revealed! He studied bees and lice, and when he was about

40 he wrote a description of the sting, mouth and eye of a bee.

Other scientists were so impressed that he quickly became famous. Many scientists from other parts of Europe visited him to see the fascinating world revealed by his microscope. They, in turn, started to use microscopes in their own work. Nowadays nearly all scientists use microscopes of one sort or another. ■

See also

Microscopes

Biography
Hooke

Lenin, Vladimir Ilich Ulyanov

Born 1870 in Simbirsk (now Ulyanovsk), Russia
He led the Communist Revolution in Russia in 1917, and ruled the new USSR until his death
Died 1924 aged 53

Vladimir Ulyanov was the son of the director of schools in the Simbirsk region of Russia. He himself seemed set for a successful career at school and university, but when he was 17 his beloved elder brother, Alexander, was hanged for trying to kill the Russian tsar. This opened Vladimir's eyes to the problems of his country: a weak tsar, a corrupt Church and nobility, and millions of poor and angry peasants and factory workers. Some people saw revolution and the communist ideas of Karl Marx as the only solution. Vladimir soon became one of them.

Within a few months of going to Kazan University in 1887 to study law, he was expelled for taking part in a student protest meeting. After getting his degree in 1891, he continued his political activity, and was sent first to prison in the Peter and Paul fortress in St Petersburg (renamed Leningrad), and then into exile in Siberia. While he was in Siberia he married Nadezhda Krupskaya, who later became a well-

▲ After the 1917 Revolution posters and statues of Lenin were put up all over the Soviet Union. This poster shows him at the wheel of a ship, steering a steadfast course for his people.

known teacher and education expert. It was in Siberia that he took the name 'Lenin', from the River Lena.

While Lenin was in Siberia, the Russian Social-Democratic Workers' Party was formed in 1898. Lenin did not think all its members were true to Marx's ideas, so he helped to split the party in 1903, leading the *Bolsheviks* ('Majority') against the *Mensheviks* ('Minority'). The Bolsheviks later became the Russian Communist Party.

From 1905 until 1917, Lenin lived in exile. His chance to return to Russia came when the tsar was overthrown and a new government (headed by the son of Lenin's headmaster from Simbirsk) came to power. On his return, Lenin called for a revolution to put a Bolshevik government into power. This he led in October (by the

new calendar, 7 November) 1917. As chairman of the Council of People's Commissars, Lenin became the real ruler of Russia. He made peace with Germany and resisted the opponents of the Bolsheviks in the civil war. It was during Lenin's rule that the old Russian empire was transformed into the Union of Soviet Socialist Republics. He died of a stroke seven years after the Revolution. The USSR, also known as the Soviet Union, lasted from 1922 until 1991.

On the hundredth anniversary of his birth, a third of the people of the world were living in countries run by communist governments inspired by Lenin's first successful communist revolution. ■

See also

Communists
Russia's history
USSR 1922–1991

Biography
Marx
Stalin

Leonardo da Vinci

Born 1452 near Vinci, in Tuscany, Italy
An artist, scientist and inventor at the
time of the Renaissance
Died 1519 aged 67

The young man Leonardo was described as handsome, strong and charming, a talented musician and excellent conversationalist. At 15 he was apprenticed to a leading Italian artist who taught him painting, sculpture, metal casting, mosaics, jewellery and costume design. Leonardo was a master painter at 20 and considered himself as much an engineer as an artist.

He began many grand paintings but actually finished very few. Although his artistic output was small he brilliantly solved the problem of how to make faces and people look three-dimensional on a flat surface by cleverly shading light into dark. His picture of the Mona Lisa is probably the most famous portrait in the world. His other masterpiece, a wall painting of the Last Supper, is unfortunately in extremely poor condition.

Leonardo had enormous curiosity. He restlessly roamed from one interest to another, tackling one problem and then moving on to the next. He was one of

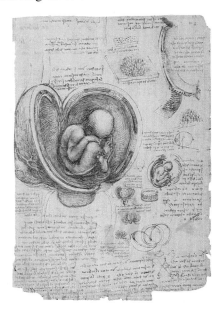

▲ Leonardo produced very detailed anatomical studies but this drawing shows how he imagined the baby in the womb.

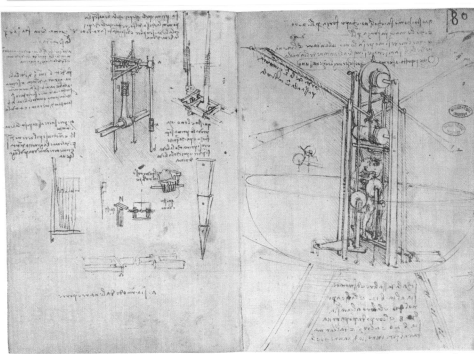

▲ Leonardo's scientific ideas were more advanced than those of his contemporaries. This is a design for a flying machine, made years before the first powered aircraft flew. Leonardo made his notes in mirror writing.

the first to dissect human bodies and understand how muscles and bones really work, and how the baby grows in the womb.

He examined all of nature; how plants and trees grow, how rocks are formed and what laws govern the wind and oceans. He even suggested that the Sun stood still, and did not move round the world as most people believed. He planned buildings, he worked out how to divert a river and how to construct canals. He invented weapons and acted as military adviser to the Duke of Milan. His skills also included arranging festivals and grand theatricals and inventing amusing mechanical toys. He wanted to understand and know about everything he saw. He was an astonishing man.

Although Leonardo was both greatly admired and highly respected he was not really understood. His scientific work was far ahead of that of his contemporaries, and most of his ideas remained in his notebooks and were not developed. He designed a flying machine nearly 400 years before the first powered aircraft flew. It is amazing to us that one man could have

discovered so much. He was a genius, and not only a famous artist but also a scientist, an engineer, botanist and musician. ■

See also

Portraits
Renaissance

Lewis, C. S.

Born 1898 in Belfast, Northern Ireland
A very popular children's writer
Died 1963 aged 64

After a lonely childhood, partly spent playing imaginative games with his older brother Warren, Clive Staples Lewis became an outstanding scholar who taught at both Oxford and Cambridge universities. He wrote learned books and science fiction for adults and then decided to write for children too, mainly because he felt there were not enough children's books of the type he liked.

The Lion, the Witch and the Wardrobe was the first of a series of seven stories which describe the activities of a family of children who stray into the fairyland world of Narnia. In each story they are faced by a choice between good and evil. The adventures that follow are so exciting that many young readers miss the fact that Lewis is using the stories as an allegory to preach a Christian message. His great hero, Aslan the lion, is a symbol for Jesus Christ. ■

See also

Allegories

▲ Illustration for the cover of a paperback edition of the first book in the *Chronicles of Narnia* series.

Lincoln, Abraham

Born 1809 at Nolin Creek, Kentucky, USA
President of the United States during the American Civil War
Assassinated 1865 aged 56

Born in a log cabin, Lincoln spent his childhood doing all the hard and lonely jobs of a frontier farm boy. He could hardly ever go to school, but loved reading. A relative said, 'I never seen Abe after he was twelve 'at he didn't have a book in his hand or in his pocket.' Books were scarce and expensive then; Lincoln read the Bible and *Aesop's Fables* over and over again.

Lincoln's family, always poor, moved several times. In Illinois, Lincoln tried various jobs, then taught himself to be a lawyer. He wanted to be a politician. But he always spoke and voted as he

▲ The statue of Abraham Lincoln at the Lincoln Memorial in Washington, DC is 5·8 m (19 ft) tall. It stands as a permanent reminder to the American people of one of their greatest presidents.

thought right, so he did not always win elections.

Lincoln worried about the split between Americans who thought slavery was wrong, and those who thought it was right. In an election speech in 1858, he said 'I believe this government cannot endure permanently half *slave* and half *free*.' Two years later he was elected president.

After the Civil War began in 1861, Lincoln was criticized because the North did not win quickly. But he kept trying. He wrote the Emancipation Proclamation, freeing all US slaves on 1 January 1863. (Southerners, of course, did not free their slaves until they had lost the war.)

Few people noticed Lincoln's speech later in 1863 when he dedicated a soldiers' cemetery after the terrible battle of Gettysburg. But later, Americans realized Lincoln had summed up the spirit of democracy. He said the soldiers had died so 'that government of the people, by the people, for the people, shall not perish from the earth'.

Lincoln had plans for healing the wounds caused by the war, but he was killed before he could carry them out. He was shot dead at the theatre by John Wilkes Booth, a fanatical supporter of the southern states in the Civil War. ■

See also

American Civil War

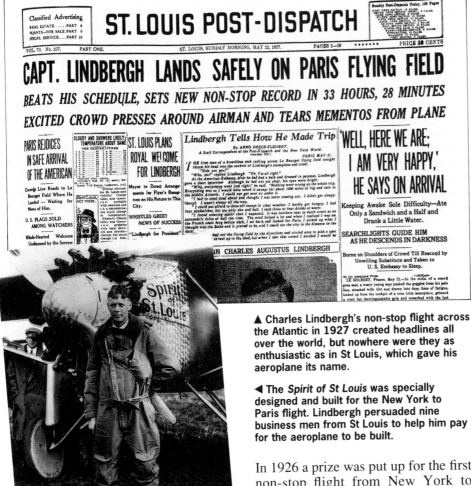

▲ Charles Lindbergh's non-stop flight across the Atlantic in 1927 created headlines all over the world, but nowhere were they as enthusiastic as in St Louis, which gave his aeroplane its name.

◄ The *Spirit of St Louis* was specially designed and built for the New York to Paris flight. Lindbergh persuaded nine business men from St Louis to help him pay for the aeroplane to be built.

Lindbergh, Charles Augustus

Born 1902 in Detroit, USA
The first person to fly solo non-stop across the Atlantic Ocean
Died 1974 aged 72

Charles Lindbergh's father was a politician, and his family moved about a great deal. This meant that Charles often changed schools. He was also rather stubborn and did not like discipline very much, and as a result he did not do well at school.

He always had the ambition to be a flyer. To please his mother he went to college in 1920, but he soon left and went to learn to fly. After a time in the Army Air Service he had a regular job flying the mail across America.

In 1926 a prize was put up for the first non-stop flight from New York to Paris. Several famous airmen decided to attempt this. Some were killed in the attempt. On 20 May 1927 Lindbergh took off in a specially built aeroplane called *Spirit of St Louis*, after the town where his employers had their headquarters. He landed at Le Bourget Airport, Paris, 33½ hours later, having flown 5,800 km (3,600 miles).

Lindbergh became a tremendous hero on both sides of the Atlantic, and went on to be an important adviser during the growth of long-distance air travel. Towards the end of his life he became interested in conservation, and opposed the development of supersonic aeroplanes as he believed they would have a bad effect on the Earth's atmosphere. ■

See also

Aircraft

Biography
Wright brothers

Linnaeus, Carolus

Born 1707 near Kristianstad, Sweden
Established the modern scientific method of naming and classifying plants and animals.
Died 1778 aged 70

Carolus Linnaeus was the son of a Swedish clergyman. Even as a tiny child he was fascinated by plants. When he went to school he neglected his lessons and often played truant so that he could go and look for them.

He lived at a time when many new plants and animals were being discovered. Linnaeus worked out a method of giving two-part names to every different species. In this way each kind of plant and animal had a name which was not used for any other. It was said at the time 'God created; Linnaeus set in order', for his system made it possible for each new discovery to be slotted into an arrangement of similar species.

While still a student Linnaeus visited the wild country of Lapland. Later he went to The Netherlands, Germany and England. When he returned to Sweden he was made professor of medicine and then of botany at Uppsala, where he had been a student. He was a very popular teacher; up to 1,500 students crowded in to hear him lecture. In 1753 he became a Knight of the Polar Star in recognition of his work, and later he was made a count.

Wherever he went he collected plants and made notes on all that he saw. He published over 180 works on plants, animals and minerals. The most important of these is *Systema Naturae*, which is written in Latin and is still used today by scientists who classify the living world.

Linnaeus was born Carl Linné but became known as Carolus Linnaeus as all his works were in Latin. ■

See also

Animals
Botanists
Classification
Plants
Species

Lister, Joseph

Born 1827 in Upton, Essex, England
Appreciated the importance of cleanliness and the sterilization of equipment during operations, and dramatically reduced death rates following surgery.
Died 1912 aged 84

Joseph Lister was born into a Quaker family, the son of a wealthy wine merchant. His father was fascinated by science, ground his own lenses, and had invented a type of microscope. He sent Joseph to University College hospital to train to be a doctor. There, he worked on the structure of the eye, showing that two muscles control the size of the pupil. He also attended one of the first operations to be performed under anaesthetic, at Edinburgh medical school.

Lister was appalled at the huge number of people who died after surgery. Surgeons, working in their ordinary clothes, and with unwashed hands, boasted that they could cut off a leg in 25 seconds. Not surprisingly, many of the patients died.

Lister tried moving the patients' beds further apart to prevent infection, but things were no better. Then he read Louis Pasteur's findings about bacteria in the air, and began to look for something to keep operating theatres perfectly clean.

Lister observed that as sewage was purified with carbolic acid, perhaps it would kill bacteria in surgery too. Carbolic acid was sprayed into the air during operations; and heat was used to kill bacteria on knives and instruments. At first no one believed Lister's success, but by 1879, most of the London hospitals were using his methods, and many patients lived who would have died without them. In 1902, King Edward VII was taken ill with appendicitis and operated on, using Lister's methods, to recover for his coronation. ∎

◉ See also

Hospitals
Hygiene
Operations
Surgeons

Biography
Pasteur

▼ Lister developed a carbolic spray which was used to kill bacteria during operations. He was the first to realize how important clean, sterile conditions were for surgery.

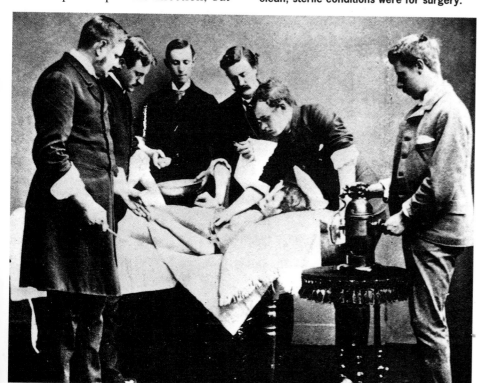

Liszt, Franz

Born 1811 in Raiding, Hungary
A great piano virtuoso and pioneering composer
Died 1886 aged 74

Music came naturally to Liszt. He began to play the piano when he was only 5, and gave his first public concert when he was 9. This so impressed a group of Hungarian noblemen that they gave money for him to study in Vienna and Paris. By the time he was 12 he was being compared with the greatest adult pianists of the day. Soon he had conquered Europe. He was a 'star'.

Liszt was more than just a great virtuoso. He was a fine composer. His music was not only technically brilliant, it was also very adventurous and pointed the way to new musical developments. One of his inventions was the symphonic poem, an orchestral work that told a story in terms of music. *Les Préludes, Mazeppa*, and *Hamlet* are examples, but he also wrote vast quantities of music of all kinds. ∎

Livingstone, David

Born 1813 in Blantyre, Scotland
A missionary and explorer whose three long expeditions to Africa made him a Victorian hero
Died 1873 aged 60

This famous Scottish explorer was born in a crowded tenement home in a mill town near Glasgow. When he was 10 he began work in a local cotton mill, but he found time to educate himself, and often read until midnight. He saved enough money to train as a doctor, and in 1841 sailed for South Africa to join a Christian mission station in Botswana (then called Bechuanaland).

Livingstone's missionary work involved danger and hardship. Once he was attacked by a lion and almost lost an arm. Despite the risks, he took his wife Mary and their young children on many long hard journeys. In 1851 he discovered that the slave trade,

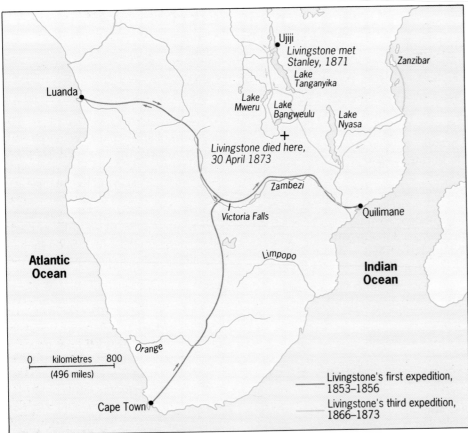

which Britain had acted to abolish in 1807, was still flourishing. Livingstone thought that the best way to stop slavery was to open Africa to trade and commerce. So he began a search for new trade routes.

In 1853 Livingstone began his first great expedition. He walked from the middle of Africa to the Atlantic coast, then turned round and headed east until he reached the Indian Ocean. He was the first European to see the Victoria Falls. When Livingstone returned to Britain in 1856 he was hailed as a hero, the first European to cross Africa from west to east.

Livingstone's second expedition, up the Zambezi River by steamboat, was a disastrous failure. His wife Mary died of fever and many other lives were lost before the expedition collapsed in 1864.

Livingstone's third expedition, to find the source of the River Nile, began in 1866. He vanished and some people wondered if he had died. But in 1871 the American journalist Henry Morton Stanley found Livingstone at Ujiji on

▲ David Livingstone's three expeditions into the heart of Africa made him the most knowledgeable European of his day about Africa's customs and geography, and about the slave trade.

the shore of Lake Tanganyika. 'Dr Livingstone, I presume,' said Stanley at the famous meeting.

Livingstone died in 1873 about 800 km (500 miles) south of Ujiji. Carrying his body, his loyal African servants led by Chuma and Susi reached the coast five months later. Livingstone's body was shipped to England and buried in Westminster Abbey. ■

See also

African history
Explorers

► Lloyd George was considered one of the greatest public speakers of his time, both in and out of the House of Commons. Here he is addressing a crowd at Lampeter Station, west Wales in 1919.

Lloyd George, David

Born 1863 in Manchester, England
Prime Minister of Britain from 1916 to 1922
Died 1945 aged 82

David Lloyd George was born in Manchester, but his father died before he was two years old, so he was brought up in his uncle's home near Criccieth in north Wales. When only 27 he became a Liberal Member of Parliament and began to fight for a better life for poorer people. In 1908 he was appointed Chancellor of the Exchequer, and in his budget of 1909 he said he would change the law, making richer people pay much more in taxes in order to give more help to the sick and unemployed. His budget was strongly opposed in the House of Lords, and only after the Liberals, helped by other parties, had won a general election in January 1910 was the budget passed.

When World War I broke out in 1914, Britain was poorly prepared. Lloyd George was given the job of organizing the production of weapons and materials. But still Britain did badly. In 1916 the prime minister Asquith was pushed out and Lloyd George took his place. He now set about winning the war. It was not easy to make people and especially the army generals change their old-fashioned ways. In 1918 victory came, and Lloyd George won the general election that followed with a large majority. He began the

task of rebuilding Europe, and was one of three main peacemakers at the Paris peace conference. He helped set up a League of Nations to keep the peace. At home, with Ireland at war, he agreed to split the country into an independent Irish state and six of the counties of Ulster still under British rule in the north. In 1922 he was forced to resign by his opponents. Never again did he hold government office, but he remained an important figure in British politics until the 1940s. ■

See also

British history 1919–1989
Ireland's history
World War I

Lloyd Webber, Andrew

> **Born** 1948 in London, England
> An enormously successful composer of musicals for the stage

Dr William Lloyd Webber, Andrew's father, was an organist and a composer of church music. Both Andrew and his brother Julian have grown to be successful musicians: Andrew as a composer, Julian as a well-known performer on the cello.

Andrew was a rather aloof boy at school. This was partly because he seemed more interested in pop music than in the classics. When he left, he tried to become a pop composer, and he was joined in this by Tim Rice, who was interested in writing lyrics. The two of them were asked by one of their old teachers to write a short 'cantata', based on a Bible story, for a school performance. The work they produced was *Joseph and the Amazing Technicolor Dreamcoat*. A repeat performance was arranged in the Methodist Central Hall in London, and luckily, though fewer than 50 people were there, one of the parents who attended was Derek Jewell, a music critic. Jewell wrote an enthusiastic review about *Joseph* in the *Sunday Times*, and Lloyd Webber and Rice were on their way to success. The rock opera *Jesus Christ Superstar* followed in 1970.

Since then Lloyd Webber has produced a series of tremendously successful musicals, including *Evita* in 1976, *Cats* in 1981, *Starlight Express* in 1984 and *Phantom of the Opera* in 1986. ■

See also

Musicals   **Biography**
                         Joseph

Llywelyn ap Gruffudd

> **Born** date unknown, somewhere in north Wales
> The first and last Welsh 'Prince of Wales'
> **Killed** 1282 age unknown

Llywelyn ap Gruffudd was a grandson of Llywelyn the Great, the famous prince of Gwynedd in north Wales, who had united Wales. But by 1246, when Llywelyn became prince, even Gwynedd was divided.

Llywelyn was determined to recreate an independent Wales. He strengthened his position in Gwynedd and by 1258 was recognized as their leader by all the Welsh princes.

Taking advantage of a weakened England under Henry III, he attacked English lands and castles in south Wales. In 1267 the English were forced to accept that Llywelyn was Prince of Wales and lord of the Welsh princes.

Llewelyn did not go unchallenged. In 1276 the young King Edward I launched all-out war to unite Wales with England. Welsh resistance was crushed and Llywelyn had to surrender. But peace could not last for long, and in 1282 a revolt broke out. During the fighting, Llywelyn was killed by a Shropshire soldier who did not even recognize him. Without Llywelyn, the revolt collapsed and the dream of Welsh independence was lost. ■

See also

Welsh history   **Biography**
                      Edward I
                      Llywelyn the Great

Llywelyn the Great

> **Born** about 1172 in north Wales
> The greatest of the medieval Welsh rulers
> **Died** 1240 aged about 67

Although he was heir to the kingdom of Gwynedd (Snowdonia) in north Wales, the young Llywelyn spent his childhood in exile. But he fought back, and by 1194 he had deposed his uncle David and by 1200 he had become master of most of northern Wales. Five years later he married the illegitimate daughter of King John of England, and began to threaten English lands in the south. This was too much for King John, who invaded Wales in 1211.

Fortunately for Llywelyn, John's troubles with his barons in England meant that he had little time to deal with the Welsh. Seizing his chance, Llywelyn forced Welsh rulers throughout the country to recognize his leadership. Two years after John's death, the English acknowledged that Llywelyn was ruler of most of Wales. Even a powerful attack led by Henry III in 1231 could not shake him. Llywelyn created a strong government based in Gwynedd to control the princes. Shortly before his death, he became a monk, after a lifetime spent encouraging the Welsh to think of themselves as a united people. ■

See also

Welsh history   **Biography**
                   John, King
                   Llywelyn ap Gruffudd

Lorenz, Konrad

> **Born** 1903 in Vienna, Austria
> The 'father of ethology', the scientific study of animal behaviour
> **Died** 1989 aged 85

As a young man, Konrad Zacharias Lorenz studied zoology and medicine, but he was always interested in birds and he made a particular study of the family life of jackdaws. His most famous work showed the way that birds, soon after they hatch, learn or are 'imprinted' with the sight of their mother. Working with geese, Lorenz was able to imprint them himself, so that the goslings followed him instead of their parents. He also studied dogs, the fish of coral reefs, and aggression in animals.

Konrad Lorenz became the co-director of the Max Planck Institute for the Physiology of Behaviour near Munich, and then director of the Research Station for Ethology in Austria.

Lorenz was a large man, who radiated excitement about the work he was doing, so that the many students that he met, from all over the world, were drawn in to share his enthusiasm. He wrote many scientific papers and his book *King Solomon's Ring* is one of the most widely read natural history books of the 20th century. During his long and active life he received many honours, including the Nobel prize awarded jointly with Niko Tinbergen and Karl von Frisch. ■

⊙ See also

Animal behaviour

Louis IX, Saint

Born 1214 in Poissy, France
He was a holy king who ruled France with justice and died on crusade.
Died 1270 aged 56

Louis had three elder brothers, but they died young, leaving Louis as heir to the French throne. His mother, Blanche of Castile, took great care over his education. She made him go to church every day, and told him again and again that he must try to lead a holy life without sin. Louis also learnt from a friar whom he met that the way to rule a kingdom in peace was to give the people justice.

Louis became king when he was only 12, so Blanche ruled for him. The French nobles did not at first warm to the boy king and his Spanish mother, but Louis managed to win their loyalty by not taxing them too hard, and by putting into practice the friar's lesson. In the gardens of his summer palace,

▲ This painting of St Louis shows him in a ship on his way to the crusade. The halo around his crown shows that he is a saint as well as a king.

he would sit under an oak tree with his advisers, and pass judgement on the cases brought to him.

As he took on more power, Louis began to grow away from his mother. In 1234, when he married, Blanche felt so jealous that Louis and his wife had to plan to be together in the palace without her knowing. Servants would tell them when she was coming!

In 1244, he decided to go on crusade. He wanted to serve God not only through his peaceful ruling of France, but also through making war on the Muslims in the Holy Land. He was a brave leader, but the campaign of this, the seventh crusade, was not a success. In 1249 he landed in Egypt, was defeated in battle when plague broke out in his army, and was taken prisoner. He had to be ransomed for a large sum. Twenty years later, Louis decided to try again, but this time he himself fell ill and died of plague in Tunisia. About 40 years later, a knight called John of Joinville, who was a close friend of the king, wrote the *History of St Louis*. ■

⊙ See also

Crusades

Louis XIV

Born 1638 at Saint-Germain-en-Laye, France
A king who ruled France for 72 years from 1643 to 1715
Died 1715 aged 76

Louis became King of France at the age of 4 on the death of his father. His mother, Anne of Austria, at first ruled for him, helped by her powerful chief adviser, Cardinal Mazarin. As a child Louis was often neglected. Once he almost drowned in a pond because no one was looking after him.

Mazarin died in 1661, and Louis was determined from now on to rule alone. As he said himself, 'L'état, c'est moi' ('I am the state'). He believed that he was God's representative on earth. He had many good ideas for improving the towns and countryside. He also encouraged brilliant writers and artists to come to his court.

But there was a darker side to his reign as well. He fought expensive wars in The Netherlands and Spain, but was defeated when other countries joined together against him. At home he was cruel to the Huguenots (Protestants), who after a century of freedom were told in 1685 that they had to become Roman Catholics. Two hundred thousand of them refused and left the country.

Louis had ordered a palace to be built in Versailles, and he moved his court there in 1682. The life of luxury angered those who were struggling to survive. Known as the Sun King, because he chose the Sun as his royal badge, Louis died a lonely figure. His body was buried to the jeers of a crowd who no longer respected his single-minded belief in himself. ■

See also

France's history   Huguenots

Louis XVI

Born 1754 in Versailles, France
The last French king before the Revolution; he ruled from 1774 to 1792.
Executed 1793 aged 38

Louis came to the throne at the age of 19. A weak man, he often relied on the advice of his strong-minded wife, the beautiful Marie Antoinette of Austria. But she was unpopular because of her high spending. Louis himself failed to impress the French nobles, who began to oppose much that he tried to do.

In 1788 he summoned the estates-general (a sort of parliament) to help him get his way against these nobles. This parliament was made up of representatives from the Church, the aristocracy and ordinary people, and had not met since 1614. Soon it too was causing him trouble, demanding reforms. Not knowing where to turn, Louis increasingly retreated to his favourite hobbies of hunting and making locks. When the French Revolution started in 1789, he and his family were taken away and kept under guard.

All was not yet lost, but instead of trying to come to an agreement with the new forces in France, Louis attempted to escape with his family. They fled from Paris in a horse and carriage in 1791, but he was recognized from his picture on French banknotes and brought back. In 1792 documents which showed his dealings with

enemies of the revolution were found in a secret cupboard, and Louis was tried for treason. Addressed in court merely as 'Citizen Capet', he was condemned to death and beheaded by guillotine in 1793. Nine months later his wife Marie Antoinette was also guillotined. ■

See also

France's history

Luther, Martin

Born 1483 in Eisleben, Germany
A monk who broke away from the Catholic Church, and began the Protestant Reformation in Germany
Died 1546 aged 62

Martin Luther decided to become a monk after he was nearly killed by lightning in a terrible storm. He was a serious, unhappy person, and very worried by his own sins and by the evil he felt was everywhere in the world. He was worried too that the Catholic Church had become so wealthy and powerful. He felt many churchmen had forgotten the teachings of Jesus.

Luther became a priest in 1507 and a teacher of theology (religion) at the University of Wittenberg in Saxony. In 1517, he decided to protest against the sale of indulgences in Germany. Indulgences were pieces of paper which people could buy, which said their sins were forgiven. Luther believed you could not buy forgiveness like that, and he wrote out a list of 95 theses (reasons) why indulgences were wrong. He nailed his list to the door of the main church in Wittenberg. The 95 theses were also printed, so many more people outside Wittenberg read them.

A great argument began between Luther and other churchmen. Luther had studied the Bible and teachings by early Christians, and now at last he felt sure that people must have faith that God would save them from their sins. They must study the Bible for themselves, and believe in Christian teaching. Then they would lead good and holy lives. They did not need to

buy indulgences, say a certain number of prayers, or go to special church services. So priests, and the whole organization of the Catholic Church, were much less important.

Soon Luther was in trouble. In 1520 the Pope sent him a Bull (a proclamation) which said he was expelled from the Church. Luther burnt it publicly, in the market place in Wittenberg.

Then, in 1521, the Holy Roman Emperor Charles V ordered Luther to appear before a special meeting, called a Diet, of all the princes in Germany, at Worms. Luther still refused to give up his beliefs, though the emperor condemned him, and he was in danger of being imprisoned and burned to death.

However, the ruler of Saxony protected Luther. Some other German princes supported him too. For the rest of his life, Luther taught and wrote. He translated the Bible into German. He wrote several beautiful hymns. He gave up being a monk and married a woman who had been a nun.

By the time Luther died, his followers (called 'Lutherans') had formed a new Protestant Church which was separate from the Catholic Church. ■

See also

Catholics   **Biography**
Christians   Charles V
Protestants
Reformation

Luthuli, Albert John

Born 1898 in Southern Rhodesia (now Zimbabwe)
A leader of his people, he was awarded the Nobel Peace Prize for his non-violent opposition to racial discrimination.
Died 1967 aged 69

Albert Luthuli was born into a Christian Zulu family. His father was a Christian missionary. Albert was educated at Adams College, near Durban in South Africa. He then went on to teach at Adams College for fifteen years before being elected tribal chief in his family home at Groutville, Natal.

As tribal chieftain, he did much to help the black farmers in his home village get a better price for the sugar they grew. After World War II, he joined the African National Congress (ANC) which was working for black people to be given full political rights in South Africa. Albert Luthuli did not believe in violence; instead he led campaigns of peaceful disobedience against the 'apartheid' laws that kept races apart in his country.

When he was elected President of the ANC, the government responded by taking away his chieftainship. Later he was arrested, and in 1959 he was banned from leaving his home district for five years. The following year the ANC was banned. Despite the ban Luthuli was allowed to go to Oslo in 1961 when the Swedish government awarded him the Nobel Peace Prize for all that he had done in opposing discrimination against black people in South Africa.

Many people throughout the world got to hear about Albert Luthuli after this. He wrote his autobiography, *Let My People Go*, in 1962. ■

See also

Apartheid
South Africa

▲ Albert Luthuli in his early 50s, during his presidency of the African National Congress.

Macdonald, Flora

Born 1722 on South Uist, in the Scottish Hebrides
She helped Charles Stuart (Bonnie Prince Charlie) escape from the English.
Died 1790 aged 68

Flora was brought up on a farm in the Hebridean islands off the west coast of Scotland. When she was 23 she heard that Bonnie Prince Charlie had landed in Scotland. He hoped to raise an army that would march on London and restore his father, James Stuart, to the throne. A few months later he and his men were defeated at Culloden, and the English placed a reward of £30,000 on his head. Charles went into hiding on the Isle of Uist, where Flora lived.

On a night of full moon in June 1746 she went to sleep in a lonely shelter half-way up the mountain, where she

Macdonald, Sir John Alexander

Born 1815 in Glasgow, Scotland
The chief architect of Canada's confederation and Canada's first prime minister
Died 1891 aged 76

John A. Macdonald emigrated with his family to Kingston, Upper Canada (now Ontario) when he was 5 years old. When he was 10 he was sent to a boarding school. At the age of 15 he began to work in a law office. Before he turned 21 he opened his own office and became a successful lawyer.

He was first elected to government in 1844. In 1865, he and a former rival, George Brown, began persuading others to unite Britain's six North American colonies to form a single country. He chaired the London conference of 1866 to create the Dominion of Canada. He was chosen to be Canada's first prime minister when it became independent on 1 July 1867. He went on to encourage the building of a railway across the continent and the development of industry.

was driving her cattle for their summer grazing. She was woken by four men, one of them the Prince, who asked if she would help him escape. She agreed to let him come with her, disguised as her Irish maid. Seven boatmen rowed the small party over the sea to the Isle of Skye, and from there Prince Charles escaped to France.

Flora herself was captured and taken to London, where she was held prisoner for a year. On her return to Scotland she heard that she had become a heroine, and that songs and poems had been made up about her.

She married a young farmer and they emigrated to America. Later they returned to Scotland, where they settled down to farm once more. ■

See also

Biography
Charles Edward Stuart

His personal life was not always happy. His first son, John Alexander, had died as a baby. His first wife, Isabel, spent most of her life sick in bed. A daughter from his second marriage was an invalid. Macdonald took to drinking, and was sometimes drunk in public. He would joke about himself and managed to make people accept him even with this failing. ■

See also

Canada's history

Magellan, Ferdinand

Born 1480 in Sabrosa, northern Portugal
The first man to find a route from the Atlantic Ocean to the Pacific
Killed 1521 aged 41

Ferdinand Magellan was the son of a noble Portuguese family, and his name was originally Fernão de Magalhães. He was a page at the Portuguese court before serving in the army, and sailing with merchants to the Moluccas, in Indonesia.

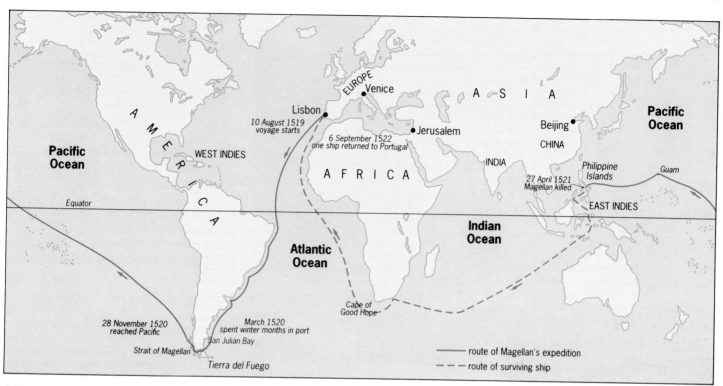

▲ **Magellan commanded the first expedition that sailed around the world. Although Magellan did not live to see the voyage completed, it provided the first proof that the Earth is round.**

Magellan thought there must be a way around the Americas to the Indies. But he fell out of favour with the king, Manoel I, who rejected his plan for a voyage of discovery. So he offered his services to King Carlos of Spain.

Magellan set sail in 1519 with five small ships and 568 men. Magellan's Spanish captains distrusted him, and when the fleet anchored for the winter in San Julián Bay, in Argentina, they mutinied. Magellan hanged one of the ringleaders.

One ship was wrecked in a storm, and another turned back to Spain. With the others Magellan battled against the bad weather conditions through the straight between Tierra del Fuego and the mainland of South America. (The strait is called the Magellan Strait after him.) He emerged into calm sea, which he named the Pacific (peaceful) Ocean.

The ships sailed for sixteen weeks without making a landfall. The crews were short of stores, and survived on foul, stinking water, old ship's biscuit,

rats, and stewed leather. At last they reached the island of Guam and fresh food and water. From there they sailed on to the Philippines. There, at Mactan, Magellan was killed in a skirmish. But he had succeeded in reaching the East Indies by sailing westwards.

One ship made the complete voyage round the world. Its commander, Sebastián de Cano, arrived back in Spain with just seventeen men. Eighteen other men returned later. ■

◑ **See also**

Explorers

Mandela, Nelson

Born 1918 at Umtata in the Transkei, South Africa
South African leader imprisoned for his work towards ending the system of apartheid

When he was born, Nelson Mandela was named Rolihlahla which means 'stirring up trouble'. Little did his parents know what a good name they had chosen for their son! After a childhood herding cattle, Mandela was

sent away to be educated. Eventually, with the help of his first wife Evelyn, he qualified as a lawyer in Johannesburg.

From the start Mandela was angry about the 'apartheid' laws that made black people second-class citizens. He joined the African National Congress and, with Walter Sisulu and Oliver Tambo, led peaceful protests against apartheid. Many thousands of ANC supporters were arrested in the 1950s.

In 1960, 69 protesters were killed by police at Sharpeville. Such violence led Mandela and others to form 'Umkhonto we Sizwe' (Spear of the Nation). This secret organization used sabotage against government property.

Mandela, now married to Winnie, went 'underground' using false names and disguises to continue his work. In 1962 he was arrested and sentenced to five years. Then, at a second trial, he was imprisoned for life in 1964. At his trial he said: 'I have cherished the ideal of a democratic and free society in which all persons live together in harmony. It is an ideal which I hope to live for and achieve. But if needs be it is an ideal for which I am prepared to die.'

Mao Zedong

Born 1893 in Hunan, China
He was one of the founders of the
People's Republic of China in 1949.
Died 1976 aged 82

Mao Zedong's father was a peasant at a time when life was desperately hard for village people. As a boy Mao loved the stories of rebel leaders who stood up for the peasants. He was one of the first to join the new Chinese Communist Party in 1921. It worked alongside the Guomindang (Nationalist Party) led by Jiang Jieshi until Jiang had many communists killed in 1927.

Mao helped the rest to survive by setting up a 'soviet' (elected council) in Jiangxi where the peasants ruled themselves. Mao taught them to fight

▲ Nelson Mandela about to burn his pass book in 1960 as a protest against apartheid. Pass books had to be carried by all black South Africans, and shown at the request of any white official.

◀ The colour photograph shows Mandela after his release from prison in February 1990.

▼ After the 'people's liberation army' won control of China in 1949, Mao became one of the world's most famous leaders. In the People's Republic of China pictures of him appeared everywhere. Young and old studied his writings and learned his sayings. This poster from 1976 shows crowds marching through the streets praising Mao, holding aloft a picture of him and banners with slogans such as 'Long live great leader Chairman Mao!' At the foot of the poster is the slogan 'Hurrah for the Revolutionary Council!'

The years in jail did nothing to change Mandela's mind about the evil of apartheid. Winnie Mandela was frequently detained and interrogated for her activities, but more and more people throughout the world heard of Nelson Mandela and joined the campaign to free him and to end apartheid. On 11 February 1990, Mandela was finally released from prison and he immediately launched himself back into the political struggle against apartheid, as Deputy President of the ANC. ■

👁 **See also**

Apartheid
South Africa

革命委员会好

off Jiang's attacks with ambushes and lightning raids. In 1934 the attacks were so strong that Mao led the communists on the 'Long March', nearly 10,000 km (6,000 miles) over mountains and deserts to a new base. Thousands died on the way of exhaustion and exposure as well as enemy attacks.

In 1937 the Japanese invaded China. Jiang retreated to the mountains, but Mao sent the 'people's liberation army' to fight an underground war. They helped people in occupied villages to run their own schools, clinics and law courts. When the Japanese left, the memory of the behaviour of Mao's soldiers meant that more and more people supported him in a civil war against Jiang.

In 1949 Mao's forces captured Beijing and set up a People's Republic. The peasant's son had become leader of a quarter of all the people on Earth. He encouraged the peasants to overthrow the landlords and work together on collective farms. He led campaigns to help women stand up for themselves. His colourful speeches used stories from China's past to explain his ideas.

In 1957 he ordered the peasants to join their collective farms into large 'communes'. Some had to work in 'brigades' on the fields, but many were given tasks such as building new dams. Others were told to open factories or furnaces to make iron. These were part of Mao's plan for a 'Great Leap Forward' in industry. Many of the schemes did not succeed, and other communist leaders said this was because Mao had not ordered enough money to be spent on new technology or education for the most skilled workers. In 1966 Mao started the 'Cultural Revolution' to try to prove them wrong. His supporters were young people who got together in mobs, waving little red books of Mao's sayings and attacking their teachers and managers. The Cultural Revolution finally ended when Mao died. ∎

See also

China's history   **Biography**
Communists   Jiang Jieshi

Marconi, Guglielmo

Born 1874 in Bologna, Italy
The great pioneer of radio
Died 1937 aged 63

Marconi's father was Italian and his mother Irish. When he began his experiments on sending radio signals in Italy he found that no one was very interested, so he moved to England.

He found that if signals were to travel long distances he needed to have a very high aerial, so he began to use balloons and kites. In 1897 he sent a signal just over 14 km (9 miles) from one side of the Bristol Channel to the other. But still not many people were interested until in 1899 he set up his apparatus in two American ships and was able to report how the America's Cup yacht race was going. Suddenly everyone was very excited and Marconi became very famous. But some scientists still did not believe that you could send signals very far, because they thought the waves would go straight up and get lost in space.

In 1901 Marconi finally convinced everyone by sending a signal all the way from Cornwall to Newfoundland. It was later proved that the waves bounced back off special layers in the atmosphere and that was how they were able to travel round the world. ∎

See also

Atmosphere
Radio

Marlborough, John Churchill, 1st Duke of

Born 1650 in Devon, England
English general and statesman who led the fight against Louis XIV of France
Died 1722 aged 72

John Churchill became powerful under the patronage of James II. But he was an Anglican not a Catholic, and disliked James's attempt to turn the country back to the Catholic religion. When William of Orange landed in England in 1688 Churchill deserted

James for William. At first he was a leading general in William's army, but he was not trusted and William dismissed him. He was suspected of conspiring with the Jacobites and was imprisoned for a time in the Tower of London. But at the end of his life, William saw that Marlborough was the man to lead the fight against Louis XIV's France and appointed him Commander-in-Chief.

In the early years of Queen Anne's reign Marlborough was the most famous Englishman in Europe: the statesman who held together the Grand Alliance against Louis, and the general who led their armies to a string of dazzling victories, Blenheim (1704), Ramillies (1706), Oudenarde (1708) and Malplaquet (1709). But by 1711 the mood had changed, Europe was ready for peace and Marlborough was dismissed. He lived on till 1722, dying in the partly completed great palace of Blenheim which was the grateful nation's gift for his victories and his most conspicuous memorial. ∎

See also

Stuart Britain

Biography
Anne, Queen
Louis XIV
William III

Marley, Bob

Born 1945 at Rhoden Hall, St Ann, Jamaica
A singer who made Jamaican reggae music popular throughout the world
Died 1981 aged 36

Bob Marley was born to a black mother and a white father, who left home before Bob was born. When he was 10, he and his mother moved from the village to Trenchtown, Kingston. The harsh living conditions made a big impression on him. When he joined the 'Wailin' Wailers' in 1960, he wrote many songs about life in Trenchtown.

In 1965 Bob married Rita Anderson from the group. By then the Wailers' reggae music was attracting listeners

▲ Bob Marley was instantly recognizable to his millions of fans throughout the world, thanks to his Rastafarian 'dreadlocks' and his fine reggae music.

far beyond Jamaica and the members of the group were now getting involved in Rastafarianism.

A recording contract in the UK brought world fame in the 1970s, but because he would not take sides in gang violence, in 1976 some gunmen tried to kill Bob Marley. Then, in 1977, he contracted cancer in the foot. It spread throughout his body and he died in Miami in the USA. His grave in Rhoden Hall is now a national shrine. ■

👁 See also

Rastafarians
Reggae

Marx, Karl

Born 1818 in Trier, Germany
One of the founders of communism; his ideas helped to shape the modern world.
Died 1883 aged 64

Karl Marx was born in Trier and spent five years at high school there, where he met and fell in love with Jenny, the daughter of Baron von Westphalen, a Trier city councillor.

As a student at the University of Bonn, Marx was more interested in drinking and writing poems than in studying. His father became so worried that he moved him to Berlin in 1836. Here Marx discovered ideas that changed his life.

In 1843 Marx, now a journalist, married Jenny and they began a journey round Europe. After a spell in Paris, they moved to Brussels where Marx met Friedrich Engels. Together they worked for the Communist League and in 1848 wrote *The Communist Manifesto*. This pamphlet said that working people should take over the governments of the world, and ended with the words: 'The workers have nothing to lose but their chains. They have a world to win. Workers of all countries, unite!'

Ideas like these led to Marx being expelled from Brussels and then from France and Germany. In 1849 he fled with his family to London. There he worked as a journalist, but spent most of his time, with the help of Engels, developing his communist ideas.

'Communism (is) the positive abolition of private property,' Marx wrote. Under communism, people would own all things in common and share them fairly. Marx thought that this ought to happen and he believed it would happen, but only if working people organized themselves to make it happen.

That is why he became one of the leaders of the International Working Men's Association ('the First International') in 1864. By 1869 it had 800,000 members and Marx had published Volume I of *Das Kapital* ('Capital'), the most important work of his life. After Marx's death, Engels published Volumes II and III, making sure that Marx's revolutionary ideas reached people all over the world. ■

👁 See also

Communists
Revolutions

Biography
Lenin
Stalin
Trotsky

▲ Throughout his later years, Karl Marx suffered from ill health. Had it not been for the money that Engels gave him, he would not have been able to support his family or continue his work. This is a drawing of him when he was 50 and living in London.

Mary I

Born 1516 at Greenwich Palace, London, England
Daughter of Henry VIII and Catherine of Aragon; Queen of England and Wales from 1553 to 1558
Died 1558 aged 42

Mary was an affectionate, obedient child, but her happiness ended when she was 15, and her father banished her mother from court. Mary never saw Catherine again. But although she was lonely and unhappy, she never forgot her mother, or her Catholic faith, even when England became Protestant under Edward VI, her half-brother.

When Mary became queen in 1553, she married Philip II of Spain. She hoped he would help her make England Catholic again. But Philip left not long after the wedding. Mary was determined to stamp out Protestant belief, and during her short reign over 300 Protestants, including Archbishop Cranmer, were burnt because the queen considered them heretics (for not accepting Catholic teaching). But Protestant beliefs did not disappear.

Spain dragged England into war with

France, and Calais was lost. Above all, Mary wanted a son to follow her, instead of Protestant Elizabeth. But she was a sick woman, and she died, sad and disappointed, after a reign of only five years. ■

See also

Protestants
Reformation
Tudor England

Biography
Cranmer
Edward VI
Elizabeth I
Henry VIII
Philip II of Spain

Mary II

Born 1662 in London
She ruled with her husband William of Orange, after the Glorious Revolution of 1688.
Died 1694 aged 32

Mary was the eldest daughter of the Catholic King James II, but she married William of Orange and went to live in Holland in the Netherlands. She was homesick and unhappy at first, but became a devoted and loyal wife. She willingly agreed that she and William should rule England together, when James II lost his throne in 1688.

Mary was always popular in England. She had to rule when William was abroad fighting the French, though she never enjoyed it much. She was interested in gardens, and helped to plan the building of Kensington Palace and parts of Hampton Court. She enjoyed dancing and music; the composer Henry Purcell wrote songs for her.

Mary had no children. When she died quite young of smallpox after only six years as queen, William was heartbroken. ■

See also

Glorious Revolution
Stuart Britain

Biography
William III

► Mary, Queen of Scots, was the daughter of Margaret Tudor's only son, James V. Many thought she had a better claim to the English throne than Elizabeth I. Elizabeth was born from Henry VIII's second marriage, to Anne Boleyn. Catholics did not recognize this marriage.

Mary, Queen of Scots

Born 1542 in Linlithgow, Scotland
Queen of Scotland who was forced to abdicate. She was later beheaded on the orders of Elizabeth I of England.
Executed 1587 aged 44

Mary was the daughter of King James V of Scotland, who died a week after her birth. She was born at a time of conflict between Scotland and England, and was brought up in the French court for safety. In 1558 the English throne passed to Elizabeth I, but many Catholics viewed Elizabeth as illegitimate and thought Mary had a better claim to the throne. She returned to Scotland in 1561, but with ambitions in England.

At first Mary managed to remain a Catholic queen without offending the powerful Scottish Protestants. But in 1565 she married her cousin Lord Darnley, who turned out to be a childish fool. When she drew closer to her adviser David Rizzio, her Protestant enemies involved the jealous Darnley in a plot to kill Rizzio. The murder increased her loathing of Darnley, and she supported a plot in which he was blown up. Barely three months later she married the Earl of Bothwell, a prime suspect in Darnley's murder. People thought this was an outrage and in 1567 she was forced to abdicate (give up the throne). She sought safety in England, but Elizabeth

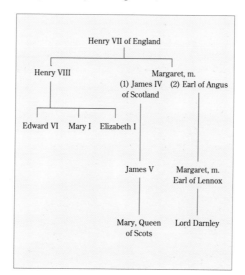

feared her and kept her in captivity for nineteen years. Eventually Mary was found guilty of involvement in a Catholic plot to kill Elizabeth, and she was beheaded in Fotheringhay Castle, Northamptonshire, in 1587.

Mary did many foolish and wicked things, but her beauty, the drama of her life and the bravery of her death have ensured a lasting fascination in her. ■

See also

Scotland's history
Biography
Elizabeth I

Matisse, Henri

Born 1869 in Le Cateau, Picardy, France
One of the greatest artists of this century
Died 1954 aged 84

Matisse began a career in law and took drawing classes only as a hobby. At the age of 20, when he was recovering from appendicitis, his mother gave him a paint box to keep him amused. He first copied the landscape examples on the box lid, and then painted his first two original pictures, both arrangements of books. He kept these all his life.

He soon decided he must become a painter and quickly proved exceptionally talented. He constantly experimented and developed a colourful free style, often considered shocking. He made a famous portrait of his wife, nicknamed 'Green Stripe' because he boldly painted the shadows on her face in bright green, not at all what people expected!

Paintings of the human figure dominated Matisse's work. His drawings, prints, book illustrations, paintings and sculpture all show his experiments with the quality and energy of the human body.

Later in life he travelled widely and was fascinated by North African patterns and shapes, which he used in

▲ *The Dance* by Matisse, Hermitage Museum, St Petersburg, Russia. The movement and energy of the dancers is the main theme in this painting and there are few details to distract from it. The picture consists of flat forms in bright colours, like cut-out paper patterns. The simplicity of the figures gives them great intensity.

many of his pictures. Later still he cut and pasted paper to create powerfully coloured pictures of simplified shapes. He almost eliminated detail, so his work was often flat patterns of colour and line.

Matisse said that for more than 50 years he had not stopped working for an instant, from morning to nightfall, seven days a week. He seemed tireless, although he had two major operations for cancer when he was 71, and after that he had to work from his wheelchair. ■

See also

Portraits

Matsushita, Konosuke

Born 1894 in Wakayama Prefecture, central Japan
Founder of one of Japan's most successful electronics companies, famous also for his belief that business should be used to bring peace and happiness to the world
Died 1989 aged 94

Matsushita was the third son of a farmer. He started work in the city of Osaka at the age of 9 and had several jobs while studying at night school. In 1918 he opened his own electrical workshop, and was very successful

► Konosuke Matsushita opened a workshop making bicycle lamps when he was 24. His company grew to become one of the world's most successful manufacturers of electronic and electrical goods.

making battery lamps for bicycles. The electrical industry was growing fast in Japan at that time, and Matsushita's company was one of the most important up to the end of World War II. The war seriously damaged the Japanese economy, and Matsushita had to work hard to rebuild his company, but business grew very fast from the 1950s. The company produced domestic electrical appliances, such as televisions, washing machines, fridges and audio-visual equipment.

Matsushita himself became one of Japan's richest men. He tried to make workers in his company feel they belonged to one large family; work discipline was strict, but in return the company tried to look after the workers. Matsushita also started the PHP movement. PHP stands for 'Peace and Happiness through Prosperity', and means that business should work to make the world peaceful and happy. ■

See also

Electronics
Japan

Maxwell, James Clerk

Born 1831 in Edinburgh, Scotland
Developed the theory that magnetism, electricity and light are all connected.
Died 1879 aged 47

Maxwell became a professor at Aberdeen University when he was only 24, and just ten years later he decided to retire to write his famous book on electricity and magnetism. When he was 40 he was invited to become the first professor of experimental physics at Cambridge. There, with money given by the Duke of Devonshire, he was able to build the famous Cavendish Laboratory in which an enormous number of important scientific discoveries have been made.

Michael Faraday, the scientist who invented the transformer and the dynamo in the year Maxwell was born, talked about magnets and electric currents having 'lines of force' and made pictures of them. This is very easy to do. You lay a piece of paper over a magnet and scatter iron filings over it. The filings all link up into curved lines that run from one pole of the magnet to the other.

Maxwell heard about this and developed a marvellous mathematical theory that explained it. He suggested that if the magnet moved back and forth it would make waves run along the lines of force, just like the waves you can make on a long piece of rope if you wobble the end.

He then made the amazing suggestion that light is in fact incredibly rapid waves on the lines of force. The waves are called 'electromagnetic waves'. He was able to prove that this is true. His mathematics also seemed to suggest that there ought to be other kinds of electromagnetic waves with shorter and longer wavelengths than light. Sadly he died before any of the others could be discovered, but we now know that radio, infra-red and ultraviolet rays, X-rays and gamma rays all belong to Maxwell's electromagnetic wave family, and his theory is still used by scientists. ■

See also

Light
Magnets
Radio
Waves
X-rays

Biography
Faraday

McAdam, John Loudon

Born 1756 in Ayrshire, Scotland
The best-known road-maker in the golden age of the English stage coach
Died 1836 aged 80

McAdam was nearly 60 when he took the job which was to make him famous. For most of his life, he had been a merchant and a country gentleman. Then in his middle forties he became interested in roads. He spent years travelling many thousands of miles at his own expense to study the appalling state of Britain's rutted, muddy roads.

At last, in 1815, the chance came to put his ideas into practice. He was made General Surveyor of the Bristol roads. McAdam believed that most of the roads should be dug up and remade by laying 25 cm (10 in) of small broken stones, no bigger than 2·5 cm, on a flat well-drained bed. The carriage wheels would then compact the stones until the surface was smooth, hard and easy to maintain.

McAdam's system worked so well in Bristol that soon it was known all over the country, and a new word for it, 'macadamizing', had entered the language. Even today the word 'tarmacadam', or 'tarmac' for short, preserves his name. ■

See also

Roads

Meir, Golda

Born 1898 in Kiev, Ukraine, Russian empire
Prime Minister of Israel from 1969 to 1974
Died 1978 aged 80

Golda Meir was born Golda Mabovitch, the daughter of a carpenter. In 1906 the family moved to Milwaukee, Wisconsin, in the USA. Golda was brought up there and became a schoolteacher. In 1917 she married Morris Myerson, and the couple emigrated to Palestine in 1921. Myerson had a badly-paid job, and Golda took in washing to make ends meet.

In 1934 Golda Myerson became an active member of the labour movement in Tel Aviv, and later of the Zionist movement, which fought for a homeland for Jews in Palestine. On the eve of Israel's independence in 1948 she was sent to the USA to raise funds for defence, returning with $50 million.

She became Israel's first diplomatic representative in Moscow, but was soon recalled to become minister of labour in the cabinet of David Ben-Gurion. In 1956 he appointed her foreign minister. Now a widow, she changed her name to the Hebrew form Meir.

Golda Meir held this post for nine years. In 1966, aged 68 and in poor health, she retired. In 1969 the prime minister, Levi Eshkol, died suddenly, and at the age of 70 she was asked to take over for a few months until elections were due. She was such a

▼ Golda Meir is seen here at the age of 75 talking to an injured Israeli soldier who had been returned after being captured by the Egyptians in the 1973 war. Six months later she resigned from office.

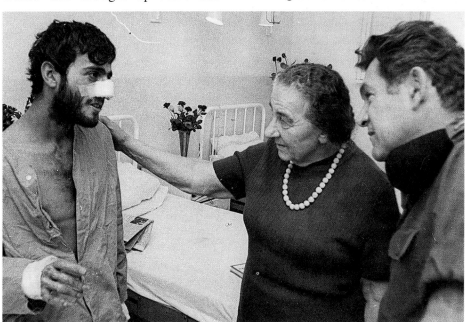

success that after the election she was asked to carry on.

Golda Meir took a tough line with Israel's Arab enemies, while trying to reach a lasting peace. In 1973 the Yom Kippur War, the fourth conflict between Israel and the Arab countries, broke out. Although peace was soon negotiated, her government was severely criticized because of early defeats, and she resigned. ■

See also

Israel   **Biography**
Palestine   Ben-Gurion

Mendel, Gregor Johann

Born 1822 in Austrian Silesia (now in Czechoslovakia)
His study of generations of pea plants led him to discover how certain characteristics, such as size and colour, are inherited.
Died 1884 aged 61

Mendel came from a very poor family and as a child looked after fruit trees for the lord of the manor. As a young man he joined a monastery and became a monk. The monastery supplied schools with teachers, and Mendel was sent to university to train as a science teacher. He spent his life teaching science in a local school and living a quiet religious life in the monastery.

Mendel had his own little garden in the monastery where he grew peas, of the sort you eat, and also sweet peas with pretty coloured flowers. He became interested in how the different characteristics, such as size and colour, were passed down from parent plants. He kept careful records of what all the parent plants looked like and what sort of young plants their seeds produced. He grew many generations of pea plants and worked out a set of rules which explained how different characteristics were passed down (the subject we now call heredity).

He published his work in a local magazine for botanists. Nobody took any notice of it, which was a great pity

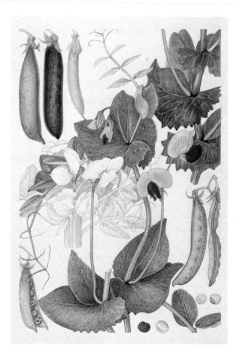

because Mendel's work helped explain some of Darwin's theory of evolution, which had been published just a few years earlier.

Sixteen years after Mendel's death, and eighteen years after Darwin's, the Dutch botanist Hugo de Vries discovered the paper written by Mendel, and Mendel's Laws of Heredity became the basis of all studies of heredity. ■

See also

Botanists   **Biography**
Evolution of living things   Darwin
Evolution of people
Genetics

Mendeléev, Dimitri Ivanovich

Born 1834 in Tobolsk, Siberia, Russian empire
He arranged all the chemical elements into a pattern called the 'periodic table' and predicted the discovery of new elements.
Died 1907 aged 72

Mendeléev was the youngest of about fifteen children. His father had been a headmaster but lost his job when he became blind. His mother set up a glass

◄ Mendel carefully studied the sizes and colours of pea plants which he had grown. From his observations he was able to discover the rules which explain how characteristics are passed on from one generation to the next.

factory to earn money to keep her large family. When Mendeléev was about 15 years old his father died, and his mother's death followed a few years later.

Mendeléev studied science in France and Germany and then became a professor of chemistry in the Russian university of St Petersburg. He was interested in the atomic weights of different elements and made a list of all 63 of the chemical elements known at that time, putting them in order of increasing atomic weight. He then rearranged the list into a continuous pattern of rows and columns and found that all the elements in the same column were similar to each other. This arrangement is called the 'periodic table'.

When Mendeléev worked out this table he found there were gaps, and he predicted that new elements would be discovered to fill these gaps. He looked at the sort of elements in the same column as the gap and was able to say what the new element would be like.

At first scientists were rather suspicious of Mendeléev's predictions, but within a few years some new elements were discovered and Mendeléev became a world-famous scientist. ■

See also

Atoms   **Biography**
Chemists   Dalton
Elements

Mendelssohn, Felix

Born 1809 in Hamburg, Germany
One of the great 19th-century composers of symphonies, chamber music and oratorios
Died 1847 aged 38

Mendelssohn was a man who had everything. He was handsome, intelligent, highly educated, and born into a very wealthy Jewish family. He gave his first public concert when he was 9. By the time he was 16, when he completed his octet for strings, it was clear to everyone that he was also a musical genius.

Good fortune followed him through the rest of his life. He became one of the most popular composers of the day in England as well as in Germany. His music, such as the 'Italian' Symphony, the 'Hebrides' Overture, the music for 'A Midsummer Night's Dream', the Violin Concerto, and the oratorio *Elijah*, pleased everyone. But he took his duties seriously. He worked so hard as a teacher and conductor that he undermined his health. When he heard that his beloved sister Fanny had died, he seems to have lost the will to live. ■

See also

Chamber music
Symphonies

Michelangelo Buonarroti

Born 1475 in Caprese, Italy
A great sculptor, painter, draughtsman, poet and architect who lived at the time of the Renaissance
Died 1564 aged 88

At the age of 13, against his family's wishes, Michelangelo became apprenticed to a painter. He studied the great paintings and sculptures of the past, and learned how to paint frescos. When he was 14 he left to go to a school for sculptors.

Michelangelo longed to understand exactly how the human body worked. He dissected corpses at a hospital, and what he learned from his dissections made him able to paint, draw or sculpt figures in all sorts of complicated

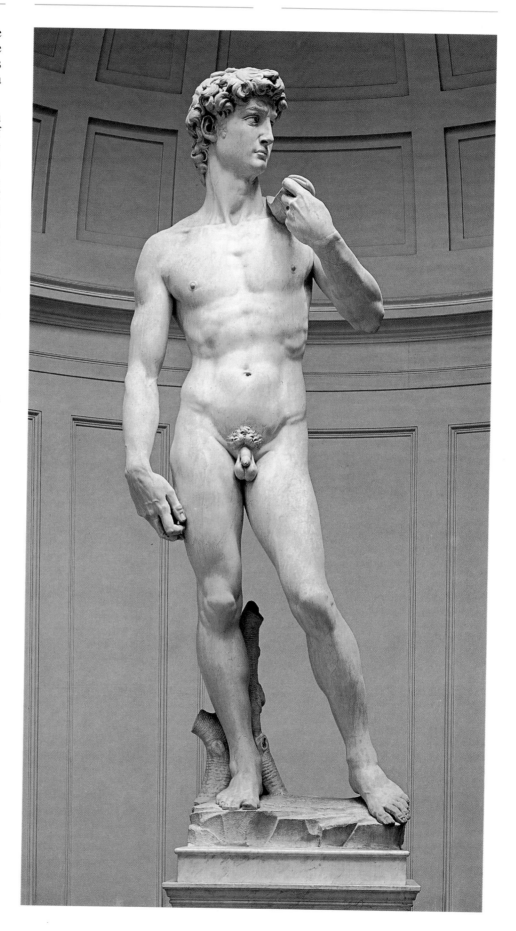

▶ *David* by Michelangelo, Museo Accademico, Florence, Italy. This is one of the most famous pieces of sculpture in the world. The carving of the marble body demonstrates Michelangelo's deep knowledge of anatomy. He shows David as a young man, carrying a sling behind his shoulder, alert and ready to defeat Goliath. Most of Michelangelo's sculptures and paintings were inspired by Bible stories.

positions with an accuracy that astounded everyone around him.

When he was sculpting, he felt he was 'releasing' the figures that were trapped inside the stone. He had a passionate love for the materials of his art and he spent months in the marble quarries in order to choose exactly the right stones.

For all his great gifts, Michelangelo was a difficult personality. He quarrelled easily, and was often bitter and depressed, imagining enemies everywhere. He was furious when Pope Julius II asked him to paint the ceiling of his chapel. He thought it was a plot by his enemies to keep him away from sculpting. But the painting which he did on the ceiling of the Sistine Chapel turned out to be one of the most astonishing creations in the history of art. It took four years of agonizing effort and is one of the best-known works of art of all times.

Michelangelo worked for some years at the great church of St Peter in Rome and is mainly responsible for the magnificent dome. Later in his life his work changed in feeling, and his late painting in the Sistine Chapel is sombre and heavy. His poetry also becomes sad. In sculpture his forms merge into each other and are very emotional compared to the serenity of his earlier work. But he never stopped working all his life, and was busy hammering away at a sculpture until just before his death. ■

See also

Frescos
Renaissance
Sculpture

Biography
David, King

Milton, John

Born 1608 in London, England
A great poet of the 17th century
Died 1674 aged 65

At Cambridge University John Milton first thought of becoming a clergyman, but decided instead to put his great gifts into poetry. One of his first major poems was *Lycidas*, a poem about the death of his friend Edward King. Like other poets he was greatly influenced by Latin and Greek literature, but Milton also brought to this poem his own Christian vision of life. He created a new form of poetry, both passionate and scholarly at the same time.

When the English Civil War began, Milton sided with Parliament against King Charles I. Because of this, his first wife, Mary, left him. He wrote many articles and pamphlets attacking the monarchy and defending people's freedom to choose their own leaders as well as to read what they liked.

He shocked many people by arguing that married couples should be allowed to divorce. But he did not marry again until several years after Mary died.

Milton's work led to serious eye-strain, and in 1652 he went blind. When Charles II was restored to the throne in 1660, Milton was arrested, but then set free again. At about this time he wrote one of the greatest poems in existence, *Paradise Lost*. This is a very long poem re-telling the Bible story of how Satan tempted Adam and Eve into disobeying God. The first lines are:

Of man's first disobedience, and the
  fruit
Of that forbidden tree, whose mortal
  taste
Brought death into the world, and all
  our woe,
With loss of Eden.

Composed entirely in Milton's head and dictated to his daughter and various others, *Paradise Lost* uses poetic language to create an effect that is both magnificent and moving in a way that has never been equalled. ■

See also

English Civil War
Stuart Britain

Moctezuma II

Born about 1480 in the Aztec empire
Emperor of the Aztecs for eighteen years
Killed 1520 aged about 40

The Aztecs controlled most of Mexico and parts of Central America for over 100 years before they were conquered by the Spanish. Aztec emperors were elected by government, army and religious leaders. They ruled with the help of a group of nobles to advise them. They had every possible luxury, but they and the people who served them were restricted by many rituals and customs. Emperors remained remote mysterious figures, rarely showing themselves to the common people.

Moctezuma II became emperor in 1502. He was greatly feared, ruling his people with an iron will. Unlike

On his Blindness

When I consider how my light is spent
  Ere half my days, in this dark world and wide,
  And that one talent which is death to hide,
Lodged with me useless, though my soul more bent
To serve therewith my Maker, and present
  My true account, lest he, returning, chide;
  'Doth God exact day-labour, light denied?'
I fondly ask: but Patience, to prevent
  That murmur, soon replies, 'God doth not need
Either man's work, or his own gifts; who best
  Bear his mild yoke, they serve him best; his state
  Is kingly: thousands at his bidding speed,
And post o'er land and ocean without rest;
  They also serve who only stand and wait.'

the previous emperor, he gave greater power to his own family and the nobility, and took it away from other people such as members of the important merchant class. During his reign, his army conquered many other cities, and he brought lands ruled by the Aztecs more firmly under his control. He went on several military campaigns himself.

In 1519 the Spanish, led by Hernán Cortés, entered the Aztec capital of Tenochtitlán, and Moctezuma was eventually killed during a battle. ■

The name is also spelt Montezuma.

See also

Aztecs
Spanish colonial history

Biography
Cortés

Molière

Born 1622 in Paris, France
A very witty French playwright who lived in the 17th century
Died 1673 aged 51

The son of a successful upholsterer, Molière was named Jean-Baptiste Poquelin. He first studied law at university, then left home to become an actor and soon adopted the stage name of Molière. With a group of friends he toured France and began to write plays for the company.

In 1658, after about twelve years of touring, the group was given a permanent theatre in Paris by King Louis XIV. In return Molière wrote many more delightful plays. Although most of these were comedies, they often had a serious side too, attacking human failings such as snobbishness, hypocrisy and meanness.

One of his funniest plays is called *Le Malade Imaginaire* (The Imaginary Invalid). It is about someone who always thinks he is more ill than he really is. One night Molière, who was acting the main part, collapsed and died a few hours later. He left behind numbers of brilliantly witty plays, many of which are still performed all over the world. ■

Monet, Claude

Born 1840 in Paris, France
One of the greatest French Impressionist painters
Died 1926 aged 86

Claude Monet was the eldest son of a grocer who moved to the port of Le Havre in northern France when Claude was 4 years old. He hated school and spent his time making cartoon-style pictures of his teachers; he became so clever at it that at the age of 16 he was earning pocket money making quick portraits. He loved to explore the cliffs, beaches and jetties and wanted always to live near water. Much later, water

and light became the subjects of very many of his pictures.

He struggled for many years in poverty while his art was ignored, laughed at and considered the work of a lunatic. He insisted on working outdoors to make on-the-spot pictures, but as the weather is always changing he had to work quickly, and he energetically applied pure, bold colour straight onto the canvas. His colourful pictures do not attempt to 'copy' a scene; they give an impression of it, concentrating on the effects of light and atmosphere.

From his mid-fifties, he was the famous grand old man of Impressionism. His output of paintings was enormous. He particularly liked to paint the same subject many times in different weather conditions and seasons. He painted the Thames in London in different lights, and at home in his garden he made a series of wonderful pictures of water-lilies. Cézanne described him as 'Only an eye – but my God what an eye!' ■

See also

Paintings

Biography
Cézanne

► *La Gare Saint Lazare* by Monet, Musée du Louvre, Paris, France. Trains and railway stations were exciting new experiences when Monet lived. He painted a series of pictures in which the new iron monsters emerged out of the smoky haze of a Paris railway station, giving a marvellous atmospheric effect.

Montagu, Lady Mary Wortley

Born 1689 in Nottinghamshire, England
Remembered for her entertaining letters
and for introducing to England an early
form of immunization against smallpox
Died 1762 aged 73

Lady Mary was the eldest daughter of
the Earl of Kingston. Her mother died
when she was 4, and she made up for
the boredom of her governess's lessons
by teaching herself Latin and reading
widely in her father's library. She was
particularly fond of romantic novels.

At 22, to avoid an arranged marriage
with a man she detested, she eloped
with Edward Wortley Montagu. Her
beauty and wit made her popular in
society, but Lady Mary found little in
that life to interest her.

When in 1716 her husband was sent
on a diplomatic mission to negotiate
between the Emperor of Austria and
the Sultan of Turkey, she and their 3-
year-old son went with him to Istanbul,
the capital of the Ottoman empire. This
ancient city gave scope for her curiosity
and powers of observation. She learnt
to speak Turkish, and explored Istanbul
veiled and disguised in Turkish dress.

Lady Mary learned the Turkish method
of 'ingrafting' to immunize against the
disease of smallpox. Ingrafting
involves taking a small amount of
infected pus from someone with
smallpox and inserting it into a scratch
on the skin of a healthy person. This
causes a mild attack of smallpox and
immunizes the patient against the
illness.

On her return to England Lady Mary's
findings were rejected by doctors and
she was criticized for experimenting
on her two children, even though her
experiments were successful. At the
age of 50 she separated from her
husband and went to live in Europe. ■

See also

Ottoman empire
Vaccinations

Biography
Jenner

Montessori, Maria

Born 1870 near Ancona, Italy
She developed a system of educating
young children which encouraged the
children to choose their activities and
organize their own day.
Died 1952 aged 81

Maria Montessori was the only child
of a civil servant. She was clever,
strong-willed and determined to follow
the life of her own choice. In 1890 she
became Italy's first woman medical
student. Despite the opposition of her
male colleagues and her horror at
dissecting corpses, she graduated with
distinction.

As a doctor she publicized the plight
of disturbed and retarded children kept
in asylums meant for insane adults. In
1900 she became director of Rome's
first special school for 'degenerates'
as children with severe learning
difficulties were then called in Italy.
She taught these children by new
methods, and they did as well in the
state examinations as 'normal
children'.

In 1906 she opened a school for 3- to
6-year-olds on a slum estate. She
noticed that the children's urge to
master their surroundings was so strong
that they could be left to organize their
own learning when given the right
equipment and materials. She provided
furniture and tools of a size that they
could use, plants and animals that they
could care for, and toys that would
help them solve problems about the
physical world. Visitors from abroad
were astonished to find the children
calm, tidy, courteous, and absorbed in
what they were doing. They learned to
read and write without difficulty.

From 1912 until her death she travelled
and lectured on her methods and
worked hard to keep up the standards
of the many Montessori schools that
opened all over the world. The methods
she developed proved to be just as
successful with normal and clever
children. ■

▼ Even in her later years Maria Montessori
still loved to visit children in kindergartens
and schools, where she was always treated
as an honoured guest. The enjoyable
activities of the children here would have
been unusual in schools at this time.

Montgolfier brothers

Designed and made the first successful hot air balloon
Joseph Born 1740 in Vidalon-lez-Annonay, France
Died 1810 aged 69
Jacques Étienne Born 1745 in Vidalon-lez-Annonay
Died 1799 aged 54

The Montgolfier brothers were paper-makers, who owned a factory at Annonay, near Lyon. At that time nobody believed that people would ever fly, but that did not stop the Montgolfiers experimenting with hydrogen gas, or testing parachutes by jumping off the factory roof. They discovered that a smoke-filled bag would rise above a fire of straw and wool, and thought they had discovered a new gas, 'electric smoke'. In fact this was only hot air, as they realized later.

On 5 June 1783 they flew a silk balloon, lined with paper, and filled from a burning brazier. It travelled over a kilometre in its ten-minute flight.

That August, Professor Jacques Charles, of the Paris Academy, launched a hydrogen balloon. Jacques Étienne saw his experiment, and the brothers were determined to beat him and be the first to fly.

In September, they sent a sheep, a duck, and a cockerel on an eight-minute flight. They crashed into a tree, and the sheep trod on the cockerel, but they survived. On 15 October, François Pilâtre de Rozier went up in the brothers' tethered balloon. All was ready for the free-flight attempt, to take place in Paris.

The intrepid Pilâtre de Rozier, and his friend the Marquis d'Arlandes, made the first free flight in a balloon on 21 November 1783, travelling 9 km (5½ miles) in 25 minutes, until the brazier they carried burnt a hole in the balloon. Souvenir hunters tore their jackets to pieces.

A fortnight later, on 1 December, Professor Charles flew 43 km (27 miles) in a hydrogen-filled balloon. He proved that a hydrogen balloon was easier to control than one with the Montgolfiers' 'electric smoke'.

Jacques Étienne returned to the paper mill. Joseph worked in the paper industry, but went on inventing, including ways of preserving fruit by drying it under reduced temperature and pressure. ■

See also

Balloons and airships

Montgomery, L. M.

Born 1874 at Clifton (now New London), Prince Edward Island, Canada
She achieved lasting fame for her children's novel *Anne of Green Gables*.
Died 1942 aged 67

Lucy Maud Montgomery was just two years old when her mother died. She was sent to live with her grandparents in their farmhouse. When she grew up she became a teacher, but she left this job to take care of her grandmother after her grandfather died.

She had kept a journal for many years, and eventually she began writing stories and poems, which were published in a local newspaper. Her first novel, *Anne of Green Gables*, was published in 1908. It was an instant best seller. In the book, an elderly brother and sister ask for a boy from an orphanage to help on their farm. They are sent a girl, Anne, by mistake, and they come to love her very much. The story echoes Montgomery's own childhood.

In 1911 she married a Presbyterian minister, Ewan Macdonald, and moved from Prince Edward Island to Ontario. She continued to write a great deal and produced seven sequels to *Anne*, other novels for children and adults, an autobiography, and many poems and short stories. She left a journal of over 5,000 pages, covering 53 years of her life. ■

Montrose, James Graham, 1st Marquis

Born 1612, in Scotland
A general who was hanged for supporting the king during the English Civil Wars
Executed 1650 aged 38

Montrose, a Scottish noble, was drawn into the events that divided Scotland during the English Civil War. When King Charles I attempted to interfere with the Scottish Church, Montrose joined with most of Scotland in opposing the king, and signed a protest known as the National Covenant. He led the Covenanters in skilful military campaigns during 1639 and 1640 which greatly weakened the king.

But the intolerance of the Covenanters began to worry Montrose, and in 1644 he offered Charles his support. Montrose assembled a motley army of Highlanders and Irish, and circled the Highlands from one victory to another. But Lowland Scotland refused to support him, especially after his men were allowed to rampage through Aberdeen and Dundee. His army was defeated by the Covenanters at Philiphaugh near Selkirk in September 1645, where many of his men were massacred to the cry of 'Jesus and no quarter'. Montrose managed to escape abroad.

When Montrose returned to Scotland in 1650, he was captured, taken to Edinburgh and hanged. His dignified bearing earned the respect of the watching crowds, who had been expected to stone him as a traitor. Even the hangman wept as he did his work. Eventually his remains were recovered and buried with honour in St Giles' Cathedral.

He is remembered as a brilliant soldier, but also as a tolerant and civilized man. He wrote a little poetry which is still read, including some lines written on the eve of his execution. ■

See also

English Civil War
Scotland's history

Moore, Henry

Born 1898 in Castleford, Yorkshire, England
One of the most famous sculptors of the 20th century
Died 1986 aged 88

Henry Moore was born in an industrial area of Yorkshire, surrounded by factories, mills and wild countryside. He was one of eight children; his father was a miner. All the family were keen on education. It was at Sunday school that he first heard about Michelangelo, and by the time he was 11 he had decided to become a sculptor.

To avoid a future working in the coal-mines, he trained as a teacher. During World War I he joined the army. He fought in the trenches in France, was gassed and discharged. On his return to Yorkshire he started teaching but disliked it so much that he enrolled at Leeds School of Art. Here the long hours of continuous work suited him. After a scholarship to the Royal College of Art in London, he travelled to Italy to widen his understanding of sculpture.

Henry Moore's work was always based on nature: rock formations, stones and bones, landscape itself and the human figure. He never tried to copy precisely the source of his ideas, but rather to suggest a likeness. 'Form should be used and felt *as shape* not to describe something,' he said, 'and there are universal shapes to which everyone responds.' He was interested in the sculpture of the early civilization of the Aztecs of central America and loved the simple forms of their work.

He was 50 before he was inter-nationally recognized. He had exceptional energy, finally completing about 800 sculptures in wood, stone and bronze, 4,000 drawings and 500 prints. Perhaps his best-known works are his monumental figures, massively solid, simplifying the human form in smooth rhythmic shapes. ∎

See also

Sculpture

▼ **Henry Moore standing by one of his sculptures in his garden in Stroud, Gloucestershire, in 1951.**

More, Sir Thomas

Born about 1477 in London, England
A famous scholar who dared to disagree with Henry VIII, and died for his beliefs
Executed 1535 aged 58

Thomas More was a successful lawyer and a scholar who lived at the time of the Reformation and Renaissance. He wrote a best-selling book called *Utopia*. This described an imaginary island where there was no money, and no one was greedy or lazy because they shared their work and their possessions.

Thomas was deeply religious and a strong Catholic. As a young man he nearly became a monk. He was a lively, amusing person, devoted to his family, and he gave a good education to his daughters, which was unusual at that time. Many interesting people visited his home in Chelsea, including his friend Erasmus. Henry VIII enjoyed Thomas's company too, but Thomas was not deceived by the King's favour. He once said, 'If my head could win him a castle in France, it would not fail to go.'

▲ This picture by the artist Rowland Lockey shows Sir Thomas More and his family. Lockey painted this picture in 1593 when Sir Thomas and several other members of his family were already dead. The artist copied a portrait of Thomas More's family painted in his lifetime, and added his descendants living in Elizabeth I's reign. That is why John More II, the son, looks younger than the Elizabethan Thomas More II, the grandson.

The people from left to right are:

Sir John More, father
Anne More, wife of John More II
Sir Thomas More
John More II, eldest son
Cecily Heron, daughter
Elizabeth Dauncey, daughter
Margaret Roper, daughter
John More III, great-grandson
Thomas More II, grandson
Christopher Cresacre More, great-grandson
Maria More, Thomas More II's second wife

After Cardinal Wolsey had failed to get the king his divorce from Catherine of Aragon, Henry made Thomas More his chancellor. But Thomas believed the king was wrong to divorce his wife, and to take over the Church to get his way. He refused to swear an oath accepting Henry's actions. He was imprisoned in the Tower of London for seventeen months, and still did not give in. Then he was beheaded. He said on the scaffold: 'I die the king's good servant, but God's servant first.' ■

See also

Reformation
Renaissance
Tudor England
Biography
Erasmus
Henry VIII
Wolsey

Morgan, Sir Henry

Born about 1635 in Glamorgan, Wales
A cruel pirate who grew rich and famous by attacking Spanish towns and treasure ships in the Caribbean
Died 1688 aged about 53

Henry Morgan's greatest adventure was the capture of Panama City in 1671. With 1,400 men, he made a nine-day dash from the Caribbean Sea to the Pacific coast, across the jungle-clad isthmus (narrow strip of land) of Panama. The Spaniards tried to drive a herd of cows into Morgan's ranks. But the cows stampeded and threw the Spanish soldiers into confusion. Morgan and his men burnt Panama City to the ground after looting all its treasures.

It needed 175 mules to carry the gold and silver coins and jewellery away. When the men got back to their ships, they were given only £10 each. Morgan seems to have kept the bulk of the treasure for himself. Treasure hunters today are still trying to find the place where he might have buried it.

Afterwards, Morgan was arrested and sent back to London because England and Spain were officially at peace. But he was soon released. King Charles II knighted him and made him lieutenant-governor of Jamaica. There he hunted down both English and Spanish pirates. ■

See also

Pirates

Morgan, William

Born about 1545 in Caernarvon, Wales
He translated the Bible into Welsh.
Died 1604 aged about 59

The son of a farmer in north Wales, Morgan went to Cambridge University in 1565. There he studied Latin, Greek and Hebrew, the ancient languages that all Bible scholars had to know. Already his ambition was to be the first Welshman to translate the Bible into his mother tongue. Once ordained as vicar of Llanrhaeadr-ym-Mochnant in Denbighshire (now in Clwyd), in 1578, he began his task. Far from libraries and without the help of other scholars, he took ten years to complete his translation. The Archbishop of Canterbury gave his support to the work, and in 1588 *Y Beibl Cyssegr Lan* was published and dedicated to Queen Elizabeth I.

Morgan's achievement was enormous. Not only was he a great writer and scholar, but through his work he made sure that the Welsh language did not die. The Welsh people came to love the beautiful language of their own Bible, and Morgan's translation was used in Wales for the next 400 years.

Morgan became Bishop of Llandaff in 1595, and six years later Bishop of St Asaph. Throughout these years he continued with his work as a religious translator. He died a poor man, buried in an unmarked grave. But his work had helped to keep the Welsh language vigorously alive. ■

See also

Bible   Welsh history

Morris, William

Born 1834 in Walthamstow, England
A famous Victorian designer, artist and poet who also became a socialist politician
Died 1896 aged 62

After getting a degree from Exeter College, Oxford, William Morris started work as an architect, but he soon gave up architecture to become a painter like his friends Burne-Jones and Rossetti. Later he helped to set up a firm of fine art craftworkers who designed furniture and wallpaper. He was also interested in Iceland and some of his many poems and stories are based on ancient sagas.

In 1883 he joined a socialist political party, the Social Democratic Federation, and travelled the country to speak at meetings and lead marches. He was with the playwright George Bernard Shaw on the 'Bloody Sunday' march to Trafalgar Square by unemployed workers in 1887, and was arrested by the police. When he quarrelled with the leaders of the Social Democratic Federation, he helped to start another party, the Socialist League.

Five years before he died he began yet another venture, setting up the Kelmscott Press to publish beautifully bound and illustrated books. ∎

⊙ **See also**

Patterns
Biography
Shaw

▲ This design for wallpaper is just one of many created by William Morris for fabrics and wallpapers. He hated anything 'sham', and combined accuracy of drawings from nature with a strong sense of design. He loved colour and brought new brightness into the décor of many houses.

Moses

Dates of birth and death unknown. He probably lived in the 13th century BC. A great leader, lawgiver and prophet of the Hebrews, the ancestors of the Jews.

According to the Bible, Moses was born while the Hebrews were slaves in Egypt. Pharaoh, the ruler of Egypt, had ordered that all boy Hebrew babies must be killed. So Moses' mother hid him in a basket in the bulrushes (reeds) on the banks of the River Nile. Pharaoh's daughter found him and he grew up in the palace.

After attacking an Egyptian who was ill-treating a Hebrew slave, Moses had to run away to Midian in Arabia. There he felt the presence of God when he saw a burning bush, and he knew that he had to return to his people.

Back in Egypt he and his brother Aaron asked Pharaoh to 'Let My People Go'. Pharaoh refused and God sent ten plagues to Egypt. After this, Pharaoh agreed to let the people go and Moses led the Hebrews in the 'Exodus' (departure) across the Red Sea.

They wandered in the wilderness for 40 years, living on manna (food dropped from heaven) and quails (birds), often criticizing Moses for bringing them out of Egypt. At Mount Sinai Moses received the Ten Commandments on two tablets of stone and bound the people to God in a covenant (agreement) that they would keep His laws. They also made a special tent called a tabernacle in which to worship God. Moses died before the people reached the 'promised land' of Canaan.

The story of Moses is found in the Books of Exodus, Leviticus, Numbers and Deuteronomy in the Old Testament of the Bible. So far, no archaeological evidence has been found to support the stories. ∎

⊙ **See also**

Bible
Hebrews
Jews
Biography
Joseph

Mountbatten of Burma, Earl

Born 1900 in Windsor, England
He was a naval officer and cousin of George VI, and became the last viceroy in India before it became independent.
Murdered 1979 aged 79

Louis of Battenberg was a great-grandson of Queen Victoria. In 1913 he entered the Royal Navy, and during World War I his family changed their name from Battenberg to Mountbatten because of the anti-German feeling in Britain at that time.

He remained in the navy between the wars, qualifying as an interpreter of French and German. Then, at the start of World War II, he returned to sea, commanding the destroyer *Kelly* and the aircraft-carrier *Illustrious*. In 1940–1941 he commanded a flotilla of destroyers in the Mediterranean; these were badly bombed in the battle of Crete. He became Chief of Combined Operations in 1942 and helped to plan the landings (of allied troops) in North Africa and Italy. In 1943, as an acting admiral, he was made Supreme Allied Commander for South-East Asia. Some people thought he only got this job because he was the cousin of King George VI, but Mountbatten's armies successfully recaptured Burma from the Japanese.

After the war he became viceroy (the king's representative) in India and carried out the arrangements for India and Pakistan to become independent countries, free of British rule. It was then that he was made Earl Mountbatten of Burma. Later, in the 1950s and 1960s, he had a number of important jobs in the Royal Navy and on Britain's Defence Staff.

It was while Mountbatten was on holiday in Ireland that the IRA planted a bomb on his fishing boat. The explosion killed him and two of his grandchildren. ∎

⊙ **See also**

Indian history
World War II

Biography
Nehru (photograph)

Mozart, Wolfgang Amadeus

Born 1756 in Salzburg, Austria
The greatest of all composers of opera and concertos
Died 1791 aged 35

When the Salzburg violinist Leopold Mozart realized that his children, Anna and Wolfgang, were exceptionally musical, he set about teaching them all he could. But even he must have been surprised when he discovered just how talented his son was. By the time Wolfgang was 5 he was able to compose quite respectable pieces of music, and as a performer he could outshine musicians many times his age.

In 1762 Leopold took his children on tour, to Munich and then Vienna. In the following year they went further afield, to Germany, France and England. In 1770 they toured Italy. Everywhere they went, young Mozart caused a sensation. He met all the leading musicians and competed with them on equal terms. Whether he intended it or not, Leopold Mozart had

▲ In Paris in 1763 Wolfgang Mozart, then only 7 years old, performed with his father, Leopold, and his sister. He is seen sitting at the clavier, a keyboard instrument like a piano.

provided his son with the finest musical education a composer ever had.

When eventually the touring had to stop, Mozart joined his father as one of the Archbishop of Salzburg's court musicians. But he hated being treated like a servant. In 1781 he left and set out for Vienna, determined to earn a living as best he could.

He taught and gave concerts. He composed music of all kinds and, for a while, was successful. But things began to go wrong, and his last few years were spent in comparative poverty. He was given the cheapest of funerals and his grave was soon forgotten.

Mozart wrote 41 symphonies and 27 piano concertos, besides much chamber and piano music. The complete list of his works contains over 600 titles. Finest of all, perhaps, are his operas: *The Marriage of Figaro, Così fan tutte, Don Giovanni* and *The Magic Flute*. His music is elegant and charming, and yet is full of deep feeling. It seems effortless. Not a note could be improved upon. To many musicians he is, quite simply, the greatest of all composers. ■

See also

Chamber music
Concertos
Operas
Symphonies

Mugabe, Robert

Born 1924 at Mutama, Southern Rhodesia (now Zimbabwe)
After many years as a freedom fighter, he became the first prime minister of independent Zimbabwe.

Robert Mugabe was born at a Catholic mission north of Salisbury, the capital of Southern Rhodesia. He spent his childhood tending cattle, fishing and boxing with his friends. His mother hoped he would become a priest, but he trained to be a teacher instead.

Rhodesia was then a colony ruled by Britain. Robert Mugabe travelled to other countries in Africa in the 1950s and was impressed by people who were

fighting for independence from British rule. This led to him being gaoled in 1963 for his beliefs. With others, he founded the Zimbabwe African National Union to fight for majority rule by black people in his country. ZANU was banned and Mugabe was sent to prison. He spent his time studying, and gained six university degrees by the time he was released.

He then joined the ZANU guerrillas who were attacking Rhodesian forces from Mozambique. The guerrilla fighters succeeded in winning a cease-fire and free election in 1980. Robert Mugabe was elected prime minister by an overwhelming majority of the votes cast. He has been one of the strongest critics of the South African policy of apartheid. ■

See also

Zimbabwe

▲ Robert Mugabe's portrait is carried aloft by thousands of his supporters during the 1980 Zimbabwe election campaign.

Muhammad

Born about AD 570 in Mecca, Arabia
Prophet and founder of Islam, the religion of Muslims
Died 632 aged about 62

Muhammad's father, Abdullah, died before he was born, and his mother, Aminah, died when he was only 6. He was brought up under the protection of his grandfather, Abdul Muttalib, and his uncle, Abu Talib. They came from the powerful Quraish tribe who looked after the Kaaba, the central religious shrine in the city of Mecca in Arabia.

The fact that Muhammad was an orphan has always meant that the care of orphans has a special place in the Muslim religion. As he grew up Muhammad worked as a shepherd, and later with the trading caravans that travelled all over the Arabian peninsula. He was known as *al-amin*, the trustworthy one. He worked for a widow, Khadija, who later asked him to marry her when she was 40 and he was 25.

Muhammad used to pray alone in a cave on Mount Hira outside Mecca, and there he received the first revelations from God. Muhammad believed that he had to preach to the people of Mecca that there is only one God, Allah, and that they were wrong to worship idols (images). The people laughed at him and insulted him. Khadija and a few others believed in his message and encouraged him to continue to preach.

In 619 Khadija and Abu Talib, the powerful uncle who had protected him, died. With the loss of these two important supporters, some of the Meccans plotted to kill Muhammad. He decided to accept the invitation of some people from Yathrib (later called Medina) to live there. In 622 he emigrated from Mecca to Medina with his followers. This move is called the *hijra* (migration) and marks the beginning of the Muslim calendar.

In Medina Muhammad acted as a leader when the people needed help with disputes. He taught them about religion, and he organized armed resistance to anyone, including the Meccans, who was hostile to the new Muslim community. He led various campaigns and defeated the Meccans. In 630 Muhammad entered Mecca peacefully. The people there became Muslims and destroyed the idols. By the time of Muhammad's death most of the tribes in the Arabian peninsula had acknowledged his authority. He was buried in Medina.

For all Muslims Muhammad is the example of a person whose life was rightly guided by God. He is their model husband, parent, statesman, soldier, honest trader and man of God. ■

See also

Koran
Muslims

Prophets

Mussolini, Benito

Born 1883 in Dovia, Italy
Leader of Italy's Fascists and dictator of his country from 1926 to 1943
Executed 1945 aged 61

As a schoolboy, Benito Mussolini was famous for his bad temper. From an early age he was involved in politics and was often arrested for his activities. He began to believe that the only way to change society was through violence. In 1914, he wrote in a socialist newspaper that Italy needed a 'bath of blood'.

However, he was expelled from the Socialist Party for supporting Italy's participation in World War I. After the war, many people were scared that there would be a revolution in Italy, so they gave Mussolini funds to set up the Fascist Party to oppose the socialists and communists. His Fascists attacked trade unionists, broke up strikes and then marched on Rome.

There, the king asked Mussolini to become prime minister in 1922. Gradually he took more power for himself until, by 1926, *il Duce* (the Leader), as he was now known, was dictator.

In 1935, to increase Italy's power and his own glory, Mussolini invaded and conquered Ethiopia in north-east Africa. His great friend in Europe was Hitler, and they formed an alliance, which took Italy into World War II on Germany's side in 1940. However, Mussolini's armies suffered defeats in Greece and Africa, and Italy itself was invaded by British and American troops in 1943. By this time Mussolini had been overthrown and placed under arrest. German paratroops rescued him and put him back in power in northern Italy. The end, though, was not long in coming. When Italy was finally defeated, Mussolini was shot by his Italian enemies and his body was hung upside-down in the Piazza Loreto in Milan. ■

See also

Dictators
Fascists
Italy's history
World War II

Biography
Hitler

▼ Mussolini was a powerful speaker and a charismatic leader. This picture shows him in Rome, making a speech to the Italian people. He kept power by such methods as murder, exile and prison camps.

Nanak, Guru

Born 1469 in Talwandi, Punjab, northern India
The first of ten leaders of the religious community of Sikhs. The word 'guru' means teacher.
Died 1539 aged 70

Nanak was born a Hindu, but when he grew up he worked for a Muslim and learned about the Muslim religion too. While he was a young man he had an experience of God and became a religious teacher. There is a story that, while he was bathing in the river, he disappeared for three days. They dragged the river and when they could not find his body they thought he must be dead. Then he returned. We do not know very much about his experience except from one of his early songs which is in the Sikh holy book, the *Guru Granth Sahib*. Here is a part of it. 'He' is God, whom Nanak believed he had seen.

On me he bestowed nectar in a cup,
The nectar of his true and holy name.
Those who are at the bidding of the
  Guru (God)
Feast and take their fill of the Lord's
  holiness,
Attain peace and joy.

Nanak travelled a great deal to teach people about God's path. After several years he settled in the village of Kartarpur and lived as the teacher of ordinary men and women. They shared morning and evening devotions to God, listened to Nanak's teachings and followed his example. Before he died, Nanak appointed Angad to be the next Guru. ■

See also

Sikhs

Biography
Gobind Singh

Nansen, Fridtjof

Born 1861 at Christiania (now Oslo), Norway
Zoologist, explorer, oceanographer and later diplomat who was awarded the Nobel Peace Prize in 1922
Died 1930 aged 68

Nansen began his varied career as a zoologist. On a whaling voyage he saw Greenland, and decided to lead an expedition to cross it. With five other men he made the first crossing of the island in 1888–1889.

Later Nansen led a more daring expedition, letting a specially designed ship, the *Fram*, freeze into the polar ice and drift across the Arctic Ocean. Nansen left the ship drifting slowly and tried to reach the North Pole on foot. He had to turn back, but had got nearer the Pole than anyone before him.

Nansen then settled down as a scientist. He became first a professor of zoology, and then of oceanography, the study of oceans. In 1908 he began his diplomatic career. After World War I he became the Norwegian delegate to the League of Nations. He negotiated the return of more than 400,000 prisoners of war from the USSR to Austria and Germany, and then organized relief work in Russia. In 1921 he was appointed League of Nations High Commissioner for refugees. ■

Napier, John

Born 1550 near Edinburgh, Scotland
Invented logarithms, and also designed a simple method for doing multiplication and division known as 'Napier's bones'.
Died 1617 aged 67

When Napier's book of logarithms (numbers set out in tables so addition and subtraction sums are used instead of multiplication and division) was published in 1614 it was as exciting to scientists as the modern invention of the calculator. With the help of logarithms they could perform complicated multiplication and division quickly and easily for the first time. Napier went on to try and introduce calculating rods that could be manipulated to produce even simpler ways of doing multiplication and division. They were called 'Napier's rods' or 'Napier's bones' and were used for about a century. His logarithms are still used today. While inventing logarithms Napier invented the decimal point.

Napier spent his life working on mathematics. As the son of a wealthy Scottish laird (a nobleman) Napier never needed to find a job. He became Laird of Merchiston and died where he was born, in Merchiston Castle, his family home near Edinburgh. ■

See also

Mathematics

Napoleon Bonaparte

Born 1769 in Ajaccio, Corsica
Emperor of France from 1804 to 1814 and again in 1815; one of the greatest generals of all time
Died 1821 aged 51

Napoleon's life history is so remarkable that it has inspired more books than there have been days since his death.

When he was only 10, he entered a French military school, and was commissioned in the artillery at the age of 15. When the French Revolution broke out he agreed with many of the new ideas, but he hated disorder.

He was first noticed at the siege of Toulon in 1793, where he commanded the artillery (large guns) with great daring. Then, in 1796, at the age of 26, he was given command of the army in Italy. In just over a year, he drove the Austrians out and conquered northern Italy for France. Next he invaded Egypt in 1798, but his fleet was defeated by Nelson at the battle of the Nile. Napoleon heard that all was not well in France and hurried back to Paris.

He decided that, after ten years of revolution, France needed firm government and that he was the man to provide it. In November 1799, after a *coup d'état* (overthrow of a

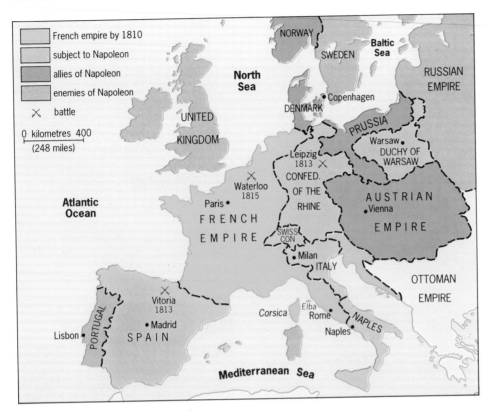

▲ By 1810 Napoleon had created the largest European empire since that of the Romans. Some countries were united directly with France, some were subject to Napoleon, while others were allies. From 1812 the whole empire began to collapse.

government), he became First Consul, the new leader of France. Over the next five years, working fifteen or more hours a day, Napoleon changed the taxes, reduced the price of bread, set up new schools and universities and organized a new code of laws.

His armies were also defeating France's enemies abroad. In 1804 he became emperor, and by 1807 his was the largest empire in Europe since the days of Rome. But then things began to go wrong. He made his brother Joseph King of Spain, but the Spanish fought against this insult, and when the British sent an army under Wellington to help, the French were driven out of Spain.

In 1812 Napoleon made his worst mistake. He invaded Russia with an

enormous army of half a million men. The Russians steadily retreated, burning their crops and drawing Napoleon's army deeper into Russia and further from its supplies. Napoleon reached Moscow, which the Russians

abandoned and burnt. Still they refused to make peace, and Napoleon saw that he had to retreat. His army was now caught by the bitter Russian winter, and his frozen and starving men died in their thousands.

By now many French people were weary of Napoleon's rule, with its censorship, secret police and the constant need for yet more soldiers. His army was crushed in the battle of Leipzig and France was invaded in 1814. Napoleon was banished to the island of Elba in the Mediterranean.

In 1815 he escaped and landed in France with only 700 men. The soldiers who were sent to stop him welcomed him with shouts of 'Long live the Emperor!' and he returned to Paris. But Britain, Prussia, Russia and Austria combined to defeat him at the battle of Waterloo. This time Napoleon was exiled to the island of St Helena in the south Atlantic, where he died six years later. ■

See also

Battles (Waterloo map)
France's history

Biography
Nelson
Wellington

▶ This picture shows Napoleon's Grande Armée (Great Army) on the retreat from Moscow in 1812. Some soldiers were so desperate to get away that they tried to cross the frozen river and fell through the ice.

Napoleon III

Born 1808 in Paris, France
He ruled as France's last emperor from 1852 to 1870.
Died 1873 aged 64

Napoleon III was born Louis Napoleon, the nephew of Napoleon Bonaparte. When the French king was put back on the throne in 1815, the whole Bonaparte family was banned from France. Louis spent this time in Italy, Germany and Switzerland, and dreamed of returning to France as a great ruler himself. In 1836 he tried to start a rebellion in Strasbourg against King Louis Philippe. This failed and he was exiled to America. He tried again in Boulogne in 1840, and this time he spent six years in prison before escaping to England.

In 1848, King Louis Philippe was expelled from France, and Louis Napoleon returned, this time to be elected president. Many people voted for him because he was the nephew of Napoleon Bonaparte. Although he promised to keep France a republic, he became Emperor Napoleon III in 1852. (Napoleon I's son was reckoned to be Napoleon II though he never reigned.) He censored the press and arrested many thousands of his critics. But he strongly encouraged industrial development, particularly the construction of railways and the rebuilding of Paris. His foreign policy was less successful, since he was never able to resist interfering in other countries' affairs.

From 1856 he suffered from ill health, and by 1863 he began to let his ministers take over the government. This led to some changes which made France more democratic. Then in 1870 France declared war on Prussia and her armies were heavily defeated. Louis Napoleon was once more thrown out of France, and he died three years later in England after an unsuccessful operation. ■

See also

France's history
Biography
Napoleon Bonaparte

Nasser, Gamal Abdel

Born 1918 in Alexandria, Egypt
President of Egypt from 1956 to 1970 and a leader of the Arab world
Died 1970 aged 52

As a boy Nasser joined demonstrations against the British, who ruled Egypt with the help of the Egyptian king. Then, in the army, he joined a secret group called 'the Free Officers' who managed to overthrow King Farouk and get rid of the remaining British troops in 1952. Some of the rebels wanted to execute Farouk, but Nasser persuaded them to exile him instead. Two years later Nasser became prime minister and then, in 1956, president.

In that year Egypt was invaded by Britain, France and Israel when Nasser took over the Suez Canal from its foreign owners. The invading countries were criticized by many other nations and soon withdrew, leaving Nasser even more powerful in Egypt.

He tried to use this power to unite Arab countries, but the joining of Egypt and Syria only lasted from 1958 to 1961. Six years later, Egypt was defeated in the Six Day War by Israel, and in 1970 Nasser died of a heart attack. ■

See also

Arabs
Egypt
Middle East

Nehru, Pandit Jawaharlal

Born 1889 in Allahabad, in Uttar Pradesh (then called the United Provinces), India
Became the first prime minister of independent India in 1947.
Died 1964 aged 74

At the age of 15, Jawaharlal was sent away from home to study at Harrow, the well-known boarding school in England. He took a degree in science at Cambridge University and later studied law in London. He returned to India in 1912 and joined his father's flourishing law practice.

Nehru was an early supporter of Mahatma Gandhi and became one of the most prominent leaders of the Indian nationalist movement. In 1920, he gave up the law practice and started working actively for the Indian National Congress, an organization that led India's struggle to gain freedom from British rule. He was elected president of the Congress in 1929 and served again as its president in 1936–1937. He was frequently sent to prison for his opposition to British rule.

▼ Nehru played a key role in the negotiations to prepare for India's independence from Britain. The photograph shows him with Earl Mountbatten, viceroy of India, in 1947.

In 1946, he was again elected president of the Indian National Congress. He led the team that negotiated with the British government the terms and timetable for India's independence. He became the first prime minister of independent India in 1947, and remained prime minister until he died.

Nehru strongly believed in parliamentary democracy and in the rapid economic development of his country. His government began a series of five-year economic development plans that concentrated on establishing large-scale industrial units and new hydroelectric projects to generate power to meet India's needs.

He was a keen supporter of the Commonwealth and the United Nations. He helped to set up a group of non-aligned countries that were not in a military alliance with either the United States or the Soviet Union during the Cold War of the 1950s. Nehru's success in foreign policy suffered a severe blow when China invaded India in 1962. Many Indians blamed Nehru and his policies for the unprepared state of the Indian army at the time of the invasion. He died two years later after a stroke.

His daughter, Indira (Mrs Gandhi), became prime minister in 1966. ■

See also

Commonwealth
Indian history

Biography
Gandhi, Indira
Gandhi, Mahatma
Mountbatten

Nelson, Horatio

Born 1758 in Burnham Thorpe, Norfolk, England
Britain's greatest sailor and the victor at the battle of Trafalgar
Died 1805 at sea aged 47

The son of a country vicar, Nelson was never a strong child. But from an early age he was determined to go to sea. He sailed boats on the local rivers, and at the age of 12 he accompanied

▲ In this painting by Denis Deighton, Nelson is shown dying on the deck of *Victory*. His last words were said to be, 'Thank God I have done my duty.'

his sailor uncle on a voyage to the Falkland Islands. At 15 Nelson joined the navy full-time, and six years later was given command of his own ship.

Despite frequent illnesses, Nelson continued to make a name for himself as a commander who was both skilled and also popular with his men. His big opportunity came when Britain declared war against the French in 1793. Despite being blinded in his right eye in a battle off Corsica, Nelson was soon made an admiral. More injuries followed, leading to his right arm being cut off at the elbow. But still he pursued the French, destroying their navy in 1798 in the battle of the Nile. Another victory followed at Copenhagen, even though Nelson's ship was at one stage in such danger that he was ordered to withdraw by his commander. Nelson avoided this order by carefully putting his telescope to his blind eye, then announcing 'I really do not see the signal!'

His most famous success was sadly his last. Near the coast of Spain, off Cape Trafalgar, in 1805, Nelson's 27 ships encountered 33 French and Spanish vessels. Nelson signalled to his own fleet: 'England expects that every man will do his duty.' Then battle commenced, and once again the French navy was completely beaten. But during the fighting Nelson was shot by a French sniper and died on the deck of his ship, the *Victory*. England was now safe from invasion but had lost one of its greatest heroes. ■

See also

Battles

Biography
Napoleon Bonaparte

Nero

Born AD 37 in Italy
Emperor of Rome
Committed suicide AD 68 aged 30

Nero was adopted by his mother's uncle, the Emperor Claudius, in AD 50. He married Claudius' daughter Octavia and so became part of the imperial household. Nero's mother Agrippina made sure that her son became emperor after Claudius by poisoning the true heir, Britannicus.

Nero was said to be a cruel man, even arranging for his own mother and wife to be murdered. We do not know for sure that he actually started the Great Fire of Rome in 64, but he used the opportunity to rebuild large parts of the city and to build an enormous palace for himself, called the Golden House. He blamed the Christians for the fire and used it as an excuse to persecute them. Many were massacred in amphitheatres, fighting gladiators or torn apart by wild animals.

He was very interested in the arts and wrote and recited poetry himself. He also sang in festivals and considered himself a fine charioteer.

In AD 68 there were uprisings against him starting in southern Gaul (now France). He committed suicide when he realized that everyone, including his own bodyguard, had deserted him. ■

See also

Roman ancient history

Newcomen, Thomas

Born 1663 in Dartmouth, England
He built one of the first steam-engines.
Died 1729 aged 66

Thomas Newcomen was a blacksmith. In 1698 he used his skill in working with metal to build a steam-engine. Seven years earlier a military engineer called Thomas Savery had built the first steam-engine. It could be used to pump water out of a mine or well, but it was very dangerous to use because it required enormous steam pressure which could easily burst the pipes. Newcomen developed a much safer engine, but it was rather slow and could not do a lot of work. About 60 years later James Watt found a way of making Newcomen's engine work much better, and this new type of engine was used to drive machines in many different industries. The steam-engine was one of the important developments that led to the Industrial Revolution. ■

See also

Industrial Revolution   **Biography**
Steam-engines   Watt

Newton, Sir Isaac

Born 1642 in Woolsthorpe, Lincolnshire, England
One of the greatest scientists that ever lived, best remembered for his ideas on gravity
Died 1727 aged 84

Many people have heard the story of Newton sitting in the orchard and seeing an apple fall. He was only 23 but was already thinking in a new way about the movement of the Earth, the Moon and the planets. He realized that, just as the force of gravity pulled the apple to Earth, gravity kept the Moon in its orbit. It is rather like a piece of string tied to a stone you whirl round your head; if the string breaks the stone is flung away. Without gravity the Moon would fly off into space.

Newton went to Cambridge University when he was 19, and was already doing important research in his second year. But then, because of the great plague, he had to go home to Lincolnshire for two years until the danger was past.

Newton tried to make a telescope to study the stars, but found that if he used lenses the bright images had

▲ Newton was the first person to make a mirror telescope. This one, which has a 9 in (23 cm) curved mirror at the lower end of the tube, can be seen at the Science Museum in London.

coloured edges. In trying to find out why this was, he invented the mirror telescope. This does not give coloured edges, and many of our present-day telescopes are based on Newton's design. He was so persistent in asking questions about the coloured edges that he was the first person to realize that white light is a mixture of all the colours. Raindrops make a rainbow and a prism makes a spectrum by splitting up the white light. Before Newton people thought that the prism or the raindrops added the colour.

Newton's greatest book, written in Latin, and usually called *The Principia*, has had an enormous effect on the way scientists, and especially physicists, have thought ever since.

Newton was knighted in 1705. At one time he was Master of the Royal Mint, which is why his portrait was on the back of the last English one-pound notes. He was very absent-minded and there is a story that he invited a friend to dinner and then forgot to come home himself. His servant put a cooked chicken under a cover on the table, and the friend ate it and put the bones back under the cover. When Newton eventually came home he lifted the cover, saw the bones, and said he had forgotten that he had eaten dinner already. ■

See also

Colour   Telescopes
Gravity
Light   **Biography**
Motion   Huygens
Rainbows   Young

Nightingale, Florence

Born 1820 in Florence, Italy
She was a national heroine and the founder of modern nursing.
Died 1910 aged 90

Florence Nightingale, who was named after her birthplace, was the daughter of wealthy parents who hoped that she would grow up to marry a rich husband. But when she was 17, she heard God calling her. She was not sure what He wanted her to do, but by 1844 she had decided to be a nurse.

This caused bitter arguments with her family, who thought that nursing in those times was not a job for respectable women, and it was not until 1851 that Florence got her own way. Her work in a small London hospital was so successful that the Secretary of State for War asked her to go to the Crimean War to take charge of the nursing of wounded British soldiers.

She set sail in 1854 with 38 nurses. Within a month they had 5,000 men to look after. Florence worked 20 hours a day to improve the nursing of ordinary soldiers. Every night she visited all the wards, and the soldiers loved her as 'the lady with the lamp'.

▼ Florence Nightingale, 'the lady with the lamp', pictured doing her nightly rounds of the wards in Scutari, where she and her staff nursed the soldiers injured in the Crimean War.

Her story was published in newspapers back home and she became a national heroine. £45,000 was collected from the public for her to spend as she saw fit. In 1860 she spent it on the Nightingale training school for nurses at St Thomas's Hospital, London.

The strain of her work in the Crimea caused her health to get worse, but she carried on training hospital nurses, midwives and district nurses to take medical care out into people's homes. And she still had an interest in the welfare of British soldiers, doing much to improve their health, housing and food.

By 1901 she was blind, but still she worked and in 1907 she became the first woman ever to be awarded the Order of Merit. ■

See also

Crimean War
Nurses

Biography
Seacole

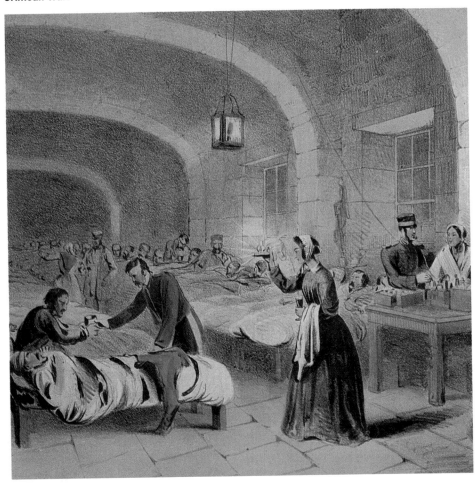

Nijinsky, Vaslav

Born 1890 in Kiev, Ukraine, Russian empire
The best known male ballet-dancer of his time
Died 1950 aged 60

Nijinsky's parents were dancers, and both he and his sister followed in their footsteps. When he was 10 he was enrolled in the Imperial Ballet School in St Petersburg. By the time he was 20 he was touring the world. People who saw Nijinsky say he was unforgettable. He was handsome, with a beautifully muscled body. He was famous for tremendous leaps, so high that some people were sure he could hover in the air. The great ballet producer, Diaghilev, made him the star of many of his ballets, a large number of which were specially created for him. Nijinsky was always looking for new techniques and styles, and he often offended classical ballet fans. Much of what he did, though, was later recognized and used in modern ballet.

Nijinsky's later life was tragic. By the time he was in his thirties he was showing signs of mental illness. This became progressively worse and he spent much time in hospital. He died, after much sadness and suffering, in London in 1950. He was reburied in Paris in 1953. ■

See also

Ballet

Nixon, Richard Milhous

Born 1913 in Yorba Linda, California, USA
The only President of the USA to resign from office

Nixon began his career as a lawyer, and served as a naval officer in World War II. In 1946 he was elected as a Republican to the House of Representatives, and after four years there he became a senator.

When Eisenhower became president in 1953, Nixon was his vice-president. He failed to win the election for president in 1960, but won in 1968. During his presidency, US astronauts became the first men on the Moon.

American troops were heavily involved in the Vietnam War. At first Nixon increased the bombing attacks against North Vietnam, Cambodia and Laos. But gradually he recognized that the communists could not be defeated. So from 1971 American forces began to be withdrawn from South Vietnam. Afterwards he improved relations with China and later visited that country. He also visited the USSR and signed an agreement to limit the production of nuclear weapons.

Nixon was easily re-elected in 1972, but his second term of office was rocked by scandals. In 1973 Vice-President Agnew resigned after he was accused of taking bribes. Also during the 1972 election campaign some of Nixon's supporters burgled the Watergate Hotel, the headquarters of the opposing Democratic Party. At first Nixon denied all knowledge of the break-in, but eventually he had to admit that he had helped to cover up the scandal. He resigned in 1974 and handed over the presidency to Vice-President Gerald Ford. ■

See also

USA: history
Vietnam

Biography
Eisenhower

Nkrumah, Kwame

Born 1909 at Nkroful, Gold Coast (now Ghana)
He led the fight for freedom and independence for African nations.
Died 1972 aged 62

Nkrumah was given the name 'Kwame', which means Saturday, the day of his birth. After a happy childhood when he gained a lifelong interest in wildlife, he became a successful student at Achimota College. He wanted to go to Lincoln University, Pennsylvania, but had no money. Luckily, relatives gave him the £150 he needed to get to the USA. There he worked his way through university, taking any jobs he could get to pay his fees. Often he had to sleep in railway stations and on park benches.

In 1945 he left the USA for Britain. In both countries he met people who were working for the rights of black people, and they inspired him. He returned to the Gold Coast to fight for his country's independence.

He founded the Convention People's Party in 1949 with the slogan 'Self-Government Now!' He called for 'positive action', similar to that taken by Gandhi to make India free. This led to his imprisonment in 1950. While in prison, he won an election so easily that not only was he released, but he was also made 'Leader of Government Business'. Then in 1954 he became prime minister. Ghana won its freedom in 1957, and in 1960 Nkrumah became its president.

There then followed many problems for Nkrumah's government and it became increasingly unpopular. While he was on a trip to China in 1966, he was deposed. He died in exile in 1972. ■

See also

Ghana

▲ As prime minister of the country that was soon to become Ghana, Nkrumah liked to wear traditional West African clothes to show his respect for Africa's history.

Nobel, Alfred Bernhard

Born 1833 in Stockholm, Sweden
He made a fortune from his invention of explosives, and in his will left a fund for prizes (Nobel prizes) to be given to people who helped humankind.
Died 1896 aged 63

▲ Each Nobel prize winner receives an award of money and a medal. The medals carry a picture of Alfred Nobel on one side. Prizes are awarded for special achievements in literature, chemistry, physics, physiology and medicine, world peace, and economics.

Nobel's father invented a submarine mine, and went on to manufacture explosives. His son Alfred became obsessed with explosives. He tried to manufacture a powerful explosive called nitroglycerine, which had been discovered about ten years earlier. It was a very dangerous substance, and Alfred Nobel's factory blew up, killing his brother. But he continued experimenting with explosives and invented a much safer explosive which he called 'dynamite'. This was used for blasting through rock. He also invented another explosive which was used for shooting bullets or shells out of guns.

Nobel died a very wealthy but very sad man. He had no friends, and everyone thought of him as a man who manufactured destruction. He had hoped that terrible weapons would prevent war because no one would dare use them. He was wrong. In his will he left a fund of over $9 million to give prizes (Nobel prizes) in five fields: literature, physics, chemistry, physiology and medicine, and peace. (In 1969 a sixth prize was added: for economics.) They have become the highest award anyone can be given. ■

See also

Bombs
Explosives
Weapons

Nuffield, Lord

Born 1877 in Worcestershire, England
Car manufacturer and generous
supporter of charities and research
Died 1963 aged 85

When William Richard Morris left Cowley village school near Oxford, he began repairing bicycles in a shed near his home. As his business grew, he began to make bicycles as well as to repair them. From bicycles he moved on to motor cycles; then, in 1911, he built his first motor car.

Morris was convinced that a cheap, dependable motor car would be bought by ordinary people, and his Morris Cowley, costing £165, was a challenge to all the expensive motor cars bought only by the rich. It was so popular that Morris had to open a new factory to cope with the demand.

By 1925, Morris was mass-producing 50,000 cars a year, on production lines like those of Henry Ford's factories in America. While the cars moved through the factory, each worker completed one small task on them, repeating this task with each car on the 'track'.

Morris bought the Wolseley car company in 1927, and merged with the makers of the sporting Riley car. By 1938 the Morris factory covered 50 hectares (120 acres), and gave work to 16,000 people. William Morris was made a viscount, the first Lord Nuffield.

Throughout his life, Morris was enormously generous. By 1938, he had already given £11·5 million for research, education, and charity. But his factories continued to make money, and a year later the millionth Morris was made. After World War II, his factories continued to grow, and he produced popular cars like the Morris Minor and the Morris Oxford. In 1952, the Morris and Austin companies merged to become the British Motor Corporation. They produced such cars as the Austin and the Morris Mini. William Morris, Lord Nuffield, was chairman of the corporation.

Morris's generosity continued. In 1943, he established the charitable Nuffield Foundation with a gift of £10 million. This gave money for research into people's health and behaviour. Money was also given to set up the radio telescope at Jodrell Bank, and for work in nuclear physics. Over £8 million was given to Oxford University, including a grant to establish Nuffield College, the first Oxford college for both men and women. The Elizabeth Morris Fund was established to help women to complete their education.

By 1957, Lord Nuffield had given away £27 million of his own money. Cars are not made with the name Morris any longer, but the car factory at Cowley, where cars are built by robots, is still producing cars. ■

See also

Motor cars

Biography
Ford
Issigonis

Nureyev, Rudolf

Born 1938 in Irkutsk, Siberia, USSR
A ballet-dancer who has become famous
throughout the world

When Nureyev was a child he was interested in folk dancing. He was a member of a children's troupe which travelled about performing traditional dances. Later he joined his local ballet

company. In 1955 he went to the Kirov ballet school in Leningrad (now St Petersburg), one of the top ballet schools in Russia. From there he joined the Kirov Ballet and became a principal dancer.

In 1961 Nureyev went to Paris with the Kirov. While he was there he decided not to go back to the Soviet Union. He asked for 'political asylum' (protection and refuge from a country) and stayed on in the West. Since then he has become famous throughout the world, dancing all the great ballet roles. He is admired for his powerful personality and the strength which shows in his dancing. ■

See also

Ballet

Biography
Fonteyn

Nyerere, Julius

Born 1922 at Butiama, Tanganyika (now Tanzania)
He became one of the most respected statesmen in Africa.

Julius Nyerere was born the son of a chieftain at a village on Lake Victoria, Tanganyika. He was educated at Makerere University College and later at Edinburgh University, where he became a Master of Arts in 1952.

He returned to teach at a Roman Catholic school near Dar es Salaam. In 1954 he helped to start the Tanganyika African National Union (TANU), which did very well in Tanganyika's first elections of 1958. Tanganyika became independent in 1961 as a result of TANU's success. Nyerere was elected prime minister. He resigned after a short time, but became President of the Republic of Tanganyika in 1962. In 1964 Tanganyika and Zanzibar decided to merge to form 'the United Republic of Tanganyika and Zanzibar'. The name was changed to Tanzania and Nyerere became its president. He was regularly re-elected at five-yearly intervals, and became one of the longest serving leaders in Africa until he retired in

1985. His views are listened to throughout the world and he has done much to bring peace and freedom to other parts of Africa.

Despite being very busy as a statesman, he still found time for his love of literature, translating Shakespeare's plays into the Swahili language. ∎

◉ See also

Tanzania

▲ Julius Nyerere's supporters carry him shoulder high through the streets of Dar es Salaam to celebrate Tanganyika's independence in 1961. Three years later he became president of the new united country of Tanzania.

Oakley, Annie

Born 1860 in Darke County, Ohio, USA
The sharp-shooting star of the Wild West
Died 1926 aged 66

Phoebe Anne Moses was born on a farm. She learned to shoot when she was very young, and was very good at it. When she was a child she hunted game which she sold for money to pay off the mortgage on the family farm. She married a marksman whom she met in a shooting competition. They started their own trick-shooting act, and together they toured variety shows and circuses.

When Annie Oakley (her stage name) was 25 she and her husband joined the famous 'Buffalo Bill' Cody's Wild West Show. For seventeen years, Annie Oakley was the main attraction. She amazed audiences with her shooting skills. She was such a good shot that she could split a playing card held edge on from 30 paces away. She could hit a coin thrown in the air, and even shoot cigarettes held in her husband's lips. Annie Oakley travelled to Europe with the Wild West Show. When she was in Berlin, the Kaiser

(Emperor) William insisted that she shoot a cigarette from his lips.

When Annie Oakley was 41 she was injured in a train crash, but she recovered and continued to amaze her audiences for many years. ∎

◉ See also

Biography
Buffalo Bill

▲ Annie Oakley's extraordinary shooting skills brought her fame in many countries. In 1946, years after her death, a musical comedy *Annie Get Your Gun* was written about Annie Oakley. However, she was much quieter in real life than the character portrayed in the musical.

O'Connell, Daniel

Born 1775 in County Kerry, Ireland
Known as 'the liberator', he led campaigns to win political rights for Irish people when their country was ruled by Britain.
Died 1847 aged 71

Daniel O'Connell was a tall, broad-shouldered lawyer who worked fifteen hours a day. He had a great gift for speaking in public, and he used it to lead campaigns for rights which most Irish people believed they had lost when their country was joined to Britain in 1801 and their parliament in Dublin was closed.

His first campaign was to change the law forbidding Catholics to hold positions as Members of Parliament, judges, town councillors and so on. He set up a Catholic Association,

which even the poorest peasants were invited to join, and toured the country holding people spellbound with his speeches. In 1828 he won an election even though it was illegal for him, as a Catholic, to be a candidate. The British parliament gave in and passed a law for Catholic emancipation in 1829.

In the 1840s O'Connell led his second great campaign, to repeal the 1801 Union of Britain and Ireland. He spoke to huge crowds at open air meetings, but it was only the start of a struggle which went on until 1921, long after his death. He is remembered for his efforts to unite all classes of Irish people, and because he always stood for political campaigns, not violence, to win what he thought was right. ∎

◉ See also

Ireland's history

Olivier, Laurence Kerr

Born 1907 in Dorking, England
One of Britain's greatest actors
Died 1989 aged 82

Laurence Olivier's father was a clergyman, and Olivier has said that his love of acting came from taking part in church services. Even when he was still a child people noticed how good he was at acting, and when he left school he went to the Central School of Speech and Drama in London.

The first 'hit' that he acted in was *Private Lives* by Noel Coward, but he became really well known in 1935 when he played Romeo in Shakespeare's play *Romeo and Juliet*.

▼ Although he later played many parts on the stage and in films, Laurence Olivier was still best remembered by many people for his role as Henry V in the 1944 film of Shakespeare's play.

A year later he was the leading actor at the Old Vic, an important London theatre, and took several major parts in Shakespeare plays. He became an international star when he appeared in films such as *Wuthering Heights* and *Henry V*, and he was knighted in 1947.

As well as being an actor, Olivier directed many plays and in 1962 he was made the first Artistic Director of the National Theatre company. He was made a life peer, becoming Lord Olivier, in 1970. ■

Orwell, George

Born 1903 in Bengal, India
A writer with a nightmare vision of the future
Died 1950 aged 46

George Orwell was the pen-name of Eric Blair, a brilliant novelist and journalist who only became famous in his last few years. In 1945 he wrote

▲ The pig-rulers in the cartoon film of *Animal Farm*. They ran the farm in the same heartless way that Communist Party officials ran the Soviet Union when Stalin was in charge. George Orwell was a socialist all his life, but he disapproved of communist dictatorship.

Animal Farm, an allegory describing how some farm animals first get rid of their harsh master, Mr Jones, only to suffer even worse cruelties from their own ruthless pig-rulers. In fact, Orwell was really attacking the way that the Russian Revolution of 1917 was betrayed by the tyrant Stalin, who ended up behaving even worse than the former Russian tsar.

Four years later Orwell wrote *Nineteen Eighty-four*, a novel set in what was then the future. It describes a bleak world where workers must exercise every day in front of a 'tele-screen' which also spies on them. Anyone showing any signs of independence is caught and executed. It is a powerful novel describing the horrors of total dictatorship. ■

See also

Allegories
Dictators
Russia's history

Owen, Robert

Born 1771 in Newtown, Montgomeryshire (now in Powys), Wales
A rich factory owner and a reformer of social conditions
Died 1858 aged 87

Robert Owen's father had a small shop. He sent his son to school until he was 9 and then out to work. Robert moved to Manchester and, after years of

▲ At his factory in New Lanark, Robert Owen paid good wages and provided decent houses for his workers. He ran a school for the children, which was also unusual. Here you see important visitors watching as the children dance in a light airy room with pictures. Owen thought teachers should be kind and keep the children happy so that they could learn better.

hardship and struggle, became manager of a spinning-mill employing 500 workers. He fell in love with the daughter of a Scottish millionaire, married her and settled in New Lanark, near Glasgow, as manager and part-owner of a textile mill.

There he proved that he could treat his workers well and still make a profit. He stopped employing children under 10, reduced the working day to 10½ hours and built houses. New Lanark and its model village became famous in Europe and America.

In 1825 he went to America, where he started a socialist community called New Harmony in Indiana. Everyone shared their work and possessions, but quarrels soon broke it up and Owen returned to Britain. He lost about £40,000 on that venture.

Times were hard for working people. In 1833 Owen tried to form one huge Grand Consolidated Trades Union for all workers, but this collapsed the

following year. He also campaigned for the Tolpuddle Martyrs (a group of farm labourers who tried to form a trade union). Owen's ideas were far ahead of his time and only some of them worked. His greatest influence was on a small group of workers in Rochdale, Lancashire, who began the first co-operative society. ■

See also

Co-operative societies
Factory reform in Britain
Tolpuddle Martyrs

Owen, Wilfred

Born 1893 in Oswestry, England
A poet renowned for the poems he wrote in the First World War
Killed 1918 aged 25

Wilfred Owen was already a poet when World War I began. After he enlisted in 1915, the atmosphere in his poems soon changed from romance to bitter anger against the slaughter then going on in the trenches. As he puts it himself in his poem *Anthem for Doomed Youth*:

What passing-bells for these who
    die as cattle?
Only the monstrous anger of the
    guns.

In 1917 he returned to England with injuries, but went back to France next year. He was shot dead one week before the end of the war. His poems, published after his death, did much to change the notion that war was still a brave and noble thing. Instead, he painted an unforgettable picture of the pointless waste, stupidity and cruelty that had led to the deaths of so many young men on both sides in the trenches. ■

See also

World War I

▼ Extract from *Exposure* by Wilfred Owen.

Our brains ache, in the merciless iced east winds that knive us ...
Wearied we keep awake because the night is silent ...
Low, drooping flares confuse our memory of the salient ...
Worried by silence, sentries whisper, curious, nervous,
But nothing happens.

Watching, we hear the mad gusts tugging on the wire,
Like twitching agonies of men among its brambles.
Northward, incessantly, the flickering gunnery rumbles,
Far off, like a dull rumour of some other war.
What are we doing here?

The poignant misery of dawn begins to grow ...
We only know war lasts, rain soaks, and clouds sag stormy.
Dawn massing in the east her melancholy army
Attacks once more in ranks on shivering ranks of gray,
But nothing happens. ...

◀ Emmeline and Christabel in prison uniform. They cannot have actually been in prison when this photograph was taken, because the authorities would not have allowed it. The picture was meant to rouse sympathy and admiration for them, and was used in the suffragette campaign. Even in these dowdy clothes the two women manage to look impressive leaders.

Park, Mungo

Born 1771 near Selkirk, Scotland
The first European to locate the River Niger in West Africa and to travel much of its length
Believed **drowned** in the River Niger, 1806 aged 34

Mungo Park was the son of a farmer, the seventh of thirteen children, a tall sturdy boy with a serious mind. He studied medicine and went to London, where a group of gentlemen interested in African exploration chose him to search for the River Niger.

In 1795 he set out on horseback from the mouth of the River Gambia wearing a frock coat and a tall hat in which he kept his notes, and carrying an umbrella. He travelled inland from one African kingdom to the next, finding that 'There was no difference in the genuine sympathies and characteristic feelings of our common nature.' He was captured by Muslim nomads, who reduced him to begging for his food and drinking from the cattle trough. Park escaped and on 21 July 1796 had his first sight of the River Niger near Ségou. He followed it to Sansanding, where the onset of the rainy season forced him to return.

In England his book of *Travels in the Interior Districts of Africa* was very successful, and in 1805 he was asked to lead a military expedition to follow the Niger to the sea. He set out with 42 British volunteers, but the rains came and despite his courageous leadership the men sickened and died. At Sansanding he built a boat made from two canoes. By the time he launched it, only four men remained alive. Ill and in fear of the Muslim tribesmen,

Pankhurst family

Emmeline and her daughters led the violent suffragette campaign to win votes for women in Edwardian Britain.
Emmeline Born 1858 in Manchester, England
Died 1928 aged 69
Christabel Born 1880 in Manchester
Died 1958 aged 77
Sylvia Born 1882 in Manchester
Died 1960 aged 78

Emmeline Goulden was a clever, elegant woman. She married a lawyer, Richard Pankhurst, who believed that women should have the same rights as men. After he died, she and her forceful eldest daughter Christabel (who was training to be a lawyer) founded in 1903 the Women's Social and Political Union, the 'suffragettes'. They and their supporters interrupted political meetings, smashed shop windows, and did all they could to win women the right to vote. When they were arrested they went on hunger strike; Emmeline made herself seriously ill. Christabel escaped to Paris in 1912 so that she could stay free to organize the campaign. They became very ruthless, and even broke with Emmeline's younger daughter Sylvia because she worked independently from them, with poor women in London's East End.

When war came in 1914, Emmeline and Christabel urged women to work for their country. Sylvia, however, believed the war was wrong.

Women over the age of 30 were given the vote in 1918, and then in 1928, a month after Emmeline Pankhurst's death, all women were given the same voting rights as men. ■

⊙ **See also**

Edwardian Britain
Suffragettes
Women's movement
World War I

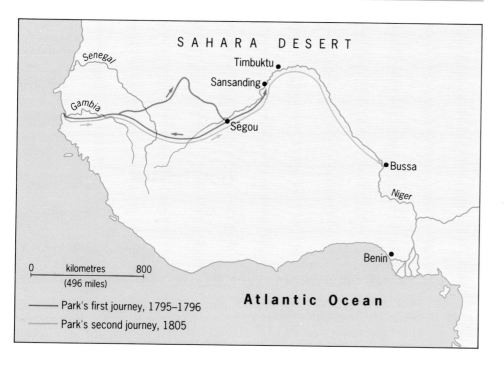

▲ Mungo Park led one of the first European expeditions to investigate the course of the River Niger in West Africa. He played an important part in early European exploration of Africa.

they travelled down river firing indiscriminately at the canoes that came out to meet them. At Bussa they were attacked and Park was last seen jumping overboard. ■

See also

African history

Parker, Charlie

Born 1920 in Kansas City, USA
A jazz saxophonist and composer, famous because he was one of the founders of the jazz style called 'bebop'
Died 1955 aged 34

Charles Christopher Parker Junior was always called either 'Charlie' or by the nickname 'Bird' or 'Yardbird'. As a small boy he played baritone horn in his school band. When he was 11 his mother bought him an alto saxophone, and he left school at 15 to try to become a professional musician. His style was unusual, and he was not really accepted by other jazz musicians until he was working in New York in the 1940s with other players such as Dizzy

Gillespie. In 1945 he made a series of records with Gillespie and others. These recordings became famous as perhaps the beginning of the 'bebop' style. Parker went on to make more records and concert appearances with many other modern jazz musicians, including Miles Davis and Erroll Garner.

Parker's early death was brought about by his lifelong addiction to drink and drugs. ■

See also

Jazz

Parnell, Charles Stewart

Born 1846 in Avondale, County Wicklow, Ireland
An Irish political leader who worked to win Home Rule for his country
Died 1891 aged 45

Charles Parnell was a landowner in Ireland. Like most wealthy landlords he was a Protestant and had connections with England, where he went to school. But he sympathized with the poverty of Catholic farmers and believed that the Irish should have

their own government instead of being ruled by the United Kingdom.

By his mid-thirties he was spoken of as 'the uncrowned king of Ireland'. He became an MP in the British Parliament at Westminster in 1875, and soon became noted for holding up debates by making long speeches. This made sure that English politicians took notice of the small Home Rule Party. In 1880 he became its leader. He was also president of the Land League which backed farmers who refused to pay rents. The government put Parnell in prison, but he had so much support in Ireland that they had to agree to free him and help the farmers with money to pay their debts and buy their own land.

By 1885, Home Rule had become so popular in Ireland that Parnell's party had 86 MPs and the Liberal prime minister, Gladstone, needed his help to stay in power. Gladstone decided to give Home Rule to Ireland. Yet it did not come for another 35 years, because some Liberal MPs wanted to keep the Union with Ireland and voted against the Home Rule Bill. Parnell led more campaigns for Home Rule up to 1890. Then he was named in a divorce case by the husband of the woman he was living with (the husband and wife had separated). The Home Rule Party voted against Parnell as leader after a long argument which ruined his health and led to his death. ■

See also

Ireland's history

Biography
Gladstone

▲ One way of gaining publicity for the Land League was to make boxes of matches with slogans about the Land League on them. Many thousands of these matchboxes were sold in Ireland in Parnell's day.

Pascal, Blaise

Born 1623 in Clermont-Ferrand, France
He proved how barometers work.
Died 1662 aged 39

Pascal was a mathematical genius. By the age of 12 he had worked out by himself the first 32 theorems of Euclid. At 16 he published a geometry book about parts of cones called conic sections. The great French philosopher and mathematician Descartes hardly believed that a 16-year-old could produce such advanced mathematics.

At 19 Pascal had invented a calculating machine for adding and subtracting. Unfortunately it was too expensive to make and was never used.

Pascal was very interested in Torricelli's work with barometers. Pascal proved that the atmosphere really has weight by sending his brother-in-law up a mountain with a barometer. The level of mercury dropped in the tube the higher he went.

Ten years before his death Pascal became a devout Catholic, abandoned his scientific and mathematical work and devoted his time to writing about religion and philosophy. ■

See also

Barometers
Calculators
Geometry
Biography
Descartes
Euclid
Torricelli

Pasteur, Louis

Born 1822 in Dole, France
One of the really great scientists of all time, who discovered that bacteria cause disease. His process of 'pasteurization' is still used today to make milk safe to drink.
Died 1895 aged 72

Louis Pasteur's father was a poor man who worked as a tanner, preparing animal skins for the leather industry. His son was not a very clever boy at school and was mainly interested in painting. But Louis's life changed when he went to some chemistry classes given by an excellent teacher. He became fascinated by the subject, worked very hard and in his twenties had already become famous for his experiments in chemistry.

In 1856 Pasteur was asked to help the French wine industry, which was losing millions of francs a year because much of the wine was going sour. He showed that this was caused by a tiny living organism, a yeast, which could be killed by heat. This heating process was named 'pasteurization' and is used today to make milk safe to drink.

Pasteur's most important work was his study of what causes disease. He showed that microscopic living organisms, 'germs' (bacteria), carried disease from one person to another. He made a special study of a disease called anthrax which kills cattle and sheep. He isolated the anthrax bacteria and prepared a weak form which he injected into sheep; then when he gave them a full dose of anthrax they did not get the disease. A similar method had been used by Edward Jenner for preventing smallpox in people.

▲ **Pasteur at work in his laboratory. Pasteur showed that some diseases were spread by tiny living organisms, visible only through a microscope. We now call these bacteria.**

Louis Pasteur then made a life-saving vaccine for treating and preventing the deadly disease called rabies. Rabies makes dogs and other animals go mad, and is passed on to people when they are bitten by infected animals.

Pasteur spent his whole life dedicated to his work, and died a respected and well-loved man. ■

See also

Bacteria
Germs
Immunity
Milk
Vaccinations
Biography
Jenner
Montagu

Patrick, Saint

Born about AD 390 in western Britain
He is the patron saint of Ireland.
Died about 461 aged about 70

Patrick was born into a family of well-to-do Christians in Roman Britain. At the age of 16 he was captured by Irish pirates. He spent the next six years as a slave in pagan Ireland. Then he escaped back to Britain. According to his own later writings, he was now a much changed person. He trained to become a priest, and in about 435 he returned to Ireland. From then on he devoted his life to converting the Irish people to Christianity. He worked mainly in the north, where he had his own bishopric at Armagh.

No one is sure where he died and was buried. But he is still the most popular saint in Ireland. Many churches in the English-speaking world have been dedicated to him too, including the main cathedral of New York. His feast day is 17 March, and in pictures he is often shown treading on snakes. This is because, among many other legends, he is supposed to have driven all the snakes out of Ireland. ■

See also

Ireland's history
Roman Britain

▲ The 17th-century Spanish artist, Murillo, painted this dramatic picture of the conversion of St Paul on the road to Damascus. Jesus appears from the heavens and his words are written in Latin: 'Saul, Saul, why do you persecute me?'

Paul, Saint

Born date unknown, at Tarsus in Asia Minor (now Turkey)
One of the early Christians; a missionary, writer and thinker who had a great influence on the development of Christian teaching
Beheaded about AD 65, age unknown

This Christian saint was originally named Saul, after the first king of Israel. He was Jewish by birth and was also a Roman citizen. His trade was making tents, but he was so gifted that he was sent to Jerusalem to train as a rabbi (a Jewish religious teacher). In the years after the crucifixion of Jesus he joined in persecuting Jesus's followers. According to the Bible he was there when Stephen, the first Christian martyr (a person who suffers or dies for a belief), was stoned to death.

The story of Saul's conversion tells how he was travelling to Damascus one day when he saw a light and heard the voice of Jesus asking, 'Saul, Saul, why do you persecute me?' Blinded for a while by the great light, he was led to Damascus and there he was baptized as a Christian.

He spent three years quietly praying and thinking, and then joined other Christians in Jerusalem. This was the beginning of a life of missionary journeys to places around the Mediterranean Sea, teaching people about Jesus. Paul, as he was now called, taught in Cyprus, Asia Minor (Turkey), Athens, Corinth and Rome. He also wrote letters to the Christian congregations in those places, to help them to understand their new religion and follow its teachings. These letters are among the epistles in the New Testament of the Bible.

Paul's life was very difficult and dangerous. He was shipwrecked, beaten for his beliefs, and often criticized by those who had been followers of Jesus right from the beginning. Paul became disappointed in those he had converted when they behaved badly.

Roman soldiers arrested him in Jerusalem after a mob of people attacked him because they thought he had ignored Jewish laws. He used his right as a Roman citizen to 'appeal to Caesar', which meant going to Rome to be tried. It was on the voyage to Rome that he was shipwrecked at Malta. In Rome he was imprisoned for two years. He was probably killed in the reign of the Emperor Nero.

The story of Saint Paul's career is found in the Acts of the Apostles in the New Testament of the Bible. ■

⊙ See also

Bible
Christians

Pavlov, Ivan Petrovich

Born 1849 in Ryazan, Russia
His famous experiments with hungry dogs led to the study of behaviour in animals.
Died 1936 aged 86

Pavlov's father was a priest and assumed that his son would become one too. But Pavlov became interested in science, and left the college where he was preparing for the priesthood and went to study science and medicine at university.

Pavlov became very interested in the way we digest food and did lots of experiments with dogs. He knew that when a dog is hungry and is shown food it will start to dribble saliva straight away. This is called a reflex action. Pavlov cut open the cheeks of his dogs to reveal their salivary glands, to observe the dribbling more clearly. Then he rang a bell every time food was brought to the hungry dog. After a while ringing the bell alone was enough to make the dog dribble. The dog had learnt to expect food when the bell rang. Dribbling had become a reflex response to the bell ringing as well as to food.

This simple but cruel experiment made scientists really think about why animals (including us) behave the way they do and how they learn different types of behaviour. ■

⊙ See also

Animal behaviour
Vivisection

Pavlova, Anna

Born 1881 in St Petersburg, Russia
Russian-born ballerina who became
famous throughout the world
Died 1931 aged 49

Anna Pavlova was a delicate child from
a poor family. Her unusual talent for
dancing was spotted while she was
still at school. Like Nijinsky, she was
enrolled at the St Petersburg Imperial
Ballet School. In 1906 the Imperial
Russian Ballet gave her the title of
prima ballerina. A year later she danced
The Dying Swan, a ballet specially
created for her, and her most famous
role.

By 1913 Pavlova had decided to leave
Russia to set up her own company.
Her aim was to bring ballet not only to
the great European and American
cities, but to countries such as India,
Africa and South America where it
had hardly ever been seen.

Over a period of 20 years she covered
some 550,000 km (350,000 miles) and
gave nearly 5,000 performances,
amazing audiences with her lightness
and grace. From 1912 she was based
in London, where she inspired many
younger English dancers. ■

See also

Ballet

Biography
Nijinsky

▲ Surrounded by her ballet shoes, Anna
Pavlova sits in her dressing room at the
Théâtre des Champs-Élysées in Paris in
1924.

Pearce, Philippa

Born 1920 in Cambridgeshire, England
A wonderful modern novelist for children

Philippa Pearce did not start writing
for children until she was over 30.
When recovering from a long illness,
she started remembering her childhood
spent near Cambridge, where her father
was a flour-miller. She and the rest of
her family were brought up in the mill-
house, which had a garden running
down to the river.

Out of these memories Philippa wrote
Minnow on the Say, a lively adventure
story set on an imaginary river. But
her next book, *Tom's Midnight
Garden*, was her masterpiece. It
describes how a lonely boy called Tom
managed to make contact every night
with the ghost of Hatty, a little girl
living in the same house some 70 years
before. They met in a garden that was
once there but had since been built
over. Unlike other ghost stories there
is nothing frightening here. Instead it
is a touching tale with a marvellous
surprise ending. ■

Pearson, Lester Bowles

Born 1897 in Newtonbrook, Ontario,
Canada
A Canadian politician who played an
important role in international affairs
Died 1972 aged 75

Pearson's early years were marked by
many changes. As the son of a
Methodist minister he moved several
times during his childhood. During
World War I he was a stretcher-bearer
in Greece with the Canadian army. He
joined another regiment in 1917 and
went to England, where he was hurt in
an accident with a London bus. On his
return home he completed a degree at
the University of Toronto and then
tried careers in law, business, and
teaching before he joined the
Department of External Affairs.

Eventually he became a diplomat,

working in London and Washington.
He represented Canada when the
United Nations Organization was set
up in 1945, and was president of the
UN General Assembly in 1952. He
tried to help end the war in Korea.
When there were problems between
Israel and Egypt he suggested sending
in a UN peacekeeping force. The idea
worked well, and Pearson won the
Nobel Peace Prize in 1957.

Pearson became leader of the Liberal
Party in 1958. His party was in
opposition at first, but in 1963 it won
the election and Pearson became prime
minister. Before he retired in 1968 he
introduced welfare programmes,
including a pension plan and a
scheme to provide medical care for
everyone. ■

See also

Canada's history

Peel, Sir Robert

Born 1788 in Bury, England
British prime minister from 1834 to
1835 and from 1841 to 1846; he also
founded the first police force.
Died 1850, after a fall from his horse,
aged 62

Robert Peel was a tall, handsome man,
and a brilliant scholar at Oxford.
Thanks to his father's influence, he
became a Member of Parliament at
the age of 21, supporting the Tory
(Conservative) Party. He held a
number of government posts both in
Britain and in Ireland. When he was
Home Secretary, in charge of law
and order, he started the London
Metropolitan Police force, and
policemen were called 'Bobbies' and
'Peelers' after him.

Peel became a baronet in 1830, and
was briefly prime minister from 1834
to 1835. Then, as leader of the
Conservative Party, he became prime
minister again in 1841, staying in
power until 1846. To help poorer
people, Peel reduced the taxes on
goods, especially food, and brought
back income tax instead. His party

split, though, when he repealed the Corn Laws (which had kept the price of bread high by putting taxes on imported grain), and he resigned as prime minister. He was afterwards thought of as the founder of modern conservatism. ■

See also

Police
Victorian Britain

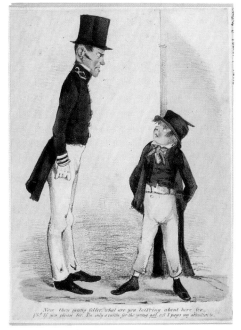

▲ Of all his achievements, Sir Robert Peel is best remembered for starting the police force in London. The arrival of 'Peelers' helped to stop a lot of petty crime, particularly amongst street boys.

Penn, William

Born 1644 in London, England
He founded Pennsylvania in America.
Died 1718 aged 73

Penn was the son of a naval officer who later became an admiral. From early on he was very religious and was eventually converted to the Quaker faith. This believes that each person must look for true religion in their own heart and in their own way. The Anglican Church (Church of England) at the time found this hard to accept, preferring instead that everyone should worship in the same style. Expelled

▲ William Penn, the founder of Pennsylvania, is shown here making his first treaty with local Indians in 1682.

from university for refusing to go to compulsory Church of England services, Penn was later imprisoned four times for preaching his own faith.

On his release he met other Quakers both in Britain and Europe all looking for a place where they could follow their own beliefs in freedom. So in 1680 Penn asked King Charles II for a gift of land in America in return for a large debt the king owed Penn's father. The gift came, made up of land on the east coast between Maryland and New York. It was called Pennsylvania, another way of saying 'Penn's woods'. Penn sailed out there with numbers of other Quakers. Once established, he was so honest and just in his dealings with the local Indians that there was very little trouble between them. Instead, he had many difficulties with

his own often unruly followers, and by the time of his death Penn was actually planning to sell Pennsylvania back to the British government once again. ■

See also

American colonial history
Quakers

Pepys, Samuel

Born 1633 in London, England
He wrote one of the most famous and interesting diaries ever published.
Died 1703 aged 70

On 1 January 1660, a young Londoner called Samuel Pepys (pronounced 'peeps') started a diary. He wrote it in code, probably because he did not want his wife to read it. His diary shows he was fond of her, but also that he grumbled because she was untidy and forgetful, and he enjoyed flirting and having affairs with other women.

Pepys had a good job organizing supplies for the navy. He travelled in the ship which brought Charles II back to England in 1660, and attended his coronation. Pepys's boss was the King's brother, the Duke of York (later James II), so he knew all the court gossip, as well as navy affairs. He lived through the terrible plague of 1665, and the Fire of London the following year.

Pepys kept his diary for nine years. When you read it, you step straight back into the London of Charles II. ■

⊙ **See also**

Fire of London
Stuart Britain

▲ Samuel Pepys's spectacles, which were designed to shield his weak eyes from the light.

Pericles

Born about 495 BC, place unknown
The most famous statesman of ancient Athens
Died 429 BC aged about 66

Pericles became a political leader in Athens after the defeat of the Persians. He helped to make Athens a great city in many ways. He developed the way it was organized, so that all the citizens (male adults) could meet in a large assembly and make decisions about peace and war and new laws. These decisions were inscribed on stone and

publicly displayed. It was the first democracy we know about.

Pericles also made Athens strong by extending the city's walls and by making sure that the navy was capable of controlling the seas around Greece. Athens was then able to build an empire from the cities and islands that looked to her for protection. He made Athens magnificent to look at by arranging for some beautiful new buildings on the hill of the Acropolis. The most famous of these is the Parthenon, a large temple to the city's goddess Athene, which took fifteen years to build.

Pericles had enemies, and not everyone thought that the democracy was the best way of running the city or that he was spending public money in the right way. Many of the comic plays written at the time made cruel fun of him, and his friends were often accused of dishonesty. But Pericles was such a good speaker in the assemblies that he remained in control for many years. He was elected 'general' (a political office as well as a military one) fifteen times.

Pericles wanted Athens to be at peace for as long as possible, but in the end he could not avoid a war with Sparta, a city in southern Greece. War broke out in 431 BC and Athens was eventually defeated. Pericles died in a great plague that hit Athens soon after the beginning of the war. ■

⊙ **See also**

Greek ancient history

Peter the Great

Born 1672 in Moscow, Russia
Peter I was Russia's greatest tsar, ruling for 42 years and turning Russia into a world power.
Died 1725 aged 52

Peter came to the throne as joint tsar with his half-brother Ivan at the age of 10, but spent his childhood playing soldiers and being educated in the countryside outside Moscow. His

▲ To begin with, Tsar Peter tried to get rid of beards from his court by clipping them by force. When this did not work, he put a tax on beards in 1698. He was determined to modernize dress as well as customs and attitudes.

stepsister Sophia ruled in his place until she tried to take power for herself. Peter then took charge and sent Sophia to a nunnery in 1689.

After Ivan's death in 1696, Peter was sole ruler. Although he read little, he loved to know how things worked and became a skilled boatbuilder. He spent two years in western Europe studying various industries, and brought back to Russia teachers of all the arts and crafts which his country most needed. To make his court more modern, he made his advisers shave off their traditional long beards. At just 2 metres (6 ft 7 in) tall, Peter towered above all around him, and if anyone argued he would beat them with a stick.

He was also a soldier tsar and spent much of his life at war. His greatest victory was against the Swedes at Poltava in 1709 during the 21-year 'Northern War'. His victories in this war enabled him to build a new capital city for Russia on the Baltic coast, St Petersburg.

The reforms he introduced with the help of foreign statesmen and craftsmen turned Russia into a more modern country, with an army and navy, schools and universities and its first public newspaper.

Peter had a son, Alexei, by his first wife Eudoxia, but Alexei plotted against Peter and was put to death in 1718. So Peter's wife Catherine became Catherine I, Empress of Russia, when he died in 1725. ■

See also

Russia's history

Peter, Saint

Born date unknown, probably in Galilee, Palestine (now Israel)
Leader of the twelve apostles, the first followers of Jesus
Crucified about AD 64

Peter was originally called Simon, and he and his brother Andrew were fishermen who lived near the Sea of Galilee. One day when they were out fishing, Jesus called to them to follow him and become 'fishers of men'. From then on Peter and Andrew were especially close to Jesus until his death. Together with James and John, they often accompanied Jesus when the other disciples did not.

Jesus gave Simon the name Cephas, which means a stone. Peter comes from the Greek equivalent, *petra*. Simon Peter seems to have been the first person to say that Jesus was the Messiah (the Jewish leader prophesied in the Old Testament of the Bible). In Matthew's gospel Jesus says that Peter and his faith are the rock on which the Church will be built.

There are many stories about Peter in the gospels. He seems to have been a person who made mistakes as well as showing great faith. When Jesus was arrested in Jerusalem and taken away to be tried, Peter in a moment of panic denied three times that he knew him. And then he wept bitterly for his betrayal.

After the crucifixion of Jesus, Peter preached that Jesus was alive. He was imprisoned twice, but escaped and travelled round the Mediterranean telling people about Jesus and his teaching. He may have written one of the epistles (letters) in the New

Testament of the Bible; but the epistle entitled 2 Peter was probably written in the next century by someone else.

There is a tradition that Peter spent the last years of his life in Rome as the first bishop of Rome, and that he was crucified head downwards as he did not think himself worthy of dying in the way Christ died. There is a tomb under the cathedral of St Peter in Rome where he may have been buried.

The gospel of Saint Mark gives most description of Peter's contact with Jesus, and some scholars think Peter may have dictated parts of it to Mark. ■

See also

Apostles   **Biography**
Bible   Jesus
Christians

Philip II of Macedon

Born 382 BC
King of Macedonia in the 4th century BC
Assassinated 336 BC aged 46

Philip, King of Macedonia, conquered large areas of northern Greece and extended his kingdom into Thrace and the Black Sea area. He also brought most of the important Greek cities to the south under his control. He began a campaign against the Persian empire which his son Alexander the Great continued.

Philip made Macedonia powerful by reorganizing the army and developed the system of using the phalanx, a huge block of heavily armed foot-soldiers. He was able to campaign throughout the year, and took many cities by surprise because they were used to a break in the fighting during winter. Philip picked off the northern cities one by one. He gained control of the Thracian gold mines, which brought him huge amounts of money. He was a shrewd politician and knew how to make use of the rivalries and jealousies of the cities. He was ruthless and brutal and destroyed cities (such as Olynthus in northern Greece) if it suited him.

His success marked the end of the freedom of the Greek cities. His main enemies were Athens and Thebes, and he defeated them in a decisive battle at Chaeronea in central Greece in 338 BC. Two years later he was assassinated at his daughter's wedding, and his son Alexander succeeded him.

Archaeologists have discovered the royal Macedonian tombs at modern Vergina, and one of them is almost certainly Philip's. It contained rich and beautiful jewellery and ornaments, and shows that Macedonia was much more advanced in art than people used to think. ■

See also

Greek ancient history
Biography
Alexander

Philip II of Spain

Born 1527 in Valladolid, Spain
King of Spain, Naples and Sicily from 1556 to 1598, and also of Portugal between 1580 and 1598. Married Mary I, Queen of England in 1553.
Died 1598 aged 71

From 1556 to 1598 Philip II of Spain was the richest, mightiest ruler in Christian Europe. His empire included parts of Italy, the Netherlands and vast stretches of South and Central America, as well as Spain and Portugal. But after 1559 he never left these last two kingdoms. As his reign went on he spent more and more time in his specially built monastery-cum-palace, the Escorial, several miles from the capital, Madrid. He was a clever king, but he took too much work on himself, because he found it hard to trust his own servants and ministers.

Philip was a very serious Roman Catholic, at a time when the wars of religion were ravaging Europe. 'I would lose all my states and a hundred lives, if I had them,' he once told the Pope, 'rather than allow the least damage to the Catholic religion and the service of God.'

He involved his peoples in many wars, against the English, Dutch, French and Turks, but he rarely let his religious aims get in the way of more worldly ones. When he sent the Spanish Armada to attack England in 1588, it was for military and not religious reasons. His reign was part of the so-called 'Golden Age' of Spain. But Philip spent so much of Spain's gold on his wars that the Spanish age of power and prosperity was almost over by the time he died. ∎

See also

Armada
Spain's history

Biography
El Greco
Mary I

▲ **This stunning suit of armour was made for Philip in Augsburg, Germany, in 1552.**

▲ *Guernica* **by Picasso, Prado Museum, Madrid, Spain. Guernica was a small Basque town in northern Spain which was almost totally destroyed by a bombing attack in 1937 during the Spanish Civil War. Picasso painted pieces of human bodies with screaming, open mouths, despairing gestures and monster animal shapes. All these convey his feelings of horror at the terrible evils of war.**

Picasso, Pablo

Born 1881 in Málaga, Spain
An outstanding painter and sculptor of the 20th century
Died 1973 aged 91

Picasso showed truly exceptional talent when very young. His first word was *lápiz* (Spanish for pencil), and he learned to draw before he could talk. By the age of 11, he was creating art magazines as a hobby, all written and illustrated by himself. He hated school and never learned to write well. He knew little of mathematics, and later admitted that he 'was even unsure of the order of the alphabet'. But he loved painting and worked at nothing else.

He often helped his father, a painter, with his work. One evening his father left the young Pablo to finish a picture of pigeons. On his return, he saw an astonishingly lifelike painting. He gave his son his own palette and brushes and never painted again. Pablo was just 13.

Many people realized that Picasso was a genius, but he wanted to do things in his own way, even if he disappointed many who expected him to become a traditional painter. At first he suffered years of real poverty, but he was both courageous and self-disciplined, with an enormous appetite for hard work.

As his extraordinary talents developed, he was constantly breaking the rules of artistic tradition; he often shocked the public with his strange and powerful pictures. He often did not try to 'copy' real life in his paintings. He designed new forms to give fresh ways of seeing things in the world around us.

His style changed many times. He had enormous energy; he made drawings, paintings, collages, prints, theatre sets, sculptures, pottery and ceramics. He is probably best known for his 'Cubist' pictures, which used simple geometric shapes and only a few colours.

His life's work entirely changed our ideas about art. To millions modern art means the works of Picasso.

Picasso himself wrote, 'Basically I am very curious. My curiosity is greater than that of any other man. I am curious about every aspect, moment and phenomenon of life. I am curious about every dream. My curiosity crosses over every frontier of curiosity.' ■

See also

Sculpture
Spain's history

Pitt, William (the older)

Born 1708 in London, England
One of Britain's greatest statesmen, and prime minister from 1766 to 1768
Died 1778 aged 69

William Pitt the older was the son of a Member of Parliament. He hated school, and left university after one year. Entering Parliament at the age of 27, he soon made his name as a fine speaker, never afraid to criticize the most famous in the land including the king. Unlike other Members of Parliament, Pitt was very honest and stayed a fairly poor man, never accepting the bribes common at the time. At 46 he became happily married to Lady Hester Grenville.

In 1756 Britain was at war with France (in the Seven Years War) but doing badly. Pitt was given the job of heading the war effort, and did so with great success. The fleet was strengthened, and the French were eventually beaten in India, America and the West Indies as well as in Europe. In 1766 Pitt was made Earl of Chatham and was prime minister, but resigned two years later in ill health. ■

Pitt, William (the younger)

Born 1759 in Hayes, Kent, England
Prime Minister of Britain from 1783 to 1801 and from 1804 to 1806
Died 1806 aged 46

William Pitt, the younger son of the Earl of Chatham, entered Parliament in 1781 at the age of 22. Like his father, he was a brilliant speaker. Impressed by his abilities, King George III invited him to become prime minister in 1783. This was a job he was to hold for the next seventeen years. During this time he raised taxes to pay off Britain's debts, and reduced widespread smuggling.

When France declared war on Britain in 1793 after the French Revolution, Pitt fought back hard. He censored the press and sometimes imprisoned without trial those who wanted a revolution in Britain too. Abroad he formed an alliance with Russia, Sweden and Austria against France, but died in his second term of office as prime minister. Never marrying and with few friends, he lived entirely for politics. ■

See also

France's history
Georgian Britain

Pizarro, Francisco

Born about 1474 in Trujillo, Spain
Conquered the Inca empire of Peru for Spain.
Assassinated 1541 aged about 67

Pizarro was a Spanish adventurer who conquered the Inca empire of several million people in South America with an initial force of just 180 men. He was the illegitimate son of a Spanish colonel, and was apparently abandoned by his parents. He worked as a swineherd for some time, before going to Hispaniola in the Caribbean to try his fortunes there. He took part in several exploring expeditions.

In 1522 he was trying to scratch a living as a landowner in Panama when he heard rumours of the Inca empire and its fabulous wealth. Having made an expedition to check that it really existed, he went home to Spain in 1528 and asked permission from the king (Emperor Charles V) to conquer it.

In 1532 Pizarro arrived in Peru to find the country split by civil war. He seized the emperor, Atahualpa, and demanded a huge ransom of gold and silver. When it was paid he had Atahualpa executed on the grounds that he was plotting against the Spaniards. Spain now ruled the Inca empire. But Pizarro himself did not enjoy his victory long. In 1541 he was assassinated in Lima, Peru, by rival Spaniards. ■

See also

Conquistadores   **Biography**
Incas   Atahualpa
Spanish colonial history   Charles V

▼ In this engraving Pizarro is shown supervising the collection of Atahualpa's treasure by Spanish soldiers. In the background a priest is baptizing Indians as Christians while soldiers stand by to assist.

Plato

Born 429 BC in Athens
This famous Greek philosopher founded the Academy in Athens and was responsible for putting into writing the ideas and teachings of Socrates.
Died 347 BC aged 82

Plato was born into an important Athenian family. He was well educated and at the age of 20 became a pupil of Socrates. The teachings of Socrates had enormous influence on Plato's thinking and on what he wrote.

When Socrates was put to death in 399 BC, Plato left Athens and lived for a time in Megara to the west of Athens. He also travelled for the next twelve years throughout Greece and to Egypt, Italy and Sicily. In 387 he returned to Athens and started a school of philosophy. Most schools were held in the open air, in shady walks or under the colonnaded verandas of public buildings. His school was established in a park and gymnasium (sports ground) about two kilometres outside the city walls. This park was sacred to Academus, and so Plato's school became known as the Academy (a word still used today for some types of school). The Academy of Plato was still there until AD 529.

Plato believed, like Socrates, that the right way to teach was to ask questions and let the pupils discover the truth for themselves. A great deal of this teaching was published in his *Dialogues*, discussions between various people. Probably Plato's most famous work was *The Republic*, in which he discusses the ideal state or society. Plato describes the last hours and thoughts of his master Socrates in a book called *Phaedon*. ∎

See also

Greek ancient history
Philosophers

Biography
Aristotle
Socrates

Pocahontas

Born 1595 at Chesapeake Bay, Virginia, USA
An Algonquin Indian who befriended English settlers and used her influence to keep peace between them and her own people. Her name means 'The Little Playful One'.
Died 1617 aged 22

Pocahontas was the favourite daughter of Powhatan, chief of the area where the first English settlement was established at Jamestown, Virginia in 1607. She was 12 when Captain John Smith was dragged before her father to be clubbed to death. Pocahontas laid her own head upon his and pleaded successfully for his life. Later she visited Smith at Jamestown, and 'vied with the boys, in turning handsprings'.

When Smith returned to England, fighting broke out again. Pocahontas was taken hostage and chose to stay in Jamestown, where a tobacco planter, John Rolfe, made her his 'strange wife'. He took her and their baby son to London for a year. Pocahontas attended court in European dress. She met John Smith again and told him she wished to be 'for ever and for ever your countryman'. As her ship set sail for Virginia, she was taken ill and put ashore at Gravesend, where she died. ∎

See also

American colonial history

▶ This charming portrait of Pocahontas, painted by an unknown artist in 1616, shows her dressed like an English lady.

Polo, Marco

Born about 1254 in Venice, Italy
A merchant who spent many years in China and wrote the first account of that country by a European
Died 1324 aged about 70

In the 13th century, Cathay, as people then called China, was a romantic, unknown land to Europeans. So when 18-year-old Marco Polo was invited by his father and uncle, Niccolò and Maffeo Polo, to go with them to the court of the emperor Kublai Khan at Khanbalik (Beijing) he was delighted. Niccolò and Maffeo had already visited Kublai Khan, the first Europeans to do so, and the Khan had asked them to return.

The three merchants set out in 1271. They went by ship to the Mediterranean coast of Turkey, and the rest of the way over land. They took the southern branch of the Silk Road, along which merchants from China regularly brought silk to Europe. The road runs north of the Himalayas, and across the Gobi Desert. The whole journey took nearly four years.

Kublai Khan received them warmly at court. Niccolò and Maffeo seem to have settled down as traders, but Marco, who had a gift for languages, became a civil servant and travelling diplomat. He kept his eyes and ears open, and reported back to Kublai all that he had seen and heard. He was sent on many missions, visiting India, Burma and Sri Lanka.

After 17 years the Polos decided it was time to go home. At first the Khan refused to let them go, but in 1292 they obtained his permission on condition that they took charge of a Mongol princess whom he wished to send as wife to his grand-nephew, the ruler of Persia. They went by sea, by way of Singapore, Sri Lanka, and the Persian Gulf. When they had safely delivered the princess they returned to Venice. They arrived back in 1295, having been away 24 years. They had a fortune in jewels.

Marco spent the last 30 years of his life as a Venetian merchant. At one

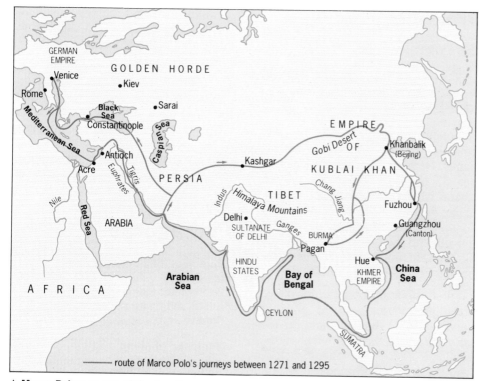

▲ Marco Polo was one of the few Europeans in the Middle Ages to journey into the heart of the Chinese empire. The book he wrote on his return contained descriptions of the splendours of Kublai Khan's court and of the countries he visited.

time he was captured in a sea fight by the Genoese, became a prisoner of war in Genoa, and there dictated the story of his travels. This is not a story of his personal adventures but a description of the almost unknown Mongol Empire. He begins by describing Kublai Khan, and the magnificent state in which he lived. He has chapters telling of the Summer Palace, and the hunting parties in the country south-east of Beijing. There are fascinating chapters too about his travels inside China, particularly his visit to Hangchow, which was the capital before the great Khan conquered the country. Many readers thought he was making things up, and Venetians called Marco *Il Milione*, meaning 'he of the million lies'. But later people realized that his account was mostly true. It influenced Christopher Columbus's decision to look for a westward route to China and Japan. ■

See also

Explorers

Biography
Ibn Battuta
Kublai Khan

Potter, Beatrix

Born 1866 in London, England
She wrote *The Tale of Peter Rabbit* and other famous children's stories.
Died 1943 aged 77

Beatrix Potter had a lonely childhood. Her parents were rich and she lived in a big house in London. But she was never sent to school, and very seldom met other children. She spent much of her time in the nursery upstairs and had no toys except for one wooden doll called Topsy.

The family and their servants used to go for long summer holidays to Scotland, and it was here that Beatrix discovered an amazing new world, away from London. She found that the countryside was full of mysterious small animals that burrowed under leaves, lived in hedgerows, or darted through streams. She began to imagine what it felt like to live on a tiny scale.

When she grew up, she used to send letters to her friends' children; when she ran out of news, she filled the pages with pictures and a story about a rabbit called Peter. The children loved them.

She sent *The Tale of Peter Rabbit* to a publisher, but he returned it. She sent it to five other publishers, but none of them accepted it for publication. So she had the book printed with her own money, and gave copies of it to children. Then children that she did not know wanted copies, too, and in 1902 the first publisher, Frederick Warne, agreed to reprint *Peter Rabbit* for her. The books became very popular and thousands of copies were sold. With the royalties from *Peter Rabbit*, *Squirrel Nutkin*, *The Tailor of Gloucester*, and other books, she bought a small farm in the Lake District. During the next ten years she wrote *The Tale of Tom Kitten*, *The Tale of Jeremy Fisher*, and many more, using the landscape and the animals around her for inspiration.

She married at the age of 47 and settled down happily as a sheep-farmer. With that, Beatrix Potter's life as a writer came to an end, but her books are still read by millions of children all around the world.

She gave Hilltop, her Lakeland home, and many acres of farmland to the National Trust on her death. ■

▲ An illustration from an edition of Beatrix Potter's first book, *The Tale of Peter Rabbit*, which she had printed herself after it was rejected by six publishers.

Priestley, Joseph

Born 1733 near Leeds, England
Discovered oxygen.
Died 1804 aged 70

Joseph Priestley was a minister in the Unitarian Church and very interested in politics. He was on the side of the Americans who were trying to free themselves from British rule, and he also supported the French people who during the French Revolution fought against the French king and his noblemen.

Priestley had no scientific education, but he did have the desire to experiment. He lived next to a brewery, from which he got large supplies of carbon dioxide, the gas which makes bubbles in beer. He began a series of experiments with the gas, and produced a bubbly drink called soda water, which is still enjoyed today.

But Priestley's real claim to fame is his outstanding work studying many other gases, and particularly his discovery of oxygen, which he called 'dephlogisticated air'. The importance of oxygen in burning was shown by the great French chemist Lavoisier.

Priestley's political opinions got him into a great deal of trouble. Many people in Britain were opposed to the growing success of the French Revolution, and a mob burned down Priestley's house in Birmingham. He fled to London with his family, but France declared war on England and the new French people's government made Priestley a French citizen. He could no longer live safely in England and quickly left for the United States of America.

The USA was now independent of England and warmly welcomed Priestley. He spent the rest of his life working mainly for the Unitarian Church. ■

See also

American Revolution
Gases
Oxygen

Biography
Lavoisier

Prokofiev, Sergei

Born 1891 in Sontsovka, Ukraine, Russian empire
One of the leading Russian composers of operas, symphonies and ballets
Died 1953 aged 61

Prokofiev had his first music lessons from his mother, who was an excellent pianist. He began composing when he was 5, and could play Beethoven sonatas when he was 9. When he was 13 he went to the St Petersburg Conservatory of Music. He did not get on well with the other students, or the teachers. He found them dull, and they thought he was too full of himself.

His first important compositions, two piano concertos, caused a great scandal. People thought them far too noisy. But later works, such as the popular Classical Symphony, helped them to change their minds.

Prokofiev did not like the results of the 1917 Russian Revolution, and after the founding of the USSR he spent many years in America and France. But in the end he could not keep away from his mother country. One of the first pieces he wrote on his return to Russia was the delightful children's tale *Peter and the Wolf*. ■

See also

Ballet   Sonatas
Concertos   Symphonies
Operas

Proust, Marcel

Born 1871 in Paris, France
Author of the longest novel in the world
Died 1922 aged 51

Marcel Proust was the son of a successful doctor. Throughout his life he suffered from asthma, and his growing ill health led him gradually to withdraw from people into his own company. But by this time he had wide knowledge of the ways of rich French society, all of which he used in the writing of his seven-part novel *Remembrance of Things Past*. He also used this book to make a study of memory itself and the way tastes or smells can suddenly take us back to things that happened years ago.

Proust's work is not easy, and was originally refused by so many publishers he eventually had to pay for its publication himself. But over the years it has come to be seen as one of the great classics of literature, full of revealing ideas about human thoughts, feelings and relationships. ■

Pythagoras

Born about 582 BC on the Greek island of Samos
Remembered for his study of musical sounds and his mathematical ideas
Died about 497 BC aged about 85

At the age of about 40 Pythagoras set up a strange religious community in southern Italy. It was called the Pythagorean Brotherhood and its members lived according to rules made by Pythagoras. They did not eat any meat, because they believed our souls could enter animals when we died. They also did not eat beans, because Pythagoras believed they also had souls. Pythagoreans lived a very strict, simple life and spent much of their time doing mathematics. Pythagoras believed that mathematics held all the secrets of the universe, and he believed some numbers were magical.

He is remembered for 'Pythagoras' theorem', a simple rule in geometry about the sides of right-angled triangles. But Pythagoras also did some of the very first scientific experiments, by listening to the sounds of stretched strings of different lengths and working out the mathematics of octaves and harmony. Pythagoras' mathematical ideas became important to the philosopher Plato, and through him influenced other scientists such as Galileo, Kepler and Sir Isaac Newton. ■

See also

Geometry   **Biography**
Mathematics   Galilei
Music   Kepler
                    Newton
                    Plato

Ralegh, Sir Walter

Born about 1552 near Budleigh
Salterton, England
A courtier, soldier, explorer, pirate,
scientist and writer, and a favourite of
Queen Elizabeth I
Executed 1618 aged about 66

▲ This tiny miniature portrait (diameter 4·8
cm) shows Sir Walter Ralegh dressed in the
height of fashion. It was painted by Nicholas
Hilliard, probably soon after the queen
knighted her favourite in 1584. Although
Elizabeth I enjoyed Ralegh's company, she
did not think he was reliable, and never
gave him any real power.

Walter Ralegh is supposed to have first
pleased Elizabeth I when he laid his
fine velvet cloak over a puddle, so the
queen would not get her shoes muddy.
He was certainly a great favourite of
the queen's after he came to court in
1581. But he did not always please
her, especially when he married
Elizabeth Throgmorton, a lady in
waiting. He was sent to the Tower of
London, and then banished from court
for a time.

Walter Ralegh was not just a charming,
witty courtier. He was an accomplished
soldier who had fought in France
and Ireland, and helped to prepare
England's defences against the Spanish
Armada.

He was fascinated by the riches of
America, then mainly controlled by
Spain. His attempt to start a colony at
Roanoke in North America failed. He
never went there himself, but his

expeditions probably brought potatoes
to Britain for the first time, and whether
he brought tobacco from America or
not, Ralegh made pipe-smoking
fashionable at court. In 1595 he went
to South America and searched
unsuccessfully for El Dorado, an
imaginary land full of gold. He tried
(but failed) to make his fortune by
attacking Spanish treasure ships in the
Caribbean.

James I, who became king in 1603,
distrusted Ralegh, and imprisoned him
in the Tower of London for over twelve
years. Ralegh wrote a *History of the
World*, and did many scientific
experiments. The king's eldest son
Henry became his friend, and said 'No
king but my father would keep such a
bird in a cage.'

In 1616, James allowed Ralegh to go
back to South America to search for
gold, on condition he did not cause
trouble by attacking the Spanish. But
his expedition found no gold. They
got into a fight with the Spanish, and
Ralegh's son Wat was killed. Ralegh
returned a sick, sad man. In 1618,
James finally ordered his execution. ■

Ralegh spelt his name this way. The spelling
Raleigh is also used.

See also

Stuart Britain   **Biography**
Tudor England   Elizabeth I
      James I

Raphael

Born 1483 in Urbino, Italy
With Leonardo da Vinci and
Michelangelo, Raphael was one of the
three great artists of the Renaissance.
Died 1520 aged 37

Raffaello Sanzio (his Italian name) was
born into a very educated family. At
about 7 years old, he was apprenticed
to his father, an artist, to learn his
father's trade of painting. He began by
learning to mix up colours for his
father's pictures.

By 17 he was already a master painter.
He worked in Florence and then in
Rome. He was employed by the Pope

to work on his palace (the Vatican)
and his chapel (the Sistine), for which
he designed tapestries.

His great interest was in painting the
human figure, especially the Madonna
and Child (Mary and Jesus). By
showing tender glances and reaching-
out gestures, he made them look
loving, unlike the cool and formal
pictures people were used to. He had
amazing skill at taking ideas from
others and, by varying and changing
them, making something quite new of
his own. His work shows exquisite
beauty and harmony. He painted
nothing ugly, horrible or shocking. His
own gentle character seems to show in
his paintings, which look effortless,
but were the result of endless hard
work.

He crammed an astonishing amount
of artistic achievement into his short
life, and received many honours for
his work in fresco, portraits, huge
figure compositions, engravings and
tapestry design. He died on his 37th
birthday, and left behind an idea of
'perfection' in painting. For centuries
after his death he was generally
regarded as the greatest painter of all
time. ■

See also

Frescos
Paintings
Renaissance (reproduction of a painting)

Reagan, Ronald

Born 1911 in Tampico, Illinois, USA
American film star who became
president of his country from 1981 to
1989

The Reagan family was poor. After
working his way through college,
Ronald became a radio sports
announcer. His good looks and voice
soon got him a Hollywood contract,
and he made many films.

He joined the air force in World War
II. Witty and energetic, for several
years after the war he was president of
the Screen Actors Guild. He also
worked in television. He was so good

at making speeches that people told him he should be a politician.

Reagan was elected Governor of California in 1966. He believed that government had become too big and powerful. It also cost too much, and was hindering instead of helping most Americans. These ideas did not win him the presidency in 1976, but he tried again and won the presidential elections in 1980 and 1984. He was not only the oldest, but one of the most popular and conservative American presidents. During his presidency, military expenditure increased enormously while less money was spent on welfare benefits for the poor. ■

See also

USA: history

Rembrandt van Rijn

Born 1606 in Leiden, The Netherlands
One of the greatest portrait painters the world has ever known
Died 1669 aged 63

Rembrandt was the eighth of nine children born to a miller and a baker's daughter. He was a very gifted child and his parents sent him to university when he was 14. A year later, he left to develop his artistic talent. He used his own family as models, and mastered the skill of painting facial expressions. He loved to paint portraits. Indeed he painted himself 60 times, leaving a record of how he looked from a young man to old age. He became famous in his twenties, married a rich wife, bought a grand house and collected art works and oddities.

Unfortunately he could not manage money at all. His sufferings began with the death of three of his children, then of his mother, then of his wife, Saskia, leaving him with one son, Titus. His pictures became less popular, and debts made him practically bankrupt. But still he worked on.

As he grew older Rembrandt became extra-sensitive to the real person

behind the face. He no longer bothered with people's clothes or backgrounds, but concentrated on the true personality, what people were like and what they had been through. Truth became more important than beauty.

After the death of his beloved son Titus and of his mistress, Hendrickje Stoffels, the only close relation left was their daughter, Cornelia. Though she was devoted to him, he was often lonely. This is reflected in his last sombre paintings. His fellow artists painted the world around them; Rembrandt painted the world inside ourselves: the human spirit. ■

See also

Portraits

▲ *Self-portrait* (1642) by Rembrandt, Kenwood House, London. Rembrandt's self-portraits face you squarely looking out from the canvas with a searching honesty in the eyes. This is a powerful and dignified image of an artist who always looked below the surface of things. His own self-portraits became more and more revealing as he grew older.

Renoir, Pierre Auguste

Born 1841 in Limoges, France
One of the most popular of the French Impressionist painters
Died 1919 aged 78

Renoir was the son of a tailor, and grew up knowing that good craftsmanship was essential in the making of quality work. At the age of 13, he was apprenticed to a porcelain manufacturer to produce hand-painted designs. But soon machines were invented to do this cheaply, and Renoir moved over to painting fans and then to decorating blinds. He was dissatisfied with this work, and soon saved enough money to study figure drawing and anatomy at evening classes. He worked in a famous studio where he met other budding young artists who were also interested in capturing the dappled effects of light and shadow in their paintings. With them he founded the group of painters known as the Impressionists, who held their first exhibition in 1874. As with the others, his early work suffered ridicule, but he soon became successful as a portrait painter. He also enjoyed painting busy scenes of ordinary people in bright gay colours, using bold brushstrokes without fussy detail.

When an old man he painted with the brush strapped to his stiff arthritic wrist, and directed assistants to make his sculptures. He never ceased working; in all he produced an astonishing 6,000 pictures. ■

See also

Paintings

Biography
Monet

▶ *Ball at Le Moulin de la Galette* by Renoir, Musée d'Orsay, Paris, France. *Le Moulin de la Galette* was an open-air dance hall where Parisians met to enjoy themselves. Renoir has caught the flickering light filtering through the branches of the trees and shows how it dapples the faces and dresses of the girls and the dark cloth of the men's coats.

Revere, Paul

Born 1735 in Boston, Massachusetts, USA
Famous for rousing the patriots of Massachusetts at the outbreak of the American War of Independence
Died 1818 aged 83

At the age of 13 Paul Revere was apprenticed to his father, a Boston silversmith. Later he set up his own workshop and became an ardent patriot who wanted his country to be free of British rule. Disguised in war-paint and feathers, he destroyed crates of tea at the 'Boston Tea Party' to protest against British taxation.

On 16 April 1775 a single lantern in the North Church steeple signalled that the British troops were marching inland to capture a munitions store at Concord and two patriots, Hancock and Adams, who were hiding at Lexington. Paul Revere rode through the night to warn the country people and to urge them to resist. At Lexington the soldiers were fired on by armed farmers, and they were forced to retreat from Concord by a larger force. ■

See also

American Revolution

Rhodes, Cecil John

Born 1853 in Bishop's Stortford, England
He was one of the great builders of the British empire in Africa.
Died 1902 aged 48

As a boy Cecil Rhodes suffered from weak lungs, so instead of going to university he went to southern Africa where the climate would be better for him. At first he worked on a cotton farm with his brother, Herbert, but then moved to Kimberley to mine for diamonds.

Between 1873 and 1881, Rhodes spent some of his time at Oxford University studying for a degree. It was during these years that he decided that the British should extend their rule throughout Africa. Back in Kimberley, he began to make the money to turn this dream into reality. By 1891 his company, De Beers, owned 90 per cent of the world's diamond mines.

Rhodes had already entered parliament in the Cape Colony in 1881, and he became prime minister in 1890. Against opposition from Paul Kruger and the Boers of the Transvaal, he pushed British rule northwards into

▲ The *Colossus of Rhodes* was one of the seven wonders of the ancient world. It was a giant statue of Helios, the sun god, built on the island of Rhodes. This cartoon from the British magazine *Punch* is saying that Cecil Rhodes was so important in Africa in 1892 that he, too, was a 'colossus'.

Mashonaland and Matabeleland. The new colony was called Rhodesia (now Zimbabwe) after him. He dreamed of building a railway across Africa from Cairo to the Cape.

His success caused further quarrels with Kruger. In 1895, Rhodes supported the 'Jameson raid', which was an attempt to overthrow Kruger's government in the Transvaal. It failed, and Rhodes had to resign as prime minister.

In later life he was involved in a scandal with Princess Radziwill, who forged letters and documents in his name. Before her trial was over and while the Boer War was still being fought, Rhodes died. In his will, he left £3 million to pay for overseas students to go to Oxford University. ■

See also

Boer War   **Biography**
Zimbabwe   Kruger

▶ Richard I portrayed in combat. He was remembered for his bravery in battle as Richard the Lionheart. The illustration is on a tile made in the 13th century for Chertsey Abbey in Surrey, England.

Richard I

Born 1157 in Oxford, England
A warrior king of England from 1189 to 1199, he fought for his lands in France, and for the Holy Land as a crusader.
Died 1199 aged 41

Richard was the third son of Henry II and Eleanor of Aquitaine. He grew up closer to his mother than his father, and in 1173 she persuaded him to rebel with two of his brothers against Henry. The revolt was a failure, but sixteen years later Richard forced his ageing father to make him heir to all his lands in England and France, leaving nothing for John, Richard's younger brother.

Once in power, Richard went on the Third Crusade with the other kings and nobles of Europe. They failed to capture Jerusalem, but Richard defeated Saladin, the Muslim leader, at Arsuf. On the way back to England, Richard was taken prisoner by one of his enemies, the Duke of Austria. His government in England had to raise the huge amount of £100,000 to pay the ransom of their king.

Although King of England for ten years, Richard spent a total of only five months in his kingdom, and the last five years of his reign were devoted to fighting the King of France. Richard died of blood poisoning, caused by an arrow in his shoulder, while besieging a town in Aquitaine. ■

See also

Crusades

Biography
Henry II
John, King
Saladin

Richard II

Born 1367 in Bordeaux, France
The last of the Plantagenet dynasty, he was crowned at the age of 10, in 1377, and deposed at 32, in 1399.
Murdered 1400 aged 33

Richard was the son of the Black Prince and grandson of Edward III. His father's early death in 1376 meant that Richard found himself crowned King of England at the age of 10. Older men, of course, governed instead of Richard while he was so young. But once in power, they were unwilling to give up governing, and Richard had to spend his adult life trying to rid himself of them and rule on his own.

Too often Richard acted on impulse. At the most dangerous moment of the Peasants' Revolt, in 1381, for example, he rode into the centre of the mob, shouting, 'Take me as your leader.' That risk paid off and the peasants dispersed, but Richard did not win any lasting independence.

As his reign went on, Richard took more and more desperate measures to keep his nobles under control, sending them to exile or even having them murdered. Finally one of the nobles in exile, Henry Bolingbroke, returned with an army, seized the throne as King Henry IV, and had Richard murdered.

Although his reign was a troubled one, Richard's court was a centre for poets, painters, musicians and master builders. Richard himself was an outstanding patron of the arts. ■

See also

Canterbury Tales   **Biography**
Peasants' Revolt   Chaucer

Richard III

Born 1452 in Fotheringhay, England
His brief reign, from 1483 to 1485, brought to an end the Wars of the Roses.
Killed in battle 1485 aged 32

Richard lived in the shadow of his elder brother, who became King Edward IV in 1461, while Richard was

created Duke of Gloucester. In the continuing feud of the house of York against the house of Lancaster, Richard helped his brother defeat Lancastrian challenges to the throne.

When Edward died in 1483, Richard did away with the nobles who could become his enemies, imprisoned his brother's two sons, the rightful heirs, in the Tower of London, and had himself proclaimed king – all within three months. Until then, he had been a popular and trusted man, but now he began to lose support. When England was invaded by Henry Tudor, a Lancastrian bethrothed to the Yorkist heiress, Richard was deserted by many of his followers. He was killed on the battlefield at Bosworth and his crown was found on a thorn bush. ■

See also

Wars of the Roses   **Biography**
                         Henry VII

Rivera, Diego

Born 1886 in Guanajuato, Mexico
He was one of Mexico's greatest artists, famous for his colourful murals (paintings that decorate walls and ceilings).
Died 1957 aged 70

Diego Rivera studied art and politics in Europe from 1907 to 1921. At that time he was much influenced by Pablo Picasso, the famous Spanish master of modern art. But when Rivera went home to Mexico, he deliberately turned his back on fashionable European styles of painting. He said he was more interested in 'art for the people'. He revived older methods of painting such as fresco (using water-colours on wet plaster) and encaustic painting (using heat to fuse wax colours onto a surface).

▲ *The Tarascan Civilisation: Dyeing Cloth,* **National Palace, Mexico City. This is one of a series of frescos by Rivera in the National Palace in Mexico City. It portrays and celebrates the industries and national identity of the Tarascan people of Mexico before they were conquered by Spain in the 16th century.**

Rivera loved to paint scenes from Mexican life and history, particularly the history of ordinary people. He also much admired the American Indians, and painted huge murals in vivid colours, showing how the Aztecs were destroyed by the Spaniards. His sympathy for communism sometimes got him into trouble. His huge mural for the American Rockefeller Center in New York was removed because it contained a picture of Lenin, the first leader of the communist USSR. ■

See also

Aztecs   **Biography**
Mexico   Picasso

Robeson, Paul

Born 1898 in Princeton, New Jersey, USA
A black American who became internationally famous as a classical actor and singer
Died 1976 aged 77

Paul studied law at university, but in the 1920s, when he qualified, it was difficult for black people to get work as lawyers. So he became an actor and also began to sing African American folk songs. He played in Shakespeare's *Othello* in London and New York. He also appeared in films, the best-known being *Sanders of the River*, in 1935, and *Show Boat* in 1936.

Robeson had a wonderful, natural bass voice which captured the attention of all who heard him. The song 'Ol' Man River' from *Show Boat* is always associated with him, as are such folk songs as 'Water Boy' and 'Ma Curly Headed Babby'.

After visiting the Soviet Union in the 1930s, Robeson became interested

▼ Paul Robeson was always interested in politics, and he was ready to use his fame to support causes he believed in. Here he was speaking out against nuclear weapons in Trafalgar Square, London in 1959.

in communism, and in 1950 the government of the USA took away his passport because he would not deny being a communist. This caused him great grief and bitterness and seriously affected his career. He eventually left the USA and stayed away until 1963, when he returned for health reasons. ■

Robespierre, Maximilien

Born 1758 in Arras, France
One of the most famous leaders in the French Revolution
Executed 1794 aged 36

'Under Robespierre blood ran and we had bread.' That is how a carpenter from Paris remembered him.

Maximilien Robespierre was the son of a lawyer, and after school in Paris he returned to Arras, where he remained an unknown small-town lawyer until he was 30. Then, in 1789, Robespierre was elected as a deputy to represent his province in the Estates-General (a sort of parliament). Unlike many other deputies, he saw himself as representing all the people, even the *sans-culottes*, the poor people who

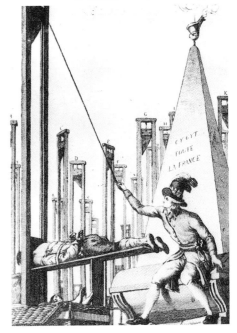

▲ Most people remember Robespierre not for his honesty or for his ideas and speeches. It is the guillotine they remember and the thousands of people he had executed before he himself was beheaded. This cartoon shows Robespierre beheading the executioner because he has run out of victims. The huge tombstone reads: 'Here lies all France'.

wore trousers, not knee-breeches (*culottes*) like the wealthier people.

Robespierre made a name for himself in the Revolution which followed through the power of his speeches. He pressed for the ideas of the Revolution, liberty for all, equality for all and fraternity (brotherhood) of all. The *sans-culottes* loved him and called him 'the Incorruptible' because of his honesty.

By 1793 there was civil war in the west, an invasion in the north-east, and people were starving. Robespierre and his supporters, the Jacobins, decided that ruthless action was needed to feed the people, to raise a citizen army and to get rid of the Revolution's enemies. He joined the Committee of Public Safety, which organized these activities.

This was the time of 'the Terror' when anyone might be accused of treason, quickly tried and executed. Robespierre thought this was necessary, but as thousands were killed, many saw it as brutal tyranny.

By the summer of 1794, people were sick of the Terror. The deputies turned on Robespierre and his supporters and ordered their arrest. No one tried to save him from the guillotine, which had been used on so many others. ∎

See also

France's history

Rockefeller, John D.

Born 1839 in Richford, New York, USA
He made a fortune as the founder of Standard Oil and gave millions of dollars away.
Died 1937 aged 97

John Davison Rockefeller was working as a business man when the first oil well was drilled in the USA in 1859. Four years later he started an oil refinery near Cleveland, Ohio. By 1870 his company had become the Standard Oil Company, which began to buy up many other oil companies.

By 1882 Rockefeller's company had beome almost the only refiner of oil in the USA, with 95 per cent of all business. This monopoly made him into a multimillionaire. Once he had made his fortune he began to look for good and useful ways to spend it. In 1891 he paid for the University of Chicago to be set up. Later he also set up the Rockefeller Institute for Medical Research (which became Rockefeller University) in New York City. In 1913, after he retired from the oil business, he began the Rockefeller Foundation to finance many charitable activities. ∎

Rodin, Auguste

Born 1840 in Paris, France
A great French sculptor
Died 1917 aged 77

Rodin's father, a police official, sent him to boarding school for a short time to improve his poor studies, but Rodin's only interest was drawing. His mother shopped at a general store

where plums were wrapped in paper cones, rolled from the pages of art magazines; these were Rodin's first inspiration. Later he began work as a stonemason, carrying out the designs of others for decorations on buildings. His techniques became highly skilled and he began to study the works of famous sculptors in museums.

He was powerfully influenced by the statues of Michelangelo and visited Italy to see more of them. His own figures eventually became famous for their unusually lifelike quality and sense of movement. They were so realistic that he was accused of taking a cast from a live model to achieve accuracy.

Rodin's sculptures caused constant opposition and endless quarrels amongst his critics. Often his pieces were accepted only after long argument. Many changes were usually requested before his figures could take up positions in public places. One of his most famous, 'The Thinker', was attacked by a vandal with a chopper. Like other artists at the time, he discovered that sculpture need not look entirely finished to be effective or powerful. ∎

See also

Sculpture

Röntgen, Wilhelm Conrad

Born 1845 in Remscheid, Germany
He discovered X-rays, one of the most powerful tools to help doctors see inside the human body.
Died 1923 aged 77

In 1895 Röntgen was doing some experiments in which he applied a strong electric current to some metal plates inside a glass tube from which most of the air had been removed. His tube was covered with black cardboard and the room was dark, but to his amazement, he noticed that a chemical on the bench across the room was glowing. After many different experiments he decided that the tube

must be giving out rays that went through both the glass and the cardboard. They were so mysterious that he called them X-rays. The letter x often means unknown. Nowadays most people have had an X-ray at the hospital or the dentist and so they have lost some of their mystery. It was not until about 1910 that scientists showed that they were electromagnetic waves like light but with a much shorter wavelength. ∎

The name is also spelt Roentgen.

See also

Light
Waves
X-rays

Roosevelt, Eleanor

Born 1884 in New York City, USA
The first wife of an American president to become famous in her own right
Died 1962 aged 78

Eleanor was orphaned at 10 and brought up by her strict grandmother. She was taught at home, until at 15 she went to school in England. There she found friends, but she was still easily hurt all her life, although she tried not to show it.

Eleanor married a distant cousin, Franklin Delano Roosevelt, and supported him when he became a politician. Then he caught polio. To save his career, Eleanor became 'the legs and eyes of a crippled husband'. She visited mines, slums, hospitals: places he could not go to himself.

Eleanor always spoke up for the poor, blacks and women. Many thought she should keep quiet when her husband was elected president in 1932. Others admired her honesty.

After Franklin's death in 1945, Eleanor continued to make speeches and write for newspapers. She was a US delegate to the United Nations. At her funeral, a friend said 'She would rather light a candle than curse the darkness.' ∎

See also

Biography
Roosevelt, F. D.

Roosevelt, Franklin Delano

Born 1882 in Hyde Park, New York State, USA
The only President of the USA to be elected four times; he led the country out of the Great Depression and during World War II.
Died 1945 aged 63

Like his uncle, President Theodore Roosevelt, Franklin D. Roosevelt had to fight hard to overcome a physical handicap. He developed polio at the age of 40, and his legs were paralysed. He partly recovered the use of them through swimming.

By this time Roosevelt, a Democrat, had already served in the New York State senate, and as Assistant Secretary for the Navy. Although he was badly crippled he soon returned to politics. In 1928 he was elected Governor of New York State, and four years later became President of the USA.

The country was in a terrible state. One worker in four was out of work, and many families were too poor even to buy food. Five thousand banks had failed. Roosevelt promised a New Deal, and told Americans: 'The only

thing we have to fear is fear itself.' He launched a programme to put the country back on its feet. It enabled banks to reopen and gave jobs to the unemployed. He also began radio broadcasts to the nation, known as his 'Fireside Chats'. The success of these and later measures made him president again in 1936.

In 1940, with World War II raging in Europe, Roosevelt was elected for a third term, the first and last president to be so. In December 1941 the USA entered the war. Roosevelt guided the country through its darkest days, working closely with the leaders of Britain and the Soviet Union, Winston Churchill and Joseph Stalin. He won a fourth election in 1944, but in April 1945, with war victory in sight, he died suddenly. ∎

◉ See also

USA: history
World War II

Biography
Roosevelt, Eleanor

▲ This photograph of Franklin Roosevelt was taken in November 1944, just after he had voted in the Old Town Hall, Hyde Park, New York. He died only five months later.

Roosevelt, Theodore

Born 1858 in New York City
Youngest man to become President of the USA, soldier, explorer and international peacemaker
Died 1919 aged 60

Roosevelt was born into a wealthy family. A weak child who suffered from asthma, he built up his health and muscles. He was always known as 'Teddy', and cartoonists likened him to a bear. Toymakers began making stuffed animals they called 'Teddy Bears'.

Roosevelt entered politics at the age of 23, but the death of his wife and his mother on the same day in 1884 shattered him, and he became a cattle rancher in Dakota instead.

In 1898 Roosevelt led a cavalry regiment, the Rough Riders, in the Spanish American War. Then he became vice-president in 1900. Six months later President McKinley was assassinated, and Roosevelt became president.

As president, Roosevelt broke up trusts (big business monopolies), settled a damaging coal strike, and bought a strip of land to build the Panama Canal. Through his efforts, Panama became independent from Colombia.

After he was re-elected in 1904 Roosevelt helped to bring about peace

▼ Theodore Roosevelt always liked the outdoor life almost as much as he enjoyed being president in the White House. Here he is standing with the naturalist John Muir above Yosemite Valley, California.

in a war between Russia and Japan. For this he was awarded the Nobel Peace Prize in 1906.

When he retired Roosevelt hunted big game in Africa, and led an expedition to explore the River of Doubt in Brazil, now called the Roosevelt or Teodoro River. ■

👁 **See also**

Panama
Toys
USA: history

Rothschild family

Rothschild, Mayer Amschel
Born 1744 in Frankfurt, Germany
He founded the Rothschild banking empire and ran it with his five sons.
Died 1812 aged 68
Amschel Mayer Born 1773
Died 1855 aged 82
Salomon Mayer Born 1774
Died 1855 aged 80
Nathan Mayer Born 1777
Died 1836 aged 58
Karl Mayer Born 1788
Died 1855 aged 66
Jakob or James Born 1792
Died 1868 aged 76

Mayer Amschel Rothschild had to give up being a student when his parents died. He went to work in a bank instead. Gradually he built up his own banking business in Frankfurt and, with the help of his sons, he started branches all over Europe. His eldest son, Amschel Mayer, worked with him in Frankfurt. Nathan Mayer started the London branch in 1804. Then Jakob, the youngest son, set up the Paris branch in 1811. In the 1820s, after their father's death, Salomon Mayer and Karl Mayer opened new branches in Vienna and Naples.

They all followed two main guidelines. Firstly, they carried out their business activities together as one family. And secondly, they would never try to make too much profit.

The family fortune was made during the wars against Napoleon, when they lent money to the warring countries. Later during the Industrial Revolution they made money buying and selling the stocks and shares of the new companies in Europe. All five sons were rewarded by becoming barons of the Austrian empire.

In London, Nathan Mayer Rothschild was followed by his son Lionel Rothschild (1808–1879), who became the first Jewish Member of Parliament in 1858. Later he lent £4 million to prime minister Disraeli for Britain to become the main owner of the Suez Canal.

A number of Rothschilds became scientists, including Lionel Walter Rothschild, the 2nd Baron Rothschild (1868–1937), who opened a Natural History Museum at Tring, near London, in 1892. On his death he left it to the British Museum. ■

Rubens, Sir Peter Paul

Born 1577 at Siegen, near Cologne in Germany
He was a famous painter and ambassador.
Died 1640 aged 62

Rubens was always successful at everything he did. At 14 he began as an apprentice painter in Antwerp, and seven years later was a master. When he was 23, he travelled to Italy to learn about art and to develop his own extraordinary talents. He stayed there for nearly eight years and returned to Antwerp only because his mother was seriously ill.

He had a particularly charming personality, and was able to make friends easily. He became adviser as well as court painter to the Spanish rulers of Flanders, and they sent him to Spain and England. Rubens travelled from one royal court to another, trying to make good feelings between countries and to prevent war. He spoke several languages well and combined the two careers of painter and diplomat.

He was a good organizer. When the demand for his paintings became too great for him alone to cope with, he set up a studio with several first-class assistants. The studio kept up a huge output of paintings which Rubens planned and finished off himself.

He could easily produce huge, confident paintings (usually on biblical or mythological subjects) crowded with figures, but seeming spacious and light. His work is bold, energetic, full of colour, splendour and optimism.

At the age of 53, four years after the death of his first wife, he married his second wife, a 16-year-old girl, Hélène Fourment, whose face can be seen in

◄ *The Garden of Love* by Rubens, Prado Museum, Madrid, Spain.
This crowded painting shows richly dressed men and women enjoying themselves in a garden full of strange buildings and statues. Cherubs (child angels) add to the gaiety of the scene. This is a picture full of movement and colour and it reflects the splendour of the courtly life of the time.

many of his pictures. His interest in his new young family can be seen in the more domestic painting of his last ten years. ■

Rumford, Count

Born 1753 in Woburn, Massachusetts, USA
His experiments with cannon-making helped scientists understand what heat is.
Died 1814 aged 61

Count Rumford was born Benjamin Thompson, and at the age of 13 began his working life as a shop assistant. At 19 he married a rich widow and went to live with her in Rumford, New Hampshire. At that time America was ruled by Britain, and when Americans began to fight for the right to rule themselves, Benjamin Thompson decided to spy for Britain. After the war he went to work as minister of war and adviser to the ruler of Bavaria (now in Germany). He was made a count in 1791 and chose the title Rumford.

Rumford was always interested in science. At that time scientists thought

heat was a liquid, but Rumford noticed that when cannon were made the metal glowed red hot as the hole was bored down the centre. He did a series of experiments which showed heat was not a substance at all; he said it was 'a kind of motion', which it is.

For a short time Rumford settled in London, where he founded the Royal Institution in 1799. ■

See also

Heat

Biography
Faraday

Rutherford, Sir Ernest

Born 1871 near Nelson, New Zealand
Revealed the structure of atoms and heralded the nuclear age we live in.
Died 1937 aged 66

Rutherford came from a large family of eleven children and grew up on his family's small farm in New Zealand. He did very well at school and was especially good at mathematics. After going to university in New Zealand he went to Cambridge in England.

At Cambridge he began work on the exciting new subject of radioactivity. He discovered that radioactive substances produce three different types of radiation. This was an especially exciting time for scientists, because they were beginning to study the inside of atoms. For more than 2,000 years atoms had been thought of as like tiny marbles, but Rutherford performed some very important experiments which showed that in the centre of an atom there is a tiny, heavy blob, the nucleus, and that most of the atom consists of empty space.

Rutherford continued to study atoms, and he gathered round him in his laboratory in Cambridge other brilliant scientists who were fascinated by atoms and the particles found inside them, scientists such as Chadwick (who discovered the neutron) and Cockcroft (who built an atom-smashing proton accelerator). The work of these and others, like Marie and Pierre Curie, Enrico Fermi and Niels Bohr, began a new age of physics: the 'nuclear age'. It has produced radiation for treating cancer, nuclear power-stations which generate electricity, and also, sadly, nuclear weapons. ■

See also

Atoms
Nuclear power
Particles
Radiation

Biography
Bohr
Chadwick
Cockcroft
Curie
Fermi

Saladin

Born 1137 in Tekrit, now in Iraq
He united the Muslims in the Near East
and led the holy war against the
Christian crusaders.
Died 1192 aged 54

On the night that Saladin was born, his family moved to Aleppo. His education there taught him how to fight and how to honour his God. In the years to come he was to do both, by waging *jihad* (holy war), the Muslim equivalent to the Christian crusade.

Saladin began his life as a soldier when he was 14 years old, fighting against other Muslims in Egypt. Before he could attack the Christians, he had to unite all the different Muslim kingdoms. This took him fifteen years to achieve, but he succeeded in his ambition. By 1187, he was able to lead the Muslims against the Christians in the Holy Land. Saladin destroyed the Christian army at Hattin, recaptured Jerusalem, and held his forces together to resist the new Christian attack led by Richard the Lionheart, King of England.

Although he was a great soldier, Saladin could also be kind and gentle. When his enemy Richard the Lionheart was ill, Saladin sent him fruit and snow from the mountains. Soon after Richard returned to Europe, Saladin died. His people saw him as a hero who revived memories of the first Muslim conquests under Muhammad. ■

See also

Crusades
Muslims

Biography
Muhammad
Richard I

Samson

Dates of birth and death not known. He
was a hero of the Hebrews and probably
lived in the 11th century BC.

According to the Bible, Samson had very great strength which came from a vow he had taken to God not to cut his hair. This strength helped him to defeat the Philistines, who at that time were attacking the Hebrew people of Israel. However, he fell in love with a woman named Delilah. The Philistines gave her money to find out the secret of Samson's strength. She eventually persuaded him to tell her and while he was asleep she cut off his hair. The Philistines then captured him, put out his eyes and kept him a prisoner, 'eyeless in Gaza'. They brought him out on display for a great feast, but Samson prayed to God and mustered one last effort of strength to pull down the central pillars of the building so that the whole lot collapsed, killing many thousands of Philistines and himself.

The story of Samson is found in the Book of Judges, chapters 13 to 16. ■

See also

Bible
Hebrews
Palestine

Schubert, Franz Peter

Born 1797 in Vienna, Austria
A great and very prolific composer,
particularly of songs
Died 1828 aged 31

Schubert's father was a schoolmaster. All but five of his twelve children died in childhood. Franz Peter was the fourth to survive, and he showed a remarkable talent for music. His father taught him to play the violin, and his elder brother taught him the piano. When he was 9 he began to study harmony and counterpoint (the way of adding melody as an accompaniment).

In 1808 he became a chorister of the Imperial Court chapel. This meant that he could also attend the college that was attached to it. Here he founded a students' orchestra. Besides playing in it, he was sometimes allowed to conduct. By this time he was also writing music, including quartets for himself and his father and brothers to play.

When Schubert left college, he too became a schoolmaster. But he did not enjoy teaching, and soon gave it up in order to earn his living as best he could while he made his way as a composer.

In his short life Schubert wrote an amazing amount of music, including nine symphonies, several operas, much fine chamber music and over 600 songs. Although he seldom had any money, he lived happily enough. He

▼ This picture by the artist W. A. Rieder shows Schubert in 1825, just three years before his death.

had many friends who admired his music, and they did their best to help and encourage him. His music is full of splendid tunes and wonderful touches of harmony. For the most part it seems sunny and carefree, but it has moments of great sadness, as if he knew how short his life would be. ■

See also

Chamber music
Symphonies

Scott, Robert Falcon

Born 1868 at Devonport, England
His expedition to the South Pole ended in tragic failure, but made him a British hero.
Died 1912 aged 43

Robert Scott was a British naval officer who became famous as an Antarctic explorer. In 1900 he was placed in command of a British Antarctic Expedition, and in 1901 sailed south in the ship *Discovery*. His party

▼ Captain Scott (second from the left) led a party of five on the final stretch of their journey to the South Pole. On the return trip, all five died from cold and hunger.

returned two years later, having reached further south than anyone else at that time.

In 1910 Scott, by then a captain, once again travelled to the Antarctic, this time in an attempt to be first to the South Pole. The expedition was dogged by bad planning and bad luck, but by the beginning of 1912 it was within 200 miles of the Pole. Captain Scott set out on the final stretch with four colleagues: Oates, Wilson, Bowers and Evans. They reached their objective on 18 January only to find that the Norwegian explorer Amundsen had beaten them to it by a month. Bitterly disappointed, they turned back, but were overtaken by blizzards, and died from starvation and exposure.

The bodies of Scott and his colleagues were recovered eight months later by a search party, who also found notebooks, letters and diaries describing the brave but grim events. The gallant manner of Scott's failure was admired by the British, and he became a national hero. ■

See also

Antarctica   **Biography**
Letter writing   Amundsen
                            Shackleton

Scott, Sir Walter

Born 1771 in Edinburgh, Scotland
A famous writer and poet, best known for his novels about Scottish history
Died 1832 aged 61

Walter Scott, the son of an Edinburgh lawyer, became one of the most famous romantic writers in Europe. He was so popular that a railway station (Waverley) and a football team (Heart of Midlothian) were named after his novels, and a monument to him towers over the centre of his native city.

Young Scott had an illness that made him lame, and he was sent to his grandfather's house in the Scottish Borders to recover. He never lost his limp, but he became a great walker and grew to love the Border country with its many legends. After training in Edinburgh as a lawyer, he married and returned to the Borders. He enjoyed collecting the old Border ballads, and tried writing poems of his own, such as *Marmion* and *The Lady of the Lake*. Their mixture of romance, history and action was very popular, but he next tried writing novels.

His first novel, *Waverley*, mixed real people such as Bonnie Prince Charlie with characters that Scott had invented. It brought history to life in a way that no other writer had ever managed. Readers felt transported back to the din of old battles, the sights and smells of old streets, and the passions of old arguments. *Waverley* was an instant success, and so were the many novels which followed, especially those with Scottish settings such as *Old Mortality*, *The Heart of Midlothian* and *Rob Roy*.

Scott's historical novels were the first of their kind, and made him world-famous. Streams of people came to see him at Abbotsford, the mansion he had built on the banks of the Tweed. Tourists began visiting Scotland because they had read about it in Scott's books. But in 1826 his publishing company collapsed, leaving huge debts. Scott bravely decided to clear them by writing. He succeeded, but he died at Abbotsford after six years of dogged hard work. ■

Seacole, Mary

Born 1805 in Jamaica
A Jamaican who helped care for sick and wounded soldiers in the Crimean War
Died 1881 aged 76

Mary's mother was black and her father was a Scottish officer with the British army in Jamaica. Her mother taught her African cures for tropical illnesses, and Mary became known as a 'doctress' in Jamaica.

In 1854 the British army was sent to fight Russia in the Crimean War. Mary went to England to join the nurses whom Florence Nightingale had taken to the Crimea. She was turned down because she was coloured, so she went out to the Crimea at her own expense and opened a store and eating-place near the front lines.

Mary showed great bravery, going among the men with medicine and supplies of food. When the fighting was fierce she bandaged the wounded and comforted the dying. Her work was remembered by many soldiers who, after the war, gave money to save her from poverty. ∎

⊙ **See also**

Crimean War

Biography
Nightingale

Shackleton, Sir Ernest

Born 1874 in Kilkea, County Kildare, Ireland
British sailor who led two expeditions to Antarctica and nearly reached the South Pole
Died 1922 aged 47

Ernest Henry Shackleton was an officer in the merchant navy. In 1901 he joined an expedition to Antarctica led by Robert Falcon Scott. During this trip he nearly died of starvation. Undeterred, he decided to lead an expedition himself, setting out in 1907. He got to within 156 km (97 miles) of the South Pole before shortage of food

forced a retreat. For this exploit Shackleton was knighted.

In 1914 he set out to try to cross Antarctica from one side to the other. His ship, the *Endurance*, was trapped in ice, was crushed and sank. Shackleton saved his men and the ship's boats, and they spent five months on an ice floe until it was possible to launch the boats. After a hazardous voyage they reached Elephant Island.

Shackleton and five men set out in one boat to fetch help from Stromness, in South Georgia, 1,280 km (800 miles) away. They landed on the wrong side of the island, but Shackleton and two companions trudged across glaciers and mountains to Stromness and saved the rest of the party. ∎

⊙ **See also**

Antarctica

Biography
Scott, Robert

▼ Lord Shaftesbury worked hard to collect information about the terrible conditions in which children worked in the mines. The report he helped to produce for Parliament in 1842 was unusual because it had pictures, which made people realize what mines were like. This picture shows Lord Shaftesbury seeing conditions for himself and talking to a child working down a mine.

Shaftesbury, 7th Earl of

Born 1801 in London, England
An upper-class landowner who spent his life helping the poor, especially children
Died 1885 aged 84

Anthony Ashley Cooper was an unhappy child. His father was cold and distant, and his mother was selfish. Only his nurse Maria Millis loved him; she taught him his Christian faith which inspired everything he did. At the age of 7 he went to a dreadful boarding school, and became even more unhappy when Maria died. Later, as a teenager, he saw the funeral of someone who had died poor and alone. Some drunken men had been paid a few pence to carry the coffin. He was so shocked that he decided to spend the rest of his life helping the poor.

He went into Parliament in 1826 and campaigned long and hard to bring in laws which helped many people in Britain's industrial cities. These laws meant that children were no longer employed in textile mills; women and children did not work in coal-mines; and boys did not climb dangerous sooty chimneys to sweep them. He also helped to cut down the working day for adults in factories to ten hours.

He helped to start 'ragged schools' for very poor children, and the 'Arethusa Training Ship' to train boys for the merchant navy. He ran soup kitchens for the hungry, and improved conditions for the mentally handicapped. Though his family was rich (he became Earl of Shaftesbury when his father died in 1851) he was often quite short of money because he gave so much away. ∎

See also

Factory reform in Britain
Victorian Britain

Shaka, the Zulu

Born about 1787 on the White Umfolozi River in what is now South Africa
The first great chief of the Zulu nation in southern Africa
Murdered 1828 aged about 41

Shaka was born the son of Senzangakona, a chieftain of the Zulu clan in southern Africa. His mother, Nandi, was an orphaned princess of the Langeni clan. When he was a child, Shaka and his mother were banished from the Zulu villages by Senzangakona and had to go back to the Langeni. There they were treated very badly, often being teased and attacked. Eventually they were banished by the Langeni too.

They found shelter with the Mtetwa clan, and there Shaka became a warrior. Then, when Senzangakona died, Shaka returned to the Zulu as chieftain. He set about reorganizing the Zulu army into regiments known as the *impi*, giving them more deadly assegais (stabbing spears), changing their battle tactics, and training them to march up to 80 km (50 miles) a day. In this way he made the Zulu the strongest clan in southern Africa.

When Shaka became chief, there were fewer than 1,500 Zulu; by 1824 he had fifteen regiments and ruled over 50,000 people because he incorporated defeated clans into the Zulu nation. He was, though, a very cruel leader. When his mother died in 1827, he had 7,000 Zulu put to death as a sign of his grief and he would not allow any crops to be planted or any milk to be drunk for a whole year. Shaka was murdered in 1828 by his own half-brothers. ∎

See also

Clans   Zulus
South Africa

▼ The Zulu warriors trained by Shaka defeated many other tribes, which Shaka then forced to join the Zulu nation. Their assegais and shields made them better armed than most of their enemies. Some of his defeated enemies fled into the Transvaal and to Matabeleland.

Shakespeare, William

Born 1564 in Stratford-upon-Avon, Warwickshire, England
The world's most famous writer
Died 1616 aged 52

William Shakespeare's father, John, had a business selling gloves and he later became bailiff (mayor) of Stratford. His mother, Mary, was from the Arden family, who were well known in the area at that time. William was the oldest child and probably attended the local grammar school, where he would have learned Latin and Greek.

In 1582, when he was 18, Shakespeare married Anne Hathaway, eight years his senior, from the nearby village of Shottery. Their first child, Susannah, was born the following year and twins, Hamnet and Judith, followed in 1585. Hamnet died when he was 11.

Nobody knows what Shakespeare was doing for a living in his early twenties, but it is certain that by 1592 he was earning money as an actor and playwright in London while his wife and family remained in Stratford. He soon became a leading member of a theatrical company called the Lord Chamberlain's Men, with whom he remained for the rest of his working life. In 1603, when James I succeeded Queen Elizabeth I on the throne, the company changed its name to the King's Men and often performed at court. Between 1599 and 1613 their main base was the Globe Theatre on the south bank of the River Thames; and in 1609 they also acquired the Blackfriars Theatre in the City of London.

Shakespeare seems to have taken little or no interest in the printing or publication of his work, and one or two of his plays may have been lost. A complete edition was not published until seven years after his death, when his friends and former fellow actors, John Heminges and Henry Condell, produced the so-called First Folio which included all his plays except for *Pericles*. The number of plays which

▲ A scene from the Royal Shakespeare Company's production of *Richard III* in 1984.

have come down to us wholly or mostly written by Shakespeare is generally agreed to be 37.

Shakespeare's most famous plays are probably the four great tragedies, *Hamlet*, *Macbeth*, *Othello* and *King Lear*. He also wrote popular comedies, such as *A Midsummer Night's Dream* and *Twelfth Night*, and many history plays. The best-known of these are *Julius Caesar* and *Antony and Cleopatra*, which deal with Roman history, and a long cycle of eight plays dealing with English history from the reign of Richard II to the reign of Richard III. Other favourites in the theatre are *The Merchant of Venice*, *Romeo and Juliet* and *The Tempest*.

Shakespeare's plays are mostly written in verse, although there are some scenes in prose, or a mixture of verse and prose, especially in the comedies. The metre (rhythm) used in the verse is known as the iambic pentameter. In this metre each line normally consists of ten alternately unstressed and

▲ In 1616, the year of Shakespeare's death, an artist sketched this picture of a Thames bankside theatre. He titled it the Globe Theatre at Southwark, but people now think it was the Rose Theatre.

stressed syllables. In the early plays, but not so much in the later ones, Shakespeare also used rhyme, as he did in the 154 sonnets he wrote.

By 1597 Shakespeare was so successful that he was able to buy one of the finest houses in Stratford, New Place; and it was here that he retired with his family for the last few years of his life. He died on 23 April (traditionally, but not definitely, his birthday too) in 1616, and was buried in Holy Trinity Church in Stratford. ■

See also

Drama
Poems and poetry
Theatres

Shaw, George Bernard

Born 1856 in Dublin, Ireland
The most famous playwright of his time writing in English
Died 1950 aged 94

George Bernard Shaw moved from Ireland to London at the age of 20 and tried writing novels, but these were not very successful. People did begin to take an interest in his magazine articles, though. Many of these were about politics, as the young Shaw was a keen supporter of the Fabian Society, a group of socialists.

His first successful play was *Widowers' Houses*, which was performed in 1892. The play attacked slum landlords, and it upset those people who did not like to see themselves or their society criticized on stage. In the years that followed, Shaw wrote many plays that have since become famous. *Saint Joan* is about Joan of Arc, the courageous young woman who led the French army against the English in the Middle Ages. Many people know the story of *Pygmalion* because of the musical version, *My Fair Lady*. However, there is more to Shaw's plays than just the stories. They contain powerful arguments against things and ideas that Shaw considered unfair, dangerous or silly.

When Shaw published his plays, he added prefaces or introductions in which he explained his ideas. He was awarded the Nobel prize for literature in 1925. ■

Smeaton, John

Born 1724 near Leeds, England
One of the first engineers, at the time of the Industrial Revolution; famous for rebuilding the Eddystone lighthouse
Died 1792 aged 68

As a child, John was always making things. He had his own workshop at home, where he learned to work in wood and metal. Once he built a miniature pumping engine, with which he drained one of his father's fishponds and, unfortunately, killed all the fish.

Smeaton decided not to become a lawyer like his father, but instead to become a mathematical instrument-maker in London. There he carried on experimenting and went to meetings with other scientists at the Royal Society. This contact brought him his big chance. In 1755 the Eddystone lighthouse burnt down and he was asked to rebuild it.

The Eddystone rocks are a low jagged reef on the route to Plymouth harbour. At high tide the waves boil over them. So, to stand up to the pounding waves, Smeaton decided to build the lighthouse of stone, with each block cut so that it locked into the blocks next to it. The bottom layer of stones were shaped so that they fitted into recesses cut in the rock itself. The lighthouse took three years to build. When it was finished, it was so strong that it survived the Channel gales for over 100 years. Then it was taken down because the rocks on which it was built were becoming undermined. The lighthouse has been rebuilt on Plymouth Hoe.

For the rest of his life Smeaton was busy on schemes to build bridges, canals and harbours. ■

See also

Industrial Revolution
Lighthouses

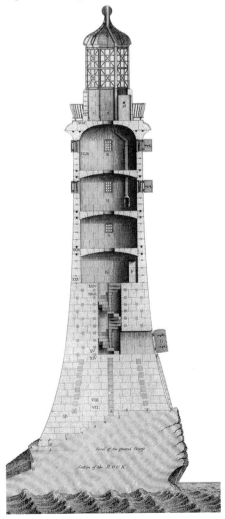

▲ Smeaton's design for the lighthouse which he built on the Eddystone rocks in 1755. The lighthouse can still be seen today on Plymouth Hoe, where it has been rebuilt.

Smuts, Jan Christiaan

Born 1870 at Riebeeck West, Cape Colony (now part of South Africa)
He was Prime Minister of South Africa twice and a world-famous statesman.
Died 1950 aged 80

After going to school at Stellenbosch in southern Africa, Jan Christiaan Smuts went to Christ's College, Cambridge, where he was a brilliant student. In 1895 he returned to Cape Town and began work as a lawyer. To make extra money, he also wrote for newspapers.

In 1899, a war started between the British, who ruled the colonies of southern Africa, and the Boers (Afrikaners), white settlers of Dutch descent. Smuts fought against the British, and at the end of the war in

▲ The Boers, who fought the British in the Boer War, wore clothes similar to those worn here by General Jan Smuts. However, at the time this photograph was taken (1914) Smuts was about to become an ally of Britain in World War I.

1902 he began to work for the colonies to become self-governing instead of being ruled by Britain.

When Transvaal got its own government in 1907, Smuts became a member of it. The next step, he believed, was to unite all the colonies into one country, the Union of South Africa. This was achieved in 1910, and the new Union remained part of the British empire.

During World War I, Smuts became a member of the War Cabinet in London. After the war, he became Prime Minister of South Africa in 1919, and held this post until 1924.

He did not become prime minister again until 1939, when South Africa allied itself to Britain in World War II. This time Smuts stayed in power until 1948, when he was defeated in the elections by Daniel Malan, who put forward 'apartheid' policies to keep the different races apart in South Africa. Smuts was leader of the opposition at the time of his death in 1950. ■

See also

Boer War
South Africa

Socrates

Born 469 BC in Athens, Greece
This Greek philosopher left no writings
but is probably the best-known of the
ancient thinkers.
Poisoned 399 BC aged 70

Socrates did not choose to become a philosopher and teacher when he was a young man. At first he followed his father's profession as a sculptor of statues. Like most men at that time in Athens he served in the army, where he gained a reputation for great courage. After that he held government office. He was a strong character both in his mind and body. It is said that he did not mind either extreme heat or cold. He went barefoot all year round.

Philosophers and teachers in Athens at this time used to open schools, which were usually conducted in the open air. Socrates did not open a school, or even give public lectures as some philosophers did. He simply felt he had a mission to correct people's ignorance. His method was to engage people in 'question and answer' sessions. He was the first to use a set of rules, or logic, to discuss important matters. He questioned the way people thought and acted. We know about his ideas and teaching methods from his follower Plato. Plato wrote down Socrates' ideas and published them.

Socrates upset some people in government and important positions in Athens. In 399 BC he was accused of being contemptuous of the gods and of corrupting young men, by making them ask awkward questions about the society in which they lived. He was found guilty and the judges condemned him to death.

His execution was delayed for 30 days because of a religious festival. During this time he refused all offers to escape into exile. He seemed to be content to die, and took the poison (it was hemlock) given to him. ■

See also

Greek ancient history
Philosophers

Biography
Plato

Solomon, King of Israel

Born about 990 BC in Jerusalem
King of Israel, famous for his wealth and
his wisdom
Died about 930 BC aged about 60

Solomon was the son of King David and of Bathsheba, the most powerful of David's wives. He succeeded his father to the throne of Israel when he was about 20 years old.

Solomon strengthened the fortifications of Jerusalem and other cities and enlarged the army by adding horsemen and chariots. His reign of about 40 years was mostly peaceful. He made alliances with the ruler of Egypt and other nations, and planned a large programme of trade, industry and construction.

The first Jewish temple in Jerusalem was built during his reign. Foreign rulers such as the Queen of Sheba came to visit his court. He also had a reputation for being wise.

But the wisdom of Solomon was not shown in the way he ruled his land. He was extravagant and used heavy taxation and forced labour for his building programme. This caused hardship and unrest among the people.

There was rebellion during his lifetime, and after he died Israel was divided again. The northern kingdom kept the name Israel. The south was called Judah.

The account of Solomon's reign is told in chapters 1 to 11 of the First Book of Kings in the Old Testament of the Bible. There is a tradition that he wrote the Book of Proverbs, the Song of Songs and Ecclesiastes, but in fact these were written centuries later. ■

See also

Bible   **Biography**
Palestine   David, King

Stalin, Joseph

Born 1879 in Gori, Georgia, Russian
empire
Ruthless dictator of the USSR for nearly
30 years from 1924 to 1953
Died 1953 aged 73

Joseph Vissarionovich Dzhugashvili was born in the hillside village of Gori in Georgia. His father, who died when he was 11, was a shoemaker and his mother a washerwoman. They sent their son first to a church school and then to a Christian college to become a priest. But he was expelled at the age of 20 for his 'disloyal ideas'. Later he joined the Russian Social-Democratic Workers' Party and became a full-time revolutionary. His bank raids and other daring escapades often landed him in prison or exile, but he always managed to escape from his place of exile. He proved himself to be tough, brave and dedicated, and was invited by Lenin to join the Bolshevik Party leadership in 1912. It was then that he took the name 'Stalin' (man of steel).

In 1917, Stalin was a loyal supporter of Lenin's seizure of power. He was made the minister for nationalities but suppressed a democratic republic in Georgia, where he was born. Then, in 1922, he became secretary of the Communist Party (as the Bolsheviks were now known). As Lenin lay dying, however, he asked his comrades to remove Stalin from the post because 'he is too rude and uncomradely'. But Lenin died in 1924 before any action could be taken.

In the years that followed, Stalin helped to build a strong nation through a series of Five-Year Plans intended to industrialize and modernize Soviet Russia. His greatest achievement was to lead his country, as 'Generalissimo', to victory over the Nazis in World War II. After this, communist influence spread through much of Europe.

But all this was done at great human cost. Stalin had all his rivals killed until he became dictator. Soviet people lived in fear of arrest, torture and execution by the notorious secret police (later called the KGB). In the countryside, millions of people were sent to labour camps for opposing Stalin's wishes, and millions more died of starvation during the 1920s and 1930s.

It was only after his death in 1953 that people felt free to criticize Stalin. The leaders of the Communist Party then denounced him in 1956, and in 1961 his body was removed from its place of honour in the Lenin Mausoleum in Red Square. ■

See also

Communists
Georgia
Russia's history
USSR 1922–1991

Biography
Lenin
Trotsky

▲ 'The Rocket' was built by George Stephenson's son Robert. The front wheels were turned by steam-driven pistons. Coal and water for the boiler were carried in the truck on the back.

Stephenson, George

Born 1781 in Wylam, near Newcastle-upon-Tyne, England
Designed many of the earliest railway locomotives and built the world's first public railway.
Died 1848 aged 67

George Stephenson's father was a colliery fireman, and as a teenager George had various jobs working with mining engines. He had never been to school, but he taught himself to read by attending night-classes. He became a colliery engineer, and in 1812 was appointed as engine-builder at Killingworth colliery, near Newcastle. In 1815, Stephenson invented a miner's safety lamp. But Sir Humphry Davy, who produced a similar lamp at the same time, is generally regarded as the safety lamp's inventor.

Stephenson spent the rest of his working life designing and building railways and railway locomotives. Between 1814 and 1826 he built at least twelve railway engines. These engines were for pulling coal, but in 1823 he was put in charge of building a railway from Stockton to Darlington that would carry people. When it opened in 1825, Stephenson himself drove the engine which pulled the world's first steam-hauled passenger train. From 1826 to 1830 he supervised the building of the Liverpool to Manchester railway. Before it opened, a competition was held to find the most efficient locomotive. The £500 prize was won by 'The Rocket', designed by Stephenson and built by his son Robert.

Stephenson's successes led to the building of railways throughout Britain. From 1830 until he retired in 1845, he acted as engineering consultant to several railway companies. He used the money he had made from his inventions to set up schools for miners' children and night-schools for the miners themselves.

George Stephenson's fame has tended to overshadow the achievements of his son Robert, who assisted his father as railway-builder and locomotive-designer and became a famous bridge-builder. ■

See also

Industrial Revolution
Railways
Steam-engines

Biography
Davy
Trevithick

▲ In his younger days (top) Stalin had the look of a daring revolutionary who was always living outside the law. Later, when he became leader of the Soviet Union, his public image became much more respectable, until some people began to refer to him as 'Uncle Joe' (bottom).

Stevenson, Robert Louis

Born 1850 in Edinburgh, Scotland
The author of *Treasure Island* and
Kidnapped
Died 1894 aged 44

This famous writer was brought up
in Edinburgh. As a child he was
frequently ill, and he decided to devote
his life to writing. When he left
university he travelled abroad to escape
the Scottish climate. Stevenson's first
books described his tours in Belgium
and France, and his journey to
California to marry an American,
Fanny Osbourne. He also produced
many essays and poems.

Treasure Island was published in 1883.
This thrilling adventure brought
Stevenson his first real success, and
has been popular ever since. Three
years later his fame soared when

Kidnapped and *The Strange Case of
Dr Jekyll and Mr Hyde* were published.

In 1889 Stevenson and his family
settled in the Polynesian island of
Samoa. He continued to write, and the
islanders called him *Tusitala*, meaning
the Storyteller. He died suddenly in
Samoa while working on his great
unfinished novel *Weir of Hermiston*,
and was buried there beneath a stone
with his own words:

Here he lies where he longed to be;
Home is the sailor, home from sea,
And the hunter home from the hill. ■

Stopes, Marie

Born 1880 in Edinburgh, Scotland
She started the first birth control clinic in
London.
Died 1958 aged 77

Marie Stopes was a very clever
woman. She studied science in England
and Germany and later also studied
philosophy. She married when she was
31, but her marriage was unhappy and
she and her husband soon separated.

At the time many people thought it
was wrong to talk about sex and birth
control. As a result they were ignorant
when they got married, and this often
caused problems. Because of her own
unhappy marriage, Marie Stopes
decided to do something about this.
She wrote two important books:
Married Love and *Wise Parenthood*.
The books explained sex, birth control
and family planning clearly. Some
people were shocked by the books,
but others were pleased and many
wrote to Marie Stopes thanking her
and asking for more information. In
1918 she married again. With her
second husband she opened the first
family planning clinic in London in
1921. It is largely due to the work of
people like Marie Stopes that people
today understand and can talk openly
about sex. ■

See also

Sex

Stowe, Harriet Beecher

Born 1811 in Litchfield, Connecticut,
USA
She wrote *Uncle Tom's Cabin*, the
greatest and most influential anti-slavery
book.
Died 1896 aged 85

For the first 41 years of her life Harriet
was unknown to anyone except her
close family and friends. Then
suddenly, through the publication of
her book *Uncle Tom's Cabin* in 1852,
she became the most famous woman
in America and, shortly afterwards, a
world celebrity.

She was born the seventh of nine
children. Her mother died when she
was 4 years old. Her eldest sister,
Catherine, set up a school at Hartford,
and Harriet went there, first as a pupil
and then as a teacher. In 1832 the
family moved to Cincinnati, where
Catherine and Harriet set up one of the
first colleges for women.

Harriet married Calvin Ellis Stowe, a
professor, and for the next eighteen
years she shared at close hand in one
of the most dramatic periods in
American history. In the Southern

▲ Although her novel, *Uncle Tom's Cabin*,
made her welcome amongst anti-slavery
groups all over the world, Harriet Beecher
Stowe was hated by those people in the
Southern United States who wanted to keep
their slaves.

states slave-owning was legal, but many of the Northern states had abolished slavery. Slaves from the South would often try to escape to the North where they could be free. Only the River Ohio separated Harriet from a slave-holding community, and runaway slaves were sometimes sheltered on their way north by Harriet and her friends.

While she was looking after her seventh child she began work on *Uncle Tom's Cabin*, a book that describes in vivid, moving language the hardships and tragedy of a slave's life. It was read by more people than any other novel of its time, and influenced people very strongly to abolish slavery for good. ∎

See also

American Civil War
Slaves
USA: history

Biography
Tubman

Strauss, Johann

The name of the two most important members of a famous family of dance musicians
Johann I Born 1804 in Vienna, Austria
Died 1849 aged 45
Johann II Born 1825 in Vienna
Died 1899 aged 73

The first Johann Strauss began his musical career as a violinist. Shortly after the birth of his son (Johann II) he formed his own orchestra and played in the inns and dance-halls of Vienna. Soon everyone was dancing to the waltzes and galops he composed. Even Wagner described him as 'the magic fiddler'. His fame rapidly spread throughout Europe and he undertook many successful tours. He visited England in 1838 and took part in the coronation celebrations of Queen Victoria.

Johann II began writing music when he was 6 years old, but his father did not want him to take up a musical career. He therefore studied in secret. When he appeared before the public for the first time in 1844 with six of his own compositions, it was clear that

▲ In this Viennese silhouette picture, Strauss is shown conducting waltzes in heaven. Both Mozart and Brahms are among the dancers.

he was the only man who could rival his father. Poor Johann I simply had to accept the situation.

When it came to waltzes, no one could rival Johann II. He was the 'Waltz King' of Vienna. 'The Blue Danube' and 'Tales from the Vienna Woods' delighted everyone, as did his polkas, quadrilles and marches. His operettas, such as *Die Fledermaus* (The Bat), were equally successful.

Johann I had other musical sons, Josef (1827–1870) and Eduard (1835–1916), who also wrote splendid dance tunes, but neither of them could rival their famous elder brother. ∎

Stravinsky, Igor

Born 1882 in Oranienbaum, Russia
One of the most remarkable and influential composers of the 20th century
Died 1971 aged 88

Although Stravinsky showed an early talent for music, it was some time before he found his feet as a composer. His first great success came with the ballets he wrote for the Diaghilev company between 1910 and 1913. *The Firebird*, *Petrushka* and *The Rite of Spring* made him the most talked-about composer in Europe. But many people

were outraged by *The Rite of Spring* and thought it was simply a horrible noise.

Because of World War I and the Russian Revolution, Stravinsky decided to leave Russia. He lived first in Switzerland and then in America. His music also took a new turn. It still used interesting harmonies and exciting rhythms, and was still unmistakably Stravinsky, but it was no longer as savage as it had been in *The Rite of Spring*. It was all much simpler. Some works, such as the concerto 'Dumbarton Oaks' and the opera *The Rake's Progress*, sounded as though an 18th-century composer had suddenly stepped into the 20th century.

Everything Stravinsky did was news. Even at the end of his life he was still experimenting with new ways of writing music. When he died, the world felt that it had lost one of the most courageous and adventurous musical explorers of all time. ∎

See also

Ballet
Concertos

Stroud, Robert

Born 1890 in Seattle, USA
A convicted murderer and lifelong prisoner who became an internationally known expert on birds
Died 1963 aged 73, in prison

Robert Stroud was the grandson of a judge, but his mother made a very unhappy marriage, and Robert's childhood was full of fear and uncertainty. He grew up with a deep loathing of bullying, and a wish to protect the weak.

Stroud became a railway labourer in Alaska, and at the age of 17 he killed a man who had beaten and robbed his girlfriend, Kitty O'Brien. He gave himself up to the police, and was sentenced to twelve years on McNeil Island, a prison island. He began to study and read in prison, but in 1912 he was transferred to a harsher prison, Fort Leavenworth.

Stroud and other prisoners were attacked by a bullying guard, whom Stroud killed in a fight. He was sentenced to hang, but at the last moment the sentence was changed to life imprisonment. He spent much of that time in solitary confinement.

In June 1920, the weather drove some baby sparrows into his cell. He adopted and cared for them. He saw in the defenceless birds something of his own condition, and studied to understand more about their lives. He was allowed to keep cage birds in his cell. He studied, bred and sold them, and wrote a book on the diseases of canaries.

In 1933 he married Della May Jones, whom he had met through their shared interest in birds.

In 1942 he was moved to Alcatraz Island, a prison in San Francisco Bay, and became prisoner number 594. He was allowed no letters and had no radio. He had never even seen a television. But he became famous as the Bird Man of Alcatraz. His health was failing, and in 1959 he was transferred to a prison hospital in Springfield, Missouri, where he died. ■

Suleiman I, the Magnificent

Born about 1494 probably in Istanbul, Turkey
Muslim ruler of the Ottoman empire from 1520 to 1566 and one of the greatest rulers of his time
Died 1566 aged about 71

Suleiman was the only son of Sultan Selim I. As a young man he served as *sancak beyi* (governor) of Kaffa in the Crimea during the reign of his grandfather Bayezid II. Then when his father was sultan he became *sancak beyi* of Manisa in Asia Minor. Here he learnt the skills that he needed when he became sultan of the Ottoman empire in 1520.

Immediately he had a military success, conquering Belgrade in 1521. The following year he also conquered Rhodes, and then in 1526 he defeated the Hungarian armies in a battle at Mohács where the Hungarian king was

▲ This contemporary miniature shows Suleiman the Magnificent surrounded by his army commanders during his Hungarian campaign of 1541–1543. Turks and Hungarians are seen confronting each other across the River Danube.

killed. He tried to capture Vienna too, but failed. His victories increased the size of the Ottoman empire, which took in parts of Hungary, Transylvania and Persia. The Ottomans also became a mighty sea power at this time and were feared throughout the area of the Mediterranean Sea.

Suleiman gathered around himself many great statesmen, lawyers, architects and poets. He liked to write poems himself, and the architect Sinan built mosques, bridges, aqueducts and fortresses for him throughout the empire. Because he tried to modernize their laws, the Ottomans gave Suleiman the name *Kanuni*, which means 'Lawgiver'. In Europe, though, his opponents called him 'Suleiman the Magnificent'.

In his later life, Suleiman's reign was troubled by the arguments that broke out between his three sons. Suleiman himself was still actively involved in military matters when he died during the siege of a fortress at Szigetvár in Hungary in 1566. ■

⊙ See also

Hungary
Ottoman empire

Sullivan, Sir Arthur

Born 1842 in London, England
The composer of some of the world's finest operettas
Died 1900 aged 58

Sullivan's musical career began when he was 12 and joined the choir of the Chapel Royal. He then went on to study at the Royal Academy of Music and at Leipzig.

He first became known as a composer of serious music, including several oratorios and a very fine 'Irish' Symphony. But in 1875 he met the playwright W. S. Gilbert, and from then on serious music had to take a back seat. Between them they wrote a string of operettas that delighted everyone. Gilbert's witty words were the perfect match for Sullivan's

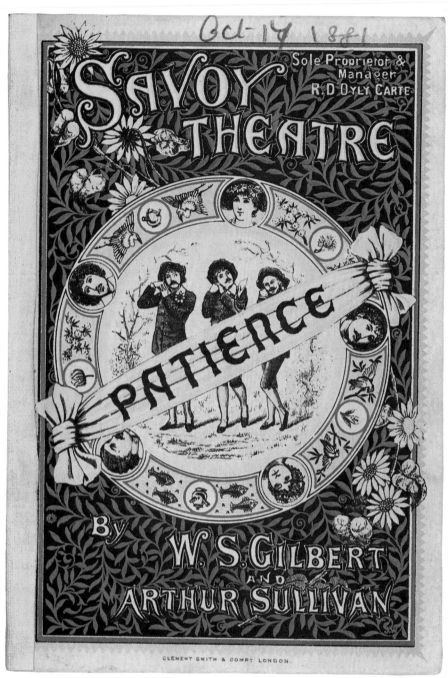

▲ The programme cover of a performance of Gilbert and Sullivan's *Patience* at London's Savoy Theatre.

sparkling music. *HMS Pinafore*, *The Mikado* and *The Gondoliers*, to name but three, enchanted everyone when they first appeared. They still do.

Sullivan was a very sociable man. He liked to gamble and go to the races. But he was never very strong, and much of the music that now seems so carefree was written when he was in great pain. ∎

Sun Yixian

Born 1866 near Canton, China
He created the Guomindang (Nationalist Party), which ruled China before the communists.
Died 1925 aged 58

Like most village children, Sun Yixian (Sun Yat-sen) worked in the fields, but at 13 he went to his brother who had emigrated to Honolulu. As a

teenager Sun saw how backward his own country was. He wanted a Western education, and studied medicine in Hong Kong before going back to China. There he joined revolutionaries trying to overthrow the rule of the emperors of the Qing dynasty. To escape the police he had to travel abroad. Eventually, he was called back to China in 1911 to be president, because there had been a revolution at last.

The new republic broke up into districts ruled by warlords' armies, so Sun was president in a part of south China only. He set up the People's National Party to carry out his 'Three Principles of the People'. Sun's first principle was nationalism, or a China which was united. The second was democracy or people's rights. The third was the people's livelihood, by which he meant a land where industry was modernized and peasants had enough land to feed their families. Sun began to build up an army to march against the warlords, but he died before it set out. His wife, Song Qingling, joined the first communist government in 1949. ∎

See also

China's history

Suzuki, Shin'ichi

Born 1898 in Nagoya, Japan
Violinist and founder of the Suzuki Method

Suzuki's father was an instrument manufacturer. His company eventually became the largest violin-making firm in Japan. After studying the violin in Japan, and later in Berlin, Suzuki got together with three of his brothers and formed a string quartet. Later he founded the Tokyo String Orchestra.

But he was not content. He wanted everyone to play an instrument. It occurred to him that if children could learn their native language by repeating simple words and phrases and gradually moving on to more complicated sentences, they might also be able to learn to play an instrument in the same way. He therefore devised a method whereby very young children could learn to play in easy stages, starting with simple tunes and repeating them day after day until playing became second nature to them.

The Suzuki Method spread, and not only for string instruments. It is now used all over the world. ∎

▲ Children from Suzuki's talent education institute perform for the President of the Japanese Red Cross in 1956.

Swift, Jonathan

Born 1667 in Dublin, Ireland
Author of *Gulliver's Travels*
Died 1745 aged 77

Jonathan Swift was born in Ireland of English parents. For 30 years he was Dean of St Patrick's Cathedral in Dublin, but was more famous as a writer of satire, highly fanciful fiction that is sometimes comic, sometimes serious but always deeply critical of human beings and the society in which they live.

His best-known satire is *Gulliver's Travels,* which describes four imaginary journeys to invented countries of a ship's doctor named Lemuel Gulliver. He first visits Lilliput, where everyone is quite tiny, then travels to Brobdingnag, a land of

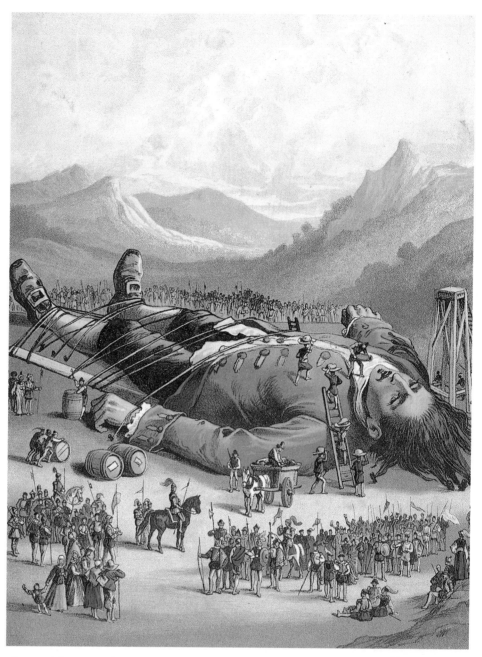
▲ In this illustration for Jonathan Swift's most popular book, Gulliver wakes up in the land of Lilliput to find himself surrounded by tiny people. This illustration was made for an edition of *Gulliver's Travels* printed in Victorian times.

giants. After more journeying, Gulliver arrives at a country ruled by gentle, talking horses. These behave towards each other so much better than do humans that Gulliver longs to stay with them, dreading the return to his own world of back-biting, poverty and war.

Although Swift mocked his fellow humans in this and other books, he also worked tirelessly for Ireland against the oppressive rule of the British government. ∎

👁 **See also**

Gulliver's Travels

Tagore, Sir Rabindranath

Born 1861 in Calcutta, India
A great Indian poet, philosopher and musician
Died 1941 aged 80

Rabindranath Tagore was born into a rich Bengali family and was sent to England to study law. He started writing poems at a very young age, and published his first poems when he was 17 years old. He also wrote a number of plays and novels. During the years he spent in England and in Europe, he was greatly influenced by European literature. He tried to blend together the best traditions of Indian and European literature. Tagore also wrote a large number of songs which he set to music himself. He played an important part in the revival of the theatre in India. He also took up painting rather late in life.

Tagore established a school at Bolpur in his native province of Bengal, which became an important centre of art and literature. He wrote in Bengali, but his works have been translated into many other languages. He won the Nobel prize for literature in 1913, and was given a knighthood by the British government in 1915.

He renounced his title in 1919 in protest against the Jallianwala Bagh incident, when a British general ordered troops to fire on an unarmed crowd, killing about 400 people. From then on he became involved with the Indian independence movement. A song written and composed by Tagore was adopted as the national anthem of India in 1950. ■

See also

Indian history

Talbot, William Henry Fox

Born 1800 in Dorset, England
An all-round scientist chiefly remembered for his work on photography
Died 1877 aged 77

Fox Talbot was a very bright boy, interested in science, and while he was at school at Harrow he caused explosions and created frightful smells with chemical experiments. His housemaster forbade him to do further experiments in the school, so he found a friendly blacksmith who, in the housemaster's words, 'lets him explode as much as he pleases!'

When Talbot was 33, on holiday in Italy, he was looking at a camera obscura (rather like a pin-hole camera) and thought how wonderful it would be if the pictures could be recorded on paper.

Six years later he had invented the photographic process in which a negative is made first and then a print is made from the negative. We still use the same idea today.

Talbot then tried to find a way of making many copies quickly. In 1851 he had the idea of breaking up a picture into tiny dots so that photographs could be produced on a printing machine. If you look through a magnifying glass

at a photograph in a newspaper you will see it is made up of tiny dots.

Talbot was the squire (chief landowner) in the village of Lacock, where his family had lived for about 400 years, and he was so concerned about the poor working conditions of the local people that he became the local Member of Parliament for Chippenham as a Liberal. He was also a keen botanist, had his own apparatus for experiments in electricity, and knew many different languages. He was one of the few people in England who could read the writing used by the ancient Babylonians called cuneiform. ■

See also

Cameras
Photography
Printing
Writing systems
Biography
Daguerre

▲ These two pictures show Talbot's negative and positive of his home, Lacock Abbey in Wiltshire, in about 1843.

Tamerlane

Born about 1336 near Samarkand, now in Uzbekistan
The last great central Asian conqueror
Died 1405 aged about 69

Timur, later known in the West as Tamerlane or Tamburlaine, was the great-grandson of a minister of Genghis Khan. His ambition was to rebuild the empire of that great conqueror. As a boy he learnt how to fight, but also how to read and to play chess, a game which he loved.

When he was about 20, Timur began to claim power over the other tribes in the area around Samarkand. By 1369, he had brutally defeated all his rivals. He now decided to move further afield. For the next 35 years he raided, conquered and plundered the regions from the Black Sea to the Indus. In 1404, at Samarkand, he staged an immense celebration of his victories, displaying his spoils and captured treasures. His next great expedition was to be against China, and in 1405 he set out, but died on the way of a fever.

Timur was lame in his right leg, and so the Persians called him 'Timur lenk', meaning 'Timur the lame', which became 'Tamerlane'. ■

See also

Mongolia
Uzbekistan

Biography
Genghis Khan

Tasman, Abel Janszoon

Born about 1603, probably at Hoorn, The Netherlands
Dutch explorer who discovered Fiji, New Zealand, Tasmania and Tonga
Died about 1659 aged about 56

Tasman was a sailor who worked for the Dutch East India Company, one of the great trading companies of the 17th century. He was based in Java, then a Dutch colony and now part of Indonesia. In 1642 Van Diemen, the governor of the Dutch East Indies, sent Tasman to explore the seas further south in the hope of finding new markets and a route across the Pacific Ocean to Chile.

Tasman sailed west across the Indian Ocean, then turned south-east. Eventually he came to a forested coast, and named the territory Van Diemen's Land. It is now called Tasmania. He then carried on east and found more land, which he named Staten Land (we now know it as New Zealand).

Tasman decided to head back to Java, but lost his way. He sighted Tonga and then Fiji before returning to his home port of Batavia. He had sailed right round Australia without knowing it. ■

See also

Australia
New Zealand
Tasmania

▼ In 1642 Tasman set out to explore the South Pacific from Java. He became the first European to reach the island now called Tasmania and to see New Zealand.

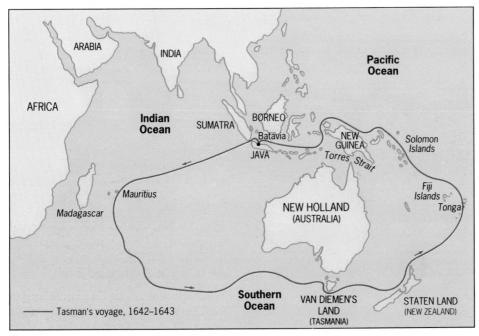

Tchaikovsky, Peter Ilich

Born 1840 in Votkinsk, Russia
He composed some of the most beautiful music ever heard: the ballets *Swan Lake*, *Sleeping Beauty*, *Nutcracker*, and several symphonies and concertos.
Died 1893 aged 53

If you like ballet or like listening to music, you will probably know and love Peter Tchaikovsky. His is the music of the heart, warm and full of joy and love and sorrow. Songs and symphonies, operas and ballets, concertos and serenades all poured from his pen.

Pyotr (Peter) Tchaikovsky was born into a wealthy Russian family and grew up in the town of Votkinsk near the Ural Mountains. He was sent to boarding school in St Petersburg when he was 8, and eventually became a student of law. It was not until he was 23 that he decided to devote his life to music, and he enrolled in Russia's first Conservatory of Music in St Petersburg, run by the brilliant pianist Anton Rubinstein.

When he was 26 he wrote his first symphony, and followed it with some piano pieces, the *Children's Album*, written for his nieces and nephews. He also wrote difficult piano works, like the piano concertos, which even Rubinstein and other top pianists could hardly play at the time. But it is his fairytale ballets that many people know: *Swan Lake*, *Sleeping Beauty* and *Nutcracker*.

Oddly, when *Swan Lake* was first performed at the St Petersburg Imperial Theatre in 1877, with the composer present, it was met in puzzled silence and was not seen again until after Tchaikovsky's death. His next ballet, *Sleeping Beauty*, was a great success, partly due to the wonderful dancing, costumes and scenery created by the French choreographer Marius Petipa. It was staged in the St Petersburg Marinsky Theatre in the presence of the tsar in 1890. The same theatre witnessed the triumphant première of

Nutcracker two years later, also with the tsar and composer present.

Despite his great success and fame, Tchaikovsky was often unhappy. He suffered from depression. He also tried to hide his homosexuality from society at a time when being gay was thought to be shameful. Five days after conducting his moving 6th Symphony, the 'Pathétique', he died. He had caught cholera after drinking a glass of polluted water. ■

See also

Ballet
Concertos
Symphonies

Te Kanawa, Kiri

Born 1944 in North Island, New Zealand
An opera singer who rose to great fame in the 1970s and 1980s

Five weeks after Kiri was born in a poor Maori family, she was adopted by Tom and Nell Te Kanawa, who named her Kiri, the Maori word for bell. Kiri was singing to her mother's piano playing before she was 5. When she was 6 she sang in a talent show on the radio. Her mother then sent her to a convent school where there was a good singing teacher. She went on to win many competitions and became very well known in New Zealand.

In 1966 she left New Zealand to study in London. At first she found it hard to be an unknown student after her New Zealand fame, but she eventually settled down. Her first really big success was in the opera *The Marriage of Figaro* at Covent Garden Opera House in 1971. Everyone realized she was one of the great operatic sopranos of our time. Her biggest audience came in 1981 when she was chosen by Prince Charles and Lady Diana Spencer to sing at their wedding in St Paul's Cathedral. Six hundred million people all over the world saw and heard her. Kiri Te Kanawa was made a Dame of the British Empire by the Queen. ■

See also

Operas

Telford, Thomas

Born 1757 in Eskdale, Scotland
Helped create the profession of civil engineering.
Died 1834 aged 77

Thomas Telford was the son of a shepherd. He was brought up in a small thatched cottage, and started his working life as an apprentice stonemason. By his skills, hard work and constant thirst for knowledge Telford became one of Europe's leading civil engineers. His canals, bridges, harbours and roads can be found all over England and Scotland, still in use today.

In 1793 Telford was given his first big project: to build the Ellesmere Canal linking the rivers Severn and Mersey. This canal made his reputation, and soon he was in great demand. He solved many technical problems to build the Caledonian Canal crossing the Scottish Highlands, and planned the Gotha ship canal in Sweden linking the Baltic and the North Sea.

He was an outstanding road builder, and his Holyhead Road from London to the Welsh ferry port for Ireland was one of the most important routes in the country. His famous Menai suspension bridge still carries this road to Anglesey.

In 1820 the Institution of Civil Engineers invited Telford to be its first president. He held this post until his death, and his influence greatly helped civil engineering become a respected profession. He was buried in Westminster Cathedral, and in 1963 the town of Telford in Shropshire was named after him. ■

See also

Bridges
Canals
Engineers
Biography
Brunel

▼ **In 1826 Thomas Telford completed the great road bridge across the Menai Straits between the mainland of North Wales and Anglesey. It was rebuilt in 1940.**

Tenzing Norgay

Born 1914 in Tsa-Chu, Nepal
A Sherpa who was one of the first two men to reach the summit of Mount Everest
Died 1986 aged 71

Tenzing Norgay was a Sherpa, one of the Himalayan people who have the reputation of being hardy mountaineers. Tenzing made his first trip as a porter (load carrier) on the British expedition to Mount Everest in 1935. Over the next fifteen years he made seventeen more expeditions to the Himalayas and became an experienced mountaineer and *sirdar*, a Sherpa leader.

In 1953 he was invited to lead the Sherpas on another British expedition to Everest. This was his nineteenth Himalayan climb. By now Tenzing was a major climber in his own right and he was selected to be in one of the assault parties to attempt the final climb to the summit. On 29 May, Tenzing and Edmund Hillary of New Zealand stood on the top of Everest, the first men to do so. ■

See also

Mountains   **Biography**
               Hillary

▲ Tenzing Norgay stands proudly on the summit of Mount Everest. He and Hillary set up their final camp just 400 metres below the summit before their successful ascent.

Teresa of Avila, Saint

Born 1515 in Avila, Spain
She was a holy woman who saw visions and reformed the order of Carmelite nuns.
Died 1582 aged 67

Teresa came from a devoutly Christian family. As a child she used to read the lives of the saints and think about following their example. With one of her brothers, she decided to run away to North Africa to be martyred by the Arabs. They only got as far as the town walls before they were stopped.

In her teens Teresa started to buy make-up and perfumes. Then she became ill with fever. Believing she might die, she remembered her childhood dreams of heaven, and decided to become a nun. When she was better, she ran away from home and joined a Carmelite convent just outside the town.

The Carmelite order of nuns had been founded 400 years before. But standards of obedience to the rules had slipped and Teresa was greatly disappointed by the behaviour of the nuns. She found it very difficult to pray and for 20 years she was weighed down with a sense of guilt and failure. Then she started to read the *Confessions* of St Augustine and was inspired by his account of his conversion. Now, in her prayers, she began to hear and see God very intensely and to experience visions.

In 1562 Teresa began her mission to reform the Carmelite order. She insisted, for example, that the nuns slept on straw, wore rope sandals and ate no meat. Teresa spent the last sixteen years of her life travelling around Spain, restoring Carmelite houses to their original purity. All this time, she was writing for her followers about her travels, her life and her prayers. ■

See also

Catholics   **Biography**
Monasteries   Augustine of Hippo
Saints

Teresa, Mother

Born 1910 in Skopje, Macedonia
She has dedicated her life to caring for the poor and dying.

Agnes Gonxha Bojaxhiu grew up in a loving home. Her Albanian father ran a grocer's shop. Like her brother and sister, she went to the local school, but by the time she was 12 she became a nun, taking the name Teresa. 'And that,' she says, 'is when my life began.'

In 1928 she was sent to India to teach at St Mary's High School convent in Calcutta. One day she felt that God needed her among the poorest, forgotten people of the city. In 1948 she requested permission from the Roman Catholic authorities to leave the convent, and after two years it was granted. So she set aside her nun's habit and put on an Indian sari.

With a few rupees in her pocket she moved into the slums of Calcutta, where she gathered together five destitute children and sheltered them in a friend's flat. Numbers grew, girls and teachers from her old school came to help her and the Church allowed her to found the Congregation of the

▲ Mother Teresa, who is known as the 'saint of the gutters', has received other awards in addition to the Nobel Peace Prize. The Roman Catholic Church gave her the Pope John XXIII peace prize in 1971 and the Indian government gave her the Nehru award for international understanding in 1972.

Missionaries of Charity. She opened a Home for the Dying in Calcutta, as well as a leper colony called Shanti Nagar (Town of Peace). 'What the poor and sick need, is to be wanted. Being unwanted is the worst disease that any human being can experience,' she says.

Mother Teresa has opened over 60 more schools, orphanages, and homes for the dying in India, Africa, America, Europe, Australia and other parts of Asia. In 1963 she received permission to start an order for men called the Missionary Brothers of Charity. Those who recover under the care of her helpers are sent to settlements where they learn to live useful, productive lives. All the homes and settlements depend on gifts of money and other help.

In 1979 she received the Nobel Peace Prize, which she accepted on behalf of the poor and destitute everywhere. People who meet Mother Teresa say that she is very determined, but also humble. She is small and looks frail, but the love that shines through her gives her a joy and strength that touch everyone who meets her. In 1990, after suffering from illness, she retired from the most active work. ■

See also

Christians
Missionaries

Tereshkova, Valentina

Born 1937 near Yaroslavl, Russia
The world's first woman in space

Although she grew up on a farm, Valentina went to work after school in a tyre factory and then in a textile mill. In her spare time she took up sky diving and made as many as 163 parachute jumps. Because of her lack of fear and her dedication, she was picked for space training in 1962.

A year later, on 16 June 1963, she piloted a spacecraft, *Vostok 6*, in a group flight that lasted three days. Her spaceship made 48 orbits of the Earth.

Soon after the flight she married fellow cosmonaut Andrian Nikolayev; but the marriage did not last. Although she is a colonel in the Soviet air force, Valentina has tirelessly devoted herself to helping others in many spheres — as a Member of Parliament, as a diplomat on trips round the world, and as a campaigner for peace and women's rights. ■

See also

Astronauts
Space exploration

▲ This picture of Valentina Tereshkova at the controls of the spacecraft, *Vostok 6*, was beamed down from space during one of her many orbits of the Earth.

Thatcher, Margaret Hilda

Born 1925 in Grantham, Lincolnshire, England
Became Britain's first woman prime minister in 1979 and won the two following elections in 1983 and 1987.

Margaret Thatcher was born Margaret Roberts. She studied chemistry at Oxford University and later became a barrister. In 1951 she married Denis Thatcher, a business man, and they had twin children, Carol and Mark. Having been elected to Parliament in 1959, she gained her first cabinet post as Minister of Education in 1970. Following two election defeats for Edward Heath in 1974, she was elected Conservative Party leader the following year.

▲ Margaret Thatcher is shown here speaking during the 1987 General Election. After her victory at this election she became the longest serving British prime minister in the 20th century.

In 1979 the Conservatives won the General Election, and Margaret Thatcher became the first woman prime minister of Britain. She at once set about lowering taxes and reducing government control of businesses. A number of laws were passed to limit the power of trade unions. Later many state-owned businesses, including British Telecom and British Gas, were sold to private owners.

In 1982 Margaret Thatcher reacted quickly when Argentina invaded the British colony of the Falkland Islands. Within 74 days a British task force had recaptured the islands, but many hundreds of British and Argentinian soldiers, sailors and airmen died. In 1983 she led the Conservatives to another election victory.

In her second term of office, many of the country's miners went on strike to try to stop mines being closed down. Margaret Thatcher refused to back down, and after more than a year on strike the miners returned to work. In 1987 she became the first prime minister since the Earl of Liverpool in the early 19th century to be elected to a third consecutive term of office.

Margaret Thatcher's economic policies, which gave fewer responsibilities to the government, came to be called 'Thatcherism'. Her toughness in defence matters and foreign affairs led to her being called 'the Iron Lady' and she earned a lot of respect from people throughout the world. However, there were some in the European Community and the Commonwealth who believed that Margaret Thatcher did not co-operate enough with other leaders. She also came under attack from colleagues in the cabinet who thought that her style of government was too autocratic. By the end of 1990 her popularity had declined. There was a contest for the leadership of the Conservative Party and she resigned. ■

See also

British history 1919–1989
Prime ministers

Titian

Born about 1485 in Cadore, Italy
The greatest Venetian painter
Died 1576 aged about 91

Tiziano Vecellio (his Italian name) was born in a mountain village north of Venice, where earning a living was hard. His family was not rich but was at least respected: his father after being a captain in the army became a local official.

Titian trained to be a painter in the workshop of Giovanni Bellini, the most famous Venetian painter of his time. When Bellini died in 1516, Titian took over his post as the city's official painter. He worked on paintings for the great churches and families of Venice, and he became so successful and famous that kings and nobles from other parts of Europe commissioned (ordered) work from him.

Titian's wonderful skill in composing a painting enabled him to break all the traditional rules of how pictures should be arranged. He deeply impressed other artists in Venice by his modern bold style. No other painter had placed the Madonna and Child in the corner of a picture and not in the centre, as Titian did. He used oil paint with sumptuous,

glowing colours which suited the splendour and richness of the Venice of his time. The free style of his late works was heightened by using his fingers more often than a brush for finishing touches or highlights. His fame was such that even the Emperor Charles V bent down to pick up a brush he had dropped. This was unheard-of respect for an artist at that time. ■

See also

Italy's history

▲ *The Death of Actaeon* by Titian, National Gallery, London. When the goddess, Diana, turned Actaeon into a stag, he was torn to pieces by his own hunting dogs. On the left, the graceful figure of Diana moves across the landscape and the beauty of the glowing colours and the fine brushstrokes seem to distract from the full horror of the scene that is taking place on the right. The story comes from the Roman myth of Diana (Artemis in Greek myths).

Tito, Josip Broz

Born 1892 in Croatia
He was a Yugoslav communist who led the fight against the Germans and then became President of Yugoslavia.
Died 1980 aged 87

Josip Broz was the son of a blacksmith in Croatia, which was then part of the Austrian empire. He was called up to fight for Austria against Russia in World War I. After the war he stayed in Russia to help the communists, who had just come to power.

When he came home in 1920, Croatia was part of a new kingdom which soon took the name 'Yugoslavia'. Along with the Croats there were the people of five other national groups, each with their own history, language and culture. However, Yugoslavia was little better than a dictatorship and the most powerful leaders in it were from one of the nationalities, the Serbs.

In 1921 Josip Broz founded the Yugoslav Communist Party. The government declared it illegal, so in the 1920s and 1930s he was either in prison for his beliefs or working for communism in other countries, where he used the undercover name 'Tito'.

In 1941, during World War II, the Germans invaded and occupied

Yugoslavia. Tito built up a resistance force, the Partisans, which used guerrilla tactics. They had terrible struggles to keep alive while Germans hunted them across the mountains. In 1945 they chased the Germans out and set up a new communist state with Tito as leader. The homelands of all six national groups became equal republics in the state. At first Tito ran the government as the Soviet Union ordered, but in 1948 he broke away. His Partisan comrades stood by him, so he kept Yugoslavia free from Soviet control. Although the government was still communist, it gave the people more freedom and let workers and farmers manage their own factories and farms. ■

👁 **See also**

Communists
Croatia
Guerrillas
Yugoslavia

Tolkien, J. R. R.

Born 1892 in Bloemfontein, South Africa
He wrote the best-selling children's books, *The Hobbit* and *The Lord of the Rings*.
Died 1973 aged 81

When John Ronald Tolkien was 3 years old he and his younger brother moved to England with their mother. His father died before he could join them, and the family, which was now quite poor, set up home in a small village in Warwickshire. Here Tolkien was very happy until he was 12, when his mother died too. She left the boys in the care of a priest, who saw to it that they had a good education. As a child Tolkien loved the strange Welsh names he saw painted on coal trucks coming through Warwickshire from Wales, and for the rest of his life he remained fascinated by old languages. He married and became a professor of English at Oxford University. To amuse himself and his children, he invented creatures, like elves and hobbits, with their own languages, and gave them adventures. His first children's book, *The Hobbit*, appeared

in 1937, but it took him another twelve years to complete the three volumes of *The Lord of the Rings*. Since then, his books have sold millions of copies and have been read by people all over the world. ■

Tolstoy, Leo

Born 1828 in Yasnaya Polyana, near Tula in Russia
One of the world's greatest writers; his best-known novels are *War and Peace* and *Anna Karenina*.
Died 1910 aged 82

Leo Tolstoy was born into one of Russia's most famous noble families, on his parents' country estate of Yasnaya Polyana. His mother died when he was 2 and his father when he was 8, so he was brought up by his aunt. He did not go to school but was educated at home by a governess. He later studied at Kazan University, but left before finishing his course and spent the next few years having a good time.

At the age of 23 he became an artillery officer in the Caucasus and took part in the Crimean War. He wrote his first stories during the war, drawing on his own early life. *Childhood* was published in 1852, followed by *Boyhood* and *Youth*. After taking part in the defence of Sevastopol, he wrote his famous *Sevastopol Sketches*. After the Crimean War he travelled widely in western Europe, devoting his second trip in 1860 to a study of educational methods. During the 1860s and 1870s, he spent much of his time and energy on education. He established a school for peasant children on his country estate at Yasnaya Polyana, published a magazine and wrote stories for children.

It was in this period, 1863 to 1869, that he wrote *War and Peace,* sometimes said to be the greatest novel in the world. It gives a picture of Russia just before and during the war against Napoleon in 1812. Next he worked on *Anna Karenina,* about a married woman's tragic love affair with a

▲ Two great Russian writers, Leo Tolstoy, on the right, and Anton Chekhov who was 30 years younger.

soldier. By the time the book was finished, Tolstoy was facing a crisis in his life. He was an aristocrat, but he was beginning to reject his life of luxury for the simple life of a peasant. In spite of his marriage and great work of writing, he felt he was living selfishly. He developed a new religious philosophy based on peace, love and a humble life.

Finally, one night he felt that he must get away. He left home secretly, but died of pneumonia at a small railway station ten days later. ■

Torricelli, Evangelista

Born 1608 in Faenza, Italy
Invented the barometer.
Died 1647 aged 39

Torricelli studied mathematics in Rome, but his life changed when at the age of about 30 he read a book written by the great Galileo. He wrote to Galileo, and soon this famous scientist invited Torricelli to join him in Florence. By this time Galileo was old, blind and only had a short time to live, but Torricelli stayed with him and worked as his secretary. Right up to his death Galileo was puzzled by the fact that pumps working in mines could never raise water above a height of about 10 m (33 ft).

After Galileo's death Torricelli tried to solve this mystery by filling a metre tube with some mercury, a liquid much heavier than water. One end of the tube was closed and the open end he placed in a dish of mercury. Some of the mercury poured out of the upside-down tube, but a column of about 76 cm (2 ft 6 in) remained in the tube. Torricelli realized that the column stayed up because of the weight of the atmosphere pressing on the surface of the liquid in the dish. If he had repeated the experiment with water a column of about 10 metres would have been supported. The height of the column of mercury changed slightly from day to day. This was the first barometer. ■

See also

Barometers
Vacuums

Biography
Galilei

Toussaint l'Ouverture

Born about 1746 in St Domingue (now Haiti), Caribbean
He was leader of the black armies in St Domingue who fought to keep their freedom from slavery.
Died 1803 aged about 57

Pierre Dominique Toussaint's father is said to have been an African chief who was taken as a slave to a sugar plantation in the French colony of St Domingue. Toussaint was born there. He was clever, and his father helped him to learn to read French and Latin and study mathematics. Toussaint also became a brilliant horseman.

In 1791 the slaves rebelled against their masters and Toussaint joined them. He was so admired as a leader that he became commander and turned the rebels into a strong fighting force. Without this their freedom would have been lost, because they had to defeat

French armies and then British troops who invaded the island. By 1798 both French and British had been beaten. Toussaint's followers called him 'l'Ouverture', meaning the opener of the way to freedom. Because they respected him, they returned to work as free men on the plantations to grow sugar which was sold to the USA, whose president admired Toussaint.

In 1802 the French emperor, Napoleon, sent an army to recapture Toussaint's country. Toussaint agreed to make peace with the French commander, who promised to do him no harm. The promise was false and Toussaint was sent to prison in France, where he died. His soldiers rose up and drove the French from their country, which became free with a new name, Haiti. ■

See also

Caribbean history
Haiti
Slaves

▼ A contemporary picture by the artist, Rowlandson, of Trevithick's circular railroad on display at Euston Square, London, in 1809.

Trevithick, Richard

Born 1771 in Illogan, Cornwall, England
He developed the high-pressure steam-engine and built the world's first railway locomotive.
Died 1833 aged 62

Trevithick was born in a tin-mining district of Cornwall, where his father was a mine manager. He went to the local village school, and although he was quick at arithmetic, he was not an exceptional pupil. However, as a young man he won a reputation for great physical strength and for his knowledge of mining engines. At 19 he was appointed a consulting engineer at one of the mines in the district.

The engines used to pump water at the mines were the low-pressure steam-engines with condensers, which James Watt had invented. Trevithick was soon suggesting improvements. His greatest achievement came in 1798 with the development of the high-pressure steam-engine, which was smaller, lighter and worked faster than Watt's engine. Between 1799 and 1812, Trevithick developed his engine for many uses. In 1801 he built the

first full-sized road locomotive in Britain, which successfully carried a number of passengers up a hill. Then, in 1804, he built the first railway locomotive, which ran along a ten-mile (15-km) track at Penydarren in South Wales. But the locomotive was so heavy that it crushed the cast-iron rails, and after a similar experience with another locomotive in 1808, Trevithick concentrated on other ideas. His engine had already been used to provide power for the world's first steam dredger, and in 1812 it was used to drive a corn-threshing machine.

Trevithick's inventions never made him rich for he was a poor business man. In 1816 he went to South America, hoping to make his fortune in the silver mines in Peru, but he came back home penniless in 1827 and was still in debt when he died. ■

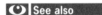
See also

Railways
Steam-engines

Biography
Stephenson
Watt

Trotsky, Leon

Born 1879 in Yanovka, Ukraine, Russian empire
He was one of the leaders of the Russian Revolution, but was later expelled from Russia.
Assassinated 1940 aged 60

When a 'hitman' sent by Stalin split open Trotsky's skull with an ice pick in Mexico City, it was the final act in a tragic life.

Lev Bronstein was born of Jewish parents on a 100-hectare (250-acre) farm in the Ukraine. After school he went to university in Odessa in 1897, but soon left to work full time for a revolution in Russia. In 1898 he was arrested and sent to Siberia. He escaped from there and fled the country under his new name, Trotsky, which he took from one of his prison guards.

When the Russian Social-Democratic Workers' Party split in 1903, Trotsky became a Menshevik (the minority) opposing Lenin's Bolsheviks (the

▲ Leon Trotsky (left) is shown here at Petrograd (now Leningrad) railway station in 1921. He used the railway system in the Soviet Union to keep in contact with the Red Army as it fought against those who were trying to overturn the Revolution.

majority). Back in Russia, he became head of the St Petersburg workers' soviet (council), which led a revolt in the city. Again he was arrested and banished, but again he escaped abroad.

Only when he returned to Russia after the tsar was overthrown in 1917 did Trotsky join the Bolsheviks. He helped to organize the Revolution, particularly the tactics for seizing power. Later he took charge of foreign affairs and defence, and built a new army, the Red Army, to fight against those forces which wanted to crush the Revolution.

Trotsky was a brilliant linguist, writer and speaker, but his impatience and bitter tongue made him many enemies in the Communist Party. After Lenin's death, he was deprived of power by Stalin. In 1927 he was expelled from the party, and two years later was driven out of the USSR. Eventually he was murdered in Mexico on Stalin's

orders. Followers of Trotsky's ideas exist today as communist groups fighting for world revolution. ■

See also

Communists
Russia's history
USSR 1922–1991

Biography
Lenin
Stalin

Trudeau, Pierre Elliott

Born 1919 in Montréal, Québec, Canada
A prime minister of Canada who made French and English the two official languages

Pierre Elliott Trudeau grew up in Montréal able to speak both French and English. As a young man he studied law at Harvard in the United States of America and at the London School of Economics in England. He also travelled a good deal and had many adventures; once he was nearly drowned trying to canoe to Cuba.

Trudeau became involved with politics during a miners' strike at Asbestos, Québec, in 1950. He supported the workers, and later helped to write a book criticizing the government for keeping their pay so low. He became well known for his views on how society should be organized.

In 1965 he was elected to Parliament and he became prime minister in 1968. At this time many French-speaking Quebeckers wanted their province to become a separate country from English Canada, but Trudeau worked hard to keep the province in Canada. He insisted on the use of both French and English by the national federal government, based in Ottawa.

A bachelor until he was 52, he astonished everyone in 1971 by marrying Margaret Sinclair. He had three sons and is a devoted father, but his marriage did not last long.

In 1982 he negotiated a law with Britain that gave Canada power over its own constitution, which had been held by the British government. The same law also gave Canadians a Charter of Rights and Freedoms, which made sure that all people, including those from minority groups, would be treated fairly. He retired as prime minister in 1984. ■

◉ See also

Canada's history

Tubman, Harriet

Born about 1820 in Maryland, USA
'The Moses of her people', she helped slaves escape from the Southern states to Canada and the Northern states.
Died 1913 aged about 93

Harriet Tubman was born into slavery. She was called Araminta, but later took her mother's name, Harriet. As a child and young woman, Harriet worked, under terrible conditions, on the slave plantations in the Southern states of the USA. Her master forced her to marry another slave called Tubman, from whom she took her surname.

A few years later, Harriet managed to escape from the plantation. She made her way north on the 'Underground Railway'. This was not a real railway but a code name for a famous escape system for fugitive slaves. They were smuggled out of the South to Canada or the Northern states, where slavery was not legal. The route was organized by black and white abolitionists, people working to end slavery. Escaping slaves were called passengers. The homes they hid in were called stations, and the people who organized the escapes were called conductors.

Harriet Tubman became the most famous 'conductor' of all. Over the next ten years she worked on the escape route and helped more than 300 slaves to escape, including her aged parents. She suffered from constant ill health, but she was a brave woman and

▼ *Rain, Steam and Speed* by Turner, National Gallery, London. This picture is Turner's attempt to represent the sensation of speed as a train rushes through the rain, enveloped by its own steam. The blurred detail and the curious light effects made by the mixture of yellow and orange colour give a feeling of distance and movement.

devoted her life to helping slaves and working for the abolition of slavery. She always managed to avoid being caught, and eventually became known as the 'Moses of her people' because, like Moses, she led so many slaves into freedom. She opened schools for black people who had been slaves, and eventually settled in New York. There she opened the Harriet Tubman Home for Aged Negroes. ■

◉ See also

American Civil War   **Biography**
Slaves   Moses
Slave trade   Stowe

Turner, Joseph M. William

Born 1775 in London, England
One of the greatest English landscape painters
Died 1851 aged 76

Joseph William Turner, the son of a London barber, was an exceptionally talented child. At the age of 14 he became a student at the Royal College of Art, and at 16 his work was first

exhibited to the public. From the beginning he worked incredibly hard; indeed he felt this to be the reason for his success, and said 'The only secret I have got is damned hard work.'

Turner went on the first of his sketching tours at 17 and was to continue this method of travelling and working for 50 years. Each year his style changed as he met with new ideas from other countries and other artists.

After touring Italy he became particularly interested in colour and light. His subject, nearly always landscape, seems to be a fantastic magical world of lighting effects, threatening weather conditions and mysterious shadows. He could make both land and sea look impressive and sometimes fearsome. A friend described his way of working: 'He began by pouring wet paint onto the paper until it was saturated. He poured, he scratched, he scrabbled at it in a kind of frenzy, and the whole thing was chaos — but gradually as if by magic the lovely ship, with all its exquisite detail came into being. By lunch-time it was finished.'

His energy was astonishing. He produced about 500 oil paintings and over 20,000 water-colours and drawings. He left most of his pictures and drawings to the nation in his will; they are displayed at the Tate Gallery in London. ■

⊙ See also

Paintings

Tussaud, Marie

Born 1760 in Strasbourg, France
She founded the famous 'Madame Tussaud's Exhibition' of waxwork models in London.
Died 1850 aged 89

When Marie was a baby her father died and her mother moved with her to Berne, in Switzerland, to become the housekeeper of a German doctor. The doctor enjoyed making wax models of parts of the human body, and soon got a reputation for making

good likenesses of people's heads as well. He moved to Paris to earn more money by modelling the heads of the rich and the famous, and in time Marie and her mother joined him. When she was 6 he taught her how to work in wax, and her portraits became so popular that by the time she was 20 she was living in the Palace of Versailles at the invitation of the royal family, as art teacher to the king's sister.

In 1789 the French Revolution broke out, and during those terrible days Marie was called upon to make models of the severed heads of the same aristocrats, many of them her friends, after they had been killed by the revolutionaries. Then she was herself taken prisoner on suspicion of being a royalist, but was released.

She married a French engineer, François Tussaud, and they had two children. In 1802 she received permission from Napoleon to take her waxwork collection to England, in order to earn more money there. With her 4-year-old son she toured Britain and Ireland, and her shows were a great success. She began making models of important English men and women, as well as of notorious criminals who had been executed. In 1835 she set up a permanent exhibition in London, where you may still see the models she made of her great contemporaries, as well as many others which have been added since. ■

Tutankhamun

Born about 1370 BC in Egypt
One of the best-known of the ancient Egyptian kings
Died 1352 BC aged about 18

The modern world discovered Tutankhamun, the boy-king, in 1922 when the English archaeologist, Howard Carter, uncovered his secret tomb.

We call Tutankhamun the boy-king because he died young, after reigning

for only nine years. Tutankhamun became the pharaoh (god-king) when he was about 10 years old. He became pharaoh through his marriage to the princess Ankhesenpaaten, who was the daughter of the pharaoh Akhenaten and his queen Nefertiti. We are not sure who his parents were. ■

⊙ See also

Egyptian ancient history

Tutu, Desmond Mpilo

Born 1931 in Klerksdorp, western Transvaal, South Africa
He became Archbishop of Cape Town and a leading opponent of South Africa's 'apartheid' policies.

Desmond Mpilo (meaning 'life') Tutu was the son of a primary school headmaster and a domestic servant. He soon discovered what it was like to be black and poor in South Africa. In his teens he spent nearly two years in hospital suffering from tuberculosis. This increased his ambition to become a doctor, but he could not afford to. He trained to be a teacher instead. However, in the 1950s the South African government decided that black children should only be given a basic education. Tutu could not accept this, so he left teaching to become a priest in the Anglican Church.

In the 1960s and 1970s he and his family spent some time in Britain, where he studied and worked for the Church. They were amazed at the civilized way they were treated compared to their experiences in South Africa. This made him speak out against 'apartheid' (the policy of racial separateness and discrimination) when he returned to his own country. In 1975 he became Dean of Johannesburg and could have lived in an area reserved for whites. Instead he chose to live in Soweto: a crowded township of a million black people.

After becoming Bishop of Lesotho and then of Johannesburg, in 1986 he was made Archbishop of Cape Town, the head of the Anglican Church for all

▲ **Archbishop Tutu is shown here celebrating in his usual exuberant way the 70th birthday of another fighter against apartheid, Nelson Mandela.**

southern Africa. Desmond Tutu has been given many honours for speaking out for black people, but the greatest was in 1984 when he was awarded the Nobel Peace Prize for his 'non-violent struggle against apartheid'. ■

See also

Apartheid
South Africa

Twain, Mark

Born 1835 in Florida, Missouri, USA
He is perhaps the most widely read of all American writers; he wrote *Tom Sawyer* and *Huckleberry Finn*.
Died 1910 aged 74

Mark Twain's real name was Samuel Langhorne Clemens. When Sam was 4 his family moved to the small town of Hannibal on the River Mississippi, where his father opened a grocery store. Sam spent his childhood watching the giant lumber rafts roll by, and the steamboats dock alongside the quay. He was fascinated by the mixture of people who came and went. When he was 11 his father died, and after that Sam stopped going to school. He did odd jobs to earn money for his family instead.

At 13 he was apprenticed to a printer, and later began writing for local newspapers. He adopted the pen-name 'Mark Twain', which was a phrase that the Mississippi pilots called out when they made soundings of the river: it meant 'two fathoms deep'. For almost four years he worked as a steamboat pilot himself, and later, when he had become world-famous as a writer, he remembered those years as the most carefree of his life. In 1861 he tried his luck as a gold-miner, and when that failed, he became a full-time writer.

He was a very great storyteller, and wrote in a brilliantly funny way about the Southern way of life. He had the knack of making his readers feel part of the story. In *Tom Sawyer* (1876) and *Huckleberry Finn* (1884) he painted a wonderful picture of life on and around the Mississippi during an exciting era, describing it exactly as the boys in the story would see it. He also wrote many other novels and a travel book, *The Innocents Abroad.* ■

Tyler, Wat

Born date unknown, in southern England
He was a leader of the Peasants' Revolt.
Executed 1381, age unknown

Wat Tyler worked as a blacksmith in Kent at a time when English labourers were very badly paid. In 1381 the government of King Richard II introduced a poll tax which required all men to pay the same, however much they earned. This was so unjust that many rebelled. The labourers of Kent rose up against their masters, choosing Wat Tyler as their leader.

First, his ragged army captured Canterbury; then it marched on London, joining peasants from Essex led by Jack Straw. Once in London, they set fire to palaces, killed royal officials and insisted on a meeting with King Richard, who was then only 14 years old. The rebels demanded lower rents and an end to their oppression at work. The young king agreed to these conditions, but Tyler and his men were still not satisfied. In a second meeting Tyler was badly wounded, and later beheaded on the orders of the Mayor of London. All the king's promises were later broken, but at least a stand had been made against injustice. Later generations of labourers often remembered Wat Tyler's revolt when it came to fighting for their own rights. ■

See also

Feudal system
Peasants' Revolt

Biography
Richard II

Van Gogh, Vincent

Born 1853 in Groot-Zundert, near Breda, The Netherlands
A Dutch painter who was ignored and misunderstood in his own lifetime
Committed suicide 1890 aged 37

The son of a pastor (minister of a Protestant church), Vincent was taught that a meaningful life meant devoting oneself to others. He was an awkward, lonely, rather difficult child who found school life depressing and unrewarding. He became deeply religious, and trained for a life as a missionary. For a while he worked in a poor mining area of Belgium. Living in poverty, he tried desperately hard to help others. But his moody personality prevented him from being successful in the Church or in any other job he tried. His beloved younger brother, Theo, although very poor himself, helped him to survive.

Vincent taught himself to draw and paint, and struggled relentlessly to improve his skills. His early paintings in The Netherlands and Belgium are

▼ *Sunflowers* by Van Gogh, National Gallery, London. This is a picture which shows how excitement and energy can be conveyed by vivid colours, thick brushstrokes and exaggerated shapes. The use of yellow 'almost as bright as the sun itself' had special significance for Van Gogh. It was connected in his mind with sunlight, warmth and happiness.

dark and sombre, showing the miserable lives of the working poor. Later he went to Paris and the south of France, where he worked with other painters, including Gauguin. Under their influence he experimented with clear, bright colours, brushed energetically onto the canvas. This technique belongs especially to Van Gogh. His excited, bold brushstrokes show deep emotion and a sort of frenzy even when the subject itself is peaceful. His pictures are of the ordinary things in life: his bedroom, a chair, a bunch of sunflowers. He never painted any grand subjects.

He spent the last two years of his life living in Arles in southern France. His days were frantically busy and productive, but also very troubled. Times of energetic creativity turned into severe depressions and periods of insanity. Van Gogh cut off one of his own ears during one such crisis. After only ten years of painting, he committed suicide. His genius was not recognized until after his death. He sold only one painting during his lifetime. ■

 See also

Paintings | **Biography**
Gauguin

Velázquez, Diego

Born 1599 in Seville, Spain
The greatest of all Spanish painters, chiefly famous for his portraits
Died 1660 aged 61

Velázquez had one of the most continuously successful careers in the history of art. He was a prodigy, producing masterpieces when he was still in his teens. When he was 24 he painted a portrait of Philip IV, the King of Spain. Philip was so impressed that he declared that from now on no other artist would be allowed to paint him.

Philip greatly admired Velázquez as a man as well as an artist and appointed him to various court posts in Madrid. They were great honours, but they took up much of Velázquez's time, so that on average he painted only about three

▲ *Las Meninas* by Velázquez, Prado Museum, Madrid, Spain. This picture shows the daughter of the King and Queen of Spain, the Infanta Margarita, with her maids of honour, tutors and dwarfs. She is watching her parents have their portrait painted by Velázquez. The king and queen are reflected in a mirror on the back wall.

pictures a year. However, these include some of the finest portraits in the world. Velázquez depicted his subjects with great sympathy, whether he was portraying king or commoner, or even the wretched court fools. These were dwarfs and mentally subnormal people who were kept to amuse the king: Velázquez's portraits give them a sense of dignity. ■

Verdi, Giuseppe

Born 1813 in Roncole, Italy
The greatest Italian opera composer of the 19th century
Died 1901 aged 87

The wonderful thing about Verdi is that the older he grew, the greater his music became. He wrote his last operas, *Otello* and *Falstaff,* between the ages of 74 and 80, when most men have long retired. They are his masterpieces.

Life did not start too well for him. His parents were poor and his musical education was paid for by a neighbour, a wealthy merchant. Even so, he failed to gain entry to the Milan Conservatory

of Music and had to study privately. His first opera, *Oberto*, was quite successful and he was asked to write more. But tragedy struck. His wife and two young children died within two months of each other. Verdi was heartbroken and vowed never to write another note.

Fortunately he was tempted to write a new opera, *Nabucco*, and its success launched his career as Italy's most famous composer.

The stories Verdi chose for his operas seemed like battle cries, urging Italians to throw off the domination of Austria, which then ruled over much of northern Italy. Verdi and his music spoke for an entire nation which wanted independence and unity. His operas are loved for their bold tunes and the wonderful way he can make his characters come alive. They are as fresh today as they were when he first put pen to paper. ■

◉ See also

Italy's history   Operas

Vermeer, Jan

Born 1632 in Delft, The Netherlands
A Dutch painter of peaceful and homely scenes
Died 1675 aged 43

Not very much is known about Vermeer's life. His father kept an inn, and Jan Vermeer may have worked there. He married at 21 and had eleven children. He became head of the Painters' Guild twice, and was well respected. But he ran up debts, particularly to his baker, to whom he gave two paintings in return for credit. After his death, his wife offered to pay the baker in full over twelve years, if he would return the paintings, but she became bankrupt.

Vermeer did not become famous until 200 years after his death, when his paintings were recognized as masterpieces. He worked extremely slowly and produced only about 40 paintings. He painted Dutch people doing ordinary domestic jobs, such as

▲ *Interior with a Maidservant Pouring Milk* by Vermeer, Rijksmuseum, Amsterdam, The Netherlands. The quiet dignity of this figure pouring milk in preparation for a simple meal is heightened by the plainness of the wall behind her.

pouring out milk in the kitchen, but he handled light and colour so cleverly that his figures are solid and strong, yet serene and gentle. ■

Vespucci, Amerigo

Born 1451 in Florence, Italy
Explorer of South America
Died 1512 aged 61

In 1507 a German cartographer (mapmaker), Martin Waldseemüller, published a map in which the newly discovered lands to the west were given a name. That name, he said, should be America, 'because Amerigo discovered it'. Amerigo Vespucci did not discover America, but he was one of the first people to realize it could be a separate continent, and not part of Asia.

Vespucci was an Italian merchant who settled in Spain as agent of the Medici Bank. He was the contractor who supplied stores to Christopher Columbus for his voyages to the west. In due course he became chief navigator for the Medici Bank, making maps of the lands discovered by Columbus and others.

As navigator he sailed west in 1499–1500 and explored the mouth of the Amazon River. In 1501–1502 he explored the coast as far south as the Río de la Plata, and it was then that he realized he was looking at another continent, not at parts of Asia as Columbus had believed. ■

See also

Explorers

Biography
Columbus

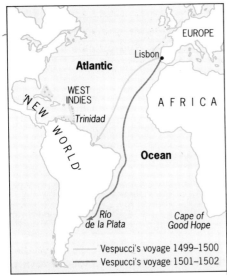

▲ Two of Vespucci's three known voyages to America. Scholars have found little evidence to support his claim that in 1497 he was the first European to see the mainland of South America.

Victoria

Born 1819 in Kensington Palace, London, England
Queen of the United Kingdom from 1837. She reigned 64 years, longer than any other British monarch.
Died 1901 aged 81

Victoria was a lonely child. Her father, the Duke of Kent, died when she was a baby. Her anxious mother protected her carefully. She was never left alone, and seldom saw anyone of her own age. When Victoria was 12, her governess and her mother decided to let her see the royal family tree. When she realized that she would be queen one day, she burst into tears; 'I will be good,' she sobbed. 'I understand now why you urged me so much to learn, even Latin . . .'

Victoria was lively and strong-willed. She could be moody, and had strong likes and dislikes, but she was sensible too. She was interested in new inventions: she enjoyed travelling on the early railways, and photography fascinated her. She was musical and could draw well. She kept a diary, so we often know how she felt. She was scarcely 1 m 50 cm (5 ft) tall, and when she was old she was fat and dumpy. But she was very dignified. Most people were rather frightened of the queen in old age.

Victoria became queen when she was only 18. Three years later, she married her German cousin Prince Albert. The queen was devoted to her 'dearest Albert', and gradually came to depend on him completely. Victoria and Albert had nine children, many of whom married into European royal families, and were strict but loving parents. When Albert died suddenly of typhoid in 1861, Victoria was desperately unhappy. She refused to appear in public, and wore black for the rest of her life.

The 'widow of Windsor' was unpopular for a time. Some people thought there was no point in having a queen nobody ever saw. The prime minister, Benjamin Disraeli, finally managed to coax her into public life again. She liked his tactful, flattering ways, but disliked his great rival, William Gladstone, who was much more serious and stiff.

Victoria took great interest in all the peoples of the British empire. Her Diamond Jubilee of 1897 was a great event in the whole empire. When she died, it seemed the end of the age to which she gave her name. ■

See also

Royal families
Victorian Britain

Biography
Disraeli
Gladstone
British Royal Family (family tree)

▲ The painting shows the young Victoria receiving the news that she was to become queen. The photograph was taken many years later in 1886, when Victoria had been queen for nearly 50 years. She is pictured with Princess Henry of Battenberg (standing), her granddaughter, Victoria, Princess Louis of Battenberg, and her great-granddaughter, Princess Alice of Battenberg.

Virgil

Born 70 BC near Mantua, Italy
Virgil is probably the best-known of the poets of ancient Rome.
Died 19 BC aged 50

Virgil's parents were not rich, but he had a good education in Cremona, Milan and Rome. He then returned to his family farm to write. Among his important poems are the *Eclogues* (the word in Latin means 'select poems'), which are about ideal countrysides and people. His poems called the *Georgics* are about farming, growing crops and keeping animals.

Virgil's most important work was called the *Aeneid*. It is a long, epic poem about the hero Aeneas and his journey from Troy to Italy. Aeneas was the son of Anchises and the goddess Aphrodite. Virgil's poem-story tells of the hero's escape from the burning city of Troy, his adventures on his journey across the sea to Carthage and then to Italy and his foundation of the city of Lavinium, a town 25 km (16 miles) south of Rome.

Virgil ordered that the manuscript of the *Aeneid* (which he had not finished) should be burnt after his death. However, the Emperor Augustus ordered it to be published. ∎

See also

Roman ancient history   Trojan War

Vivaldi, Antonio

Born 1678 in Venice, Italy
One of the most important Italian composers of concertos
Died 1741 aged 63

Little is known of Vivaldi's early life, except that he was taught to play by his father who was a professional violinist. He then trained as a priest and was ordained in 1703. In the same year he began to teach music at the Conservatorio della Pietà in Venice. The Conservatorio was an orphanage for girls, which had a famous choir and orchestra. Vivaldi helped train the girls and wrote music for them to play. As his fame spread throughout Italy, he spent more time away from the Conservatorio and finally left in 1738.

Vivaldi composed all kinds of music, including over 40 operas, but is most famous for his concertos. He wrote over 500, nearly half for solo violin; but he also wrote concertos for flute, oboe, bassoon, recorder and mandolin. Some have descriptive titles, such as *The Four Seasons* and *The Hunt,* and their music cleverly conjures up the appropriate atmosphere. Vivaldi spent money freely, and despite his success he died in poverty. ∎

See also

Concertos

Volta, Alessandro

Born 1745 in Como, Italy
Invented the first battery.
Died 1827 aged 82

The story goes that Volta's parents thought he was a very backward boy, because he did not talk until he was 4 years old. By the time he was a teenager Volta was clearly very clever and decided he wanted to be a scientist.

A friend of Volta's, a scientist called Galvani, wrote telling him about an amazing experiment that he had done. Galvani explained that he was cutting up frogs and hung a piece of muscle on a brass hook, and when the muscle came in contact with some iron wire it twitched. Some people thought that the muscle was producing its own 'animal electricity', but Volta showed that it was the contact of the two different metals that produced electricity and made the muscle twitch. Volta did many experiments with different metals. He made a pile of coins of two different metals, separated the coins with card soaked in salt solution and produced an electric current. This was the first battery. ∎

See also

Batteries   Electricity

Wagner, Richard

Born 1813 in Leipzig, Germany
The greatest of all German operatic composers
Died 1883 aged 69

Wagner was brought up in a theatrical family and until the age of 15 he seemed more likely to become a dramatist than a composer. But just as Shakespeare's plays had made him want to write for the stage, Beethoven's music made him want to write music. In the end he did both, by writing the words for his own operas.

Wagner studied music at Leipzig University, but he really began to learn his trade when he worked in various German opera houses. His own first attempts at opera failed. Then *Rienzi* and *The Flying Dutchman* were successful and turned the tide for him.

Wagner was not content with ordinary opera. He wanted something better, something that would combine all the arts into a music drama. In 1853 he began to write *The Ring of the Nibelungs,* a colossal cycle of four music dramas based on German legends.

He now found he needed a special opera house to perform his works. Fortunately King Ludwig II of Bavaria had fallen in love with his music. The king paid his debts (Wagner was very extravagant) and provided money for the new opera house at Bayreuth. Wagner completed his 'Ring' cycle in 1874 and Bayreuth opened its doors two years later.

Everything about Wagner and his music was larger than life. He was not a pleasant man. He was far too full of himself. But he was one of the greatest musical geniuses the world has ever known. ■

See also

Operas

Walpole, Sir Robert

Born 1676 in Houghton Hall, Norfolk, England
The first British prime minister, from 1721 to 1742
Died 1745 aged 68

As the son of a prominent landowner, Walpole became a Member of Parliament in 1701. Although he was briefly imprisoned in the Tower of London in 1712 for taking bribes, his hard work and attention to detail were soon recognized. He enjoyed the support of King George I and rose to great influence. In 1721 he became First Lord of the Admiralty and Chancellor of the Exchequer and so was the king's chief minister.

His policy of avoiding foreign wars and so keeping down taxes helped him keep power; so did his way of giving well-paid jobs as rewards to his own supporters. But his enemies constantly attacked him for this type of corruption, and as he grew older he became less popular. Finally in 1742 he was forced to resign.

The job of prime minister did not exist before Walpole. He helped create it by taking on the major responsibility for getting things done in the House of Commons. With the support of other 'Whig' Members of Parliament he was usually able to find enough votes to defeat the Tories, the other main party. From Walpole's time onwards, the practice of having one chief minister continued, just as it does today. ■

See also

Georgian Britain   **Biography**
Prime ministers   George I

Washington, Booker T.

Born 1856 in Franklin County, Virginia, USA
Born a slave, he founded Tuskegee Institute, a famous college for American blacks.
Died 1915 aged 59

When Booker was 9 all American slaves were freed. Booker had been a house servant, but he could read and wanted to teach. So when he was 16 he travelled 500 miles with almost no money to a school for black teachers. To pay for their studies, all the students worked. Booker cleaned the school.

Later, he started a college for blacks at Tuskegee, Alabama. The students themselves built most of it. Washington knew that many white Americans disliked and distrusted blacks, so he taught his students to be polite and to work hard, while he persuaded rich whites like Andrew Carnegie to give money to keep Tuskegee going.

In a speech in 1895, he said that blacks and whites could be separate like fingers, but that they could work together like a hand. Some black leaders disagreed, but at that time Washington thought blacks needed education and jobs more than civil rights. White people who agreed with his ideas treated him as the chief spokesman for blacks. ■

See also

Afro-Americans   **Biography**
                 Carnegie

Washington, George

Born 1732 at Bridges Creek, Virginia, USA
General who defeated Britain in the American Revolution; he was the first President of the United States of America.
Died 1799 aged 67

When George was born, Virginia was a British colony. His father farmed and owned slaves, but was not rich. He died when George was 11. George did not have much schooling, but he was always very practical. At 14 he helped to survey some frontier land. A year later he had his own surveying

▲ This painting shows Washington (standing with sword) and his troops crossing the River Delaware as they flee from the British after the battle of Whiteplains and the fall of Fort Washington in 1776.

business, and in 1752 he inherited his brother's land.

Britain and France were then rivals, both owning colonies and both trying to control North America. As a soldier in the British army, Washington was sent to tell the French commander to stop building forts on the Ohio River. The French refused. Washington fought against them for five years, and his exploits made him well known in Virginia.

After the war, Washington settled down to be a farmer on his Mount Vernon plantation. Gradually he came to believe that the American colonists had to be free from Britain. In 1775 he was made commander-in-chief of the colonists' army. His job was to recruit men for it and train them.

In fighting against the British, Washington made mistakes, but it was his grit and perseverance that kept the rebels going. Often his troops were famished and sometimes they went barefoot in the snow. In 1783, after the War of Independence had been won, Washington went thankfully back to Mount Vernon. Although he was a national hero, he did not want public office.

Nevertheless, in 1789 he was unanimously elected the first President of the USA. Dutifully he accepted the job, and his re-election in 1792, but he refused a third term. He felt very weary.

After he died, he was called 'first in war, first in peace, and first in the hearts of his countrymen'. Writers made him into an American legend. ■

See also

American Revolution
Myths and legends
USA: history

Watson-Watt, Sir Robert

Born 1892 in Brechin, Scotland
Inventor of radar
Died 1973 aged 81

Robert Alexander Watson-Watt was a descendant of James Watt of steam-engine fame. During World War I he worked on weather prediction and noticed that when there were thunderstorms about you could hear crackles on the radio. He wondered whether it might be possible to use these crackles to find where the thunderstorms were.

In the years just before World War II, the British government were worried about the danger of an enemy dropping bombs on Britain and all sorts of quite crazy suggestions were made of ways to stop bombers. Watson-Watt was asked to find out whether it would be possible to use a beam of radio waves to heat up an aeroplane so much that its bombs would explode in the air (rather as we now use microwaves to heat things in microwave cookers). Of course he very soon proved that it would be impossible. But while doing the necessary sums he realized that a narrow beam of radio waves would bounce off an aeroplane. Thinking back to the crackles on the radio he thought it might be possible to use the reflected waves from an aeroplane to find out how far away and in which direction it was. So radar (**r**adio **d**etection **a**nd **r**anging) was invented.

Many people believe that radar was one of the most important contributions to winning World War II. Now radar is used for navigation by all ships and aeroplanes, for air-traffic control and for tracking thunderstorms so that aeroplanes can avoid them. ■

See also

Airports
Radar

Biography
Watt

Watt, James

Born 1736 in Greenock, Scotland
Designed an important new, improved steam-engine.
Died 1819 aged 83

At 19 James Watt went to London to learn instrument-making. A year later ill health forced him to return home to Scotland, and he went to work as an instrument-maker in the University of Glasgow. In 1764 he was given a model of Thomas Newcomen's engine to repair. He studied the model carefully. It was clearly a clever idea to use steam pressure to drive an engine, but Newcomen's design did not work well; it was very inefficient and wasted a lot of fuel. Watt began to

▲ A model of a pumping engine which James Watt designed in 1788. Engines like this were used for pumping flood water out of mines.

make improvements, and over the next ten years he produced a really good engine. Then in 1775 he went into partnership with Mathew Boulton, a business man, and began manufacturing steam-engines.

Watt's steam-engines began to transform British industry. Iron manufacturers used them to drive the great hammers which crushed the iron. The textile industry used the engine to power the new machinery invented by Richard Arkwright. In coal-mining the coal was lifted to surface by winding-gear powered by the Watt engine. This replaced the men and women who carried sacks of coal up ladders from the coal face.

So although Watt did not invent the steam-engine it was his improvements that made it so effective. Soon other new steam-engines would be driving

even heavier machinery, such as the engine developed by Richard Trevithick, and the one designed by George Stephenson for locomotives. ■

See also

Industrial Revolution   Hero
Steam-engines   Newcomen
                             Stephenson
Biography   Trevithick
Arkwright

Wedgwood, Josiah

Born 1730 in Staffordshire, England
Set up the still famous Wedgwood pottery factory.
Died 1795 aged 64

The Wedgwood pottery firm founded by Josiah Wedgwood in 1759 is still making plates, bowls, cups and saucers of the highest quality. It is especially famous for its pottery ornaments of blue, with delicate white patterns and scenes laid on the top.

Josiah Wedgwood was born into a family who owned a pottery factory, and at the age of 9 he began his career as a potter. He became an expert at the job and invented better materials and methods for producing top-class pottery. In 1759 he set up his own factory and became famous for a cream-coloured table service, called Queen's ware, that he made for King George III's wife, Queen Charlotte.

Josiah Wedgwood's grandson was the famous scientist Charles Darwin. ■

See also

Pottery

Biography
Darwin

▲ The Wedgwood pottery firm is famed for its 'Jasper ware', which Josiah Wedgwood developed. This is a trinket-box, with white figures in relief on a blue background.

Wellington, Duke of

Born 1769 in Dublin, Ireland
One of England's greatest generals, and prime minister from 1828 to 1830
Died 1852 aged 83

Arthur Wellesley was born in Dublin just a few months before Napoleon, his great rival. He joined the army at the age of 18, but it was several years before he saw action. He served in India for eight years, where he won a number of battles and became a major-general.

But it was in Spain and Portugal that he won his great reputation (for which he was made Duke of Wellington), during the Peninsular War against Napoleon's French armies. At first his small army had to stay on the defensive in Portugal. But in 1812, when Napoleon had weakened the French armies by taking men for his invasion of Russia, Wellington was ready to attack. That year and again in 1813 the English attacked, with support from the Portuguese and Spanish troops. After victories at Salamanca and Vitoria they drove the French armies out of Spain and back into France.

When Napoleon escaped from Elba, Wellington was asked to lead the allied armies against him. At the battle of Waterloo in 1815, Wellington's cool mastery of defensive tactics and the steadiness of the English troops defeated every French attack. At the end of the day, when the Prussian army arrived to help, the French were driven from the field and defeated.

Wellington was 46 at the time of Waterloo and lived to serve his country for another 37 years, holding many positions in government, including that of prime minister from 1828 to 1830. For a time he was deeply unpopular because he did not want to give the vote to more people, fearing that it might lead to revolution as in France.

A WELLINGTON BOOT
Or the Head of the Army

▲ One of the things most people know about the Duke of Wellington is that he gave his name to a type of boot. This cartoon, from 1827, makes use of that to make 'the Iron Duke' even more recognizable.

But by the end of his long life most people had come to admire him as 'the Iron Duke'. When he died about a million and a half people stood on the icy streets of London to watch his coffin pass and to honour him. ■

See also

Battles

Biography
Napoleon Bonaparte

Wesley, John

Born 1703 at Epworth, Lincolnshire, England
He was a great Christian evangelist who founded the Methodist Church.
Died 1791 aged 88

John Wesley was the fifteenth of nineteen children and the son and the grandson of a clergyman. Not surprisingly, he too chose to enter the Church. He studied at Oxford University and was ordained as a priest in 1728. With his younger brother Charles, he formed a group of young men who tried to lead methodical lives, praying and reading the Bible together, and going to church regularly. They were nicknamed 'methodists'. In 1735 the two Wesley brothers visited the American colony of Georgia as missionaries.

Back in England in 1738, Wesley had an experience that changed his life. At a gospel meeting in London he felt his heart 'strangely warmed' and he knew that he was 'saved' by Jesus. From then on he committed himself to changing the lives of ordinary people through God's love.

For 50 years Wesley travelled all over England, holding services and preaching. Sometimes his meetings were held in churches, but often in fields and market places. He is said to have covered more than 400,000 km (250,000 miles), most of it on horseback, and preached over 50,000 sermons. Charles Wesley wrote many famous hymns for these services.

Wesley organized 'methodist' societies and used ordinary people as preachers and helpers. But still he wanted to remain a loyal member of the Church of England. Sadly the Church did not seem to care about the things that worried him, especially the conditions of poor people in cities. The split came in 1784 when Wesley broke Church rules by ordaining a group of Methodist preachers. Reluctantly Wesley watched his movement grow into a separate Church. ■

See also

Christians
Georgian Britain
Protestants

Whittle, Sir Frank

Born 1907 in Coventry, England
Developed the gas turbine into the jet engine, which is more efficient at high speeds and great altitudes than a piston engine.

In 1927, as a 20-year-old flight cadet at the Royal Air Force College, Cranwell, Frank Whittle wrote a paper on 'Future Developments in Aircraft Design'. He suggested that aeroplanes would soon be flying at more than 800 km/h (500 mph) (the fastest then was 300 km/h), at great heights, and with engines that had no propeller. Instead they would use a rocket, or a gas turbine, a type of engine that had been under development for 20 years.

In 1929, Whittle tried to persuade the Air Ministry that jet propulsion was possible. His engine would burn cheap fuel oil. The gases produced would turn turbine blades as they rushed out, compressing air into the front of the engine. The force of the gases would drive the plane forward. The Air Ministry were not interested, and Whittle registered his idea as a patent in 1930, married, and went back to flying.

Whittle went to Cambridge University to study engineering, and started a company called Power Jets Ltd. The RAF let him work full-time on his engine, and it was tried, on the ground, on 12 April 1937. A special aeroplane, the Gloster E28/39, was designed to take the engine, and on 15 May 1941

▲ Frank Whittle (right) discussing one of his early jet engines. Fuel and air burn in the cylinders around the outside of the engine. The jet nozzle is pointing to the left.

it flew for the first time, perfectly. 'Frank, it flies!' shouted one his team. 'Well, that was what it was designed to do, wasn't it?' he answered.

Other officers in the RAF knew nothing about Whittle's jet engine. 'You won't believe this, but I saw an aeroplane today without a propeller,' said one.

The jet engine was, as Whittle had predicted, more efficient at high speeds and greater altitudes, and by 1944 Gloster was producing the first jet fighter.

In 1948 Whittle left the RAF with the rank of air commodore, and was given a knighthood. He began research into equipment for the oil industry. His jet engine went on to power most modern aeroplanes. ■

◉ See also

Aircraft   Jet engines

Wilberforce, William

Born 1759 in Hull, England
He was one of the leaders of the long campaign which led to the end of slavery in the British empire.
Died 1833 aged 73

William Wilberforce was the kind of person everybody liked, even those who disagreed with him. His family was rich, and he was friendly with important politicians, especially William Pitt, the prime minister. He was Member of Parliament for Hull from the age of 21. What kept him going throughout his life was his strong Christian faith. Although he was often ill, he seldom stopped work, and he gave much of his fortune away to help spread Bible teaching.

His life's work began when he met John Newton, the captain of a slave ship, who had realized how wrong it was to buy and sell human beings as slaves. From 1785, Wilberforce kept campaigning to stop the slave trade. Finally in 1807 Parliament passed a law to abolish it. But employers in the West Indies still wanted slaves, and the trade continued secretly. So Wilberforce and his supporters decided there must be a law stopping people from owning slaves at all; then there could be no more trade in slaves. After another long campaign, a law to abolish slavery in the British empire went through Parliament in 1833, as Wilberforce lay dying. ■

◉ See also

Slaves   **Biography**
Slave trade   Pitt (the younger)

Wilder, Laura Ingalls

Born 1867 in Pepin, Wisconsin, USA
One of America's most popular authors for children
Died 1957 aged 89

As readers of her books will know, Laura lived a pioneer life as a child, moving from place to place in the American Midwest as her father looked for work. She did not start writing about her experiences until she was 65, urged on by her daugther.

Her first book, *Little House in the Big Woods*, describes the simple log cabin she remembered from her earliest days. Later books recalled everyday pleasures as well as sudden dangers from hostile Indians, wild animals or the terrible weather described in *The Long Winter*. Laura's childhood was often tough, but she remembered it with great affection, particularly the times when her father would play his fiddle while the whole family relaxed, enjoying both the music and the warmth of each other's company. ■

William I

Born about 1027 in Falaise, France
As Duke of Normandy, he invaded England in 1066 to become William the Conqueror, King of England from 1066 to 1087.
Died 1087 aged about 60

William had a difficult start. He nearly failed to become Duke of Normandy. Although his father was Duke Robert, his mother was the daughter of a tanner (leather-maker). His parents were not married, so William was not the legal heir. When he was about 8 years old, his father died, leaving no other children. The young William was chosen as their next ruler by the chief noblemen. During his childhood, a few loyal barons looked after him. Sometimes they hid him in the cottages of poor peasants to keep him safe from his enemies. William grew up to be a tall, thick-set man. He was tough, efficient, determined, and a brave fighter.

After a difficult struggle, first against rebellious lords and then against the French, he gained control of Normandy. Meanwhile the King of England, Edward the Confessor, had promised the English crown to William, his cousin. But Harold of Wessex, the strongest of the Anglo-Saxon nobles, also wanted to be king.

When King Edward died in 1066, Harold took the crown. William immediately built a great invasion fleet and crossed the English Channel. The Saxon and Norman armies met at the battle of Hastings, where Harold was killed.

William ruthlessly conquered the rest of England. He gave land to his barons and erected royal castles. The barons also built castles and took control of lands, but William made sure they stayed loyal to him. He organized the greatest land survey that had ever been made: the Domesday Book. When he died, an English monk complained about the harshness of his rule, but also declared that in the Conqueror's time a man could travel through the country unharmed, carrying a bag of gold. ■

See also

Anglo-Saxons
Bayeux Tapestry
Domesday Book
Feudal system
Normans

William III

Born 1650 in Holland, The Netherlands
He and his wife Mary ruled Britain together after the Glorious Revolution of 1688.
Died 1702 aged 51

William of Orange was the Protestant ruler of the Dutch people. He was married to Mary, the eldest daughter of James II of England.

William was not very attractive. He was small and stooping, and suffered from asthma. He seemed cold and reserved. He was also very determined. He had one great aim: to stop the powerful Louis XIV of France swallowing up more land in Europe.

William agreed to help the English get rid of their king, James II, in 1688 because he thought it would help him in his struggle with France. He refused to come to England unless he ruled equally with his wife, although it was she who had the claim to the throne.

William and Mary were crowned king and queen in 1689, and agreed to rule with Parliament. But the Catholic Irish still supported James. Finally William defeated James in Ireland at the battle of the Boyne in 1690. Many Irish Protestants today still call themselves 'Orangemen' because of William's victory.

The English liked Mary, but William was never popular; nor was his expensive war with France. But he kept his promise to rule with Parliament, and most English people thought they were better off with him than with James. William died after an accident when his horse stumbled on a molehill. ■

See also

Glorious Revolution
Ireland's history
Stuart Britain

Biography
Louis XIV
Mary II

Wilson, Woodrow

Born 1856 in Staunton, Virginia, USA
Scholar who as President of the USA led his country through World War I
Died 1924 aged 67

Wilson was an educated man with a great love of peace. He began his career as a lawyer, but soon turned to teaching. By 1890 he was a professor at Princeton University, New Jersey, and in 1902 he was elected president of the university. He introduced new methods of teaching, but other teachers and students opposed some of his changes. So he was glad to be invited by the Democratic Party to run for Governor of New Jersey in 1910. As governor he set about reforming New Jersey, ending corrupt practices in elections and improving the school system.

Wilson was elected President of the USA in 1912. Again he set about changing things, lowering many import duties and other taxes, ending child labour and cutting working hours.

When World War I broke out in Europe

▼ In 1916 this truck was driven round New York to persuade American voters to re-elect Woodrow Wilson as president. It was probably the second point on the poster that won him the most votes: 'Who keeps us out of war?'

in 1914, Wilson kept the USA out of it and was re-elected in 1916 because of this. But within a few months German submarines began sinking all merchant ships, including American vessels. Sadly, Wilson asked Congress to declare war on Germany.

In January 1918 Wilson outlined 'Fourteen Points' for a peace settlement. When the war ended Wilson persuaded other countries to agree to most of the Fourteen Points, including the setting up of the League of Nations (an earlier form of the United Nations). But Congress refused to let the USA join the League. Wilson, now a sick man, was awarded the 1920 Nobel Peace Prize for helping to found the League. ■

See also

United Nations
World War I

Wolfe, James

Born 1727 at Westerham, Kent, England
The British general who broke the French power in Canada
Died 1759 aged 32

'Mad, is he?' said King George II of James Wolfe, 'then I hope he will bite some others of my generals.' The king had recognized Wolfe's special quality. His body was frail and sickly but his energy and drive were formidable.

For most of his short life, Wolfe was a soldier. Son of a general, he was bought an officer's commission at the age of 14. At 16 he fought in the battle of Dettingen, and for the next sixteen years he was seldom away from action.

The climax came in 1759, when William Pitt chose him to lead the attack on the French in Canada. He took his expedition up the St Lawrence River to destroy the French stronghold of Québec. But Québec was well defended by troops under the command of General Montcalm and it took Wolfe some time to find a way to attack it. His plan was daring but rash. In the middle of the night he landed troops in a small cove, above the city, from

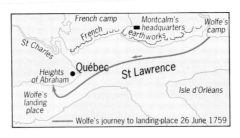

▲ Wolfe besieged Québec for three months before the night-time scaling of the cliffs known as the Heights of Abraham. Wolfe was killed during the ensuing battle on the Plains of Abraham.

where they climbed up steep cliffs to surprise the French guards at the top. When dawn broke, the French were astonished to see 4,500 redcoats lined up on the Plains of Abraham above the city, cutting them off from their supplies. When the French attacked in three columns, with drums and shouts and firing, the British lines stood unnervingly silent. Wolfe had ordered them not to fire until the enemy were 40 yards (36 m) from their bayonets. At last the British lines exploded in a shattering volley. When the smoke cleared the French were in retreat. Wolfe himself was mortally wounded and died on the field, but he knew that his troops had won a famous victory. As a result all French Canada became a British colony in 1763. ■

See also

British empire   **Biography**
Canada's history   Pitt (the older)

Wolfe Tone, Theobald

Born 1763 in Dublin, Ireland
He founded the United Irishmen to bring together Irish people of all religions in a struggle against English rule.
Committed suicide 1798 aged 35

Wolfe Tone studied law in Dublin but found politics more exciting. It was the time of the 'Ascendancy', the word used to describe how power was in the hands of a few wealthy Protestant families, who were often connected with leading Englishmen. Even though he was a Protestant, this angered Wolfe Tone. When the French Revolution

broke out in 1789 he was inspired by its belief that all men were brothers, whatever their wealth or religion. In 1791 he started the Society of United Irishmen among Protestants in Belfast. It called on people of all religions to unite against the way Ireland was ruled. A few weeks later he set up the United Irishmen in Dublin, where most members were Catholics.

In 1794 Wolfe Tone had to flee to France because an English spy found out that he had talked to an agent of the French, who were at war with England. The United Irish formed a secret society to carry on the struggle in Ireland. Wolfe Tone persuaded France to send 14,000 troops to invade Ireland, but they were forced back by bad weather. The English then began to round up United Irishmen. Fear of punishment led them to start a rebellion in 1798. The rebels were hunted down and treated with dreadful cruelty. Two small French armies came too late to help. Wolfe Tone was with them. He was captured and sentenced to death, but killed himself in prison. ■

See also

Ireland's history

Wollstonecraft, Mary

Born 1759 in London, England
She was a writer and an early believer in the right of women to control their own lives.
Died 1797 aged 38

Mary Wollstonecraft was the daughter of a weaver. His drunkenness and extravagance kept the family poor as he moved them around the country trying to earn a living.

Mary grew up to be a woman of powerful moods, resentful of her father's behaviour and the favouritism shown towards her brother. It was a difficult time for women. Very few of them owned property or followed a career; there was no effective birth control; divorce was only for the wealthy; they could not vote or have a university education. Mary, however, was determined to go her own way and lead an independent life.

Her attempts to run a school and be a governess ended stormily, but a London publisher gave her work. She wrote and translated many books, but her main work was her *Vindication of the Rights of Women* (1792), which argued for women's right to an equal education. 'I do not wish them to have power over men,' Mary wrote, 'but over themselves.'

She stayed in France during the Revolution with her American lover. When he deserted her and their baby girl, Mary threw herself from London's Putney Bridge. She was rescued, however, and in 1797 married the political writer William Godwin, although previously both had been against marriage, seeing it as a form of tyranny. She died seven months later, giving birth to Mary, who survived to become the wife of Percy Shelley and the author of *Frankenstein*. ■

See also

Women's movement

Wolsey, Thomas

Born about 1474 in Ipswich, England
Cardinal Wolsey was minister to King Henry VIII from 1513 to 1529.
Died 1530 aged about 56

Thomas Wolsey was the son of a butcher, and made his career as a priest. In Tudor England an ambitious boy from an ordinary family could still get to the top that way, and Wolsey finally got a job at court. The young Henry VIII realized that Wolsey was a man who would serve him loyally and do the boring daily work. In 1515 the king made him chancellor. Wolsey was also Archbishop of York, and a cardinal (a very senior priest), and soon became richer than the nobles at Henry's court. He built palaces, including the huge Hampton Court. Many people were jealous, but he was safe as long as he had the king's favour.

Wolsey served the king loyally at home and abroad. He enjoyed his power, but he did the tedious jobs too, and took the blame for the king when an unpopular tax caused a riot in East Anglia. When the king wanted the Pope to give him his divorce, Wolsey tried his best to get it. But he had no chance, mainly because the Pope was a prisoner of Queen Catherine's nephew, the Emperor Charles V.

Henry seldom forgave failure. Wolsey was sent to York; although he was Archbishop of York, he had never actually been there. But he could not stop meddling in politics. Henry summoned the sick, old cardinal to London to accuse him of treason. He died at Leicester Abbey on the way. ■

See also

Tudor England
Biography
Henry VIII

Wordsworth, William

Born 1770 in Cockermouth, Cumberland, England
The greatest English nature poet
Died 1850 aged 80

Both his parents died when Wordsworth was a child, and he turned instead towards the Lake District countryside for love and companionship. After university he spent some time in France, where he sympathized with those involved in the Revolution. He fell in love with Annette Vallon, the daughter of a surgeon. But although they had a child, Wordsworth left her before they could marry. His money ran out and he had to return to England.

He settled in Dorset with his beloved sister Dorothy, and in 1798 published his first collection of poems, *Lyrical Ballads*, in partnership with his great friend, the poet Samuel Taylor Coleridge. Wordsworth's poems caused a sensation because he wrote about ordinary events in plain language. One of his most famous poems starts:

I wandered lonely as a cloud
That floats on high o'er vales and
   hills,
When all at once I saw a crowd,
A host, of golden daffodils.

This new simplicity was a great contrast to more showy, artificial types of poetry then popular. Wordsworth also caused a lot of argument through his belief that truth can always be better found in nature rather than in human society. He stated too that small children possess a type of natural wisdom no longer present in many older, over-educated adults.

In his long poem *The Prelude: Growth of a Poet's Mind*, Wordsworth traces his own development from child to man, picking out incidents in his early years which had a lasting influence upon him. By this time he was living in his beloved Lake District once more, still with his sister Dorothy but now also with his wife Mary, whom he married in 1802. There he stayed until his death, famous and respected, though writing very little as he grew older. ■

... Therefore am I still
A lover of the meadows and the
   woods,
And mountains; and of all that we
   behold
From this green earth; of all the
   mighty world
Of eye, and ear, – both what they
   half create,
And what perceive; well pleased
   to recognize
In nature and the language of the
   sense
The anchor of my purest
   thoughts, the nurse,
The guide, the guardian of my
   heart, and soul
Of all my moral being.

▲ **Extract from** *Lines Composed above Tintern Abbey*, **by William Wordsworth.**

Wren, Sir Christopher

Born 1632 in East Knoyle, Wiltshire, England
A genius of many talents; mathematician, astronomer and architect. Designed St Paul's Cathedral and many other buildings.
Died 1723 aged 90

It did not take people long to realize that Christopher Wren was very clever. After studying at Oxford University, he soon became a teacher there. He was particularly good at science, especially mathematics and physics, and helped to make a reliable barometer. While still a young man, he was made a professor of astronomy in London and Oxford.

In London, in 1662, he helped to found a club of men keen to explore the world through science. King Charles II was very interested in it and it was called 'The Royal Society'. Many brilliant men were members, including Robert Boyle, Isaac Newton, and of course Christopher Wren. It still exists today.

Wren began to design buildings, and proved to be brilliant at that as well. The chapel at Pembroke College, Cambridge, in 1663, and the Sheldonian Theatre, Oxford, were his earliest buildings. Then, in 1666, the Great Fire destroyed most of London. Using his imagination and skill, Wren drew up a plan for rebuilding the entire city. Sadly his plan was never used. But St Paul's Cathedral needed to be rebuilt, and Wren was chosen to do it. The construction of his magnificent design was completed in 1710.

Wren was hard-working as well as clever. He rebuilt 52 London churches destroyed by the fire, and the list of buildings he designed seems endless. It includes Chelsea Hospital (home of the pensioners), part of Hampton Court and the Royal Naval College, Greenwich. Wren was knighted in 1672, became President of the Royal Society in 1680, and was MP for Windsor for a short time. ■

See also

Fire of London
Royal Society
Stuart Britain

▼ Even today the skyline of the City of London is dominated by the great dome of Christopher Wren's St Paul's Cathedral completed in 1710.

Wright brothers

Built and flew the first aeroplane.
Wilbur Born 1867 in Ohio, USA
Died 1912 aged 45
Orville Born 1871 in Ohio
Died 1948 aged 76

Orville was a champion cyclist, and so the two brothers set up a shop where they made and sold bicycles. Neither of the brothers had a proper education, but they had tremendous mechanical skills and a real determination to succeed. They both enjoyed the new sport of gliding, and decided to try and build a bicycle with wings and a petrol engine to drive a propeller round.

By 1903 the Wright brothers had built *The Flyer*. It was a biplane (with two sets of wings) and the pilot lay flat across the lower wing. A series of bicycle chains and gears connected the engine to two propellers which rotated at about 450 times a minute. On 17 December 1903, at Kitty Hawk in North Carolina, Orville Wright made a 12-second flight over a distance of 36 m (120 ft). This was the first aeroplane flight in history. Later that morning Wilbur flew for nearly a

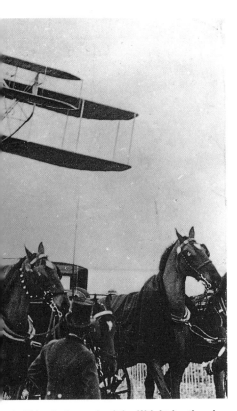

▲ This photograph of the Wright brothers' aeroplane was taken in France in 1907, four years after their first successful flight. Unlike most modern aircraft, the aeroplane flew 'tail first'.

minute. But only five people saw the flights, and there was no general interest in what the Wright brothers had done.

They carried on building better aeroplanes and in 1905 Wilbur flew 38 km (24 miles) in a half-hour flight. Three years later he flew for 2 hours and 20 minutes. Other people in Europe and America began building planes, but the Wright brothers sued many of them for using the special system that they had designed.

The brothers were the sons of a minister, Bishop Milton Wright. They never smoked or drank alcohol, and neither of them married.

Wilbur died of typhoid fever in 1912, and his brother Orville gave up building planes a couple of years later. ■

See also

Aircraft
Gliders
Internal combustion engines

Wright, Frank Lloyd

Born 1867 in Richland Center, Wisconsin, USA
The greatest of American architects
Died 1959 aged 91

Wright was the most prolific and versatile of the great architects of the 20th century. His career covered almost 70 years (he worked almost to the day of his death) and he designed about 1,000 buildings, of which about 400 were erected. He worked in a variety of styles and was highly inventive in his use of materials and architectural forms. Wright also wrote many books and articles (including an autobiography), through which he promoted his ideas. His ideal was 'organic architecture', in which buildings harmonize with their environment and their users.

Wright had achieved a considerable reputation by the time he was in his thirties, but until he was about 60, most of his commissions were fairly small; they included many houses. From the late 1930s, however, he designed many large public buildings. He was a forceful personality – one of the central figures of modern American cultural life. ■

See also

Architects (photograph)

▲ The Guggenheim Museum in New York is one of Wright's most famous buildings. It is constructed in a huge spiral, within which visitors walk around and view exhibitions.

Wyclif, John

Born about 1330 near Richmond, Yorkshire, England
He was a scholar who challenged the power of the Catholic Church.
Died 1384 aged about 54

Nothing is known about Wyclif until the 1360s. By then he was about 30 years old, studying and teaching theology at Oxford University.

Like many other medieval scholars, Wyclif made his way into public life. In 1374 Edward III sent him to Flanders to negotiate with envoys (representatives) from the Pope about the taxes that the king had to pay to Rome. Wyclif questioned the Pope's right to collect money, and went on to challenge the wealth and power of the Catholic Church in general.

Over the next ten years, in sermons and in written works, his views became more and more extreme. Wyclif attacked the authority of the Church, denied that priests were needed to save souls, and encouraged people to pray directly to God. To help his followers, he sponsored the first translation of the Bible from Latin into English, and probably translated the New Testament himself. He was condemned as a dangerous heretic, was forced to leave Oxford and had his writings publicly burnt.

From his Lincolnshire rectory, he continued to write and teach. He attracted a group of followers known as his 'poor priests', who travelled around the countryside, preaching. Wyclif's influence lasted long after his death. His ideas helped to inspire the Lollards, who protested against the power of the Catholic Church. They in turn were to inspire Protestants in the 16th century. ■

The name has been spelt in several ways, including Wycliffe.

See also

Bible
Heretics
Peasants' Revolt

Biography
Edward III

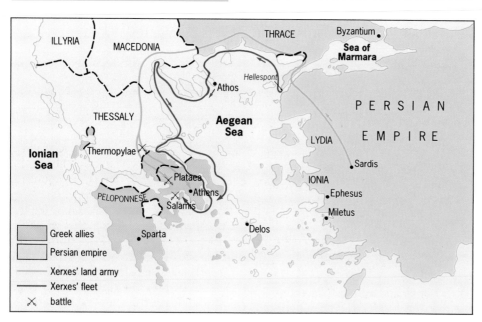

Map legend:

- Greek allies
- Persian empire
- Xerxes' land army
- Xerxes' fleet
- ✕ battle

Xerxes

Born about 519 BC
King of Persia whose navy and army
were defeated by the Greeks
Assassinated 465 BC aged about 54

Xerxes came to the throne of the huge
Persian empire on the death of his
father Darius I. Darius had invaded
the Greek mainland, but his army had
been thoroughly defeated by a small
Greek force at the battle of Marathon.

Before Xerxes could turn his attention
to the Greeks, he had to deal with
revolts in Egypt and Babylon. It was
important for him to show that Persia
was not weakened by the defeat at
Marathon. He then made preparations
for the largest invasion the Greeks had
ever seen. The army crossed into
Greece by building a bridge of boats
across the narrow straits, called the
Hellespont, which divided Greece from
Asia Minor (now Turkey). Meanwhile
the naval force sailed around the coast,
following the army as closely as it
could. At one point, in Athos, they
actually dug a canal to let the boats
cross a long narrow stretch of land,
avoiding a dangerous part of the sea.

The two armies clashed first, in 480
BC, at a narrow mountain pass called
Thermopylae. Here a small force led
by Sparta held the pass against the
Persians. However, the Persians

▲ After succeeding his father, Darius I, as
emperor of Persia, Xerxes spent several
years trying to achieve his father's ambition
of conquering Greece. Xerxes failed and his
war against the Greeks only weakened the
influence and power of the Persian empire.

managed to find a mountain track
which led them round to the rear. They
killed all but two of the 300 defenders.
The way to Athens was now open to
the Persians.

Xerxes' army did capture Athens,
though most of the inhabitants had
already fled. The only hope for the
Greeks was to defeat the Persians at
sea. They did this at the famous battle
of Salamis in 480. The Greek warships
were a bit lighter than those of the
Persians and could be manœuvred
much more easily. In the narrow straits
between the island of Salamis and the
mainland near Athens the Persian navy
was destroyed.

King Xerxes returned home, but his
army stayed and was defeated in
Plataea the next year. Persia was no
longer a threat to Greece. ■

See also

Greek ancient history
Persians

Biography
Darius

Yeats, William Butler

Born 1865 in Dublin, Ireland
The greatest of modern Irish poets
Died 1939 aged 73

Yeats went to school in London, but
for his holidays he was sent to his
grandparents in Sligo on the west coast
of Ireland. He loved to listen to the
Sligo people talk of fairies and ghosts,
and of the time when great kings,
queens and warriors inhabited Ireland.
He longed to find a similar world of
beauty and power, and to make Ireland
great again. He met and fell in love
with a beautiful young woman called
Maude Gonne, who was to inspire
much of his greatest poetry, but who
never loved him in return.

He collected the folklore and myths of
Ireland and helped to found a national
theatre in Dublin. As he grew older,
his poetry increased in power and
wisdom, drawing on ancient myths and
personal emotions. He is remembered
best for the poems of his middle and
old age, such as *The Tower*, published
1928, and *The Winding Stair*, 1933. ■

The Lake Isle of Innisfree

I will arise and go now, and go to
  Innisfree,
And a small cabin build there, of clay
  and wattles made;
Nine bean rows will I have there, a
  hive for the honey bee,
And live alone in the bee-loud glade.

And I shall have some peace there, for
  peace comes dropping slow,
Dropping from the veils of the
  morning to where the cricket sings;
There midnight's all a glimmer, and
  noon a purple glow,
And evening full of the linnet's wings.

I will arise and go now, for always
  night and day
I hear lake water lapping with low
  sounds by the shore;
While I stand on the roadway, or on
  the pavements grey,
I hear it in the deep heart's core.

Young, Thomas

Born 1773 in Somerset, England
A physicist and medical doctor who discovered how we see colour and showed that light behaves like a wave
Died 1829 aged 55

Thomas was very bright and could read when he was 2. At 16 he knew Latin, Greek and eight other languages. He was a sickly child, and this probably led him to study medicine. But he was always interested in physics. Although Newton and other great scientists thought that light was a stream of particles, Young thought they were wrong. He proved that light is really a kind of wave. He also found out that our eyes can only detect three colours and all the other colours can be made up of mixtures of these. In 1801 he was made a professor at the Royal Institution in London, but although he did some marvellous scientific work there, he was not very good at lecturing and so did not stay long.

The famous Rosetta stone was found in Egypt in 1799. It had the same announcement carved on it in three languages. The carving was done about 200 BC and was in high-class Egyptian (hieroglyphics), everyday Egyptian (demotic) and Greek. Young became very interested, and was the first to publish a translation, although it was the young Frenchman, Francois Champollion, who first deciphered the whole hieroglyphic alphabet.

Young was brilliant in so many fields that Sir Humphry Davy once said that it was difficult to say what he did not know. ◾

See also

Colour
Eyes
Hieroglyphics
Languages
Light
Writing systems

Biography
Huygens
Newton

Zhou Enlai

Born 1898 in Jiangsu, China
One of the founders of Chinese communism, he became prime minister of communist China.
Died 1976 aged 77

Zhou Enlai came from a family of scholar officials, but he came to believe that China would get rid of poverty only through following socialist ideas of sharing wealth. He went to study European political ideas in France, where he formed a branch of the new Chinese Communist Party. He returned to China and worked with other communists to build up Jiang Jieshi's Nationalist Party, until Jiang turned against them in 1927. Zhou barely escaped with his life, and joined Mao Zedong and Deng Xiaoping in the Jiangxi soviet and on the Long March.

In 1949 Zhou became the first prime minister of communist China, and held the post until he died.

He was a handsome and charming man who was admired by both Chinese and foreigners. He was so widely trusted that he was the only Chinese leader who never lost power during the arguments between those who agreed and disagreed with Mao. He helped China build up her position in world affairs by making friends with the many poorer countries in Asia and Africa. Later he built up good relations with the USA, which had been the bitter enemy of communist China.

Zhou's last words to his doctors were, 'There is little you can do for me here. Go and help others who need you.' He refused to have a monument put up in his memory. ◾

See also

China's history
Communists

Biography
Deng Xiaoping
Jiang Jieshi
Mao Zedong

◀ The Chinese people held their dead leader in such respect that many thousands of them came to Beijing to mourn the death of Zhou Enlai in 1976.

Alexandra, Princess

1936–

A cousin of Elizabeth II, Princess Alexandra was born in London and was brought up at the family home in Iver, Buckinghamshire. Her father, the Duke of Kent, was killed in a flying accident when she was only 5. She later became the first British princess to be sent to a boarding school. She studied French and music before taking a course in nursing at Great Ormond Street Hospital for Sick Children.

In 1963 she married the business man Angus Ogilvy. They have two children, James and Marina, neither of whom have titles. Her quiet, sympathetic nature makes Princess Alexandra one of the most popular members of the Royal Family. ■

Andrew, Prince, Duke of York

1960–

Prince Andrew, the second son of Queen Elizabeth II, was born at Buckingham Palace on 19 February 1960. He was christened Andrew Albert Christian Edward; Andrew after his grandfather, Prince Andrew of Greece. He went to Gordonstoun School in Scotland, the same school as his father and brothers, and like Prince Philip he went to the Royal Naval College, Dartmouth. Prince Andrew has always had a sense of fun. He was once scolded for riding down the stairs at Sandringham on a silver tea-tray.

As a helicopter pilot in the Royal Navy he took part in the Falklands War of 1982 and received praise for his dangerous work. In 1986 he married Sarah Ferguson in Westminster Abbey and on the same day the Queen granted him the title Duke of York. Prince Andrew has two other titles, Earl of Inverness and Baron Killyleagh, although he rarely uses them. Two years later their first daughter, Princess Beatrice, was born, and in 1990 the Duchess gave birth to a second daughter, Princess Eugenie. The couple separated in 1992.

Today the Duke of York combines his work in the navy with his royal duties. His favourite hobby is photography. He develops his own prints and has had several books of his pictures published. ■

Anne, the Princess Royal

1950–

Anne, the Princess Royal, is the only daughter of Queen Elizabeth II. She is one of the hardest working members of the Royal Family and undertakes over 500 engagements every year.

As a child Princess Anne was a tomboy. She was happiest when she was riding and she disliked being dressed in smart clothes. At 12 she went to boarding school and quickly won a place for herself in the school riding team. Her career flourished and she began winning horse-trials and three-day events, took part in European championships and eventually won herself a place in the United Kingdom Olympic Games team in 1976. She still rides most mornings and enjoys flat racing. She is President of the Riding for the Disabled Association.

It was through horses that the Princess met her husband Captain Mark Phillips, an experienced rider. They married in 1973, but divorced in 1992. They have two children, Peter and Zara.

Princess Anne began royal duties when she was 18. Although she supports many charities, it is as President of the Save the Children Fund that she has received the most praise. She has travelled to some of the poorest areas of the world and knows a great deal about the needs of children and ways in which poor communities can be helped to provide health care, clean water and a better diet for children and their families. She was given the title Princess Royal in 1987 by the Queen. ■

Armstrong-Jones, Lady Sarah

1964–

Lady Sarah is the daughter of Princess Margaret and Lord Snowdon, Antony Armstrong-Jones. Although the Queen is her aunt, Lady Sarah does not undertake any royal duties and has concentrated instead on building a career as an artist.

As a girl she studied ballet and later learned to sail and scuba-dive, but she loved painting more than anything and took her sketch pad everywhere. On leaving school she studied art and fashion. She loves dancing, spending time in the country and listening to jazz music. ■

Diana, Princess of Wales

1961–

Diana Spencer was born on 1 July 1961. Her parents were Lord and Lady Althorp. She was brought up with her two sisters at the family home of Althorp in Northamptonshire and also spent a lot of time in her father's house on the Queen's estate at Sandringham.

Diana's childhood was not happy. Her parents parted when she was 6 and Diana was sent away to boarding school. She did not like lessons, but enjoyed swimming and looking after animals, including her pet guinea pig 'Peanuts' and her cat 'Marmalade'. When she was 14 her father became Earl Spencer and she became Lady Diana Spencer.

On leaving school, Lady Diana moved to London and had several jobs. She became a waitress in a restaurant, a cook, a nanny and even a cleaner. She enjoyed working with children most of all and so finally began teaching under-fives at the Young England Kindergarten.

She first met Prince Charles in 1977 when he visited her family home for a shooting

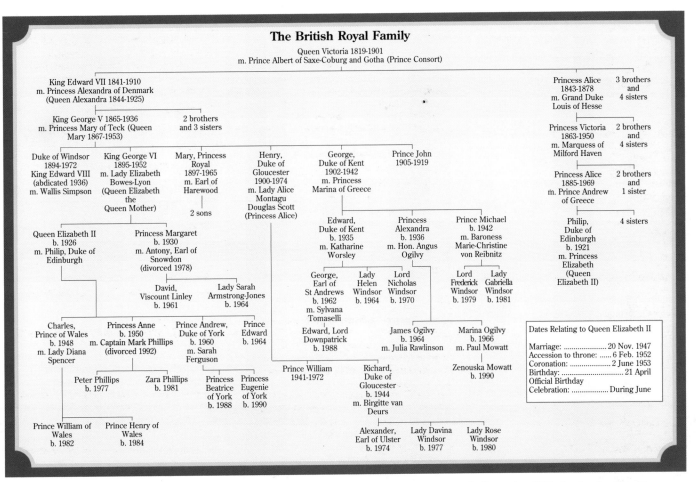

The British Royal Family

Queen Victoria 1819-1901
m. Prince Albert of Saxe-Coburg and Gotha (Prince Consort)

King Edward VII 1841-1910
m. Princess Alexandra of Denmark
(Queen Alexandra 1844-1925)

Princess Alice 1843-1878
m. Grand Duke Louis of Hesse — 3 brothers and 4 sisters

King George V 1865-1936
m. Princess Mary of Teck (Queen Mary 1867-1953) — 2 brothers and 3 sisters

Princess Victoria 1863-1950
m. Marquess of Milford Haven — 2 brothers and 4 sisters

Duke of Windsor 1894-1972 King Edward VIII (abdicated 1936) m. Wallis Simpson

King George VI 1895-1952 m. Lady Elizabeth Bowes-Lyon (Queen Elizabeth the Queen Mother)

Mary, Princess Royal 1897-1965 m. Earl of Harewood — 2 sons

Henry, Duke of Gloucester 1900-1974 m. Lady Alice Montagu Douglas Scott (Princess Alice)

George, Duke of Kent 1902-1942 m. Princess Marina of Greece

Prince John 1905-1919

Princess Alice 1885-1969 m. Prince Andrew of Greece — 2 brothers and 1 sister

Philip, Duke of Edinburgh b. 1921 m. Princess Elizabeth (Queen Elizabeth II) — 4 sisters

Queen Elizabeth II b. 1926 m. Philip, Duke of Edinburgh

Princess Margaret b. 1930 m. Antony, Earl of Snowdon (divorced 1978)

Edward, Duke of Kent b. 1935 m. Katharine Worsley

Princess Alexandra b. 1936 m. Hon. Angus Ogilvy

Prince Michael b. 1942 m. Baroness Marie-Christine von Reibnitz

David, Viscount Linley b. 1961

Lady Sarah Armstrong-Jones b. 1964

George, Earl of St Andrews b. 1962 m. Sylvana Tomaselli

Lady Helen Windsor b. 1964

Lord Nicholas Windsor b. 1970

Lord Frederick Windsor b. 1979

Lady Gabriella Windsor b. 1981

Charles, Prince of Wales b. 1948 m. Lady Diana Spencer

Princess Anne b. 1950 m. Captain Mark Phillips (divorced 1992)

Prince Andrew, Duke of York b. 1960 m. Sarah Ferguson

Prince Edward b. 1964

Edward, Lord Downpatrick b. 1988

James Ogilvy b. 1964 m. Julia Rawlinson

Marina Ogilvy b. 1966 m. Paul Mowatt

Peter Phillips b. 1977

Zara Phillips b. 1981

Princess Beatrice of York b. 1988

Princess Eugenie of York b. 1990

Prince William 1941-1972

Richard, Duke of Gloucester b. 1944 m. Birgitte van Deurs

Zenouska Mowatt b. 1990

Prince William of Wales b. 1982

Prince Henry of Wales b. 1984

Alexander, Earl of Ulster b. 1974

Lady Davina Windsor b. 1977

Lady Rose Windsor b. 1980

Dates Relating to Queen Elizabeth II

Marriage: .... 20 Nov. 1947
Accession to throne: ...... 6 Feb. 1952
Coronation: .... 2 June 1953
Birthday: .... 21 April
Official Birthday
Celebration: .... During June

---

weekend. Three years later they fell in love, and in 1981 they married in St Paul's Cathedral. Diana became the ninth Princess of Wales. She has two sons, Prince William and Prince Harry.

Although she has become a fashion leader and her clothes are copied by women all over the world, she is also an extremely hard-working member of the Royal Family. She is especially interested in children's charities, including Barnardo's, the Royal School for the Blind, and the Malcolm Sargent Cancer Fund for Children. She is also Patron of Help the Aged and of Turning Point, a charity which helps people who have problems with drugs and alcohol. ■

Edward, Prince

1964–

Prince Edward is the youngest son of Queen Elizabeth II. He was born on 10 March 1964 and christened Edward Antony Richard Louis.

Like his brothers, he had lessons at Buckingham Palace and then went away to boarding school, first to a preparatory school and next to Gordonstoun School in Scotland. After taking A levels and before going to university Prince Edward spent several months in New Zealand, where he taught in Wanganui.

He studied history at Cambridge University and, after taking his degree, was expected to join either the army, navy or air force. He chose the Royal Marines, but decided after four months that he did not want a career in the armed forces. He is now a production assistant in the theatre and at work is known as Edward Windsor (the family name). In addition to his full-time job, Prince Edward undertakes about 100 official royal engagements a year. ■

Elizabeth, the Queen Mother

1900–

Lady Elizabeth Bowes-Lyon was born in August 1900 in London. At the family home of Glamis Castle in Scotland, Elizabeth's father, the Earl of Strathmore, often entertained royalty and it was here that she first met her future husband when she was 5. They had tea and she gave him the cherries from her cake. He was the second son of King George V and when they grew up he asked her to marry him. At first she refused, but later accepted and married him in Westminster Abbey in 1923. They were titled the Duke and Duchess of York.

When the Duke of York's brother, Edward VIII, abdicated in 1936 he became King George VI, with Elizabeth as his Queen. The couple had two children, Princess Elizabeth (now Queen Elizabeth II) and Princess Margaret.

In September 1939, shortly after King George VI came to the throne, World War II began. During World War I (1914–1918) Glamis Castle had been turned into a hospital and Elizabeth had helped nurse wounded soldiers. In World War II she and the King travelled all over Britain, offering comfort to those who had been injured and lost their homes.

In 1952 King George VI died suddenly and Princess Elizabeth became Queen. As there were now two Queen Elizabeths, it was decided that the first should be known as the Queen Mother to avoid confusion. The Queen Mother moved out of Buckingham Palace to Clarence House, which has been her home ever since.

Her work has taken her all over the world. She enjoys horse racing, fishing and gardening, and likes animals of all kinds. ■

Gloucester, Duchess of

1946–

Born in Denmark, Birgitte van Deurs married Prince Richard of Gloucester in 1972. The couple met while students at Magdalene College, Cambridge, on the Prince's second day there. They now have three children: a son, Alexander, Earl of Ulster, and two daughters, Lady Davina Windsor and Lady Rose Windsor. Both the Duke and Duchess enjoy skiing. ■

Gloucester, Duke of

1944–

Prince Richard of Gloucester inherited the title Duke of Gloucester from his father in 1974. Today he is known as 'Proggy' (**P**rince **R**ichard **O**f **G**loucester) and although he does undertake some royal duties each year, his job is as an architect and his business card says simply 'Richard Gloucester'. He also runs the farm on which his family live, and in his spare time likes making models and taking photographs. He is very much against smoking, and works hard to warn people of the dangers of tobacco. ■

Kent, Duchess of

1933–

Katharine Worsley was born in Yorkshire and came from a cricket-loving family. She married the Duke of Kent at York Minster in 1961. It was the first royal marriage at that cathedral for over 600 years. Today the Duchess works very hard for a number of children's charities, not as part of her royal duties but in her own free time, because she enjoys it. The Duke and Duchess of Kent have three children: George, Earl of St Andrews, Lady Helen Windsor and Lord Nicholas Windsor. ■

Kent, Duke of

1935–

Edward, Duke of Kent, is a cousin of both the Queen and Prince Philip. His mother was Princess Marina of Greece. 'Eddie', as he is known in the family, is Princess Alexandra's brother and he inherited the title of Duke when he was just 6 years old. Because he was not always well as a child he was educated for several years in Switzerland where the air was cleaner and healthier. At school he learned to speak French, and when he later joined the army he was able to work as an interpreter.

He now undertakes some duties as a member of the Royal Family but is also a business man and promotes British businesses overseas. His two great loves are opera and tennis. ■

Kent, Prince Michael of

1942–

Prince Michael is the younger brother of the Duke of Kent and Princess Alexandra. He can speak many languages, including Russian, and spent nineteen years as a soldier with the 11th Hussars. He enjoys all winter sports and was once badly injured in a bobsleigh race. He loves cars and every year drives a car in the London to Brighton Veteran Car Rally. He has also flown across the Atlantic Ocean in an air race.

He works in banking and only occasionally performs royal duties. In 1978 he married Marie-Christine von Reibnitz, and lost his place in the line of succession to the throne because she was a Roman Catholic. They have two children, Lord Frederick and Lady Gabriella Windsor. ■

Linley, Viscount

1961–

Viscount Linley is the eldest child of Princess Margaret and her former husband the Earl of Snowdon. He has the title 'Viscount' because this is usually given to the first-born son of an earl, although he prefers to be known simply as David Linley.

At school David enjoyed making things and once gave the Queen a bird nesting box for Christmas that he had made himself. When he left school he studied furniture making and now has his own very successful business in London. He also loves cooking and owns a restaurant. ■

Margaret, Princess

1930–

Princess Margaret Rose was born on a wild and stormy August night at Glamis Castle in Scotland. As a child she was very lively. She felt that people were more interested in her sister, the Princess Elizabeth, who was heir to the throne, so tried to make herself noticed. She spent much of her childhood at Windsor Castle, where the princesses lived during World War II because it was much safer than central London.

Once the war was over she attended as many parties as possible and went to the theatre and cinema as often as she could. Unfortunately this made people think that she was not interested in work, even though she had a very full diary of working engagements.

In 1960 she married Antony Armstrong-Jones, a photographer, who was later made the Earl of Snowdon. They had two children, Viscount Linley and Lady Sarah Armstrong-Jones. The marriage ended in 1978.

Princess Margaret undertakes over 150 royal engagements every year and works especially hard with disabled children and with the National Society for the Prevention of Cruelty to Children (NSPCC). She is President of the Girl Guides Association, attends many of their activities throughout the year, and regularly holds tea parties for them at her Kensington Palace home. When not working she likes to relax at her holiday home on the small island of Mustique in the Caribbean. ■

Philip, Prince, Duke of Edinburgh

1921–

Prince Philip's father was Prince Andrew of Greece and Philip was born at the family home Mon Repos, on the island of Corfu. Because he was too tiny for a cot, he spent the first few days of his life in a padded drawer. There was fighting in Greece, so Philip was brought to the safety of England when aged just 18 months old. He travelled hidden in a wooden orange box for safety.

As a boy he was very good at all sports and enjoyed cricket, hockey, athletics and especially sailing. He went to Gordonstoun School in Scotland and then joined the Royal Navy and completed his education at the Royal Naval College in Dartmouth. It was here that he first met Princess Elizabeth, his future wife.

In 1947 he adopted his mother's surname, Mountbatten, and was given British nationality. He gave up his Greek title of Prince. That same year he married Princess Elizabeth and, on his wedding day, King George VI made him Duke of Edinburgh. Ten years later, in 1957, he was made a Prince of the United Kingdom and so could once again call himself Prince Philip.

Since his wife became Queen in 1952, Prince Philip's job has been to support her in her work, but he has always had very strong views of his own. He has a great interest in new developments in technology and engineering, especially when they result in the conservation of energy and resources. He introduced computers into Buckingham Palace and uses a battery-driven electric car for getting around London.

He still gives a lot of time to the Duke of Edinburgh Award Scheme, which gives young people opportunities for adventure, community service and personal achievement. ■

Phillips, Peter

1977–

The eldest child of the Princess Royal and Captain Mark Phillips, Peter was the Queen's first grandson. Until his birth all royal babies had been born at home, but the Princess Royal decided to have her baby in hospital, and every royal mother since has followed her example.

As the Queen's grandson, Peter Phillips is in line of succession to the throne, but is unusual because he does not have a title. As he will want to choose his own job and live an ordinary life, his parents thought it would be much easier for him not to have a title. He attended a private school near his home in Gloucestershire and then went to boarding school. ■

Phillips, Zara

1981–

Zara is the second child of the Princess Royal and Captain Mark Phillips. Like her brother Peter, Zara does not have a title. The name 'Zara' is an Arabic word which means 'morning star', and was perhaps given to her because she was born at 8.15 in the morning. She first rode a horse at the age of 3 and is now an expert rider. ■

▲ This photograph was taken at the wedding reception of Prince Andrew and Sarah Ferguson. It shows members of the Royal Family together with some of Sarah's family. The Queen granted the couple the titles Duke and Duchess of York on the same day.

Back row
James Ogilvy
Prince Michael of Kent
Hon. Angus Ogilvy
Duke of Gloucester
Duke of Kent
Earl of St Andrews

Next row
Viscount Linley
Capt. Mark Phillips
Marina Ogilvy, now Mowatt
Prince of Wales
Princess Alexandra
Duke of Edinburgh
Princess Michael of Kent
Princess Alice
Duchess of Gloucester
Duchess of Kent
Lady Helen Windsor
Hon. Doreen Wright
Major Bryan Wright
Alexander Makim

Front row
Lady Sarah Armstrong-Jones
Princess Margaret

Princess Anne
Princess of Wales and Prince Harry
Queen Mother
Queen
Duchess of York
Duke of York
Major Ronald Ferguson
Prince Edward
Mrs Susan Barrantes
Lady Elmhirst
Mrs Jane Makim

Children
Earl of Ulster
Lady Davina Windsor
Lady Rose Windsor
Andrew Ferguson
Lady Rosanagh Innes-Ker
Zara Phillips
Prince William
Laura Fellowes
Seamus Makim
Alice Ferguson
Peter Phillips
Lady Gabriella Windsor
Lord Frederick Windsor

Sarah, Duchess of York

1959–

Born Sarah Margaret Ferguson, the Duchess of York is still known in the press by her former nickname of 'Fergie'. She can trace her ancestors back to King Charles II and Robert the Bruce of Scotland. She is also related to one of the Queen's aunts, Princess Alice. Her father was Prince Charles's polo manager and it was at a game of polo that she first met her husband, Prince Andrew. They were married in 1986 but separated in 1992. They have two daughters, Beatrice and Eugenie.

Sarah was brought up with her older sister at Sunninghill, near Ascot. She was educated at a boarding school and became Head Girl, but she always preferred sport to lessons and still loves riding, tennis and skiing. After leaving school she became a secretary, worked in an art gallery, and then joined a firm of book publishers. She has written several story books for children. In 1987 she became the first woman member of the Royal Family to get a pilot's licence and can now fly a helicopter. ■

Wales, Prince Henry of

1984–

Prince Henry was born on 15 September 1984 and christened Henry Charles Albert David, but is known simply as 'Harry'. He is the second

son of the Prince and Princess of Wales and is third in line to the throne after his father and brother William. As the brothers are so important to the future of the Royal Family, the two are never allowed to travel in the same aircraft together for fear that it might crash. ■

Wales, Prince William of

1982–

Prince William was born on 21 June 1982 and was christened William Arthur Philip Louis.

From the moment of his birth, Prince William has been second in line to the throne. He is the eldest son of the Prince and Princess of Wales and is the Queen's third grandchild. Prince William has been educated at school with other children, as his parents want his upbringing to be as normal as possible. ■

York, Princess Beatrice of

1988–

Princess Beatrice is the first-born child of the Duke and Duchess of York. ■

York, Princess Eugenie of

1990–

The second child of the Duke and Duchess of York. ■

FILM

Andrews, Julie

1935–

Julie Wells appeared in musical plays in London and New York, using the name Julie Andrews, before beginning her film career. This began with two hugely popular films, *Mary Poppins* (1964), for which she won an Oscar, and *The Sound of Music* (1965), both starring Julie as a governess who sides with the children against their strict father. The energy of her acting and her beautifully clear singing voice made her a great favourite with audiences. Since then she has tried to get away from her Mary Poppins image, acting mainly in comedies for adults. She married the film director Blake Edwards, who made the *Pink Panther* comedies. ■

Astaire, Fred and Rogers, Ginger

Astaire 1899–1987
Rogers 1911–

Fred Austerlitz had a successful stage career dancing with his sister Adele from the age of 7. When Adele gave this up to get married, Fred looked for work in films. By 1933 he had changed his name to Fred Astaire and teamed up with Virginia ('Ginger') Rogers in *Flying Down to Rio,* the first of nine films they made together. Through films such as *Top Hat* (1935) and *Swing Time* (1936) they became cinema's most famous dancing couple.

Ginger also had a separate career as an actress in comedy films, winning an Oscar for *Kitty Foyle* in 1940. Fred retired for a time in 1946, but returned to star in *Easter Parade* (1948) with Judy Garland. ■

◄ **Fred Astaire and Ginger Rogers.**

Bogart, Humphrey

1899–1957

'Bogey' was the son of a New York surgeon. He suffered a lip wound in the US Navy during World War I which gave him a distinctive appearance and voice when he later became an actor. His first film appearances in the 1930s were usually in gangster movies, but he became famous as the detective Sam Spade in *The Maltese Falcon* (1941). Then came the romantic drama *Casablanca* (1942), before he teamed up with his wife Lauren Bacall in films such as *To Have and Have Not* (1944) and *The Big Sleep* (1946).

He won an Oscar for his role in *The African Queen* in 1951, another romantic drama. A very different role was the mentally-unstable Captain Queeg in *The Caine Mutiny* (1954), his last major film before his death. ■

Brando, Marlon

1924–

When Marlon Brando studied acting in New York, he learned how to identify completely with the character he was playing. He also developed a realistic style of speaking which was well-suited to the types of young people he was portraying. His early films often showed him as a rebel, as in *A Streetcar Named Desire* (1951) and *The Wild One* (1954). He won an Oscar for *On the Waterfront* (1954).

Later he played powerful, older men such as the Mafia leader Don Corleone in *The Godfather* (1972), which won him another Oscar. In *Superman* (1978) he was on screen as Superman's father for nine minutes and was paid over 18 million US dollars. ■

Cagney, James

1899–1986

James Cagney grew up in New York, where some of his schoolfriends drifted into crime. He remembered this when acting in his famous gangster films of the 1930s, which show how poor boys get involved in criminal gangs, as in *Angels with Dirty Faces* (1938). But he did not only play tough gangsters. In fact, he started his career in musical plays, and went on to sing and dance in film musicals such as the patriotic *Yankee Doodle Dandy* (1942), for which he won an Oscar. He even played the part of Puck in the film version of Shakespeare's *A Midsummer Night's Dream* (1935). ■

▲ **Cagney's shadow looms menacingly behind him in *Angels with Dirty Faces.***

▲ A scene from *The Kid*, showing Chaplin and his 7-year-old co-star, Jackie Coogan.

Chaplin, Charlie

1889–1977

Chaplin's mother was a music hall entertainer in London. From the age of 5 he began to take part in her act. When she became ill, the young Chaplin was sent to an orphanage. After some success as a teenage actor he went to America in 1910. Four years later he began to appear in films and soon became a favourite with cinema audiences, with his famous moustache, bowler hat, baggy trousers and cane. Later he took over the writing and directing of his films, and in 1919 he joined other stars and directors in founding their own United Artists film company.

In his most famous films, such as *The Kid* (1920) and *The Gold Rush* (1925), he played a sad little tramp who was bullied and confused by powerful people. Usually, though, he bounced back and was always on the side of weaker or poorer people. These films made him the best-loved comedian of the silent cinema. Even when talking pictures arrived in the 1930s, he continued to make films without words, like *Modern Times* (1936), in which he played a worker trapped by industrial machinery. He also made successful talking pictures like *The Great Dictator* (1940), a fierce but amusing attack on the German leader Adolf Hitler and his Nazi followers.

Later he was excluded from the USA because he was suspected of supporting communism, and he refused to let his films be shown there. However, in 1972 he returned in triumph to be awarded a special Oscar 'for the incalculable effect he has had in making motion pictures the art form of this century'. Two years before he died he was given a further honour in the country of his birth when he was given the title Sir Charles Chaplin. ■

Davis, Bette

1908–1989

Ruth Elizabeth Davis came from Lowell, Massachusetts, USA, and studied acting in New York. Film directors did not think she was beautiful enough for romantic roles, but in the 1930s she established herself as a powerful actress playing determined and independent women. She won Oscars for her roles in *Dangerous* (1935) and *Jezebel* (1938).

In films such as *The Little Foxes* (1941) and *All About Eve* (1950) she played cruel and selfish characters. In others, like *Now, Voyager* (1942), she played more likeable women, but her strong personality always shone through. In later life she scared audiences of *Whatever Happened to Baby Jane?* (1962) when she terrorized her crippled sister, played by Joan Crawford. ■

▶ James Dean in *Rebel Without a Cause*.
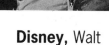

Dean, James

1931–1955

James Dean's mother died when he was just 5 years old, so he grew up on his uncle's farm. At school he loved acting, and went on to perform on stage and television before becoming a star at the age of 24 in *East of Eden* (1955). Within a few months he made two more films, *Rebel Without a Cause* (1955) and *Giant* (1956), but before they appeared in cinemas he crashed his sports car and died.

He became a hero for teenagers who were angry at the way adults misunderstood them, just like the character he played in his second film, *Rebel Without a Cause*. Many years after his death his face can still be seen on millions of posters, T-shirts and photographs bought by young people all over the world. ■

▼ Disney made a number of cartoon films, such as *Pinocchio*, which were based on popular children's stories.

DeMille, Cecil B.

1881–1959

Cecil B. DeMille started his career as an actor, but he soon became a director instead, and founded a film company which later formed part of Paramount Pictures. As a director, he started making silent comedies, but he became more famous for *The Ten Commandments,* which he made twice, first as a silent film in 1923 and then again with sound and colour in 1956. This and his other 'epic' films based on stories from the Bible and from history were famous for their huge crowd scenes and their spectacular special effects, like the parting of the Red Sea in *The Ten Commandments*. ■

Disney, Walt

1901–1966

Walter Disney grew up on a Missouri farm, and enjoyed sketching the animals. Later he worked drawing advertisements before starting on cartoon films for the Laugh-o-Gram company in Kansas. He created Mickey Mouse in 1928 and Donald Duck in 1934. These quickly became the world's favourite cartoon characters. Then he made full-length animated films, including *Snow White and the Seven Dwarfs* (1937), *Pinocchio* (1940) and *Bambi* (1942). Sometimes he was criticized for changing famous stories to suit his cartoons.

His film company was the biggest producer of cartoons, but it also made children's films with real actors, such as *Mary Poppins* (1964). In 1954 he opened Disneyland, the huge amusement park in California. He planned the even bigger Disneyworld in Florida, but this did not open until five years after his death. ■

▲ A *Fistful of Dollars* was the first of several 'spaghetti' westerns starring Clint Eastwood.

Eastwood, Clint

1930–

Clinton Eastwood worked as a swimming instructor and lifeguard while taking occasional small parts in films, before he found a regular part in the TV series *Rawhide* from 1959. His first big film success was in *A Fistful of Dollars* in 1964. It was called a 'spaghetti' western because it was filmed outside America by the Italian director Sergio Leone. This was followed by several more western films.

In the 1970s he began directing his own films, and also appeared as the detective Harry Callaghan in *Dirty Harry* and other violent films. The characters he plays are often hard men, but he has also appeared in musicals and comedies.

His directing career developed in the 1980s and he was highly praised for his film *Bird* (1988) about the life of jazz saxophonist Charlie Parker. ■

▲ Greta Garbo.

Fonda, Jane

1937–

In Jane Fonda's earliest films, like *Barbarella* (1968), the roles she played were those of beautiful women. However, she soon showed that she was an independent woman with her own opinions when she visited Hanoi to protest against America's bombing of North Vietnam in the 1970s. Many of her later films showed the problems of the modern world, like *Klute* (1971), *Coming Home* (1978) and *The China Syndrome* (1979). The first two of these films won her Oscars for best actress. She has also encouraged women to keep fit with her best-selling aerobics videos.

Her brother, Peter Fonda, acted in and directed films such as *Easy Rider* (1968), and her father was the well-known film actor Henry Fonda. Jane acted with him in his last film before he died, *On Golden Pond* (1981). ■

Gable, Clark

1901–1960

Clark Gable was a factory worker and oil-driller before he started acting. At first he appeared in films as a villain, but in 1934 he found success with the romantic comedy *It Happened One Night*, which won him an Oscar. During the 1930s he was the most popular 'leading man' in Hollywood films, famous for his muscular good looks.

His greatest role was as the handsome Rhett Butler in the American Civil War drama *Gone with the Wind* (1939). He was still acting in films at the time of his death. His last film, *The Misfits* with Marilyn Monroe, came out the year after he died. ■

▶ Clark Gable and Vivien Leigh in *Gone with the Wind*.

Garbo, Greta

1905–1990

Greta Gustafsson grew up in Stockholm, Sweden, and worked as a model before she started acting in films there. Then she travelled to Hollywood and became a star in romantic silent films such as *Love* (1927), in which she co-starred with John Gilbert. When talking pictures came in, her Swedish accent meant that she was given roles as distinguished European ladies, such as the great Swedish queen in *Queen Christina* (1933) and the tragic heroine of *Anna Karenina* (1935). She was famous for her beauty and for her serious expression.

Her films were even more popular in Europe than they were in America, but when America entered World War II in 1941 Garbo's films could no longer be shown in most European countries. She decided to retire immediately and never appeared in public again, creating a great mystery about her life. ■

Garland, Judy

1922–1969

Frances Gumm's parents managed a theatre in Lancaster, California, where she sang with her sisters as a young girl. After changing her name to Judy Garland, she appeared in *The Wizard of Oz* (1939) when she was 16, singing the famous song 'Over the Rainbow'. She became a very popular star, because audiences loved her heartfelt singing and the way she acted like an ordinary, slightly frightened girl. But the pressures of her long singing and acting career brought her unhappiness along with fame. Her health was ruined by slimming pills, and her four marriages ended in divorce. Her daughter Liza Minnelli also became a film star, singing and dancing in the film *Cabaret* (1972). ■

Hitchcock, Alfred

1899–1980

Alfred Hitchcock was the son of a London poultry dealer. He was good at drawing, and got a job writing and designing captions for silent films. He soon worked his way up to become a film director. In 1926 *The Lodger* began his long series of suspense thrillers, in which he makes a very brief appearance each time. In 1928 his film *Blackmail* was the first British talking picture. He directed *The Thirty-Nine Steps* (1935) and several other films in England, but then moved to Hollywood and became even more famous as a director of frightening thrillers like *Rebecca* (1940), *Psycho* (1960) and *The Birds* (1963).

He specialized in nasty surprises that catch the audience out, and was well known for his occasionally harsh treatment of actors and actresses. Just before his death, in 1980, he was honoured for his services to cinema and became Sir Alfred Hitchcock. ■

Hoffman, Dustin

1937–

Dustin Hoffman grew up in Los Angeles, USA, and spent the 1960s acting in New York. His third film appearance, in *The Graduate* (1968), made him a star. After that he starred in several successful American films, including *All the President's Men* (1976) and *Kramer vs. Kramer* (1979), for which he won an Oscar.

He has always enjoyed playing a wide range of different people, such as the man who impersonates a woman in the comedy *Tootsie* (1983), the much older man suffering the stress of a breakdown in *Death of a Salesman* (1985) and the autistic man in *Rain Man* (1989). In between making films, he still likes to act in stage plays and starred in Shakespeare's *The Merchant of Venice* in Britain in 1989. ■

Karloff, Boris

1887–1969

Boris's real name was William Pratt. He grew up in London but as a young man he emigrated to Canada, where he started acting. He had small roles in more than 60 films before becoming famous as Frankenstein's monster in *Frankenstein*, the classic horror film of 1931. For this part he had to spend hours having his make-up put on. He managed not only to make the monster frightening, but also to make audiences feel sorry for it. He played the monster twice more, and also acted in many other horror films, such as *The Mummy* (1932). He was still taking small parts in films the year before he died. ■

▶ The monster, played by Boris Karloff, confronts its maker, Dr Frankenstein, in the 1931 film *Frankenstein*.

Keaton, Buster

1895–1966

Joseph Keaton's parents were comedians. They trained him when he was a very young child to perform in their stage act. He was given his name 'Buster' when he fell down the stairs and survived unhurt. When he was 21 he joined the comedian Roscoe 'Fatty' Arbuckle in making short films.

From 1919 he started making his own short films and then longer films like *Our Hospitality* (1923) and *The Navigator* (1924), in which he escaped from one disaster after another with hardly a single change of expression. He was given the nickname 'the great stone face' because of this. In his greatest film, *The General* (1927), he played an engine driver caught up in the American Civil War.

Sadly, the talking pictures put an end to the kind of silent comedy which he perfected, but later generations of film fans grew to love his pictures when they were revived on television. ■

Kelly, Gene

1912–

Eugene Kelly grew up in Pittsburgh, Pennsylvania, where his mother was a dance teacher. After appearing on stage in musical plays, he started in films in 1942, singing and dancing in a fresh, cheerful style. His dancing was often very acrobatic, as in *The Pirate* (1948), and sometimes made use of ordinary objects which he seemed to bring alive, such as the famous umbrella he danced with in *Singin' in the Rain* (1952). He helped to direct this film and later found further success as a director, making the modern ballet film *Invitation to the Dance* (1956) and *Hello Dolly!* (1969). ■

▲ Laurel and Hardy in a scene of comic chaos from *Blockheads*.

Kurosawa, Akira

1910—

After the tragedy of the great Kanto earthquake of 1923, Japanese audiences were ready for light entertainment, and Akira Kurosawa remembered the imported films that he saw in the following year. They helped shape the style of his films when he became a director.

Sanshiro Sugata, his first film, was criticized by the army in 1943 for being too foreign. After the war, *They Who Tread on the Tiger's Tail* was banned by the American authorities because it was thought to be 'anti-democratic'. Many of his films tell dramatic stories from violent periods in Japanese history; some of them have been called 'eastern westerns'. Kurosawa was awarded a special Oscar in March 1990, for his unique contribution to cinema. ■

Laurel, Stanley and Hardy, Oliver

Laurel 1890–1965
Hardy 1892–1957

Stan Laurel, whose real name was Arthur Jefferson, was an English comedian who played in pantomimes before travelling to America. He started appearing in films there in 1917. Norvell Oliver Hardy came from Georgia, USA, where he first appeared on stage at the age of 8. He started film acting in 1914. Both appeared in dozens of silent films before they began their successful partnership in the 1927 silent comedy *Putting Pants on Philip*.

In the next 30 years they made over 100 silent and talking pictures, and achieved great success with films such as *Sons of the Desert* (1934), *Way Out West* (1937) and *Blockheads* (1938). Their humour came from the contrast between the small, thin and confused Laurel and the big, fat, irritable Hardy. ■

Marx Brothers

Chico (Leonard) 1886–1961
Harpo (Adolph, later Arthur) 1888–1964
Groucho (Julius) 1890–1977
Zeppo (Herbert) 1901–1979

The five Marx brothers were the sons of a poor Jewish tailor in New York. Chico, Harpo, Groucho, Zeppo and Gummo (Milton) were trained by their mother to be a singing and dancing group. They later switched successfully to comedy. When they turned from the stage to films, Gummo left the act. In five of their films Zeppo played straight, romantic roles, but the rest of their films concentrated on the three most famous Marx Brothers: Chico, Harpo and Groucho.

Each of them had a distinctive character. Groucho, with his moustache, cigar and funny walk, was always cracking jokes. Harpo, whose name came from his beautiful harp playing, never spoke. He communicated by strange noises, gestures and funny faces, which Chico interpreted for him. Chico himself always spoke in an Italian accent and the plots of the films usually gave him a chance to show his skill on the piano. Although their best films, including *Animal Crackers* (1930), *Duck Soup* (1933), *A Night at the Opera* (1935) and *A Day at the Races* (1937), show them in all sorts of crazy situations, the scripts were very carefully planned. They tried out most of the jokes and plots in their stage shows before they put them on film. ∎

Monroe, Marilyn

1926–1962

Marilyn's real name was Norma Jean Baker or Mortenson. She had a miserable childhood in Los Angeles foster homes because her mother was mentally ill. Even when she later became a famous actress, she could still feel lonely and unloved at times.

After working as a model and in minor film roles, she found her first big role in *Niagara* in 1953. Two of her best-known films, *Gentlemen Prefer Blondes* (1953) and *Some Like it Hot* (1959), show she was a fine comic actress. However she also took serious, dramatic roles in films like *Bus Stop* (1956) and *The Misfits* (1961), her last film.

She had several husbands, including baseball star Joe DiMaggio and playwright Arthur Miller. She died from a drug overdose in 1962. Even now, many years after her death, she is remembered as one of the most beautiful stars of cinema history. ∎

▶ Marilyn Monroe's short but successful film career ended tragically at the age of 36, when she died from an overdose of sleeping pills.

▲ Actors Tom Cruise (left) and Dustin Hoffman with Oscars won by the film *Rain Man*.

'Oscar'

1927–

The Oscar award was born in 1927 when the American Academy of Motion Picture Arts and Sciences began to present Academy Awards for outstanding achievements in film making. These Academy Awards are 25 cm (10 in) high and are made of bronze, covered with gold plate. They were first called Oscars in 1931 when a librarian at the Academy commented that the little statuettes reminded her of her Uncle Oscar.

Until 1936, Oscars or Academy Awards were given only for Best Picture, Best Actor, Best Actress and Best Director. Since then they have also been given to Best Supporting Actor and Actress. There are also Oscars for technical achievements in sound, music and camerawork, and since 1947 there has been an Oscar for the Best Foreign Language Film. The Awards ceremony takes place each year in Hollywood and is the most glamorous cinema occasion of all. ∎

Poitier, Sidney

1927–

Sidney Poitier was born in Miami, USA, but grew up in the Bahamas in the Caribbean. As a young man he began to take acting lessons at the American Negro Theatre in New York. This led to roles in stage plays and later to film appearances. He was in a number of films in the 1950s which showed what it was like to be black in the USA. Parts in *The Blackboard Jungle* (1955), *Edge of the City* (1957) and *Porgy and Bess* (1959) made Poitier a leading film actor. His reputation grew further in 1963 when he won an Oscar for *Lilies of the Field*.

One of his best-known films was *In the Heat of the Night* (1967), in which he played a New York detective sent to solve a murder in a small town in the south of the USA. Thanks to powerful acting from Poitier and his co-star Rod Steiger, the film won the Oscar for best film of the year. ∎

▲ Sidney Poitier arrives in a small town to solve a murder in the film *In the Heat of the Night*.

Spielberg, Steven

1947–

As a boy, Steven Spielberg began using his father's cine-camera to film toy trains. At school he made several amateur science fiction films. When he was 21 he started directing TV programmes, including the detective series *Columbo*.

His big impact on the cinema came in 1975 with the tense thriller *Jaws*, which quickly made more money than any other film ever had. After making *Close Encounters of the Third Kind* in 1977, he broke box-office records again with the success of *Raiders of the Lost Ark* (1981) and *E.T.* (1982), which made more than 700 million US dollars. In *The Color Purple* (1985) he tackled a more sensitive story about racial conflict, and he won further praise with his films *Back to the Future* (1985) and *Empire of the Sun* (1987). ∎

Taylor, Elizabeth

1932–

Elizabeth Taylor was born in London, but grew up in Hollywood as a child actress, appearing in films from the age of 10 and enjoying success in *National Velvet* in 1944.

She became one of the most glamorous stars of the 1950s and 1960s, and attracted much attention because of her several short-lived marriages. Twice she married the great Welsh actor Richard Burton, with whom she acted in *Cleopatra* (1963). She played the title role in this film and had to make 65 costume changes.

In her best films she played strong-minded women and won Oscars for her roles in *Butterfield 8* (1960) and *Who's Afraid of Virginia Woolf?* (1966). ■

▼ Elizabeth Taylor, aged 11, and Mickey Rooney in *National Velvet*.

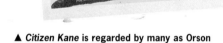
▲ *Citizen Kane* is regarded by many as Orson Welles's greatest film.

Valentino, Rudolph

1895–1926

Rudolph Valentino was born in Castellaneta, Italy. At 18, he travelled to America, working as a dancer and a film 'extra'. Suddenly in 1921 he became a star after his performances in *The Four Horsemen of the Apocalypse* and *The Sheik*.

He was adored by film fans for his handsome appearance in romantic roles such as the bullfighter in *Blood and Sand* (1922) and Ahmed in *Son of the Sheik* (1926). His early death attracted thousands of fans to his funeral to mourn the most glamorous leading man of silent films. ■

Welles, Orson

1915–1985

As a young actor Orson Welles became famous in 1938 for presenting a radio play about invaders from Mars as if it were a real newsflash. People listening to *The War of the Worlds* were terrified and thousands of them fled in panic. Welles had to apologize.

A few years later, Welles was in Hollywood making his masterpiece of film direction, *Citizen Kane* (1941), in which he also starred as a selfish millionaire newspaper owner. The new techniques he used for combining sound and pictures in this and other films, including *The Magnificent Ambersons* (1942), *Macbeth* (1948) and *Touch of Evil* (1958), inspired many other film directors. A French director, François Truffaut, has said that *Citizen Kane* is 'probably the one [film] that has started the largest number of film makers on their careers'. ■

Temple, Shirley

1928–

Shirley Temple started acting in short films at the age of 4 and was given a special Oscar when she was only 5 for her success in the film *Stand up and Cheer* (1934). Over the next few years she was America's favourite child star, usually playing the part of a little orphan who got her way with adults by smiling sweetly and dancing or singing.

Unfortunately, she did not succeed in becoming an adult actress and made her last film, *Fort Apache* (1948), at the age of 20. Later, under her married name, Shirley Temple Black, she became US representative to the United Nations in 1969 and ambassador to Ghana in 1974. ■

Wayne, John

1907–1979

Marion Morrison worked behind the scenes in film studios before taking small acting parts, first as 'Duke' Morrison and then from 1930 as John Wayne. His first leading role came in the western film *Stagecoach*, directed by John Ford in 1939. He went on to become the most famous star of westerns, through films such as *Red River, Fort Apache* (both 1948), *Rio Bravo* (1959), and many others.

He also starred in war films like *Sands of Iwo Jima* (1950), and directed two films in the 1960s. His tough patriotic roles made him a national hero for many American film fans. In all, he made more than 175 films and finally achieved Oscar success for his role in *True Grit* (1969). ■

▲ John Wayne became the best-known star of western films.

Pop & Rock

Beatles, the

Formed 1959

Pete Best 1941–
George Harrison 1943–
John Lennon 1940–1980
Paul McCartney 1942–
Ringo Starr (Richard Starkey) 1940–

The Beatles were formed in 1959 as the Silver Beatles. By 1961 they were the most popular group in Liverpool, playing songs which were a mixture of rock'n'roll and black American rhythm'n'blues music. In 1962 Ringo Starr replaced Pete Best as the group's drummer, completing the line up of John Lennon, Paul McCartney, George Harrison and Starr that became so famous. The Beatles' record for the Parlophone label, 'Love Me Do' (1962), was a minor hit, but their second, 'Please Please Me' (1963), started a run of 20 Top 10 hits before the group eventually broke up.

Their exciting music, which was written mostly by Lennon and McCartney, their rebellious attitudes and their Liverpool humour won them millions of fans in the early 1960s. The crowds that followed them about were so huge that newspapers called it 'Beatlemania'. This spread to America in 1964, when Beatles' singles held the top five chart positions all at the same time. They also made a number of successful films including *A Hard Day's Night* (1964) and *Help!* (1965).

By late 1966, audiences at their concerts were so large and noisy that the Beatles could not hear themselves playing, so they gave up live performances. The following year they released their most famous album, *Sgt Pepper's Lonely Hearts Club Band.* For this they and their producer, George Martin, introduced many unusual recording techniques, as well as new ideas in music and lyrics.

Personal and business pressures made the group split up in late 1969, just before the release of their last album *Let It Be* (1970). All four went on to further success as solo entertainers. Ringo Starr carried on singing and drumming, and also appeared in films. George Harrison raised millions of dollars to help people in Bangladesh with his 1972 concert in New York. His music career continued into the 1990s but he also became a successful film producer.

Paul McCartney formed the group Wings, who had great success with their single 'Mull of Kintyre' in 1977. After Wings split up, Paul McCartney continued to make solo recordings and do live tours. John Lennon became involved in American politics along with his wife Yoko Ono. He retired from music in 1975 but made a comeback album, *Double Fantasy*, with Yoko in 1980. Tragically, in December that year he was shot dead outside his New York home. ■

▲ The album cover for the Beatles' *Sgt Pepper's Lonely Hearts Club Band.*

Berry, Chuck

1926–

In the 1950s Charles 'Chuck' Berry invented the ringing guitar sound which inspired many 1960s pop groups, especially the Beatles and the Rolling Stones. Born in San Jose, California, he did a number of jobs while he tried to become a full-time musician. Once he got a recording contract, he had a string of hits with witty story-lines, which mixed country music with rhythm'n'blues and an irresistible dance beat.

His songs, including 'Rock'n'Roll Music' (1957) and 'Sweet Little Sixteen' (1958), are world-famous and have been performed by hundreds of other musicians. His famous crouching dance step, the 'Duck Walk', has also been much copied. Beatle John Lennon once said of him, 'If you tried to give rock'n'roll another name, you might call it Chuck Berry.' ■

▶ Chuck Berry tunes up his guitar before going on stage in 1956.

▲ Bowie often changed the way he looked, just as he did his musical styles, and sometimes appeared on stage in unusual outfits and make-up.

Bowie, David

1947–

David Robert Jones was born in Brixton, London, and as David Bowie became a songwriter and performer who remained a star by changing his looks and musical style to keep up with the times.

He was in many groups during the 1960s, but his first big hit was 'Space Oddity' in 1969. That led to a string of more than 40 hit records, including 'Let's Dance' (1983) which was No. 1 in both Britain and America at the same time.

When performing live, Bowie always liked to create a whole new personality for himself on stage, as he did in 1972 as 'Ziggy Stardust'. He also appeared in films and plays, but always returned to music. In 1983 he was paid 10·5 million US dollars for a concert in California, the highest sum ever paid to a rock star for a single show. ■

Brown, James

1928–

James Brown came from South Carolina, USA, and had a hard childhood. When he was only 16 he was jailed for armed robbery. Turning to music kept him out of trouble, and in 1958 he had his first million seller, 'Try Me', a song in the gospel and rhythm'n'blues styles. He gradually added hard, rhythmic guitars and frantic, punchy horns, creating a style which became known as funk.

His live shows, among the most exciting ever, earned him the title Godfather of Soul. Hits like 'Papa's Got a Brand New Bag' (1965) and 'Living in America' (1986) confirmed his star status over 20 years. Drug problems landed him in jail again in 1989, but he was released in 1990. ■

Collins, Phil

1951–

After a promising start as a child actor, London-born Phil Collins joined rock band Genesis as drummer in 1970, then took over singing when vocalist Peter Gabriel left in 1975. His talents as singer, songwriter and producer soon became obvious. His first solo album, *Face Value* (1981), sold over 2 million copies, followed by a No. 1 single 'You Can't Hurry Love' (1982). He starred in the film *Buster* (1988), and by 1990 had sold over 6 million LPs in Britain. ■

Dylan, Bob

1941–

Robert Zimmerman of Duluth, Minnesota, was a wild and reckless teenager who ran off to travel across America, learning the songs of his folk-singing hero Woody Guthrie. He took the name Dylan from Welsh poet Dylan Thomas and performed as a singer in New York's Greenwich Village coffee bars during the early 1960s. Two of his own songs, 'Blowin' in the Wind' (1962) and 'The Times they are a-Changin'' (1963), became anthems for the Civil Rights movement in the USA. This started a new style, 'protest music', with songs about war, religion, politics and racism.

Dylan's change from acoustic to electric instruments in the mid-1960s inspired a folk-rock craze, and he was called 'a spokesman for his generation'. On the albums *Highway 61 Revisited* (1965) and *Blonde on Blonde* (1966) he developed a new writing technique, rich in strange images, bizarre characters and hidden meanings. This inspired many imitators, and influenced the style of countless songwriters, including Lennon and McCartney of the Beatles.

After a serious motor cycle accident in 1966, Dylan returned to a simpler style with the LP *Nashville Skyline* (1969). In the late 1970s he became a Christian, which was reflected in his songs of that time on albums such as *Shot of Love* (1981). He continued to be popular throughout the world, playing to large audiences into the 1990s. ■

▲ Dylan's thoughtful, outspoken ballads have inspired many songwriters from the early 1960s to the present day.

Everly Brothers

Don 1937–
Phil 1939–

Kentucky boys Don and Phil were singing on their parents' successful country music radio show before either was 10 years old. By the mid-1950s, the brothers had developed their unique close-harmony singing style, which has since been imitated by the Beatles, Simon and Garfunkel and many others.

Their big hits, 'Bye Bye Love' (1957), 'Wake up Little Suzie' (1957) and 'All I Have to Do is Dream' (1958), combined country music harmonies with rock rhythms and greatly influenced the folk-rock boom of the 1960s. The brothers split up in 1973, and later solo recordings were unsuccessful. They continued to play occasional reunion concerts, such as the one in London in 1983. ■

Gordy, Berry

1929–

Berry Gordy Jr, an ex-boxer, became a successful songwriter in the late 1950s. He started Tamla Motown Records by borrowing 700 US dollars from his sister. Under Gordy's control, Motown developed 'the sound of young America' with over 120 hits by Diana Ross, Stevie Wonder, the Temptations, the Four Tops, Marvin Gaye, Michael Jackson and many others during the 1960s.

Gordy devised Motown's formula of a pounding beat, insistent bass guitars and catchy choruses. He also controlled the way his stars dressed, spoke, sang and danced. In the 1970s, Gordy's artists demanded and got more control of their own careers, but by this time he had already made Motown the largest black-owned organization in America. ■

Haley, Bill

1925–1981

Bill Haley, from Minnesota, USA, was originally a country and western singer, but he and his group the Comets came to fame in 1954 after switching to the rock'n'roll style with 'Shake Rattle and Roll', a Top 10 hit in America and Britain. Even bigger success followed with 'Rock Around the Clock' (1955), featured in *Blackboard Jungle*, a film about tough teenagers. Haley had a teenage audience, and for two years he was the world's most successful rock star, with twelve hits in a row. After he began appearing in films and on television, his fans realized he was actually rather old, balding and plump, and they deserted him for younger stars. ■

Hendrix, Jimi

1942–1970

Jimi Hendrix was one of the most exciting, unusual and imaginative rock guitarists ever. He began, in his Seattle home, by imitating records of blues guitarists, then played with many top soul groups. He started his own band in New York, but moved to London in 1966 to form The Jimi Hendrix Experience.

Hendrix played the electric guitar in ways that had not been attempted before, while the other members of his group played hard and fast behind him. He immediately found success with 'Hey Joe' (1967) and, despite the strangeness of his sound, followed it with five more hits and three LPs before his death in 1970. Many later guitarists have imitated Hendrix, but none have managed to play quite like him. ∎

Holly, Buddy

1936–1959

Like many early rock'n'roll musicians, Texas-born Charles Hardin Holley began by playing country music but, as leader of Buddy Holly and the Crickets, he went on to become one of rock'n'roll's greatest songwriters.

Holly was the first rock'n'roll artist regularly to write his own songs. He was also, in 1956, the first musician to use the two guitars, bass and drums, which became the standard line-up for pop groups in the 1960s; in 1957 he was the first to use studio trickery to change the sound of his music; and in 1958 he was the first to record with a string orchestra. His greatest talent, however, was the ability to write simple pop songs that were hard to forget after the first hearing. His hits, including 'That'll be the Day' (1957), 'Rave On' (1958) and 'It Doesn't Matter Any More' (1959), have been recorded by many artists and still sound fresh today.

Tragically, Holly died in a plane crash at the peak of his success, when he was only 22. ∎

Jackson, Michael

1958–

Hailed as a singing and dancing child genius from the age of 6, Michael Jackson began his show business career as the youngest of the Jackson Five in 1970. They had a string of hits in the US and Europe. Jackson's style was similar to that of such vocalists as Stevie Wonder and Diana Ross, the singing star who encouraged him in his early days. In 1971, while still with the Jackson Five, he began a solo career which brought him further international hits.

While filming *The Wiz*, a 1978 remake of *The Wizard of Oz* with a black cast, Jackson met producer and composer Quincey Jones. They worked closely together after that. Jackson's

first album with Jones was *Off the Wall* (1979), which sold 19 million copies. This was followed by *Thriller* (1982), which sold 38 million and became the biggest selling album ever, and *Bad* (1987).

Over the years he developed a distinctive singing voice and his high-speed dancing drew praise from experts like Fred Astaire. His spectacular stage shows were one of the main show business attractions of the 1980s. Rumours of plastic surgery to reshape his face, bizarre pets, like his chimpanzee Bubbles, and a life hidden away in a luxurious Hollywood mansion led to Jackson being called 'Wacko Jacko' by some newspapers. Nevertheless, he remained as popular as ever with his millions of fans. ∎

▲ Michael Jackson's singing and dancing skills made him one of the 1980s' most exciting live performers.

John, Elton

1947–

Reginald Kenneth Dwight of Pinner, Middlesex, England, was a very capable pianist who could write memorable tunes. In the late 1960s he changed his name to Elton John, and joined forces with lyric writer Bernie Taupin. Their first hit was 'Your Song' in 1970. Gradually, Elton John developed into an outrageous stage performer, wearing costumes studded with sequins and jewels, ostrich feathers and giant spectacles. In 1975 around 2 per cent of all records sold were by Elton. He was undeniably the world's best-selling pop star, enjoying six No. 1 albums in a row and many Top 10 singles.

In the 1980s he did less singing and touring, particularly after he had an operation on his throat in 1987. Instead, he spent more time on his other love, Watford Football Club; as their chairman he watched them climb from the fourth division to the first division of the Football League. ∎

King, Carole

1942–

With her husband Gerry Goffin, New Yorker Carole King was one of the most gifted songwriters of the 1960s. She had a hit in her own name with 'It Might as Well Rain until September' in 1962, but she and Gerry were best known for writing over 50 pop hits for other performers, including 'The Locomotion' by Little Eva and 'Will You Love Me Tomorrow' by the Shirelles. Carole King wrote eight No. 1 hits in the USA, more than any other female songwriter. She took up singing more seriously at the end of the 1960s and her album *Tapestry* (1971) became the best-selling rock album of that time, with 14 million copies sold. ∎

Madonna

1958–

Madonna Louise Ciccone was the most successful female singer of the 1980s. Born in Michigan, USA, she studied dancing, and then combined her dancing skills with pop singing after moving to New York. Some of her outrageous clothes attracted as much attention as her singing.

Her hits, including 'Into the Groove' (1985), 'Like a Virgin' (1986), 'Like a Prayer' (1989) and 'Vogue' (1990), had simple dance tunes, but unusual words and images. Her album *True Blue* (1986) was the No. 1 LP in 28 countries. She has also appeared in films, the best-known of which is *Desperately Seeking Susan* (1985). ∎

▲ Madonna became famous not just for her talents as a singer and dancer, but also for the extraordinary way she dressed. Many fans tried to copy the way she looked.

Orbison, Roy
1936–1988

Winner of a talent contest at the age of 10, Roy Orbison first played country music professionally in Texas dance halls but switched to rock'n'roll in the mid-1950s. His sad, high-pitched voice suited slow, heartbreaking songs like 'Only the Lonely' and 'Running Scared'. A run of 20 hits followed, the biggest being 'Oh Pretty Woman' in 1964. Elvis Presley called him 'the best singer in the world', but Orbison's career crumbled after his wife was killed in a motor cycle crash in 1966. He was just recovering when his two sons died in a fire two years later.

He returned to chart success in 1988 with 'She's a Mystery to Me', and joined the Travellin' Wilburys with Bob Dylan, ex-Beatle George Harrison and others. In a bitter twist of fate, at the height of this revival, Roy Orbison died of a heart attack. ∎

Presley, Elvis Aron
1935–1977

Elvis Presley was born into a poor white family in East Tupelo, Mississippi. As a teenager, he spent much of his time with black musicians. In 1953, he paid to make a record for his mother's birthday at Sun Records in Memphis. The owner liked his unusual mixture of country, blues and gospel styles, and offered him professional recording work.

His first local hit was 'That's All Right' in 1954, and he created a sensation on television by swivelling his hips while singing. Adults were outraged, but teenagers loved it. By 1956, he was a national star, making huge hits like 'Hound Dog', 'Blue Suede Shoes' and 'Jailhouse Rock'. Known as the 'King of Rock'n'Roll', he eventually recorded 94 gold singles and over 40 gold albums. He starred in 27 films, earning over 1 million US dollars for every role.

By the mid-1960s he had been replaced by the Beatles as the biggest name in rock music, but he continued touring and recording. His Las Vegas appearances of 1969 were particularly successful. In the 1970s he spent more and more time in Graceland, his huge Memphis mansion, where he died of heart failure in 1977. ∎

▶ Elvis Presley is still considered by many to be the 'King of Rock'n'Roll'.

Prince
1958–

Prince Rogers Nelson was the son of musician parents from Minneapolis, USA. He taught himself piano at the age of 7 and gradually learnt to play so many instruments that he was able to play all the instruments on his own recordings by the age of 18. He became an inventive songwriter, arranger, producer and performer.

His career took off with hits like 'When Doves Cry' (1984) and 'Kiss' (1986). He also starred in the films *Purple Rain* (1984) and *Under a Cherry Moon* (1986) and recorded the soundtrack album for the very successful film *Batman* (1989). ∎

▲ Prince's stage shows are as colourful, varied and inventive as his music.

Richard, Cliff
1940–

Harry Roger Webb started singing rock'n'roll music after seeing Bill Haley in 1957. A year later, he changed his name to Cliff Richard and based his act on imitating Elvis Presley. By 1959, hits like 'Living Doll' showed him developing a sound of his own, and his backing group the Shadows began having instrumental hits. Cliff's good looks made him a natural choice for pop films such as *The Young Ones* and *Summer Holiday*. Frequent changes of style brought him over 100 British chart hits, his own television series and the longest career in British pop music. In 1980 he was awarded the OBE. He became a devout Christian quite early in his career and spent much of his time sharing his beliefs with music fans throughout the world. ∎

Rolling Stones, the

Formed 1962

Mick Jagger 1943–
Brian Jones 1942–1969
Keith Richard 1943–
Mick Taylor 1948–
Charlie Watts 1941–
Ron Wood 1947–
Bill Wyman 1936–

The Rolling Stones started by singing versions of rhythm'n'blues songs in London clubs. By late 1962 the line-up had become Mick Jagger (vocals), Keith Richard (guitar), Brian Jones (guitar), Bill Wyman (bass) and Charlie Watts (drums). They grew their hair long, wore very casual clothes on stage and became almost as popular as the Beatles with records like *Out of Our Heads* (1965) and *Aftermath* (1966). Their sometimes wild behaviour earned them the disapproval of many adults but they still gained millions of fans.

Brian Jones left the band a month before his death in 1969. He was replaced by Mick Taylor and the Rolling Stones began to record much harsher and louder music, but with the same perfect dance beat. They started their own record label with the LP *Sticky Fingers* in 1971. Mick Taylor left the group in 1974 and was replaced by Ron Wood from the Faces.

During the 1970s and 1980s the members of the group began to pursue their own solo careers. Keith Richard, Mick Jagger and Bill Wyman recorded solo albums and Charlie Watts became involved in big-band jazz music. Jagger and Richard continued to write most of the Stones' songs and the band was still recording and touring in the 1990s. ■

▲ Ron Wood and Mick Jagger of the Rolling Stones.

Ross, Diana

1944–

Detroit singer Diana Earl had eighteen hits with the 1960s all-girl group the Supremes on the Tamla Motown label before she went solo in 1970, notching up over 40 more hits. Her voice is thin but radiates star quality. In a cleverly planned career, guided by Motown boss Berry Gordy Jr, she conveniently changed style from soul to pop, jazz or disco to suit the times. She also appeared in several musical films, including *Lady Sings the Blues* (1972) and *The Wiz* (1978). Eventually she became a part-owner of Motown, the label which launched her singing career. ■

▲ Diana Ross was one of the many performers who found success on Berry Gordy Jr's Motown record label.

Sex Pistols, the

Formed 1975

Paul Cook 1950–
Steve Jones 1957–
Johnny Rotten (John Lydon) 1956–
Sid Vicious (John Ritchie) 1957–1979

British pop music had become rather safe and predictable by the mid-1970s when the Sex Pistols appeared. On and off stage, they were loud, fast and abusive. They had short, spiky hair and wore ripped T-shirts and jeans held together by safety pins. This outrageous image, carefully planned by manager Malcolm McLaren, helped to bring them lots of publicity. They had several hits, including 'Anarchy in the UK' (1976) and 'God Save the Queen' (1977), which came out during Elizabeth II's Silver Jubilee celebrations and was banned by the BBC.

They paved the way for 'punk rock', but split up in 1978. Their bass player Sid Vicious died of a heroin overdose in 1979, but other members of the group, like singer Johnny Rotten, continued their careers with other groups. Many of the groups which came after the Sex Pistols helped to create a 'New Wave' in rock music in the late 1970s and early 1980s. ■

Simon, Paul

1942–

New York's folk-rock duo Simon and Garfunkel had many hit records during the 1960s and 1970s. The best known was 'Bridge over Troubled Water' (1970). They split up after this record and Art Garfunkel turned mainly to film acting while Paul Simon pursued a solo career as a singer and songwriter. Although he was often dismissed in the early stages of his career as an imitator of Bob Dylan, his work on albums like *There Goes Rhymin' Simon* (1973) and *Still Crazy After All These Years* (1975) showed him to be a sensitive and intelligent songwriter.

After reuniting with Art Garfunkel for one live concert in Central Park, New York in 1981, he recorded the album *Graceland* with many top African musicians in 1986. This celebration of the music of Africa and America is considered by many to be his finest album. ■

Spector, Phil

1940–

Phil Spector, 'The Tycoon of Teen', was the first great rock music producer. Although he was also a very good writer of songs, including 'Spanish Harlem' and 'To Know Him is to Love Him', Spector's greatest achievement was his thunderous production style, called the 'wall of sound'. To create his 'little symphonies for the kids' he packed large groups into tiny studios, using echo effects and multi-tracking to create music that sounded bigger and louder than anything else in the early 1960s. A millionaire at 21, he produced hits for the Righteous Brothers, the Ronettes, and Ike and Tina Turner.

He retired in 1966, but returned to record producing in the 1970s, working with ex-Beatles George Harrison and John Lennon. Spector's success proved that record producers could be vitally important. His style was often imitated by later producers, like Brian Wilson of the Beach Boys. ■

▲ The Sex Pistols, led by singer Johnny Rotten, shocked the music world with their outrageous behaviour and energetic music.

Springsteen, Bruce

1949–

Bruce Springsteen began his career playing in small clubs and bars around America, but later became one of the most popular live entertainers ever. Although he had great success with albums like *Born to Run* (1975), *The River* (1980) and *Born in the USA* (1984), it was his live shows that his fans remembered best. In 1984, he set off on the hardest and longest rock tour ever, playing 158 shows in 61 cities in eleven different countries of the world. On this tour he played and sang to nearly 5 million people altogether and earned millions of dollars. It was shows like these that made his fans call him 'The Boss'. ■

▲ Bruce Springsteen performing in front of thousands of fans at an open-air concert.

Stock, Aitken and Waterman

Mike Stock 1951–
Matt Aitken 1956–
Pete Waterman 1947–

In the 1980s Mike Stock, Matt Aitken and Pete Waterman wrote, produced and performed over 60 hits, making them the most successful hit production team in pop history. Voices on the hits were provided by singers like Kylie Minogue, Jason Donovan, Rick Astley, Bananarama and Mel & Kim, but Stock and Aitken were the backroom musical brains. Ex-disc jockey Waterman was the guiding light who owned their company, PWL, and ran it the way Berry Gordy ran the Motown label.

Records by Stock, Aitken and Waterman always have simple tunes, electronic rhythms and easily understood lyrics. In 1988 alone, this formula notched seventeen hits and earned them £11 million. ■

▲ Tina Turner's musical career has lasted more than 25 years, thanks to her strong, soulful singing voice.

Turner, Tina

1938–

Annie Mae Bullock of Nutbush, Tennessee, was always a fine singer, but her career began when she went on stage for a dare to sing with the rhythm'n'blues group, Ike Turner's Kings of Rhythm. She later married Ike, and together they had many hits, such as 'River Deep, Mountain High' (1966) and 'Nutbush City Limits' (1973).

After she divorced Ike in 1976, her career dipped until 1983 when she had a hit again with 'Let's Stay Together'. Her new approach to records and live shows, blending her soulful vocals with rock guitars, resulted in 'What's Love Got to Do with It' (1984) becoming 'record of the year' in the USA and establishing her as a star of the 1980s. ■

U2

Formed 1977

Bono (Paul Hewson) 1960–
The Edge (David Evans) 1961–
Adam Clayton 1960–
Larry Mullen 1961–

U2 were part of the 'New Wave' in rock music that grew out of 'punk rock' in the late 1970s. Coming from Dublin, Ireland, they soon attracted fans throughout Britain and the USA, thanks partly to the stage presence of singer Bono. Their breakthrough album was *The Unforgettable Fire* (1984), on which they created their own strong and stylish rock sound around the guitar work of the Edge.

The group's popularity grew after their appearance at the Live Aid concert in 1986, and their 1987 album, *The Joshua Tree*, went to No. 1 in Britain and America. The following year they released the film *Rattle and Hum*, and the soundtrack album became the fastest selling album of all time. ■

▶ U2 collect a Grammy award (the music industry's equivalent of an Oscar) for their 1987 album *The Joshua Tree*. From left to right are: the Edge, Adam Clayton, Larry Mullen and Bono.

Who, the

Formed 1964

Roger Daltrey 1945–
John Entwistle 1949–
Kenny Jones 1948–
Keith Moon 1947–1978
Pete Townshend 1945–

The Who became leaders of the fashionable 'Mod' teenagers of the 1960s. The group's guitarist, Pete Townshend, wrote songs such as 'I Can't Explain' (1965) and 'My Generation' (1965) about the frustrations of being young. On stage he thrashed crazily at his guitar. Singer Roger Daltrey and drummer Keith Moon were equally wild, and shows often ended with the group's instruments being destroyed. Townshend, however, was a very clever writer, who later composed *Tommy* (1969) and *Quadrophenia* (1974). These were full-length musical stories which he called 'rock operas'.

Drummer Moon died in 1978 and was replaced by Kenny Jones. Daltrey and Townshend then pursued solo careers, but still played together with bassist John Entwistle as the Who from time to time. In 1982 they decided to stop touring, but later changed their minds and were playing live again into the 1990s. ■

Wonder, Stevie

1950–

Steveland Morris of Saginaw, Michigan, was renamed Little Stevie Wonder at the age of 10 by Berry Gordy Jr, the owner of Tamla Motown Records. Stevie was blind, but played harmonica, piano, organ and drums superbly and began having No. 1 hits with 'Fingertips' (1963). Twenty hits later, Stevie struck out in a new direction in the 1970s, adding funky electronic keyboards to his sound and singing about the problems faced by black Americans. It was Stevie Wonder who led the campaign to turn Martin Luther King's birthday into a national holiday in America. He became even more successful in the 1980s with chart-toppers such as 'Ebony and Ivory' (1982), a duet with Paul McCartney, and 'I Just Called to Say I Love You' (1984). ■

SPORT

Abdul-Jabbar, Kareem

1947–

Basketball, USA

By the age of 13, Lew Alcindor was nearly 2·10 m (7 ft) tall and a brilliant basketball player. He later took the UCLA college team to three consecutive national championships and was voted Most Valuable Player each time. At UCLA he became a Muslim and changed his name to Kareem Abdul-Jabbar.

As a professional he took the Milwaukee Bucks from bottom to top of the National Basketball Association in two years. Later, with the LA Lakers, he became the top point-scorer of all time with 38,387 points from 1,560 games before he retired in 1989. He was famous for his 'sky hook' shot from high above the basket. ■

◀ Kareem Abdul-Jabbar's unusual height gave him an advantage and helped him become one of basketball's greatest players.

Ali, Muhammad

1942–

Boxing, USA

After winning the amateur 'Golden Gloves' championship in 1959 and 1960, Cassius Clay from Louisville, Kentucky, became Olympic heavyweight champion in 1960. He immediately became a professional and within four years was champion of the world.

He then became a Muslim and changed his name to Muhammad Ali. Because of his beliefs, he refused to be called up into the army. His title was taken away from him and he was banned from boxing from 1967 to 1970. He returned to the ring in the 1970s and, although he lost his title twice more, he became the first heavyweight boxer to win the world championship three times. ■

Ballesteros, Seve

1957–

Golf, Spain

Severiano Ballesteros became a professional golfer in 1974 and soon showed how skilful he was by coming second in the British Open championship of 1976 at the age of 19. In the next two years he became the leading European golfer and won the British Open in 1979. This was the first victory by a player from mainland Europe for 72 years. He won the Open again in 1984 and 1988.

He also won the US Masters championship in 1980 and 1983, and was a key member of Europe's successful Ryder Cup team in 1985, 1987 and 1989. ■

Bannister, Roger

1929–

Athletics, Britain

Roger Bannister, a medical student at Oxford, was one of the best runners in the world and wanted to be the first to run a mile (1·609 km) in under four minutes. In May 1954, he made his attempt. With the help of two runners who set the pace for him, Bannister completed the mile in 3 minutes 59·4 seconds.

In August of the same year he took on his rival, John Landy of Australia, at the Empire Games. He beat Landy and lowered the record time even further to 3 minutes 58·8 seconds. Bannister then retired from athletics to concentrate on his career as a doctor. In 1975 he was knighted for his services to sport as chairman of the Sports Council. ■

▲ Muhammad Ali defends his world title against Earnie Shavers in 1977.

Best, George

1946–

Soccer, Northern Ireland

George Best was signed by Manchester United at the age of 15, but he felt homesick and went straight back to Belfast. He was persuaded to return to Manchester and played his first game for United in 1963, aged 17. He was recognized immediately as a brilliant and skilful player with superb ball-control.

With his help, Manchester United won the European Cup in 1968 and Best was voted both British and European Footballer of the Year. Later, he began to have problems in his personal life and was sacked by Manchester United. Although he tried to make a comeback with Fulham, his career at the highest level was over by the time he was 30. ■

Bikila, Abebe

1932–1973

Athletics, Ethiopia

Running barefoot along the streets of Rome in 1960, Abebe Bikila won the marathon in a world record time of 2 hours, 15 minutes and 16·2 seconds to become the first Olympic gold medal winner in athletics from black Africa. Astonishingly, it was only his third marathon race ever.

In 1964 he had an operation to remove his appendix one month before the Olympics, but he still managed to run in the marathon. He again won the gold medal, this time wearing running shoes.

Disabled in a car accident in 1969, he took part in sport for disabled people until his death in 1973. ■

Blankers-Koen, Fanny

1918–

Athletics, Netherlands

Francina, or 'Fanny', Blankers-Koen began her career as an 800 m runner, but in the 1936 Olympics she competed as a high jumper. She then became an all-round athlete and between 1938 and 1951 she held world records in seven different events, including sprinting, hurdling, high jump, long jump and pentathlon.

Her greatest triumph came at the 1948 Olympics, when she was 30 years old. She won gold medals in the 100 m, 200 m, 4x100 m relay and 80 m hurdles. ■

Borg, Bjorn

1956–

Tennis, Sweden

Bjorn Borg was picked for his country's Davis Cup tennis team when he was only 15. Individual success followed in 1974 when he won the French Open championship. The following year he helped Sweden to win the Davis Cup and also won the French Open again. In 1976 he became the youngest Wimbledon champion for 45 years.

There then followed an incredible run of success. Borg won 41 consecutive matches at Wimbledon and remained champion from 1976 until 1981, when he was finally beaten by John McEnroe. Two years later, with six French Open wins to go with his five Wimbledon championships, Borg retired from tennis at the age of 26. ■

◄ **Bjorn Borg in action at the 1982 Wimbledon championships.**

Bradman, Donald

1908–

Cricket, Australia

As a child, Donald Bradman practised cricket on his own by bouncing a golf ball against a wall and hitting it with a cricket stump. This must have worked, because he grew up to be the greatest run-scoring batsman of all time.

In his career, he scored 28,067 runs at an average of 95 runs per innings. His highest ever score was 452 not out, for New South Wales against Queensland, when he was 21. In his last Test innings as captain of Australia, he was bowled for 0. Had it not been for that, he would have retired in 1948 with a Test average of over 100 runs per innings. ■

Chiyonofuji

1955–

Sumo wrestling, Japan

Chiyonofuji (the professional name of Mitsugu Akimoto) is probably the most successful ever sumo wrestler. He made his debut in 1970 at the age of 15, and despite being very light he quickly gained promotion through the ranks. He was at a physical disadvantage when faced by much heavier wrestlers, and so embarked on a rigorous weight-training programme to increase his muscle-size and weight.

He became a *yokozuna* in 1981, which is the highest sumo rank, and he is the only wrestler to achieve 1,000 career wins, which he did in the March tournament in 1990. ■

▼ **Chiyonofuji's speed, power and concentration have brought him over 1,000 wins in sumo wrestling.**

Comaneci, Nadia

1961–

Gymnastics, Romania

Nadia Comaneci burst onto the gymnastics scene at the European championships of 1975 when, at the age of 13, she won four of the five gold medals. The following year she made Olympic history when she became the first gymnast ever to be awarded the perfect score (10·0) for her performance on the asymmetric bars. By the end of the competition, she had won gold medals for the asymmetric bars and the balance beam and was the overall Olympic champion, all at the age of 14. In 1989 she left Romania and settled in the USA. ■

DiMaggio, Joe

1914–

Baseball, USA

Joe DiMaggio, who was also known as 'Joltin' Joe' and 'the Yankee Clipper', played baseball for the New York Yankees from 1936 to 1951. He was a superb batter and was twice the top scorer for his team. His outfielding was also excellent. In 1941, he set a new baseball record by hitting safely at least once in each of 56 consecutive games.

Even after he retired he remained in the public eye by marrying film star Marilyn Monroe in 1954. The marriage lasted only nine months. ■

Edwards, Gareth

1947–

Rugby union, Wales

As a boy, Gareth Edwards was outstanding at soccer and athletics, but as he grew up rugby became his first love. He joined Cardiff and in 1967 was chosen to play for Wales.

At the age of 20 years and 9 months, he became the youngest ever captain of Wales. He led them to no fewer than seven championships during his 53 matches for his country. When he retired in 1978 he had the satisfaction of knowing that he had scored more international tries than any other scrum half. ■

▲ Gareth Edwards playing for Wales in 1976.

Gavaskar, Sunil

1949–

Cricket, India

As a small child of 2, Sunil Gavaskar was given his first cricket coaching by his mother in their small flat. Although he never grew taller than 1·65 m (5 ft 5 in) this did not stop him becoming an outstanding batsman. He made a remarkable start in Test cricket. On his first tour of the mighty West Indies he scored 774 Test runs at an average of 154 runs per innings.

By the time he retired from Test cricket, having been captain of India 47 times, he had scored more runs than any other Test batsman of his time: 10,122 runs in all, including no fewer than 34 centuries. ■

Grace, W. G.

1848–1915

Cricket, England

William Gilbert Grace was born at Downend, near Bristol, and was taught to play cricket, along with his two brothers, by his mother. Mrs Grace must have been a very good coach, because all three Grace brothers played first-class cricket for Gloucestershire.

'W. G.', as he was known, made his debut at the age of 16. Although he later qualified as a doctor, he carried on playing cricket until the age of 60. He completely changed the way cricket was played and was so popular with spectators that notices were sometimes displayed outside grounds, saying: 'Admission sixpence [2½p]; if Dr Grace plays, one shilling [5p].'

In his career, Grace scored 54,896 runs (including 126 centuries), took 2,876 wickets and held 877 catches. ■

Graf, Steffi

1969–

Tennis, Germany

Everyone could see what a talented player Steffi Graf was when she first began to play on the international tennis circuit, but nobody could have predicted what an amazingly successful season she would have in 1988. She lost only two matches all year and did 'the Grand Slam', winning the Australian, French, Wimbledon and United States Open championships, at the age of 19. At Wimbledon, she defeated Martina Navratilova who had won a record number of Wimbledon finals, eight in all. Then, at the Seoul Olympics, Steffi added the gold medal to her four major championships to show that she was the world's best in 1988. ■

▲ Steffi Graf on her way to winning Wimbledon in 1988.

▲ W. G. Grace is one of the most famous figures in the history of English cricket.

Hailwood, Mike

1940–1981

Motor cycle racing, Britain

Known by motor cycle fans as 'Mike the Bike', Mike Hailwood started racing at 17. At the age of 20, he became the youngest rider for a works team and, in 1961, won the 250 cc world championship on a Honda. In the next six years he won eight more world championships for Honda and MV Agusta at 250 cc, 350 cc and 500 cc, before turning to motor car racing in 1967. In 1981 he was tragically killed, along with his 9-year-old daughter, in a car crash near his home. ■

Khan, Jahangir

1963–

Squash, Pakistan

The name 'Jahangir' means 'conqueror of the world'; and that is exactly what Jahangir Khan became in the world of squash. He came from a family of squash players and won the World Amateur championship in 1979 at the age of 15.

In 1981, he lost to the Australian Geoff Hunt in the final of the British Open championship. Astonishingly he did not lose another game until 1986, when he was beaten by Ross Norman of New Zealand in the world championship final. In the course of that remarkable run of victories, he was world squash champion five times in a row (1981–1985). He was world champion again in 1988. ■

Killy, Jean Claude

1943–

Skiing, France

Jean Claude Killy had very strong calves and ankles, which helped him to become an excellent ski racer. He was world champion in 1966 and was awarded the 'National Order of Merit' by France's President de Gaulle. In 1967 he won the World Alpine Skiing Cup, winning every downhill event he entered.

Then, at the Grenoble Winter Olympics of 1968, Killy won three gold medals in the downhill, slalom and giant slalom. He was world champion again that year, before becoming a professional and trying to make a living from acting in films and television commercials. ■

Korbut, Olga

1955–

Gymnastics, USSR

Olga Korbut showed such promise as a junior gymnast that she was allowed to compete in the Soviet championships, even though she was under-age. She amazed everyone by coming fifth.

She was part of the Soviet team which went to the 1972 Munich Olympics, where she caught the imagination of spectators throughout the world with her amazing routines on the floor and balance beam. Only a fall from the asymmetric bars stopped her winning a medal in the overall competition, but she came back to win gold medals for her floor exercises and balance beam routine. Later she married a leading Russian rock music star, Leonid Borkevich. ■

▲ Olga Korbut stunned the world with the speed and skill of her gymnastic displays.

Laver, Rod

1938–

Tennis, Australia

At 13, Rod Laver was selected for a tennis coaching course by a Brisbane newspaper. As a left-handed player, called 'the Rockhampton rocket' after his home town, he became good enough to win the Australian Amateur championship in 1960. Two years later he did the 'Grand Slam', winning the Australian, French, US and Wimbledon championships in the same year.

Then he turned professional, and was barred from these championships until they became 'open championships' (for both amateurs and professionals) in the late 1960s. In 1969 Rod Laver was able to do the Grand Slam once again. ■

▲ Carl Lewis.

Lewis, Carl

1961–

Athletics, USA

Carl Lewis comes from a sporting family. His father is a sports teacher, his mother and sister international athletes, and his brother a soccer player. Carl's own career is one of the most successful ever in athletics history. Not only has he had the longest run of long jump victories ever, but he has also been the world's best sprinter.

In 1983 he had three wins in the US championships and three at the Helsinki world championships. He went one better at the 1984 Olympics when he equalled Jesse Owens's record of four gold medals, triumphing in the 100 m, 200 m, long jump and 4x100 m relay. He retained his gold medals for 100 m and the long jump at the 1988 Seoul Olympics. ■

Maradona, Diego

1960–

Soccer, Argentina

Diego Maradona was born in Buenos Aires and quickly showed the skills that made him an Argentinian league footballer by the age of 15. He was voted South American Footballer of the Year in 1979 and 1980. After leading Argentina's youth team to World Cup success in 1979 he joined the full national squad in their unsuccessful attempt to keep the World Cup in 1982.

He was sold to the Spanish club Barcelona in 1982, before moving on to Napoli of Italy two years later for 5 million pounds. In 1986, as Argentina's captain, he lifted up the World Cup after brilliant performances throughout the tournament. More league and cup success followed with Napoli, but Maradona was so closely marked by opponents that he found it hard to dominate games as he once had. He led Argentina once again in the 1990 World Cup final, although they were beaten 1–0 by West Germany. ■

Marciano, Rocky

1923–1969

Boxing, USA

Rocco Marchegiano boxed as an amateur in the US army during World War II. Then he changed his name to Rocky Marciano and became a professional heavyweight in 1947. He won his first fight with a knock-out in the first round, and went on to win 43 more fights before being given a chance to box for the world title in 1952.

He knocked out Jersey Joe Wolcott in the thirteenth round to become world champion, and retired undefeated four years later with a fight record of 49 bouts, 49 wins. He was killed in 1969 when his aeroplane crashed. ■

▲ Rocky Marciano, world heavyweight champion 1952–1956.

Matthews, Stanley

1915–

Soccer, England

As a boy, Stanley Matthews kicked a small rubber ball around everywhere he went. Practising like this helped him to become one of the best dribblers of a football in the world.

Already an England player, he was sold to Blackpool by Stoke in 1947. He hoped this would give him a chance to win an FA Cup winners' medal, but it seemed that he would be unlucky when Blackpool were losing 3–1 to Bolton with only minutes to go in the 1953 final. Then Matthews helped his team to score three times to win the FA Cup. This extraordinary game is now known as the 'Matthews final'. He later rejoined Stoke and, incredibly, was still playing first division football when he retired at the age of 50. ■

Merckx, Eddy

1945–

Cycling, Belgium

Eddy Merckx lived just outside Brussels, the Belgian capital. He was a very good student at school and enjoyed playing soccer and basketball. Then, at the age of 14, he discovered cycling and made such rapid progress that he was world amateur champion at 18.

The following year he became a professional and an amazing run of success followed. Between 1966 and 1978, when he retired, he triumphed five times in the Giro d'Italia (Tour of Italy) as well as winning the Tour de France five times. But he was always the first to admit that he owed much of his success to the loyal team of riders who supported him. ■

Moses, Ed

1955–

Athletics, USA

Edwin Moses did not become a 400 m high-hurdler until 1975, but the following year he was good enough to win the gold medal at the Montréal Olympics. In 1977 he lost a race to Harald Schmid of West Germany, but then did not lose any of his next 122 races until 1987, when he was finally beaten by his fellow American, Danny Harris. This is the longest ever run of victories in track athletics, and helped to make Ed Moses one of the most popular and successful athletes in the world. ■

▶ Ed Moses leaps a high hurdle on his way to another victory.

BERG

▲ Stanley Matthews played first division football until he was 50 years old.

Murphy, Alex

1939–

Rugby league, Britain

Alex Murphy was only 16 when he played his first game of rugby league for St Helens. After many years of success with them, playing both at scrum half and at stand-off half, he moved to Leigh and then to Warrington. Each club he played for won the Rugby League Challenge Cup, and he himself played in 20 major finals and 27 times for Great Britain.

After retiring as a player, he went on to be a controversial and outspoken coach. ■

Namath, Joe

1943–

American football, USA

Joe Namath was such a good footballer at high school that he received 52 offers of places at universities and colleges. He chose the University of Alabama, who went unbeaten through the 1964 season, and then joined the New York Jets. As quarterback, he led them to a Superbowl victory in 1969.

Although his knees were so badly damaged by tackles that he needed four operations on them, he was always one of the quickest passers in the game, and his colourful life off the field made him a favourite with the fans and journalists. ■

Navratilova, Martina

1956–

Tennis, USA

Martina Navratilova was born in Czechoslovakia, but moved to the United States in 1975 when she started to become a successful tennis player on the world circuit. In 1981 she became a citizen of the United States and the following year was the first woman professional tennis player to earn more than one million dollars in a season.

Her favourite championship has always been Wimbledon, where she has won nine singles finals (1978–1979, 1982–1987 and 1990), beating the record set by fellow American Helen Moody Wills. ■

▲ Jack Nicklaus plays out of a bunker during the 1986 US Masters.

Nicklaus, Jack

1940–

Golf, USA

Taking up golf at the age of 10, Jack Nicklaus showed how good he would be by playing a round of 69 over a 6·49-km (7,095-yard) course at 13. While still at Ohio State University, he became US amateur champion. Then, when he turned professional in 1961, he began his run of tournament successes by winning the US Open championship in 1962.

Since then 'Golden Bear', as he is known to his fans, has won more major tournaments than anyone else in golfing history, including four US Opens and five US Masters championships. ■

Owens, Jesse
1913–1980
Athletics, USA

James Cleveland (J. C., thus 'Jesse') Owens from Alabama was 22 when he took part in an athletics meeting in Michigan. Within 45 minutes he had equalled the world record for the 100 yards, and broken the records for the 220 yards, the 220 yards hurdles and the long jump. His long jump world record lasted for 25 years.

The next year, 1936, was Olympic year. Adolf Hitler, the leader of Nazi Germany, wanted the Berlin Games to show the world that what he called 'the Aryan race' of white Europeans was superior to any other. When Jesse Owens demolished that myth by winning four gold medals, Hitler refused even to shake hands with the black American athlete. ■

▲ Pelé celebrates after scoring the first goal against Italy in the 1970 World Cup final.

Pelé
1941–
Soccer, Brazil

Edson Arantes do Nascimento was given the nickname 'Pelé' by the friends he played football with as a boy. He showed so much promise for his first club Noroeste that he was signed by the top club Santos and was picked for Brazil at the age of 16.

A year later, in 1958, he scored two goals to help Brazil win the World Cup final. In a career that lasted until 1977, Pelé showed that he was the complete footballer, combining speed and ball-control with fierce and accurate shooting. Before leaving Santos for New York Cosmos in 1971, he scored 1,216 goals in 1,254 games. He also played 110 games for Brazil, winning two World Cup winners' medals in 1958 and 1970. ■

Piggott, Lester
1935–
Horse racing, Britain

Lester Piggott rode his first winner in 1948 at the age of 12, and soon established a winning habit as a flat-race jockey. He had his first Derby winner in 1954 and, by 1983, had ridden a record nine winners in that Classic race.

Between 1964 and 1971 he was champion jockey each season, and he did not retire from the saddle until 1985 when he became a trainer of racehorses. Sadly, he did not pay as much income tax as he should have done and he was sent to prison for tax evasion in 1987. ■

Ruth, Babe
1895–1948
Baseball, USA

George Herman Ruth went to a school for poor children in Baltimore, which is where he began his baseball career as a pitcher with the Orioles. Then, known to all the fans as 'Babe Ruth', he became a batter with Boston Red Sox and hit 29 home runs in 1919. The next year, playing for New York Yankees, he hit 54 and became so popular that by 1925 he was earning more than the President of the USA. In 1927 he raised his record to 60 home runs in a season, and by the time he retired in 1935 he had scored a career total of 714. ■

▼ Babe Ruth poses for the cameras beside a young baseball fan.

Simpson, O. J.
1947–
American football, USA

Orenthal James Simpson was brought up by his mother, a San Francisco hospital worker, and sometimes got into trouble with the police as a youngster. However, he settled down to improve his school grades and became a promising athlete. This gave him the chance to go to the University of Southern California, where he became an outstanding running-back on the football team.

In his final year, Simpson won the Heisman Trophy as the top college player in the USA, and became a professional with the Buffalo Bills. His electrifying pace set many rushing records for them before he moved to the San Francisco 49ers at the end of his career. ■

Sobers, Garry
1936–
Cricket, West Indies

As a boy in Barbados, Garfield Sobers was excellent at all sports, but eventually he decided to devote himself to cricket. He was an elegant batsman, good enough to score a Test match record of 365 not out against Pakistan in 1958. He could bowl left handed in two different styles: fast-medium and slow spin. Under his captaincy, the West Indies became one of the most entertaining teams in world cricket.

When Garry Sobers retired in 1974, his Test match record was 8,032 runs, 235 wickets and 109 catches, making him one of the best all-round cricketers the world has seen. He was also the first player to score six sixes in one over. After his retirement, he was knighted for his services to cricket. ■

Spitz, Mark

1950–

Swimming, USA

Mark Spitz began swimming at the age of 2, and his father began to coach him seriously at 8. 'Swimming isn't everything,' he told Mark, 'winning is.'

In 1968, when he was at Indiana University, he predicted that he would win six gold medals at the Mexico Olympics. In fact, he won only two, both in the relay races. Embarrassed by this failure, he trained hard for the 1972 Munich Olympics. There he broke all records by winning seven gold medals in seven events, and in each of these events a new world record was set. ■

▲ Mark Spitz powers through the water towards another world record.

Stewart, Jackie

1939–

Motor racing, Britain

Jackie Stewart's first sporting success came at clay pigeon shooting. He won the British, Irish, Scottish, Welsh and English championships when he was 21, before turning to motor racing.

In only his second season he won the Italian Grand Prix and was third in the world championship. He became world champion driver in 1969, and repeated this success in 1971 and 1973, driving cars built for him by Ken Tyrrell.

He retired after this third victory, with 27 Formula One wins to his name, and left Britain to live in Switzerland. ■

Szewinska, Irena

1946–

Athletics, Poland

Irena Kirszenstein began her athletics career as an 18-year-old at the 1964 Tokyo Olympics, where she won silver medals in the long jump and 200 m, and gold in the 4x100 m relay. The following year she broke the world record for the 200 m, the event for which she won another gold at the 1968 Mexico Olympics. By now she had married her coach, Janusz Szewinski.

As Irena Szewinska she carried on breaking the 200 m world record regularly into the 1970s, before stepping up to win a third Olympic gold medal in the 400 m at Montreal in 1976. By the time she retired she had become one of the best athletes ever, with ten European championship medals, seven Olympic medals and four World Cup medals to her name. ■

Thompson, Daley

1958–

Athletics, Britain

The decathlon involves ten different running, jumping and throwing events in two days, so it takes a very good all-round athlete to win this competition. Britain's greatest ever decathlete is undoubtedly Daley Thompson.

After showing promise as a junior decathlete, he became Commonwealth champion in 1978. Then he finished second in the 1980 European championships. That was the last time anyone in the world beat him for ten decathlon competitions. During this long winning run, he gained two Olympic gold medals (1980 and 1984), two European championships (1982 and 1986), one world championship (1983) and no fewer than four world record scores. He was the first athlete ever to hold the world, Olympic, European and Commonwealth titles at the same time. ■

Torvill, Jayne and Dean, Christopher

Torvill 1957–
Dean 1958–

Ice dancing, Britain

Jayne Torvill and Christopher Dean first became skating partners in 1975, and won the British championship in 1978. Ice dancing at that time was dominated by skaters from the USSR, who had won the world championship twelve years in a row before Torvill and Dean triumphed in 1981.

With help from show business stars, they made their routines even more spectacular and were rewarded in 1983 when the judges gave them maximum marks for artistic impression.

As well as winning the world championship four times in a row, they won the gold medal at the 1984 Winter Olympics for their stunning performance to Ravel's 'Bolero'. They later turned professional. ■

Weissmuller, Johnny

1904–1984

Swimming, USA

Johnny Weissmuller first broke world records for swimming at the age of 17. He then won a total of five gold medals at the Olympic Games of 1924 and 1928. During his career he held 24 world records, including every distance for the freestyle, and was the first to swim 100 m in less than a minute and 400 m in under five minutes.

He left the swimming pool and moved to Hollywood to become a film actor. Starring roles in the early 'Tarzan' films made him even more famous than when he was a swimmer. ■

Zatopek, Emil

1922–

Athletics, Czechoslovakia

Emil Zatopek was the best long-distance runner of his day and possibly of all time. At the 1948 Olympics he won the gold medal for the 10,000 m and silver for the 5,000 m. Then, at the 1952 Helsinki Olympics, he won the 5,000 m and 10,000 m gold medals, and entered the Marathon for the first time in his life. He won by 800 m (half a mile) to complete a unique treble.

His wife, Dana Zatopkova, added to the family celebrations by winning the gold medal in the women's javelin competition. ■

◄ Daley Thompson throws the javelin in the decathlon, during the 1983 world championships.